Made on Earth

How gospel writers created the Christ

Lorraine Parkinson

First published in Australia in 2015
By Spectrum Publications Pty Ltd
a: PO Box 75, Richmond, Victoria, Australia 3121
t: (+61) 1300 540 736
f: (+61) 1300 540 737
e: spectrum@spectrumpublications.com.au
w: www.spectrumpublications.com.au
for Lorraine Parkinson

ISBN: 978-0-86786-254-6

Cover Design: xy arts
Typesetting by Spectrum Publications Pty Ltd
Typeface: Georgia
Cover painting: The Four Evangelists, Jacob Jordaens, 1593-1678

National Library of Australia Cataloguing-in-Publication entry:

Creator:	Parkinson, Lorraine, author.
Title:	Made on earth : how gospel writers created the Christ / Lorraine Parkinson.
ISBN:	9780867862546 (paperback)
Notes:	Includes bibliographical references and index.
Subjects:	Jesus Christ--Person and offices--Biblical teaching.
	Jesus Christ--Teachings.
	Bible. Gospels
	Bible. Gospels--Criticism, interpretation, etc
	Divine man (Christology).
	Christian life--Biblical teaching.
Dewey Number:	232.903

Acknowledgments

I wish to acknowledge the scholarly generosity and wise counsel of my three critics in the preparation of this book: the Rev Dr John Bodycomb, the Rev Dr Coralie Ling and the Rev Dr Ken Dempsey

This book is dedicated to John Bodycomb
my beloved partner in life and colleague in
exploring new possibilities for the faith

Contents

The Land of Palestine as Jesus knew it

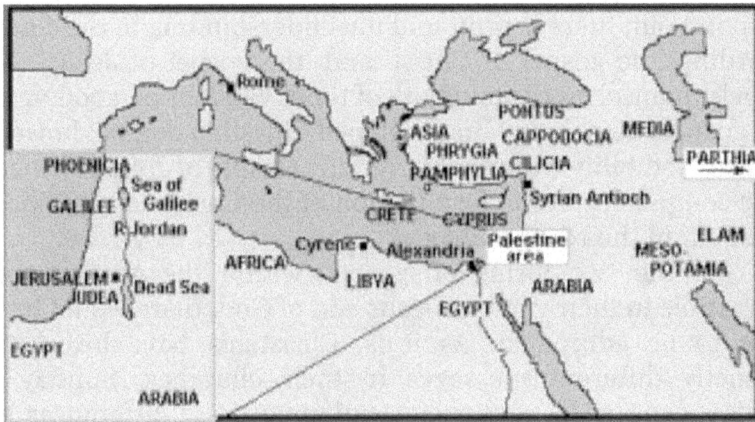

The area of the Jewish Diaspora in the 1st century CE

Preface

First an explanation of the purpose of this book. I have written it to try to bring some clarity to the considerably confusing picture of Jesus in four canonical gospels. As I will point out, there is profound misunderstanding in the church regarding 'the gospel of Christ' and 'the gospel of Jesus'. The gospels themselves contain both of those versions of 'good news'. The gospels do not contain developed Christian dogma, however biblical credibility (especially from the Gospel of John) formed a large component in the formulation of the Christology of Nicea, as set out in the Nicene Creed.

If the two forms of 'gospel' within the gospels were compatible in their views of Jesus and of God, there would be no issue to be addressed. As it is, Christians have heard two distinctly different messages in their churches, Sunday by Sunday, century by century. Questioning those differences has not been encouraged, and the two have existed, side by side, through most of the church's life. Through almost all of that time, mainstream clergy and laity have had neither the equipment nor the impetus to try to unscramble these two 'eggs'. The conventional way of dealing with this has been to emphasise one or the other, or try to conflate the two. Clergy attempts to combine the two 'gospels' have often proved to be profoundly confusing for the church-goer trying to remain loyal. In recent years this confusing combination has been seen by many as grounds for dismissing the whole lot. In addition, contemporary readers of the gospels know very well that undergirding all four of them are views of God from a pre-scientific world. They were written from assumptions about the divine that simply do not stand up to 21st century scrutiny.

In this book I will try to help my readers, whether clergy, laity, biblical scholars or those who have dropped out of church life, to see Jesus of Nazareth more clearly in gospels intentionally crafted to present him as the Messiah. There are many meanings attached to that title, as we will see. For that reason I will preface my investigation of the gospels themselves with an explanation of the concept of Messiah at the time of Jesus and at the time of the gospel writers. Then we will look at the four gospels and how their writers depicted Jesus as Messiah/Christ. Lastly, we will examine profoundly negative effects that have issued from the gospels' proclamation of Jesus as the Messiah, or Christ.

This book is intended as a guide that may be picked up and consulted as the occasion prompts, or used as a study resource for groups trying to make more sense of their faith in God as revealed by the teaching of Jesus.

Lorraine Parkinson, Melbourne, 2015.

Introduction

This book is successor to my previous work, *The World According to Jesus: his blueprint for the best possible world.*[1] There I wanted to say that the teaching of Jesus in the Sermon on the Mount and its corresponding parables, all encapsulated in the Beatitudes, is the natural foundation of the church now and in the future. In Jesus' teaching lies the wisdom to develop the best possible humanity and the best possible world. Shining through that wisdom is the way toward knowing the God Jesus loved, in whom he placed his trust through life and death. Jesus' teaching reveals that he saw God as a God of love. This seems to me and to many others an all-sufficient foundation for profound Christian evolution. Such an evolution is already taking place naturally in a world that has evolved immeasurably beyond the imperial thinking that produced the creed of Nicea (325CE).

Now is the time to set out in more detail my reasons for making that claim. In discussing *The World According to Jesus* with people from all walks of life; believers in the transcendent, agnostics, atheists, lay people and clergy, plus people of other faiths, I found in them a sometimes heartbreaking eagerness to affirm and embrace Jesus' message for the world. Along with that, most of them from the Christian tradition are in process of shaking off, like an old skin, the church's dogma about the Christ. There is a profound longing in today's people for an authentic basis and focus for their innate spirituality. The churches may be emptying, but humanity's search for the transcendent remains. The fact of dwindling church membership does not indicate a lack of interest in questions about the divine, and about the place of Jesus in the 21st century.

People who stay away from church life are signalling their disillusionment, not with the wisdom of Jesus, but with the traditional church as their guide to the sacred.

I also write this book out of questions asked of me concerning the religion *about* Jesus that I am rejecting. I write it from my own experience of theological 'archaeology' – of searching under layers of ancient christological rubble for the origins of belief in Jesus as Christ.[2] I write it to offer some reliable as possible evidence about the historical literary underpinnings of the tradition in the canonical gospels about Jesus as the Messiah/Christ. I have cited my sources for the reader's further investigation, but I have not written solely for biblical scholars or theologians. I believe this is the kind of investigation for which many lay and ordained people are searching. The withholding of this kind of knowledge about Christian origins is the cause of a world-wide and legitimate complaint from the laity about clergy 'secret knowledge'. "Why weren't we told?" they ask. Why, indeed? Swept under the rug over centuries have been countless questions and doubts, along with their appropriate and much needed answers. The clergy response has all too often been, "That's too dangerous for them to know!" The laity may well ask: "Too dangerous for whom?" Certainly it is dangerous for those who support the tenets of christological dogma[3] upon which the ecclesial (church structures) and hierarchical authority of the church have been built. Those who wish to continue to place their reliance on the traditional church will naturally do all they can to defend it from criticism.

It is important to acknowledge that failure to confront the deficiencies of Christian tradition in the 21st century does not lie exclusively with clergy who represent Christianity in parishes, schools and chaplaincies. Nor does fault lie exclusively with the teachers of the tradition in theological schools. Custodians of Christian tradition in theological schools of all sorts and stripes have mostly operated under the assumption that it was not their prerogative to 'do theology'. Rather it was for them to pass on the package labelled 'Nicea',[4] with interpretative embellishments lately called neo-orthodoxy. Yet these new interpretations of

Nicean Christology are not new ideas; they represent tinkerings around the edges of fourth century and later christological traditions. On the other hand, biblical scholars in theological schools have introduced budding clergy to critical readings of the scriptures. This has sometimes led students to an uneasy recognition that there exist not just different, but contradictory understandings of the faith. I will say more about that through this book.

Where systematic theology is concerned, clergy have emerged from theological schools armed with traditional christological views of Jesus and God, albeit interpreted by certain theologians. The theologians consulted vary in accordance with those favoured by particular denominations or by local professors of theology. Given that, the angry question, "Why weren't we told?" can indicate a lack of resources given to clergy in theological schools to enable their critical thinking. The answer to the cry of the laity is that clergy often haven't 'told it' because they haven't known it! In many cases they were not given the freedom to express alternative thinking. They were taught a corpus of theology, not how to 'do' theology.

Resultant clergy have been reticent to express from the pulpit their own thinking about the tradition's deficiencies for a living faith in the modern world. For some clergy that reticence also reflects an understandable concern about protecting their employment. Others have left the ministry precisely because they felt constrained from speaking plainly about their own beliefs. For many clergy, reluctance to speak out is about 'keeping the peace' in the parish. But increasingly there are people in the pews whose reading and discussions with others have taken them far away from expressions of the faith by parish minister or priest. Efforts to keep the peace in the parish are doomed when the views of such people are seen as inappropriate or even heretical, by the gate-keepers, the lay leaders who stand fast for tradition in theology and church life.

At the same time, meeting in someone's lounge-room or in a church meeting room on a week-night, are the 'Explorers'. This is a widely used name for groups of laity looking for wisdom about life that makes sense to them and keeps their faith alive.

For some clergy, reluctance to get involved with such groups may reflect a lack of sufficient background even to begin exploring critical ways of interpreting scripture with the congregation. Then there are the clergy who have been doing their own reading and thinking but have waited to 'come out' as dissenters from the tradition until after their retirement from full-time ministry. I have no need or intention to criticize any clergy for any of that; it is simply the way it has been.

Meanwhile, teachers in schools of theology whose primary discipline is systematic theology have defended Fort Tradition, hauling up the drawbridge when faced with the challenge to remove christological spectacles and look clear-eyed at the origins of the faith. For most, their understood role is to teach the Christian tradition to students who sit examinations based on that tradition. The most common reason for restrictions on courses taught in theological colleges and seminaries is the authority of the conferring institutions. They have the power to prescribe the core content to be taught for their degrees in theology. This state of affairs perpetuates the hiring of teaching staff who profess a traditional version of the faith. And nothing changes.

In response to that kind of imposed limit on theological studies in the Church of England, Bishop John A. T. Robinson decided to place biblical studies at the forefront of his thinking. After studying philosophy and systematic theology at Cambridge, he was appointed chaplain and lecturer in New Testament Studies at Wells Theological College. He began to suspect that christological doctrines might not be as well founded in the New Testament as is often assumed. In a book he wrote called *Jesus and His Coming*, he constructed an elaborate metaphor about the importance of biblical studies for the formulation of theology. He wrote:

> *For subterranean rumblings are heard most clearly by those who have their rooms on the ground floor, that is, at the New Testament level of the doctrinal construction. And they are the more noticeable to one who has recently moved downstairs, in the first instance from the*

floor of the philosophy of religion to that of systematic theology, and then from systematic theology to Biblical studies.[5]

It is hardly surprising that Bishop Robinson might have come to those conclusions, given that systematic theology is based not only on a literal reading of the gospels but on a reading back into them of the Christ of Nicea and later church councils. Critical biblical study does not enter into this process.

The theological/biblical archaeology this book will set out is not done without consciousness of what it might mean for those who still place their faith in traditional ideas about God and Jesus. Yet faith in the over-arching goodness of God as taught by Jesus is more than sufficient spiritual insurance to safeguard those who fear what such an exploration might unearth. I write for those who struggle quietly or loudly to reconcile traditional beliefs of the church with the God they believe in, and with their own life experience. It is definitely with hope for a renewed form of the faith that I am engaged in this exploration of Christian origins in the four canonical gospels. That hope for renewal is shared by many people in the churches, both lay and ordained. One such is Sydney pharmacist Ken Fletcher:

> *I am fortunate to associate with a progressive religious discussion group that provides the opportunity to investigate recent ideas, and work through the issues that concern us, in a non-judgmental environment. Here I realised I was not alone in my journey, that there are many others on their own similar but different pathway. My evangelical upbringing makes me want to share this new understanding.[6]*

People who see Christianity as evolving along with the rest of the world are often accused of being schismatics, of creating division. Yet differences between them and traditional Christians are not created deliberately as an unnatural diversion from the 'true faith'. The differences are part of a natural process that occurs whenever a species or system can no longer thrive in a changed environment. Evolving Christianity is a grass-roots bottom-up movement from the 20th century that cannot be halted by top-down authority in the 21st century. The church's urgent task in these times is to burst out of the old institution that places barriers in the way of following Jesus and begin to lay a foundation for the church of the future. A fearful and hesitant church will be found bunkered down and defending its shrinking institution until the bitter end.

Open investigation by scholars in church and secular institutions world-wide has revealed the mother-lode of God-inspired human wisdom received from Jesus. Scholars have exposed how that subversive teaching was appropriated and domesticated by Christian dogma formed in the crucible of the Roman Empire. Jesus' challenging wisdom was bound and gagged and re-stated in 'harmless' terms by a church initially in thrall to Rome. It hardly need be said that the church's doctrine was formulated by males, about males (starting from a male God and male Christ), for males, with the female half of the human race simply expected to tag along. The feminist biblical scholar and theologian Elizabeth Schüssler Fiorenza reiterated this as recently as 2014:

> As Judith Plaskow has argued,[7] Christian male theologians have formulated theological concepts in terms of their own cultural experience, insisting on male language relating to God and on a symbolic universe in which wo/men do not appear. Similar observations can be made regarding other world religions.[8]

Yet the disturbing wisdom of Jesus the prophet/teacher from Nazareth applies to all of humanity, female and male. Christian women and men owe it to Jesus and to themselves, to turn to his teaching free of christological encumbrance and its time-bound limitations. They owe it to themselves to embrace fully the subversive teaching for which Jesus died. There is a time when particular ways of thinking about God run their course. This has happened over and over in human history to various ways of seeing the divine. Now is the time to put to one side the exclusivist male triune God who appeared out of the mindset of male fourth century theologians and politicians. Now is the time to focus on the inclusive God revealed by Jesus in his teaching.

In his 2012 book *The Underground Church: Reclaiming the subversive way of Jesus*, US pastor/theologian Robin Meyers makes his own plea for a return to the church's subversive foundation:

> *To my way of thinking, if the church cannot return to its radical roots – driven by a truly subversive anti-imperial message and mission again – then it deserves to die. It has nothing to offer the world except something to dull the pain, circle the wagons, or lie about the number of lifeboats. For millions the church is dead already – the victim of its own intellectual, spiritual, and moral dishonesty.*[9]

I certainly acknowledge the weight and power of sixteen hundred years of Christian tradition. Yet more and more people are finding that it is possible to lift doctrinal encumbrances from their faith in God and from their desire to follow Jesus. When they do, the church roof does not fall in! The doors are opened wide and the church is filled with light and a new understanding of God.

This book will examine the four gospels for the origins of christological traditions about Jesus. It will highlight the messianic portrait of Jesus painted by the gospel writers. It will rummage around underneath and behind messianic traditions to discover their foundations. It will point out reasons why empire-based Christology took root in the first place, and why it is incompatible with expressions of faith in a non-imperialist age. It will ask awkward questions about Christian tradition. By means of my own education and experience in Christian-Jewish relations, the last chapter of this book will address the church's shocking secret regarding the Jews. A clear-eyed look at the many ways christological dogma has caused immeasurable human suffering across millennia and across the peoples of the world, will inevitably raise the question: how can this be of God?

I have conducted this investigation into the origins of the faith in the hope that readers will find the impetus for a new beginning of the church, in whatever form seems right for time and place. My further hope is that through their own thinking and writing, other scholars will pick up the challenge of liberating the church from its Christology. Paradoxically, such a new beginning can take place through a return to the oldest foundation of the faith – a reclaiming of Jesus the Prophet/Teacher and the wisdom of his God. This idea has been greeted with amusement by traditionalists – "They call themselves progressives, but they say the church should go backwards two thousand years."

Well yes, and no. Obviously I am not proposing what is impossible anyway - going back to the historical and religious context in which Jesus proclaimed the kingdom of heaven on earth. I am talking about 'turning around and going back', which is the Hebrew and Greek biblical meaning of repentance. I am talking about seeing clearly what happened to the faith of Jesus' followers in the context of the Roman Empire, close to two thousand years ago. I am talking about repenting the turning away from Jesus and the untold human suffering that turning away has caused. I am talking about giving back to Jesus his humanity and lifting from him the distorting burden of imperialist Christology. I am talking about turning back to Jesus and to the God of love he revealed. Ultimately, I am talking about rediscovering how Jesus' teachings can liberate and empower the church and all of humanity, for the good.

In that sense this is about coming full circle – turning back to the place from which the faith of the church truly began – with Jesus and his vision of the kingdom of heaven on earth. It is about uniting the past, the present and the future of the church. T. S. Eliot expressed this insight in his poem *Little Gidding*:

> *We shall not cease from exploration*
> *and the end of all our exploring*

will be to arrive where we started
*and know the place for the first time ... *[10]

Only through this process of turning back, or repentance, can the church free itself from christological dogma created within and out of imperial Rome. The traditional and apostolic church in the 21st century CE is the last gasp of the Roman Empire. Although most Christians these days agree that the alliance of church and state called Christendom has come to an end, the church clings tenaciously to Christendom's theology. Yet the end of Christendom must also mean the end of Christendom's imperialist dogma about the 'Christ'. Australian scholar Michael Morwood underlines the importance of recognizing the difference between the church's version of 'Messiah' (or 'anointed') and Jesus' own understanding:

> *We should take special note of the word "anointed", which in Greek is "christos". It is from this word that the Christian understanding of "Christ" emerged. It is important to take note of this because "christos" was applied to Jesus in a completely different context and with a very different meaning after he died. Christianity has failed and continues to fail to understand Jesus rightly because our Christian Scriptures, written decades after he died, are dominated by a different perspective about "christos", one that ignored Jesus' own understanding of the task he set for himself.*[11]

When Jesus' followers free themselves from the church's time-bound Christology, they can truly be liberated from contradiction in the expression of their faith. They can be freed to take seriously Jesus' call to create the kingdom of heaven on earth, a state of affairs I refer to as 'the best possible world'.

Through this book I aim to show my readers that such a loosening from the faith of empire is not a betrayal either of God or of Jesus. Through an investigation of the methodology and beliefs of the four canonical gospel writers, my intention is to illustrate how 'the Christ' is a humanly created concept that led to the construction of a humanly created theological and ecclesiastical edifice. Demolishing that edifice is not only possible; it is essential for the integrity of people seriously committed to following Jesus.

Section 1

Contradiction and Crisis in the church

Naming the confusion
between two gospels

Through the history of Christianity some church leaders have spoken out about Christian origins. They have dared to name and challenge what they have seen as indefensible religious traditions. The hierarchy's fear of such challenges meant that some of these dissenters were consigned by church authorities to death by fire and torture. One example among many concerned the execution by fire of the Spanish physician and theologian, Michael Servetus. He was accused by Protestant leader John Calvin of heresy for his different view of trinitarian theology. He was burned alive for that, at Champel in 1553. This kind of barbaric response to differing theological viewpoints illustrates how far the institutional church had travelled from Jesus of Nazareth and his God, by the sixteenth century.

In more recent times dissenters from tradition have been dealt with by gate-keepers of orthodoxy as if their challenging views were of no account at all. Although outspoken dissenting leaders have been read and heard and welcomed by many of the church's people, they have been determinedly ignored by many of its threatened traditional leadership. The problem was, and still is, the danger the dissenters represent. They have been and still are, chipping away at Christianity's christological foundations. The feeling from the upper rungs of traditional church hierarchies is that they must be stopped.

One attempt to stop the dissent entails carrying on 'as usual' at leadership levels as if nothing new was being said and thought by people in the pews. Yet church members continue to set up lay-led discussion groups to look at 'progressive' or evolving Christianity and its critique of the tradition. In many cases parish clergy do not attend, preferring to sit on the fence and appear neutral. Numerous clergy mental and spiritual breakdowns have resulted from this attempt to keep a foot in both camps while espousing one or both approaches to the faith. The laity are always well aware when this occurs, describing such clergy as "He/she agrees with everyone, but we don't know what he/she really believes." The result is a lack of clear leadership and the impossibility of preaching from the heart.

One clear-sighted clergyman who persisted in the face of passive and active opposition was the American preacher/theologian Harry Emerson Fosdick. Fosdick said so much of what is being said in the 21st century, yet he said it almost a full century ago:

> *There is a widespread, deep-seated, positive desire on the part of many Christians in all the churches to recover for our modern life, for its personal character and its social relationships, the religion of Jesus as distinguished from the accumulated, conventionalized, largely inadequate and sometimes grossly false religion about Jesus.*[12]

Fosdick, and 37 years later John A. T. Robinson, spoke and wrote at times when the numerical strength of the traditional church buffered its theological bulwarks against attack. These two were among the few dissenting clergy voices heard publicly, taking the brunt of fierce ecclesiastical condemnation and rejection. Some people declared that Robinson was no longer a Christian. Others confidently asserted that he was now an atheist, in spite of his clearly spelt out faith in God, albeit one much larger than the God of Christian doctrine. The problem was that Robinson had identified weaknesses in traditional doctrine long recognized in private, but denied in the public utterances of church leaders. He had hit the nail on the head when he pointed out that the church's doctrines most vulnerable to question were the doctrines of the Incarnation and the Divinity of Christ. He identified them as "the point where orthodoxy has its heaviest investment in traditional categories."[13]

The divinity of Christ is the topic most likely to surface in conversation about 'who is Jesus?' Another version of that question is, "Do you believe Jesus is the Son of God?" I have often responded to that question with, "What do you mean when you say Jesus is 'Son of God'?" A common response is confusion, and an admission that it doesn't actually make sense, even though the feeling is, "I must believe it, to be a Christian." These days reaction to theological dissent includes attempts to reinterpret christological doctrine, particularly where it pertains to the 'death of Christ'. This I acknowledge as an honest effort, but in many cases it has resulted in spectacularly unsuccessful attempts to equate love with violence. Somehow the violence of the crucifixion is meant to represent the love of God.

Why should it be surprising that such theological gymnastics are simply not bought by the vast majority of thinking people still hanging on in the churches? Many thousands of former churchgoers noted crumbling remnants of the old Christian tradition underfoot as they walked out of church life. They had been offered nothing meaningful in its place. Travelling in Europe and the United Kingdom I have observed huge crowds thronging many of the old Catholic and Anglican cathedrals. No, they were not there to worship; they were tourists from around the world eager to see what are in effect, beautiful museums of the church's past. A Catholic friend of mine described how difficult it was for her to find a Mass to attend in Europe, in cities full of magnificent but mostly unattended churches. A handful of people attended the masses she did find. By and large people called Christian still venerate Jesus and what he stands for. In the church they find that the wisdom of the Jesus they want to follow is compromised by christological doctrine.

Ideas contained in doctrines formalized at Nicaea in 325CE and in the subsequent decades of the fourth century, were congruent with their time and place and culture. They were tailor-made for the Jewish and Greco-Roman mythological, theological and philosophical milieu from which they came.

They were in fact the product of empire. Christian dogma 'fits' and supports imperialist structures and systems of power. Is it any wonder that it does not 'fit' a post-patriarchal and post-imperial world? There is no authentic option for today's church but to acknowledge its dogma as ideas whose time has long passed and reunite its people around the teachings of Jesus.

Bishop Robinson was more accurate about the effect this would have on the church than he could have imagined, when he wrote in his preface:

> *I am inclined to think that the gulf must grow wider before it is bridged and that there will be an increasing alienation, both within the ranks of the Church and outside it, between those whose basic recipe is the mixture as before (however revitalized) and those who feel compelled above all to be honest wherever it may lead them.*[14]

Waking from Confusion

Readers will have realised that my own experience of repudiating traditional doctrine lies behind my present approach to reclaiming the religion *of* Jesus, and disclaiming the religion *about* Jesus as the Christ. Something here about my own experience will help an understanding of my present stance.

My earliest questioning of previously taken-for-granted utterances from the pulpit related to what I began to see as contradictions. That initiated for me what became a crisis in my understanding of the faith. My parents were faithful members in our local Methodist church and my sister and I were regulars at Sunday School, plus morning and evening services. We could not have helped but absorb a good deal of what was said and sung and prayed. I remember a lot of talk about 'doing good works' and supporting the missionaries. Being a Methodist church, social justice and missionary work were two of the main expressions of the gospel that we heard there. I believe I thoroughly approved of the first, and was also convinced that the 'little black boys and girls in Fiji', as they were called, needed to hear about Jesus. From about age five, I would be taken by my mother to Ladies' Guild meetings where a 'bring and buy stall' was raising funds for Methodist missions in Melbourne and Methodist missionaries in the Pacific. All of that was reinforced in church and Sunday School through stories from Jesus about caring for the hungry, the naked, the ill, and so on. I had no problem with any of that and happily saved 'thruppences for mission'.

Around fourteen I had finished Bible Class and Confirmation classes and following Confirmation I became an assistant Sunday School teacher. About a year later, as a fifteen-year-old, I was given a class of nine-year-old girls and boys and a Teachers' Handbook. As an inveterate reader I was disappointed with the meagre notes provided for background on bible stories. I began to haunt ministers' libraries and ask questions about what the biblical stories *really* meant. A few years later, when I was in charge of a class of seventeen teenagers, I looked at possible reasons why a story like Noah's Ark had been written. Was there actually a big flood at some stage, which was background to the story? Well yes, scientific evidence says there had been a huge flood about 2,000 BCE in the area of Mount Ararat. It had left a deep layer of silt as evidence. Aha! That would explain the story. The people who experienced a flood of that dimension would have believed that it covered the whole world, having no knowledge of the rest of it, only their immediate environment in the Middle East.

My class lapped it up, and we had a great discussion about this as a story about God, not as a report about a world-wide flood. I remember this episode clearly because half of the parents of my class threatened to withdraw their children. The minister at the time supported me, but I learned a salutary lesson about the strength of religious convictions based on belief in the literal truth of the Bible. Through all of this I developed a taste for looking 'underneath things' in the Bible. I continued to do so in adult bible study groups I attended and eventually led.

Alongside these critical developments in my approach to the faith, I began to recognize contradictory ideas in ministers' sermons. On the one hand there would be the unpacking of a parable or story from Jesus about 'the right way to live'. The message was clear that it was up to me to put that into practice. If I did nothing to make the world a better place, it simply would not happen. I understood that, and saw around me people trying to carry out that message in daily life. My mother was a definite case in point. At least twice per week she went off with basket over her arm to visit the frail and ill in our district. She would have made scones for them, or picked flowers from her Daphne bush. At one point she cared for a woman living alone and suffering from bowel cancer at a time when palliative care hospices did not exist. The woman was also a victim of a cleft palate, having been born in a time and circumstances when no surgical aid was offered to repair it. That made her speech unattractive to hear, and in some people's eyes rendered her an 'untouchable' – a 'cripple'. My mother ignored all of that and washed her bed-linen and cleaned her up until she died. I saw and heard that as following Jesus.

Yet the Sunday morning sermon about following Jesus would often include something else – something so contradictory I could not help noticing it, and wondering why no one around me mentioned it. Into a perfectly good sermon about a parable of Jesus would be dropped a dollop of Paul's End-time Christology, often garnished with Protestant atonement theories. Apparently God had banished all evil and suffering in the world (including death itself) through the death of 'Christ' on the Cross. Now all we had to do was to wait for the 'fulfilment', which was said to mean the second coming of Jesus. Hadn't he already said all he had to say? What on earth was the first coming about, if he needed to come back? My questions about these things would fall on deaf ears. Eventually I realised that people around me managed to contain both aspects of this contradictory teaching about Jesus of Nazareth and Jesus the Christ in different compartments of their thinking. Alongside the inclusive teaching of Jesus about a loving God, they heard exclusive teaching about an unloving God who condemns 'sinners' and 'outsiders' to hell. Somehow they had to tune out one and listen to the other, and vice versa.

My readers will know that this is precisely what has been asked of churchgoers. If you ask most members of the church what they actually believe in, I think they would find it very hard to put into words, other than to say, "I follow Jesus". For as long as I can remember I have felt a mixture of outrage and despair rise within me when people have talked about 'the gospel of Christ', when what they mean is the gospel (or good news) from Jesus! Toward the end of this book I will give the reader a more lengthy explanation of why I do not see 'the gospel of Christ' as good news.

Church in those days (1950s-60s) included a lengthy and quite graphic Prayer of Confession. I was and am still prepared to recognize shortcomings in my own person and behaviour, but the church's response to that became increasingly difficult to reconcile with the God I encountered in the teachings of Jesus. Jesus' God believed first in my capacity for goodness. The church's God saw me as sinful from birth, requiring repetitious confession of sin and forgiveness. My reluctance to believe in a God who created me sinful in the first place, but required Jesus' crucifixion as payment for my sinfulness, led me to a point where a fundamental shift took place in my thinking. I could no longer agree with traditional Good Friday ideas about Jesus as the Saviour of the world who had defeated death on the Cross for my sake – at the instigation of God! It seemed to me that all of this was illustrated by a poster that hung on the wall of our Sunday School. The treatment handed out to Jesus in order for this to come about made me shudder each time I passed the poster. It depicted a crowned Jesus sitting in heaven at the right side of God's throne (God had the requisite white beard), with the words underneath: 'No Cross, no Crown'. Poor Jesus.

This internal struggle became more difficult for me at the evangelistic rallies held about every two years in our church, led by imported evangelists. I went to these with my mother, and wondered why my father always seemed to be too busy to attend – the penny dropped much later. When I was about sixteen I heard one of these evangelists deliver a particularly colourful description of what would happen to the unfortunates who did not accept Christ as their Saviour. This man seemed determined to 'scare the hell' out of the assembled company, but with his colourful language he looked to me more and more like the side-show men who spruiked their wares at the Bendigo Agricultural Show. As it was with most of them, for me his message lacked the ring of truth. I refused to go to any more of the rallies.

Those observations about contradiction between the religion *of* Jesus and the religion *about* Jesus remained with me. They stayed with me when I read and thought about this discontinuity in the heart of the faith through twenty years of marriage and motherhood and teaching Sunday School. But I loved Jesus and wanted to follow him and teach other people about him. After being widowed in my forties, I became a candidate for ordination in the Uniting Church in Australia. I then had the opportunity to study theology and ask the question in earnest: why should Christians be burdened with irreconcilable ideas about Jesus of Nazareth and Jesus as the Christ, the second person of the triune God?

Countless Christians have asked the same question. Many thousands have voted with their feet and walked out on a religion that makes no sense to them. Most of the remainder hang on in the churches because of their love for the God of Jesus, through whom they are inspired to care for the needy. That is the main reason for their continued membership; through the church they can find the people and the means for doing good in the world. They are given life and inspiration from Jesus for this, but can no longer believe in him as 'the Saviour Christ'. Many of those same people stand mutely while the Nicene Creed is being said, or during the singing of christological hymn words. They have no need to 'maintain links with the church's past', as people wanting to retain traditional expressions of the faith are inclined to advocate.

It is for those who have left the church as well as for those who remain in spite of difficulty, that I write this book. My aim is to reveal the 'Made on Earth' tag on the human product that came to be called 'Christ'. 'Christ' was initially the Greek translation of 'Messiah', but as we will see, the word came to be invested with hugely different meanings from the original Hebrew meaning: 'anointed representative of God'. Through these pages I will argue a case for unburdening Jesus from the triumphalist christological role into which the early church cast him. I signal now to the reader that this would entail the complete removal of the name 'Christ' (however reinterpreted) from association with Jesus.

I will examine the ways in which the case for regarding Jesus as Messiah/Christ was made by the three synoptic gospel-writers, Mark, Matthew and Luke, plus the writer of the Gospel of John. For the reader's clarification, I will preface that examination with background chapters about the meaning of Messiah in Judaism both pre-Easter and post-Easter.

Section 2

Where did the Messiah come from?

Messianic belief in 1ˢᵗ century CE Judaism: did Jesus think he was the Messiah?

D id Jesus think he was the Messiah, later to be called the Christ? This is the most pivotal and fundamental question Christians can ask. Upon the answer rests the legitimacy of the whole composition of Christian thought, institution and sense of self in relation to the world. If in the 21ˢᵗ century the idea of Messiah still has some counterpart in reality, there is room for consideration of who might (still) fulfil the role. If in this age the Messiah is not regarded as a king, sent down from heaven to earth to defeat empires and clean up the world, how might the concept of Messiah be explained and justified, let alone identified with Jesus? If the Messiah is sent from heaven to die to save souls from eternal hell, what does that mean for growing numbers of Christians who don't believe in hell? (Or, for goodness' sake, what does it mean for the billions who are of other faiths or of no faith?) The fact is that the Saviour Messiah/Christ idea relies on Christian belief in hell and necessitates converting all other people to Christianity. Most significantly, belief in Christ implies a disconnected inaccessible God who needed to send an emissary from heaven to rescue hopelessly worthless humanity. That same God has no compunction about sentencing human beings who do not believe in Christ to an eternity of hideous torture. But who would want to believe in a God like that?

If Jesus is in fact (not just in faith) the Messiah/Christ,

then the New Testament got it right and the church got it right. If Jesus is in fact the Messiah, he must surely have known that. If he is the Messiah, then the christological and theological structure of Christianity built on that assumption is at least partially justified. If Jesus is not the Messiah (nor is anyone else the Messiah), the Christian edifice stands on shaky foundations. If Jesus is not the Messiah, investigation of messianic assumptions about him will find those foundations to be without real substance. It will be discovered that the idea of the Messiah is a human concept, not one emanating from 'heaven'. The christological basis for traditional Christianity will then be recognized as lacking real meaning for human life. At the very least, it will be discovered that christological traditions that held meaning in geographical, religious and cultural contexts two thousand years ago, have no place in the thinking and belief of 21st century humanity. It is as simple, as important, and as extraordinarily complex, as that.

My first question must therefore be: whose version of the meaning of 'Messiah' was first proclaimed about Jesus? The church's assumption is that the Jesus of the New Testament was the fulfilment of messianic expectation in Judaism. After all, they were Jews who first made this claim about him, were they not? Jewish New Testament scholar Professor Amy-Jill Levine begins to pull the rug out from under this notion:

> *Not all Jews in the first century – or ever – have believed that a messiah was coming. Neither was there general agreement upon messianic attributes; there was no checklist that included: being born to a virgin mother, receiving a direct commission from God, defeating Satan's temptations, walking on water.*[15]

Messiahs as Kings

Messianism certainly was one aspect of Jewish hopes for the future in the period 200BCE – 100CE.[16] Jews who had messianic expectations believed that God would intervene in human history and bring a catastrophic end to the sources of evil, mainly understood as invading empires. This expectation came out of their experience of oppression and powerlessness as an occupied society. That experience covered every aspect of their life, including political, economic, social and religious spheres. Not surprisingly, they saw their circumstances as beyond their capacity to change. The only hope for relief from suffering lay in the intervention of a supernatural agency – God and a kingly leader divinely anointed.[17] This belief gave rise to messianic movements led by messianic 'kings'. These figures were believed by their followers to have been chosen by God to bring the messianic age to fulfilment, when the oppressor would be defeated through God's intervention, and an era of peace and justice would begin.

Such beliefs appear to have been held primarily by rural dwellers such as people of the Galilee region, not so much by better-educated city dwellers in Judea. There is vanishingly small evidence of kingly messianic expectation among the literate classes at leadership levels such as Sadducees and Scribes. Their writings scarcely mention messianic thinking. The Pharisees, the lay intelligentsia, did believe in a general resurrection of the dead, at which time God would send the Messiah to oversee a restored Israel. It is important to note that for the Pharisees, resurrection from the dead did not equate with immortality of the soul; it did mean the bodily resurrection of the righteous dead. They and the righteous ones living (those who had repented of their sin) would enter the kingdom of God, to be established on the appearance of the Messiah. Consequently, the Pharisees were not behind the popular militaristic (Davidic) messianic movements of the first century. They believed the initiative for the coming of the Messiah lay exclusively with God.

Accordingly it is unproductive to go looking for messianic ideas in the writings of Second Temple Judaism (515BCE – 70CE), because texts from that period come primarily from the Temple priesthood and Pharisaic lay leadership. Understandably, the greater financial security of the leadership left them with little sense that they needed salvation from the status quo, delivered by a kingly Messiah figure. The Dead Sea Scrolls do contain references to kingly and priestly messiahs, but these are due to the very different situation of the Qumran scrolls authors from that of the ruling Jewish elite in Jerusalem. The Qumran leadership regarded itself as the legitimate leadership of Jerusalem, having been dislodged from that position by a 'wicked' illegitimate Maccabean-appointed High Priest, possibly either Jonathan or Simeon Maccabeus. Even so, the Davidic (kingly) and Aaronic (high-priestly) messiahs of the Dead Sea Scrolls are not themselves agents of salvation; they are merely to appear at an apocalyptic time of fulfilment ('the Day of the Lord'). At that point the scrolls authors' self-identity as legitimate leaders of the Temple would be vindicated.[18]

On the other hand, there were people who wanted to take matters into their own hands and bring about the defeat of the Roman Empire. Popular messianic deliverers, usually called 'kings', such as Judas the Galilean (early first century CE) were consciously carrying out the role of a latter-day King David, who (Psalm 2:2,7 says) was the first anointed monarch, or messiah, also known as 'son of God'! Readers familiar with the words of Handel's *Messiah* will remember the lines: *Thou art my son; this day have I begotten thee.* That was not written about Jesus. In Psalm 2:7 it is God speaking to King David.

The primary task of the popular kingly messiahs was the defeat of Israel's enemies (Rome), the 'purification' of the Jerusalem Temple from a priesthood collaborating with Rome and the ingathering of dispersed Israelites as prelude to a messianic golden age. These messianic 'kings' gathered a following and set out to attack the strongholds of Roman and Herodian garrisons in the hope that God would support their endeavours and bring about the defeat of evil. At that juncture Israel would be delivered from its enemies and its dispersed people in the Jewish diaspora would return to a restored Zion. Although the motives of these messianic leaders (or 'kings') were theological, their *modus operandi* was militaristic. They thought it was up to them to get on with it! Then God would step in and help.

Prophets as Heralds

In the first century CE there were traditions surrounding the return of 'prophets of old' to herald either the Messiah or "the

LORD", meaning God.[19] In scriptural traditions about these prophetic figures (particularly in Malachi 3-4), they were not intended to lead their followers into battle; they were concerned with turning the people of Israel from sinfulness through repentance. Their aim was that on the apocalyptic *"Day of the LORD"* (e.g. Zephaniah 1:14) the people would have already repented and Israel could be restored to its former glory as a free unoccupied nation in covenant with God. An additional element would be the people of other nations streaming into Jerusalem from all over the world to worship Israel's God. Today many conservative Christians believe that when all Jews have converted to Christianity, this scenario will take place. Accordingly they are pouring money into Israel for two reasons: first to attract more tourists to their 'holy sites', and secondly, in the hope of making converts from Judaism. All of this reflects a supersessionist[20] reading of the Hebrew Scriptures, by which Jesus is seen as the one specifically predicted by Israel's prophets.

A common belief in the centuries before Jesus was that the continual occupation of Israel by foreign empires was caused by the sins of the Israelites. This was most often the sin of idolatry, where the people had abandoned worship of Yahweh to worship the gods of the occupying empire. For that reason the biblical prophets called the Israelites to repentance and reconciliation. An example is Malachi 4: 5-6:

> *"Lo, I will send you the prophet Elijah before the great and terrible day of the Lord comes. He will turn the hearts of parents to their children and the hearts of children to their parents, so that I will not come and strike the land with a curse."*

These prophets were also expected to perform miracles as 'signs' of the coming messianic age. The miracles attributed to Jesus in the gospels are drawn primarily from scriptural traditions about the miracle-working prophets Moses and Elijah, not from traditions about David, regarded as the first Messiah. *Contrary to gospel portraits of Jesus, miracle-working was not the expected traditional function of the Messiah.*

John the baptist, Elijah and the Messiah

Kingly/messianic and prophetic leaders were identified through clearly defined expectations. Most carried out their roles according to prescribed scriptural and extra-scriptural traditions about the apocalyptic End-time.[21] John the Baptist was one such prophetic figure looking for the restoration of Israel, but he is portrayed by gospel writers as also pointing to the coming of the Messiah. Probably much closer to the truth was that John was consciously acting out the role of an Elijah-styled prophet to call the people to repentance and (in his case) to a baptism of purification. Among the oppressed poor at that time there was an expectation that Elijah would come back to earth from the heavens to which he had ascended alive (2 Kings 2: 9-12). He would announce God's judgment on Israel's oppressors. The gospels (Mark 1:6; Matthew 3:4) state that John the baptizer wore clothes and ate foods that were similar to the clothes and food of Elijah. In accordance with predictions about the returned Elijah, John is portrayed preparing the people for "*the great and terrible day of the Lord*" (Malachi 4:5). He calls the people to repent of their sins and offers them a baptism of repentance.

John the Baptist obviously expected a fiery apocalyptic time of judgment, in which God would intervene in human history and liberate Israel. This is a plainly political, as well as a theological expectation. It did not mean John believed the world would come to an end, but that the current political circumstances would end with Rome's defeat and Israel's restoration in freedom. In accordance with the prophetic books, at that time God would judge those who had oppressed Israel. In following chapters I will have more to say about John and the role assigned to him by the gospel writers as forerunner of the Messiah. Clearly there are difficulties in reconciling the expected Jewish Messiah and the portrait of Jesus as Messiah created by the gospel writers. On the other hand, there are numerous reasons for seeing Jesus not only as a teacher of the wisdom of Torah, but as a prophet in the mould of Elijah, including his 'cleansing of the Temple':

Malachi 3: 2-3: *For he is like a refiner's fire and like fullers' soap; he will sit as a refiner and purifier of silver, and he will purify the descendants of Levi and refine them like gold and silver, until they present offerings to the Lord in righteousness.*

The identification of the *"messenger of the covenant"* (Malachi 3:1) as Elijah is confirmed by the writer of the Book of Ben Sira (or Ecclesiasticus), included in the Apocryphal books of the Catholic version of the Old Testament. In his section praising Elijah (Ecclesiasticus 48) Ben Sira refers to Malachi 4:5:

"At the appointed time, it is written, you are destined to calm the wrath of God before it breaks out in fury, to turn the hearts of parents to their children, and to restore the tribes of Jacob."

Second century CE rabbinic traditions surrounding the return of Elijah include his role as the ultimate teacher of the Torah. The explanation for this is that because Elijah has been in the heavenly realms, he now has the correct answer to every problem associated with observance of Torah.[22]

The key to Elijah's association with teaching is that he is depicted as both priest and prophet. In 1 Kings 18: 20-40, Elijah is portrayed in a priestly role, officiating at the offering of a sacrifice, and calling on God to respond with heavenly fire. In Judaism between 200BCE and 70CE, the role of a teacher was combined with those of prophet and priest. Malachi 2:7 expresses it:

"For the lips of a priest should guard knowledge, and people should seek instruction from his mouth, for he is the messenger of the Lord of hosts."

In his book Ecclesiasticus, the scribe Ben Sira describes the attributes given to the original High Priest of Israel, Aaron. Moses blessed Aaron:

"In his commandments he gave him authority and statutes and judgments to teach Jacob the testimonies, and to enlighten Israel with his law." (45:17).

The connection here between teacher and priest is unmistakable and it informed expectations surrounding a return of Elijah the prophet/teacher/priest. The gospel of Luke adds priestly qualifications to Jesus by means of the description in 1:5 of Mary's relative Elizabeth, mother of John the Baptist. Elizabeth is described as a descendant of Aaron, the first High Priest. Her lineage obviously also applies to Mary, her 'relative'. Mary then passes on her priestly lineage to her first-born son, Jesus. That detail is a piece of Luke's portrait of Jesus the Messiah.

One of the best known features of the Passover Seder meal of post-Temple Judaism (70CE onward) up to the present, is the expectation that Elijah will appear at Passover and resolve all unanswered questions regarding the Law of Moses. Later Rabbinic stories had Elijah appearing in various disguises to guide people struggling to understand the biblical Law. It is not for nothing then, that Jesus was seen by many of the people as Elijah returned, or as John the Baptist come back from the dead (Luke 9:7). They naturally saw Jesus as prophet and teacher of the Law (if not priest), but not as Messiah. He simply did not fit the kingly messianic description and expectation.[23]

There is also the strong possibility that Jesus was depicted by Matthew as fulfilment of Deuteronomy 18:18, where God speaks with Moses and says:

"I will raise up for them a prophet like you from among their own people; I will put my words in the mouth of the prophet, who shall speak to them everything that I command."

The classical prophetic role in the Hebrew scriptures[24] is to prepare the people through repentance to escape the wrath of God and receive divine blessing on the apocalyptic *"Day of the LORD"*, when all evil will be defeated and Israel restored into favour with God.

The Suffering Servant and the Messiah

Another figure often identified with Jesus the Messiah is the 'suffering servant' of Isaiah. Problematically for that interpretation, the 'servant' is not a suffering, dying Messiah. For Isaiah he represents the suffering people of Israel in Exile in Babylon, who will be vindicated in the eyes of the nations on the apocalyptic *"Day of the LORD"*. The gospel writers wrote their stories of Jesus' crucifixion in accordance with the 'suffering servant' figure of Isaiah 53 and the suffering figure in Psalm 22, identified as David, the first Messiah. Suffering Israel is now transformed into gospel-speak as the Messiah who suffers for the people.

Of course Jesus dies in accordance with depictions of a tortured, dying figure in Isaiah and Psalm 22. The gospel writers had the biblical script in front of them; they used it intentionally in order to write their crucifixion stories! The trap for Christians is reading these stylized stories of Jesus' death as vindication of prophetic 'predictions' – so Jesus really must be the Messiah! I am calling these so-called fulfilled predictions *internal proof-texting*. This explanation of similarities between the Hebrew scriptures and the death of Jesus as recorded in the gospels is resoundingly obvious, yet is hardly ever mentioned in the church as the most likely interpretation. Historically, Christianity has preferred to see Jesus as actual messianic fulfilment of the Hebrew scriptures.

Traditional biblical scholarship has peered through christological lenses at the Hebrew scriptures and taken as read a messianic fulfilment interpretation of Jesus in them. Yet a resort to the simplest explanation for the Hebrew Bible/Gospel similarities – an intentional recasting of the 'suffering servant' as Messiah Jesus – throws clear light on the origins of this messianic gospel portrait. I will set this out in more detail in the chapters on Jesus the Messiah and the gospels.

The Messiah as Son of Man

The gospel messianic portrait of Jesus also included the title *"Son of Man"*. The most obvious source is:

Daniel 7:13-14: *"I saw in the night visions, and behold, with the clouds of heaven there came one like a Son of man, and he came to the Ancient of Days [God] and was presented before him. And to him was given dominion and glory and kingdom, that all peoples, nations, and languages should serve him; his dominion is an everlasting dominion, which shall not pass away, and his kingdom one that shall not be destroyed."*(NRSV).

Son of Man is also the title of the eschatological (End time) judge in the Parables of Enoch, part of the Jewish Book of Enoch.[25] Current scholarship places the Parables in the first century BCE, about a century before Jesus.[26] There are many similarities between the Son of Man figure in Daniel and the Son of Man figure in the Parables of Enoch. Enoch is quoted in the late first century CE New Testament *Letter of Jude*, which lends weight to the argument that gospel writers were also influenced in their portrait of Jesus the Messiah by Enoch's 'Son of Man' as well as Daniel's.

A quotation from the Parables of Enoch will illustrate why this might have been so:

"And there was great joy amongst them, and they blessed and glorified and extolled because the name of that Son of Man had been revealed unto them. And he sat on the throne of his glory, and the sum of judgment was given unto the Son of Man, and he caused the sinners to pass away and be destroyed from off the face of the earth, and those who have led the world astray" (69: 26). "And from henceforth there shall be nothing corruptible; for that Son of Man has appeared, and has seated himself on the throne of his glory" (69:29).

Here the Son of Man is fulfilling the role of judge at the apocalyptic End-time (compare with Matthew 25:31).

The Greek (c.250 BCE) version of Daniel is much more clearly messianic than the original Aramaic version. A case can be made that the gospel-writers' use of the Greek version of

Daniel assisted them in crafting their portrait of Jesus as Messiah. 'Son of Man' was used in the same messianic sense in the Apocalypse of Ezra[27] (4 Ezra 13), written following the Jewish War against the Romans of 66-70CE. That may well have reflected a popular usage among Jews then of 'Son of Man' as reference to the Messiah. This is evident in Matthew's portrait of Jesus as Son of Man in the parable of the last judgment (Matthew 25: 31-46), where he fills the messianic role of End-time judge. Matthew's Gospel also was written after the Jewish War.

The Vision of Isaiah

In Jesus' time Jewish expectation of the future naturally had strong connections with prophetic writings in the scriptures, including expectation of the restoration of Israel as outlined in Micah 4: 2-4.

> *In days to come the mountain of the LORD's house shall be established as the highest of the mountains, and shall be raised up above the hills. Peoples shall stream to it, and many nations shall come and say: "Come, let us go up to the mountain of the LORD, to the house of the God of Jacob; that he may teach us his ways and that we may walk in his paths." For out of Zion shall go forth instruction, and in the word of the LORD from Jerusalem. He shall judge between many peoples, and shall arbitrate between strong nations far away; they shall beat their swords into plowshares, and their spears into pruning hooks; nation shall not lift up sword against nation, neither shall they learn war any more; but they shall all sit under their own vines and under their own fig trees, and no one shall make them afraid; for the mouth of the LORD of hosts has spoken.*

That would be an age of peace and plenty, where swords and other weapons of war are transformed into the means of producing food for all.

The 'Isaiah vision' (Is.65: 17-25) sees the ideal society as a state of affairs without war, with the expectation of long life, health and freedom from hunger. Luke has Jesus quote from Isaiah 61 when announcing his 'manifesto' for ministry:

> Isaiah 61:1-2: *"the spirit of the LORD God is upon me because the LORD has anointed me; he has sent me to bring good news to the oppressed, to bind up the broken-hearted, to proclaim liberty to the captives, and release to the prisoners; to proclaim the year of the LORD's favour, and the day of vengeance of our God; to comfort all who mourn".*

Here again there are indications of Jewish *'Day of the LORD'* expectations (*"the day of vengeance of our God"*), plus good news for the poor and those who mourn – as echoed in the Beatitudes. It must be said that Isaiah 61 was written about the people of Israel after their return from exile in Babylon around 538BCE, when they faced the rebuilding of a ruined Jerusalem. It is quoted in Luke's gospel, which was written after Jerusalem has been destroyed again in 70CE, this time by the Romans. Isaiah 61 was originally pronounced by a prophet, but Luke places a messianic interpretation on it. He has Jesus quote it as revelation of his messiahship, which (Luke believes) will fulfil the prophet's Isaiah's prediction.

It is important to note that apart from David (Psalm 2) and a reference to Cyrus the Persian ruler as 'anointed' by God for releasing the Jewish captives (Ezra 1:2-4), no messianic figure is named in the Hebrew scriptures. References there to the "Day of the LORD" are to the direct intervention of God at an apocalyptic End-time. There are messianic expectations in the Dead Sea Scrolls (200BCE – 100CE), but their writings do not represent mainstream Judaism of those times.

Jesus and traditional messianic expectation

There are many aspects of the gospel portraits of Jesus which have no antecedents in Jewish messianic expectation. Significantly, there was little or no expectation in Judaism in Jesus' time that the Messiah would die and rise again on the third day. A remote possibility is Hosea 6:1-2:

> *"Come, let us return to the Lord: for it is he who has torn,*
> *and he will heal us; he has struck down, and he will bind*
> *us up. After two days he will revive us; on the third day*
> *he will raise us up, that we may live before him."*

The drawback for that possibility is that "us" refers not to the Messiah, but to the people of Israel. Even if an unlikely possibility existed that the gospel writers knew of a tradition about a Messiah who would die and rise in three days and wrote that into their portrait of Jesus, it does not constitute proof that Jesus either knew this tradition or believed he was in fact the Messiah.

When the Jewish people heard some of their fellow Jews proclaim messianic ideas about Jesus following his crucifixion, a huge problem stood in the way of acceptance. Where was he? The messianic age to which their scriptures pointed had patently not arrived – Jesus had simply not returned in triumph as Messiah. That was sufficient for most of Jesus' fellow Jews to resist messianic proclamation about him. He had also died in the abject shame and public humiliation of crucifixion. That would never happen to the Messiah. It is important to remember that this messianic proclamation took place post-Easter, eventually from Paul and most probably not during the lifetime of Jesus. Should any pre-Easter belief in Jesus as Messiah have existed, it may have involved militaristic Zealots,[28] as I will point out when examining gospel references to Judas Iscariot.

The most critical difference between mainstream Jewish expectations of a kingly, militaristic Messiah and post-Easter believers in Jesus as Messiah/Christ, concerned the Messiah's role in the messianic age. This was the time when it was expected that evil was to be defeated. Traditional belief did not have the Messiah first appear as a teacher, healer and miracle worker, be crucified, and then reappear to reign over a messianic age. The Messiah was not expected to die and appear a second time. The post-resurrection appearances in the gospels are fleeting; they do not constitute the Messiah's triumphal appearance at the beginning of the messianic age. They are about encouraging believers in their waiting. They reflect Paul's and the gospel writers' conviction that they must wait for Jesus the Messiah/Christ to reappear.

Matthew alone tries to convince his readers of Jesus' messiahship by claiming that Pharisaic expectation of the bodily resurrection of the righteous in the messianic age happened when Jesus died. The 'proof' Matthew provides is the dead "*saints*" climbing out of their graves and walking the streets (27:52). The second coming of the Messiah at a later time was a concept alien to the Jews of Jesus' time. It required a lot of persuasion from Paul for post-Easter Jews to believe it.

The question then remains, did Jesus of Nazareth consider himself to be the Messiah? If he did, he would have measured his qualifications for this role against the traditional expectations of Messiah in his own religion and society. Did he fit those expectations? In 2003 New Testament Professor Paula Fredriksen of the Boston University School of Theology was interviewed for its *Focus* magazine. On being asked why Jesus was thought to be the Messiah, she responded:

> *Nobody has a good explanation for why the term "Christ" attaches to the figure of Jesus. Scholars don't and the Gospels don't. I mean, all the Gospels are convinced that Jesus is the Christ, yet they all give different reasons why they thought so. The problem for scholars is this: why did such a messianically improbable figure end up being known by the messianic title? He didn't do anything messianic. Messiahs don't cure people; messiahs aren't prophets. On the basis of what we have in the Gospels, Jesus is just not a messianic figure.[29]*

Keeping in mind that the gospels are deliberately created portraits of Jesus as Messiah, I will examine the gospels and (briefly) Pauline literature for signs there of intentional messianic portraits of Jesus. I will ask whether those signs are in keeping, or at odds, with Jesus' most important legacy – his teachings. In the course of this book I will propose a much more likely self-identity for Jesus, but first we will look for any messianic identification of Jesus in his own movement pre-Easter.

Messianism and the Jesus Movement Pre-Easter

The following are identifying characteristics of the pre-Easter Jesus movement that are common to all gospels and do not necessarily incorporate messianic ideas about Jesus.

Jesus came from the Galilee

Although the infancy narratives in Matthew and Luke place Jesus' birth in Bethlehem, both claim Nazareth in the Galilee as the place where he grew up. In Jesus' time Nazareth was a small village of rural workers, the majority of whom were most probably both illiterate and impoverished. Their poverty would have been caused in large part by the economic dominance of families loyal to the son of Herod the Great, Herod Antipas the Tetrarch of Galilee. Their ultimate loyalty had to be to Rome. These upper class Jews would have been regarded by the peasant class as traitors – collaborators with the oppressors. Many of these well-off people, some conspicuously wealthy, lived in the Galilee in Antipas' Roman style city, Sepphoris (re-built in 4 BCE).

The new Sepphoris was a morning's walk from Nazareth, and it would have been a study in contrasts for the poor Nazarethites. Archaeological excavations at Sepphoris have uncovered Jewish houses designed and built along the lines of Roman villas of the period, with elaborate mosaic-decorated floors and frescoes, plus fine household implements including ceramics and expensive crockery. The same kind of social division between the struggling poor and the ostentatiously rich is evident from the excavations of Antipas' Tiberias near the Sea of Galilee. To add further to that social division, the wealthy in those days amassed their fortunes from land holdings worked by Jewish peasants.

Significantly, the Jewish historian Flavius Josephus called those peasants 'Galileans'. The exploitation of the peasants/Galileans took place through exorbitant taxes and unjust demands for huge shares of the crops they grew. Naturally this sparked not merely the antagonism of the Galileans, but murderous hatred toward their oppressors, who were often also their religious and ethnic compatriots. Josephus, who collaborated with Rome, reveals some of this extreme hatred in his description of his own attempts to control Galileans involved in the sacking of Sepphoris prior to the Jewish War of 66 – 70CE:

> I marched with such troops as I had against Sepphoris and took the city by assault. The Galileans, seizing this opportunity, too good to be missed, of venting their hatred on one of the cities which they detested, rushed forward, with the intention of exterminating the population, aliens and all ... Tiberias, likewise, had a narrow escape from being sacked by the Galileans, loudly denouncing the Tiberians as traitors and friendly to the king (Agrippa II).[30]

Paradoxically, it was the relative prosperity of the Galilee region during the first century which made it the focus of unreasonable Roman and Herodian taxation, resulting in hardship for the peasant population. Studies in the economic and climatic conditions of the Galilee in the first half of the first century reveal that the area was indeed prosperous and known as the 'bread basket' of the whole region.[31] The fishing industry on the Sea of Galilee adjacent to Tiberias was also subject to taxation. In Matthew's gospel one possible illustration of this tax on fish concerns the tax collector (also called Matthew). He left the employ of the authorities and joined Jesus' core group of supporters at Capernaum, on the shore of the Sea of Galilee.

During Jesus' lifetime several messianic 'kings' from the Galilee were actively engaged in militant opposition to their Herodian and Roman oppressors. It is surely not coincidence that the peasant supporters of these messiah-kings came to believe in an apocalyptic End-time theology, whereby God would come to their aid to restore Israel to its pure religion and defeat Rome and its Herodian puppets, plus the collaborating leaders of the Temple. That environment is most likely to have been the instigation for Jesus' passionate advocacy for the poor and oppressed, through his vision of the *"kingdom of heaven"* on earth. Before Jesus began to make his vision known publicly, John the Baptist was preaching a baptism of repentance before a fiery day (*"day of the LORD"*) when God would intervene. In accordance with prophetic tradition in Malachi 3 and 4, John is depicted by gospel writers as the returned Elijah who will prepare the way for "the Lord", meaning Jesus.

In fact Malachi speaks of preparing the way for God, which is the non-messianic way the people of Galilee would have understood the biblical tradition concerning the return of Elijah. While the gospel writers cast John the Baptist in the role of the returned Elijah, it is with a crucial difference: John is depicted as preparing the way, not of God, but of the Messiah, identified as Jesus. That is a definite break with tradition.

Jesus advocated non-violent resistance

Non-violent resistance is the core of Jesus' teaching about overcoming injustice and oppression. There can be no doubt that he advocated non-violence as a way to resist the violence of the authorities in his home district of Galilee. It is also true that there is an apparent approval from Jesus of violence by sword in Luke 22:36: *"And the one who has no sword must sell his cloak and buy one"*, but the reason given for attributing these words to Jesus then follows: *"For I tell you, this scripture must be fulfilled in me, 'And he was counted among the lawless'."* This is a direct translation from the Greek (Septuagint) version of Isaiah 53 regarding the 'suffering servant': "(he) *was numbered with the transgressors"* (Isaiah 53: 12b NRSV).

Here we have Luke's use of the Greek version of Isaiah 53

to write his messianic portrait of Jesus, in this case clearly compromising Jesus' unequivocal teaching concerning non-violence. This is not a genuine teaching of Jesus; it reflects the difficult situation in which messianic Jews in Luke's community were placed when proclaiming Jesus as Messiah. Those difficulties would have included violent clashes with mainstream Jews and their Pharisaic/Temple leaders.

Luke appears in that instance to be attempting to neutralise a natural post-Easter Jewish protest that nowhere is it written that the Messiah will actually die. He counters that protest by claiming Jesus' death as fulfilment of the Isaian 'suffering servant' passage (Ch. 53), where the servant is associated with the 'transgressors', or, in the original Hebrew – the *parashim* – 'rebels'. Like the 'suffering servant' during a previous occupation of the land, Jesus is being counted here among the insurrectionists against Rome. For that reason Luke's Jesus tells his inner circle they must carry a sword for protection. That was patently not the way of Jesus as reflected in his teachings against violence in Luke chapter 6.

Luke's internal proof-texting is revealed in the words attributed to Jesus that follow the quotation from Isaiah 53: "... *and indeed what was written about me is being fulfilled.*" (22:37b). Messianic fulfilment of the Hebrew Scriptures is clearly more important to Luke than Jesus' teachings about non-violence. It is also entirely possible that this passage in Luke was added at a later date by editors intent on trying to fit Jesus into biblical predictions about the suffering servant.

Luke's gospel was written after the disastrous Jewish War, when the Messiah Jesus movement was encountering fierce opposition from both Jewish and Roman authorities. This then, is Luke giving permission to members of the movement in his day to carry swords. As was common practice in Hellenistic literature he does this by placing these words in Jesus' mouth, thereby adding to them Jesus' authority. Tragically, those words have given permission to countless followers of Jesus to use violence in his name. They illustrate the danger in turning away

from his genuine teaching about non-violence. Historical

evidence points to the likelihood that Jesus' followers pre-Easter did not stand and fight; at first they ran away. In accordance with that, there is no record of persecution of Jesus' original followers after the crucifixion. But oddly, after Luke's Jesus tells the disciples to carry a sword, he admonishes them for using it to defend him:

> 22: 49-51: *When those who were around him saw what was coming, they asked, "Lord, should we strike with the sword?" Then one of them struck the slave of the high priest and cut off his right ear. But Jesus said, "No more of this!" And he touched his ear and healed him.*

Luke (or the editor) appears to have been caught here on the horns of a dilemma. On the one hand the gospel includes Jesus' teachings about love of enemies and non-violent resistance to violence (Luke 6: 27-36). On the other hand Luke contains contrary advice to readers regarding the violent opposition the Messiah Jesus movement was encountering in the 80s of the first century CE.

There have been numerous attempts to explain Jesus' rationale for his advocacy of non-violent resistance to violent oppression. An obvious answer is that he lived in violent times, where the tragic and horrific outcome of violent resistance to empire was all too plain. From his boyhood he would have observed two responses to the oppressive authority of Rome and its puppet Jewish kings. One was to collaborate with authority and reap the material rewards. The story of Zacchaeus (Luke 19:1-10) is the perfect example of this. The riches of Sepphoris and Tiberias were the compensation some chose in return for siding with imperial power. For many of their compatriots and co-religionists, that stance was nothing short of treason and apostasy – against Israel and against its God.

When Judas the Galilean sparked a rebellion against Roman occupation in 6 BCE, he did it under the motto: "No Lord but God". For him and other military rebels the tragic outcome was wholesale slaughter of them and their followers and the destruction of the Galilean villages from which they came. Jesus would have known this, only too well. He would have observed personally the futility of violent resistance to the violence of the empire, possibly even involving family members and friends. Such personal experience cannot be ruled out as primary impetus for his teachings about love of enemy and non-violent resistance to oppression.

During the first half of the 1st century CE there were two examples of non-violent alternatives to military resistance. The first occurred around 26 – 27 CE, when Jesus was approximately thirty years of age, and would probably have been known to most inhabitants of Galilee and Judaea. Again the historian Flavius Josephus is our witness. When Pontius Pilate was appointed as the 5th Prefect of the Roman Province of Judea, his soldiers carried standards bearing images of Caesar Augustus into Jerusalem. As Josephus records it:

> *The indignation of the townspeople stirred the country folk, who flocked together in crowds"*[32] *to Pilate's headquarters at Caesarea on the Mediterranean coast. The people remained there for five days until they were surrounded by armed troops.* Josephus continues: *... the Jews, as by concerted action, flung themselves in a body on the ground, extended their necks, and exclaimed that they were ready rather to die than to transgress the law.*[33]

Their non-violent resistance was a resounding success. Pilate had the images of Caesar removed from his standards.

A second incident occurred about 10 years after Jesus' death, around 40-41 CE, when the emperor Gaius Caligula set in motion a plan to have his statue on display in the Jerusalem Temple. When the Roman-appointed Syrian governor Petronius came south from Antioch to place the statue, a non-violent popular protest was held at the Mediterranean port of Ptolemais, and another at Tiberias. Josephus and the Jewish philosopher Philo of Alexandria both described the crowds as "many tens of thousands of Jews". These people, "as if at a concerted signal",[34] offered themselves and their families for slaughter to prevent the raising of Caligula's statue. In so doing they were absent from their farms. Fearing that the crops would not be sown, Petronius gave up and returned to Antioch. Fairly obviously these people were Galileans. Who were their leaders? Who encouraged them into this form of non-violent resistance to imperial oppression? One cannot say for certain that it was the prophet/teacher Jesus of Nazareth. Neither can one argue that it was not.

John Dominic Crossan and Jonathan L. Reed offer another angle on this subject in their book *Excavating Jesus*[35]. They first make the point that the Pharisees were very influential at that time, and enjoyed popular approval. Secondly, they name the two major schools of Pharisaism, Shammites and Hillelites, and their major differences in interpreting the Law of Moses (strict Shammai versus more lenient Hillel). Crossan and Reed then ask whether these two schools of Pharisaism may have been characterized by their approval or disapproval of non-violent resistance to Rome. They come to the conclusion that if the leaders of these demonstrations were Pharisees, it is more likely for the school of Hillel to have been in favour of non-violent resistance. Jesus of Nazareth's teaching has often been identified as much closer to the school of Hillel than to the school of Shammai. It would therefore not be drawing too long a bow to see the influence of Jesus' already well-known teachings on this subject in these examples of non-violent resistance, to the point of willingness for martyrdom. It must also be said that even these examples of non-violent resistance do not include Jesus' unique instruction to "love your enemies".

Jesus was a teacher of the Law of Moses

It is curious that many Christians choose to describe Jesus as the Carpenter, when there is only one original instance in the gospels where he is described as such: "*Is this not the carpenter, the son of Mary ... ?*" (Mark 6: 3, copied by Matthew 13: 55). On the other hand the gospels contain at least 23 references to Jesus as a teacher, or as in the act of teaching. This is the primary way he was known and experienced. He was a teacher of the Law, engaged in interpreting it for his own people in his own time. Christians by and large are not aware that when following Jesus' teachings they are being guided by his interpretation of the Law

of Moses. When he quoted from the Law and then said, "*I say ...
etc.*", he was drawing out implications for applying the basic
tenets of his own religious tradition.

It is highly probable that like John the Baptist, Jesus saw
himself as a teacher/prophet engaged in calling the people of
Israel to a renewal of the Mosaic covenant. This covenant
renewal would come about through their observance of his
teachings, all of which are based on the Law of Moses. The end
result would be the kingdom of heaven on earth.

Many Christian scholars prefer to call Jesus a wisdom
teacher and concentrate on his aphorisms and parables as
windows into the kingdom of heaven. That is also a legitimate
view of Jesus' teaching, but for some it neatly avoids an overtly
clear link between Jesus' teaching and the Jewish Torah. This
kind of avoidance was practised in Christian circles until the
latter years of the twentieth century following the Holocaust,
when it finally became acceptable to acknowledge Jesus as a Jew.

First century teachers of the Law gathered students
('disciples' in Latin), who learned by means of a question and
answer format. There are ample instances in the gospels which
show that this was the way Jesus taught his own students. Most
of this would have happened in the open air where it would have
been possible for bystanders to overhear what was being said.
That would account for the gospel scenarios where Jesus'
teaching is interrupted by a question from a Pharisee standing
nearby. All of the teaching among Jews in Judea and the Galilee
would have been based on scriptures preserved in scrolls written
in Hebrew or Aramaic. These would have been very precious and
few in number, but in my opinion Jesus intentionally learned to
read in order to develop from scripture his kingdom of heaven
ideas. The teachers of the Law (the Pharisees) taught boys in
Torah schools in Jerusalem and other towns, and given Jesus'
extensive knowledge of the Law it is entirely possible that
Pharisees were his early teachers, even though it is most likely
that he would have had to go to a place other than Nazareth to
receive that instruction.

Some scholars do not see Jesus as having been literate,
but it is hard to imagine that his erudite interpretation of

scripture would not have come from his personal reading and contemplation. The fact is we do not know what he was doing until he appeared in public as a teacher. He was clearly a respected teacher in his Jewish context, given that the gospels depict the educated Pharisees wanting to engage with his ideas. Luke depicts Jesus as reading from a scroll of the Law at Nazareth (4:14-21). This indicates either that Luke had firm evidence that Jesus could read, or that Luke wished to portray Jesus as literate. In any case, if Jesus' teaching had not been thought worth questioning, the Pharisaic response would most probably have been to ignore what he was saying. He no doubt expected that other teachers would challenge his teaching, as he would naturally have challenged some of theirs. Imagine Jesus as the bystander, arguing with a Pharisee teaching a group of students! That was common practice among biblical scholars and teachers then – as it is today!

Jesus was a teacher/prophet intent on restoring Israel's covenant with God

The people's commitment to God as their ultimate and exclusive ruler is an integral and necessary foundation of the Mosaic covenant. The belief is that through the mutual commitment/covenant between God and Israel, the people will find deliverance from the oppression of the Pharaoh and (in Jesus' time) the Emperor. The Sermon on the Mount in Matthew and (to a lesser extent) the Sermon on the Plain in Luke set out blessings that will be axiomatic for those who enter the renewed covenant (or kingdom of heaven/God). In each of those scenarios Jesus looks like a new Moses delivering a renewed or restored form of the Mosaic Law. Yet it is through examining traditions surrounding a returned Elijah that the prophet/teacher Jesus of history, including his purpose, emerges most clearly.[36]

The author of the most recent case for Jesus as renewal prophet is distinguished Boston scholar Richard Horsley:

> *In sum, from the portrayals in Mark's story and the Q speeches, it is evident that Jesus was responding to the*

crisis of Galilean and Judean society under Roman rule by drawing creatively on core aspects of Israelite tradition. As we know from Josephus' accounts of prophets leading movements and other sources, memories of Moses and Joshua as founding prophets of Israel, and of Elijah as the great prophet of renewal, were operative among the people in a way that informed the generation of extensive movements of resistance and renewal. In his interaction with Galilean villagers, Jesus adapted these formative social memories.[37]

The foregoing are aspects of the pre-Easter Jesus that can be seen 'between the lines' in Mark, Matthew and Luke. They place Jesus within his own Jewish/Galilean context, as a man influenced by his own time and place and with a vision for Israel's future based firmly on his own religious traditions. As we will see, Jesus aimed to draw out those religious traditions to their ultimate meaning and potential for his people. Through his teaching and parables they were invited to imagine another world, a world of upside down values compared with the status quo. He called this alternative but possible world, the "*kingdom of heaven*" on earth. His teachings themselves indicate that this would not come about by the intervention of God in sending the Messiah, but by those who caught the dream from his teaching about the spirit and potential of the Torah.

It may disturb some of my readers to contemplate that the Gentiles were secondary in Jesus' thinking, if not mostly absent. I will expand on that in the chapter on the Gospel of Luke.

The Jesus movement post-Easter

This period has been referred to by scholars as the 'tunnel' or 'dark' era in the history of the post-Easter Jesus movement. The resources to which we can refer for information about the comings and goings of Jesus' followers in this period are few and far between, and by no means do they include reliable eye witness accounts of the nature of the Jesus groups. A lot of credence is placed on descriptions in the Book of Acts of the life of the followers in the time immediately following Jesus' death. Yet we cannot ignore the probability that Acts was written at least ninety years after the crucifixion, even in the early decades of the 2nd century CE, and that its words were passed through a profoundly messianic filter. That is not to say that all of the Book of Acts is creative writing, but its author's purpose is to encourage belief in Jesus as Messiah/Christ. Descriptions of the immediate post-Easter disciples are therefore presented as evidence that they believed Jesus was the Messiah and expected his triumphal return. That was most certainly Paul's early expectation, later promoted by the gospel writers.

However, the story of Jesus' followers in the Book of Acts has come under a good deal of examination in recent time, and in 2013 scholars of the Westar Institute (The Acts Seminar) produced a thorough investigation of Acts, including its historical provenance. Regarding its historical credibility, they state that:

> *Acts can no longer be considered an independent source for the life and mission of Paul. Rather we have found*

that the use of Paul's letters as a source is sufficient to account for all details of the life and itinerary of Paul in Acts. There is very little, if any, evidence for the use of independent sources, much less sources that can be proposed as historically reliable. As a result, we must rethink how we reconstruct the historical story of Paul without any reliance on or reference to the template created by the author of Acts.[38]

Even in the absence of credible historical evidence, the immediate post-Easter period was (according to the gospel writers) dominated by the experience and interpretation of what came to be called 'the resurrection of Christ'. The first thing to say is that this idea of a resurrection from the dead was not unheard of among the ordinary Jewish people. This was not a new and amazing, even preposterous thing to be saying. In pre-scientific first century Judaism, acceptance by Jesus' immediate post-Easter followers that he had risen physically from death did not need to necessitate their belief in something totally new and outlandishly crazy, as it would if a corpse in the 21st century were announced to have risen bodily from three days of death and decay.

The reason is that the doctrine of bodily resurrection was well established among the lay scholars of first century Judaism, the Pharisees. They were the organizers of synagogues and schools, and the educated literate scholars of both the written and oral Torah. It is therefore certain that synagogue-goers and those who attended schools run by Pharisees would have been well instructed in Pharisaic beliefs about the bodily resurrection of the righteous dead in the messianic age. Others would surely have heard of such a compelling subject by word of mouth. This belief is corroborated in Matthew's Gospel, where following the crucifixion the graves of *"the saints"* opened and the dead were wandering the streets (Matthew 27:52-53). This is also evidence for my argument that Matthew was himself a Pharisee. (See chapter on Jesus the Messiah in the Gospel of Matthew).

Josephus (also a Pharisee) is our source for the Pharisaic doctrine of bodily resurrection. He makes specific mention of it, including what look like references to reincarnation, in two books. The first quotation is from *Jewish War*:

> " *... that every soul is imperishable, but that only those of the righteous pass into another body, while those of the wicked are, on the contrary, punished with eternal torment."* [39]

The second is from Jewish Antiquities:

> " *... they hold the belief that an immortal strength belongs to souls, and that there are beneath the earth punishments and rewards for those who in life devoted themselves to virtue or vileness, and that eternal imprisonment is appointed for the latter, but the possibility of returning to life for the former."* [40]

This doctrine can also be found in Daniel 12:2: "*Many of those who sleep in the dust of the earth shall awake, some to everlasting life, and some to shame and everlasting contempt.*" The time of the awakening is at the end of days (Day of the LORD), the time of the general resurrection. In the final verse of the Book of Daniel, Daniel is told by the angel Gabriel, " *... go your way, and rest; you shall rise for your reward at the end of the days.*" (12:13).

In 2008 it was claimed by scholars in Jerusalem that a 90cm-tall stone with ink writing was proof of pre-Jesus belief in a dying Messiah who would rise after three days. The writing has many blanks and is greatly faded, but it has led a major Talmudic scholar, Professor Israel Knohl of Hebrew University, to fill in the blanks in accordance with messianic ideas. He claims the stone indicates that a 'messiah' is told by the angel Gabriel that he will die and rise in three days: "In three days, live, I Gabriel com[mand] yo[u]." [41] Given that the Gabriel stone's inscription is generally agreed to date from the late second century BCE, it likely refers to events under the Greek occupation of Jerusalem, which are also the context of the Book of Daniel. In Daniel the 'Son of Man' of chapter 7 is regarded by most scholars as the people of Israel. Because of that there is a strong likelihood that the 'one' (on the 'Gabriel' stone) who will rise in three days is in fact Israel, under the Maccabeans. This is every bit as likely as interpreting the one to whom Gabriel speaks as the Messiah.

The inscription may represent the kind of late second century BCE interpretation of Daniel from which the gospel writers drew ideas for their depiction of Jesus as the dying, rising Messiah. The gospels include Jesus referring to the Son of Man rising on the third day, as did Jonah on emerging from the whale (Matt. 12:40; Luke 11:29), but this is in accord with the writers' use of other Jewish texts and traditions to portray Messiah Jesus. It does not prove that Jesus actually said this about Jonah, or believed himself to be the Messiah who would rise from the dead.

Acts says that the Apostle Paul testified before the Jewish Council (or Sanhedrin) that he was a Pharisee (23:6). Whether that testimony includes historical fact, if Paul were in fact a Pharisee he would have subscribed to the Pharisaic doctrine of a general bodily resurrection at the end of days, in other words, at the beginning of the messianic era. After time spent post-Easter in persecuting followers of Jesus, Paul eventually came to believe that reports of Jesus' resurrection did signify his messiahship and the dawning of the messianic age: "... *in fact Christ has been raised from the dead, the first fruits of those who have died.*" (1 Cor. 15:20). Paul's messianic belief about Jesus is said (in Acts 9) to have followed a vision of the risen Messiah ('Christ' in New Testament Greek).

It is important to remember here that according to Acts Paul was persecuting followers in the late forties or early fifties CE who were led by Hellenists (Greek-speaking Jews) such as Stephen. The men chosen (Acts 6:5) as missionaries of the Christ movement were "*Philip, Prochorus, Nicanor, Timon, Parmenas and Nicolaus, a proselyte of Antioch.*" All of these are Greek names and seem to indicate that the messianic/risen Christ movement had moved quickly into well-educated Greek-speaking Jewish groups located both inside Palestine and beyond the borders of Judah and Galilee in the Diaspora.[42]

None of that rules out the continuing existence post-Easter of a Jesus movement based in Jerusalem and dedicated to following the teachings of Jesus the prophet/teacher. Such a group would probably have escaped persecution from Roman, Temple and Herodian authorities because of their non-messianic stance, while those who proclaimed Jesus as Messiah/Christ (probably Greek-speaking hellenized Jews) experienced persecution both inside and outside of Palestine. Ironically, the hellenized Jew Saul of Tarsus was initially among the persecutors.

There have been countless attempts to describe what might have led Jesus' original followers to claim he had been raised from death. Even though they most likely knew about the expectation of a general resurrection at the coming of the Messiah, it does not follow that his followers would necessarily have interpreted an experience of him after his death as fulfilment of this expectation. Unless Jesus had explicitly claimed to be the Messiah, it is unlikely that his followers would have understood reports that he had appeared after death as indication that he was the Messiah. On the contrary; the gospels emphasise that Jesus' immediate followers were not expecting anything of the sort! They were patently *not* waiting excitedly for it. The gospel writers make it clear that the followers had no expectation that the crucifixion was precursor to Jesus' resurrection as Messiah. They are not depicted as expecting to have any after-death experience of him at all. Throughout the crucifixion and resurrection narratives the disciples are devastated, terrified, amazed, and in Thomas' case – sceptical.

In reality Jesus' death was a devastating loss for his disciples; a huge personal bereavement. It was not just that they were grieving for a much loved teacher and friend; they were grieving also for the apparent death of the vision of the kingdom of heaven on earth that he had taught them, and with which they had so strongly identified. In effect, their world had come to an end, and according to the gospels their first reaction was either to go through the ritual preparation of his body for burial (the response of the female disciples), or to run away and stay in hiding. According to the gospels none of them were waiting elatedly for him to reappear on the third day, resurrected from the dead. A case could be made that the gospel writers present the original followers in this manner as proof that they just didn't 'get' him – they didn't understand who he really was. In the late first century context when the gospels were written, that would serve to explain differences between Jesus' original followers and messianic converts post-Easter. For the gospel writers, that depiction of 'dim' disciples would still allow for Jesus to have claimed messiahship, but to have been misunderstood.

If we are to accept that something happened to Jesus' closest friends that led to claims of his 'resurrection', then we are faced with questions that have no definitive answer. It is impossible to say what might have happened in post-crucifixion 'appearances' of Jesus to his closest friends; we can only speculate. Yet it is not too much to say that we in this age can compare their experience with that of people we know who have been bereaved; including, perhaps, ourselves. From that we can legitimately conclude that in their grief and longing for Jesus' presence they may well have had an after-death experience of him. In my own ministry I have lost count of recently bereaved people who have hesitantly said something like, "You're going to think I'm silly, but ...", and then gone on to describe a strong sense of the presence of the deceased. Those descriptions have sometimes included not just feelings of such a presence, but sightings of the person who has died.

There have been too many of these conversations in my own experience of working with the bereaved and in the experience of colleagues with whom I have discussed this matter, to dismiss them as of no account or reality. The point is they were real experiences to the people who had them, and they brought great comfort.[43] Given the closeness of Jesus with his loved followers, it does not stretch credibility too far to conjecture that some did 'see' him after death. Such experiences are not limited by physical barriers such as walls and doors. Neither do they entail a 'bodily' resurrection. But they do bring comfort.

The comfort that experiences such as this might have

brought to Jesus' followers could well have helped them to see the future differently. It may have enabled them to realise that what he taught them had not been destroyed by his physical death and that through those teachings he was in a sense, still with them. Luke's story of the encounter on the road to Emmaus looks like his attempt to put into words just such an experience of awareness and encouragement, albeit with messianic overtones. An experience of Jesus after his death, whatever that may mean, could have invigorated the followers to take up the task of passing on his teaching about the kingdom of heaven on earth, also known as 'the Way' (see Acts 9:2, 18:25; 19:9; 19:23; 22:4; 24:14; 24:22). 'The Way' was Jesus' socially subversive, anti-imperialist interpretation of the Law of Moses.

While I am arguing in this book that Jesus did not see himself as the Messiah, there may have been people pre-Easter who did begin to see him that way. They could have included Pharisees who became involved in the Jesus group, hoping Jesus would be revealed as the Messiah. Mark's gospel names one such person as Joseph of Arimathea, the wealthy man who asks Pilate for the body of Jesus. Mark calls him a member of the Council, that is, the Sanhedrin. The Sanhedrin was made up of Pharisees, Scribes and also the Sadducees who did not believe in the resurrection of the dead. Pharisees who had become followers of Jesus would have been eager to identify reports of after-death experiences of Jesus as the resurrection of the Messiah, herald of the general resurrection to precede the messianic age. The gospels are replete with references of this kind in relation to Jesus' death, as we will see. It is not impossible that reports of experiences grieving friends had of Jesus built up into expectations of that kind. As I have also said, belief in bodily resurrection as precursor to the messianic age was part of the theological currency of first century Judaism. The gospel writer Luke goes out of his way to present the resurrected Jesus not only as able to appear in locked rooms, but as in a 'resurrection body', meaning he could eat (Luke 24:42-3).

By the time Saul the Pharisee was involved in a Temple-backed persecution of the messianic Jesus group, belief that Jesus was the Messiah was spreading among hellenized Jews in

Jerusalem and in the Jewish Diaspora outside of Judah and the Galilee. Given the dangers associated with Jewish messianic figures under Roman dominion, that kind of belief would have been the warrant for arrests and persecutions by Temple authorities, including the stoning of Stephen (Acts 7:54-60). Acts says it was Stephen's martyrdom that precipitated the *"severe persecution ... against the church in Jerusalem ... and throughout the countryside of Judea and Samaria."* (Acts 8:1).

Even if the story is not historical, the fact that Acts says Saul was headed for Damascus (the capital of modern Syria) to arrest followers of Jesus, indicates the participation of hellenized Diaspora Jews in the Messiah Jesus movement.

The Book of Acts describes the earliest post-Easter followers trying to carry out Jesus' teachings about living in inclusive community (Acts 4:32-37). This somewhat idealised portrayal of their attempts to live in a sharing, supportive community, nonetheless seems to point to followers who are not waiting passively for Jesus' 'second coming', but are getting on with building the heavenly realm on earth. Even allowing for the apologetic and evangelical purpose of the gospels and Acts, they indicate that post-Easter there was a mixture of expectations and actions related to Jesus. Some people waited for the coming of the Messiah/Christ Jesus to announce the messianic age. Some were probably working for the creation of the kingdom of heaven on earth through the spreading of Jesus' teachings by word and example. Others possibly held both ideas concurrently. In any case the first century saw the beginnings of disparate views about Jesus that have persisted throughout church history.

Jesus the Messiah According to Paul

I want to reiterate here that, with the probable exception of Peter, the Messiah Jesus group post-Easter most probably did not include the original followers who had accompanied Jesus through his three or so years of public teaching. The gospel writers portray the twelve original disciples as incredibly slow to catch on to what each writer says is Jesus' true identity. But rather than revealing a group of people incapable of understanding Jesus, that portrayal of them may simply reflect a known non-messianic view of Jesus by his original followers. Their 'slowness' to recognize him as Messiah is more likely to be due to the simple reason that Jesus did not claim to be the Messiah. The Book of Acts says the original Jesus group was operating from Jerusalem during Paul's missionary activity and that even then (50s CE) there were variations in belief between them and Paul. One of the differences concerned the circumcision of new Gentile converts, but there may have been other clashes surrounding the identity of Jesus as Messiah, about which the author of Acts chose to write nothing.

The Players
Before proceeding with a brief description of Paul's experiences, it will be helpful if I list the major groups involved in following Jesus in the immediate post-Easter period.

- 'The apostles': the original followers of Jesus in the post-Easter period, based in Jerusalem and led by Jesus' brother James. These were 'regular' Jews, probably Aramaic-speaking, as was Jesus. The people among

whom they lived were also Aramaic-speaking Jews, probably mostly illiterate.
- The Hellenists: any Greek-speaking, Greek-educated Jew could be called a Hellenist. There were some among the upper class in Jerusalem and many outside the land of Palestine in the Diaspora.
- Some of these Hellenists were among the followers of Messiah Jesus.
- Gentiles, including Romans and natives of various countries in Asia Minor.

It is crucial in understanding Paul's evangelistic activity in the 50s and 60s CE to acknowledge that the description of this in the Book of Acts is by no means accepted universally as historical record. It would probably be more accurately described as Christian apologetic[44] that was written well into the second century. For that reason it is best not to place too much historical credence on the story of Paul in Acts. New Testament scholar Bernard Brandon Scott wisely advises what seems obvious, that it is best to consult Paul's own writings for information about Paul. Yet Scott reminds us that even that prerequisite for understanding Paul is problematic:

> *Preferably we should build Paul's story on primary evidence – in this case, his letters, which are ambiguous evidence. The problems are manifold. Which letters are Paul's? And in collecting them were they edited and if so, how much? About the first question we can be reasonably certain; about the second we are only beginning to get a handle on how to ask the question.[45]*

Traditional scholarship has insisted that Paul himself was a convert to belief in Jesus as Messiah. Converts often take a huge leap from one position to its polar opposite, even toward a position they had previously criticized very strongly. For that reason, the convert needs to continue to add credence to reasons for his or her conversion. Yet Paul says he was 'called' (not converted) to become the apostle to the Gentiles: *"But when*

God, who had set me apart before I was born and called me through his grace, was pleased to reveal his Son to me, so that I might proclaim him among the Gentiles, I did not confer with any human being ..." (Galatians 1: 15-16). Perhaps Paul's strong sense of divine calling gave him even more reason to insist on his apostolic credentials.

According to Acts, Paul declared himself to be the ultimate witness to the resurrection of Jesus the Messiah, via his 'vision' on the road to Damascus. Whether this was the way it actually happened or was the author of Acts' way of explaining Paul's radically altered point of view (after all, there is no mention of this incident in Paul's own letters), any non-messianic way of viewing Jesus would have been threatening to Paul's messianic conviction. That would have included the way the original twelve may have understood Jesus.

Even if Acts lacks historical credibility, it includes many examples of differences between groups of followers of Jesus. If those differences did not in fact exist, the writer of Acts would hardly be likely to have invented them. It is much more likely that he would be eager to present a united Christ movement, focussed on one view of Jesus as the Messiah/Christ. Instead Acts says that Paul had big problems with other teachers about Jesus who were attracting followers, including an Alexandrian Jew called Apollos. Apollos had been instructed in the *"Way of the Lord"*, apparently referring to Jesus' teachings. Acts says he *"taught accurately the things concerning Jesus"*, though *"he knew only the baptism of John."* (Acts 18: 24-25).

Here Paul's problem, recognized by his co-workers Priscilla and Aquila in Ephesus, appears to be that although Apollos had been instructed in the *"Way of the Lord"*, he did not believe in Jesus as Messiah/Christ. In other words, he had not been baptised to 'receive the Holy Spirit' (Acts 18: 26-28 and Luke 3:16). Receiving the Holy Spirit apparently accompanied conversion to belief in Jesus as Messiah/Christ.

A conversation with Priscilla and Aquila led to Apollos' conversion to belief that Jesus was the Messiah/Christ. Acts says that when Paul arrived in Ephesus (after Apollos had gone on to Corinth) he found people who had been influenced by Apollos before he was converted and whose baptism was John's baptism of repentance, not a baptism of the Spirit. Paul and his helpers quickly had those people baptized in the name of "*the Lord Jesus*", meaning in the name of Jesus the Messiah/Christ. For them receiving the Holy Spirit also involved "*speaking in tongues and prophesying*" (Acts 19:6). This is the situation as described in Acts in the second century CE. If Acts was written then, its narrative most likely reflects the second century situation for the Christ movement, not the early decades after Jesus' death. Rather than a move toward unity of belief about Jesus as the Messiah, the story in Acts indicates that quite the opposite was the case.

Whether viewed through the Book of Acts or (preferably) through his own letters, particularly 1 Thessalonians, Paul's developing apocalyptic End-time Christology, involving the return of Jesus the Messiah, was his response to a central problem – the clear-cut failure of his messianic movement's fundamental prophecy. Paul's difficulty was that by the sixth decade of the first century Jesus had not reappeared to establish the kingdom of God on earth.

Paul's earliest expectations that this would happen are set out in the first of his extant writings to the messianic communities he set up in the Greek-speaking Diaspora. His first Letter to the Thessalonians is the clearest indication of Paul's early thinking about the second coming of Jesus the Messiah/Christ. Although First Thessalonians is the earliest piece of New Testament writing (dated 50-51 CE), it was still produced approximately 20 years after Jesus' death – a long time to hold expectation of Jesus' imminent return to earth. Nonetheless, this letter to the Thessalonians is full of instructions about living as believers in Jesus the Messiah/Christ in the End-time, in the midst of persecution. The persecutors appear to be Gentile authorities (Roman) who were opposed to Paul's movement.

For Thessalonian believers in Jesus the Messiah/Christ, Paul's method of holding out hope and building courage is to preach the 'second coming' of Jesus. Paul did this both in person and through his writings. Every chapter in 1 Thessalonians ends with a reference to Jesus' return.

Chapter 1 ends by proclaiming that Jesus brings salvation and assurance. Paul speaks of people in Macedonia and Achaia who had turned away from idols:

"... to serve a living and true God, and to wait for his Son from heaven, whom he raised from the dead – Jesus, who rescues us from the wrath that is coming."

Chapter 2 ends with Paul congratulating the Thessalonians for their witness about the "Lord Jesus":

"For what is our hope or joy or crown of boasting before our Lord Jesus at his coming? Is it not you? Yes, you are our glory and joy!"

Chapter 3 encourages the followers to love one another so they will be:

"blameless before our God and Father at the coming of our Lord Jesus with all his saints."

Chapter 4 urges those who have been bereaved to believe that people who have died will be with Jesus when he comes:

"Then we who are alive, who are left, will be caught up in the clouds together with them to meet the Lord in the air; and so we will be with the Lord forever."

Paul's obviously desperate yearning for this is the scriptural basis for contemporary belief in the so-called 'Rapture', when all believers in Jesus the Christ will be taken from the earth at his second coming. The 'Rapture' is a current belief for many Christians, in both Pentecostal and mainstream denominations. That is the result of a literal approach to reading scripture. This literal belief has led to the production of the best-selling *Left Behind*[46] series of books and films concerning the dreadful fate of those left behind when believers in Christ are lifted into the air to meet the returning Jesus. Jesus is apparently 'up there' in the sky, waiting to come 'back down' to earth. The result for those left behind is catastrophic chaos and destruction and suffering, as punishment for not believing in Christ. To that thinking we can surely hear Jesus say: "Not in my name!"

Chapter 5 of 1 Thessalonians encourages the followers to support each other before the coming of:

*"our Lord Jesus Christ" because "God has destined us not
for wrath but for obtaining salvation through our Lord
Jesus Christ, who died for us, so that whether we are
awake or asleep we may live with him."*

The impetus for Paul's writing here is encouragement of
people who are beginning to doubt that Jesus will return. His use
of 'we' to describe those who will be alive to greet Jesus on his
return assumes that it will happen in his own lifetime.

Yet changes occurred in Paul's thinking which indicate
that by the time he was writing the second Letter to the
Corinthians (c.56-57 CE) he no longer believed he would be alive
at the 'second coming'. In fact, his longing is to be with Jesus
Christ, not in this life, but in the next:

*"... we would rather be away from the body and at home
with the Lord".*

That longing is repeated in his Letter to the Philippians (1:23):

*"... my desire is to depart and be with Christ, for that is
far better."*

Paul died in Rome in the mid-sixties CE, probably by
beheading under the reign of the Emperor Nero. His
expectations about the imminent second coming of Christ had
been changed by the fifties, so by the sixties he probably would
have given up anticipation that he would meet Jesus Christ
before his own death. What survived intact are his exhortations
to followers to remain faithful to what is good, and to resist evil.
By those means they will be saved from a wrathful God's
punishment for sin, into heavenly life with Jesus the Christ.

Although Paul's End-time Christology was the basis for
the burgeoning Christ movement of the post-Easter first century,
it did not represent Jewish messianic tradition about the
Anointed One. In fact it had moved far away from that. As so
many Jews in the first century would have said, traditions about
the Messiah do not indicate that he would die and reappear later.
That said, Jesus did not reappear as the expected Messiah/Christ
at all. Quite simply, (and shockingly for many today) Paul's
formulation and proclamation of christological expectations was

patently wrong. Yet Paul's messianic thought shaped the later gospels and took Jesus' followers down a very different road from the one on which the earliest disciples had first set out with Jesus.

The gospel writers, who wrote in accordance with Paul's basic beliefs about the crucified and resurrected Jesus Christ who would return when the kingdom of heaven suddenly appeared, got it wrong as well. People in today's church whisper that to each other, as if it were a terrible secret they must not let the world know about. Yet it is true and the world knows it. One response from theologians is the concept of 'realised eschatology', which claims that the kingdom of heaven has appeared already among Jesus' followers and that the church must wait for its 'fulfilment' or 'consummation', this idea obviously perpetuating End-time interventionist-God beliefs.

Why does the church of the 21st century not have the courage to admit what can be seen so clearly – that Jesus will not be returning - ever? The answer is the threat that admission would pose to the institutional church. Pre-science based Christian tradition has continued to expect the return of Jesus the Christ for two thousand years. It has not happened because it never could and it never can. That is too big and too threatening an admission for the keepers of Christian orthodoxy to make. It would undermine the whole purpose of keeping alive traditions about the Saviour Christ who will vindicate the faithful in a final 'consummation of all things'. This is the expectation of Christians who see themselves living in what theologians call a 'realised once and future' eschatology. Eschatology in this case means a time of looking toward 'last things', when the world as it was is no more and is replaced with the realm of heaven on earth, as promised by 'Christ'. That world is what Jesus of Nazareth called "*the kingdom of heaven*" (Matthew) or "*kingdom of God*" (Luke). But 'Christ' is a mythical concept. 'Christ' did not promise anything.

The fulfilment of the kingdom of heaven on earth at the End-time is the expected vindication of Christian orthodoxy. Yet as I have said in my previous book *The World According to Jesus*, that expectation is the most disempowering and dangerous doctrine of all, for Christians who want to make their own contribution to a better world. Why bother? God is going to make it happen, anyway. Jesus Christ will return and prove us to be right! There is no hope for harmony among humanity in that kind of triumphalism. Not only Christians, but all of humankind need to be liberated from the theology of Christendom.

It is important here to point out something not only interesting but potentially decisive, about the picture of the early church as preserved in the New Testament. Even in writing dedicated to making a case for Jesus as Messiah, glimpses of the post-Easter followers indicate that they were by no means of one mind, even about what it meant to claim messiahship for Jesus. Given the messianic agenda of the writer of Acts, the fact that he includes issues of dissension between apostles in Jerusalem and Paul and his Gentile converts, adds weight to suspicion that dissension was far more extensive even than reported in Acts. The writer of Acts sets out to trace what looks like a seamless transition from Peter's lone declaration of Jesus as *"the Christ of God"* (Luke 9:20), to the post-Easter twelve apostles' involvement in preaching 'Christ'.

Yet there is an apparently unavoidable spanner in the works. Whereas Peter and John are extensively reported in Acts as preaching 'Christ', the other disciples are not reported as engaged in this activity. Neither are they actually named; they are a collective called *"the apostles"*. The leadership of 'the apostles' by James the brother of Jesus (not by Peter) is not acknowledged until chapter 12:17, where Peter singles him out from the other "believers". James' leadership of the apostles' group is emphasised in Acts 15:13, where he acts as spokesman for the Jerusalem group. Why is James the leader instead of Peter? Could it be that Peter converted to belief in Jesus as the Messiah, but the other original disciples did not?

In any case there is something earth-shaking underlying the continuing existence of the apostles' group in Jerusalem. It could be their experience of Jesus after his death, but there is a huge distance between this group led by James and the mission of Paul (and Peter) to the Gentiles. The distance is not merely in miles, but in understandings of Jesus and what it means to spread his 'good news'. For Paul, the good news is the resurrection of Jesus Christ, which will pave the way for the resurrection, and reconciliation with God of all who have repented and professed belief in him.

Awkwardly, Luke's gospel is at odds with this. It says that for Jesus himself the way to peace with God is simply to repent of wrongdoing and 'turn around' (as it was for the 'prodigal son'). That, says Jesus, is sufficient to bring forgiveness and reconciliation with God. Nowhere in Jesus' teachings in the Sermon on the Mount or in his own parables, do we find reconciliation with God tied to belief that a Messiah will die and rise from the dead to open the way to God for believers in him. As I have stated, the 'death of the Messiah' was the fundamental problem facing belief in Messiah Jesus.

There is another issue that adds weight to the argument that the Jerusalem group in the early years was not preaching Jesus as Messiah. It is the absence of evidence for persecution of the followers of Jesus in Judea, Galilee and Samaria, compared with reported instances of persecution of Paul and his followers in Judea and the Diaspora. Acts 9 describes events in Damascus immediately after the conversion of Saul/Paul to belief in Jesus as the Messiah/Christ. When Paul tried to tell Greek-speaking Jews (Hellenists) in Damascus synagogues about his new-found messianic belief he encountered fierce opposition, even a plot to kill him (9:23). After escaping to Jerusalem he and his companion Barnabas again ran into murderous resistance, this time from Hellenists who had come from Antioch.

The reason for this hostility can be seen in the particular context of the Hellenists. They were Greek-speaking Jews who typically had financial and political links in Antioch with Gentile (read Roman) merchants and leaders. The last thing they needed in their situation was to be linked with a Jewish messianic group, so they alerted Roman authorities to Paul's preaching. As Acts says: *"The same thing occurred in Iconium"* (14:1) and in other places.

Early in the second century CE the Hellenists in Antioch began to call the messianic Jewish followers 'Christians', to differentiate them from Jews who did not believe Jesus was

Messiah/Christ (Acts 11:26). That differentiation made it safer for non-messianic Jews living in Gentile (Roman) societies. Because of this kind of persecution and opposition from Hellenist Jews, Paul decided that he would no longer go to synagogues first. Instead he went directly to the Gentiles.

What was happening back home?

Even taking into account reservations about its historical accuracy, Acts indicates that something very different was going on in the homeland of the Jews. As I noted, when Paul first went to Jerusalem after his conversion, he encountered hostility from Hellenists there. Some of them had possibly even worked with Paul to persecute the messianic followers of Jesus. After all, Hellenists were well-educated upper-class Jews, likely to have contacts with the Jewish ruling class in the Temple. Acts 9:30-31 describes what happened when these Hellenists threatened Paul:

> *"When the believers learned of it they brought him down to Caesarea and sent him off to Tarsus."*

In other words, they sent him out of harm's way, back home! The most intriguing aspect of all this is in the next verse (31):

> *"Meanwhile the church throughout Judea, Galilee, and Samaria had peace and was built up. Living in the fear of the Lord and in the comfort of the Holy Spirit, it increased in numbers."*

Yet Judea and Galilee were just as much part of a Roman province as was Syria. Why was there no persecution of the homeland followers? Certainly there were revolutionary groups led by messianic 'kings' such as Judah the Galilean and Zadok the Pharisee, who caused problems for both Roman and Jewish authorities during that period.

Yet it looks likely that in the earliest decades following the crucifixion, Jesus' followers in Judea, Galilee and Samaria were not proclaiming Jesus as Messiah. Because of that their situation was relatively peaceful and safe, a stark contrast with areas outside of Palestine where Paul's messianic beliefs about Jesus were spreading among Hellenist Jews and Gentiles.

Finally, I want to make it crystal clear that Paul was not 'the first Christian'. Christianity did not exist in his time, and it was another century into the future before the word 'Christian' came into common use. Also importantly, Paul was not anti-Jewish. Paul's writings may appear at intervals to be anti-Jewish when he discusses attitudes to the Law of Moses or Torah. It is essential to see each of his letters for what they are – letters. They are not only letters, they are letters written to Gentiles. They are Paul's instructions to Gentiles about how to become followers of Jesus Christ the Jewish Anointed One. Paul does not believe the Gentiles need to become Jews or to follow the Jewish Torah. Paul himself followed the Law, as a good Jew ought to do.

Now it is time to look in turn at the way each of the gospel writers crafted their portraits of Jesus as Messiah/Christ.

Section 3

The Four Gospels:
How they expressed belief
in Jesus as Messiah

Introduction to the Gospel Section

To this point I have set out the basic problem for evolving Christianity – the presence in its sacred literature and doctrine of two 'gospels' in clear contradiction – the 'gospel of Christ' and the 'gospel of Jesus'. In varying degrees, both are represented in the four New Testament Gospels. I have also given the reader some background information about messianic thought at the time of Jesus and the later gospel writers. Alongside that is a brief look at the world in which Jesus lived, including some evidence for the viewpoint of the Apostle Paul. My intention is that this information will help the reader navigate the following investigation of how the gospel writers expressed a growing belief in Jesus as the Messiah. What made them believe he was the Messiah? What evidence did they present for their beliefs? What challenges did they have to confront to make their claim?

As we will see, Mark was first cab off the rank, and as such he had no other (canonical) gospel to use as guide, although Matthew and Luke made extensive use of his. As so many have noted, the four gospel writers did not 'consult' with each other about every aspect of their gospels, despite Jacob Jordaens' depiction of them collaborating in *The Four Evangelists* (see front cover).

In reading the gospels it is important to keep in mind the fact that we have only small fragments of early copies of the original gospels, and that the earliest complete gospel texts come from the fourth century CE. I will have more to say about what that might mean in the chapters on the four gospels and in the

Conclusion to this Section. The lack of original gospel texts means we have to allow for the possibility of centuries of editing, designed to depict the gospels as in conformity with later understandings of Jesus as Messiah/Christ.

I considered setting out this section in accordance with themes common to all four gospels. Instead, I have chosen to conduct a separate exploration of each gospel. The gospels section is therefore set out as four discrete investigations, each complete in its own right. The reader will discover that this approach leads to repetition of some themes in each exploration. However, the themes are used differently by each gospel writer. It is therefore important to consider them separately in each gospel. The audience for which each gospel writer wrote is also different, which leads to different emphases in the use of similar material.

I have provided endnotes for explanations along the way, plus an Index and a Glossary of Theological and Biblical terms, at the end of the book. If the meaning of some words I have used is unclear, they will probably be found in those resources. These gospel investigations may be useful for preachers and teachers exploring ways of interpreting presentations of Jesus as Messiah in each of the four gospels. That is another reason for presenting them separately. For some people this section may function like a specialised commentary that examines the gospels as messianic literature.

The three gospels known as synoptic gospels:[47] Mark, Matthew and Luke, include similar themes and material. Yet even they have clearly different ways of claiming Jesus to be the Messiah. In particular, Mark the first gospel faces the enormous challenge of claiming Jesus as Messiah while expressing that in terms of what scholars often call the 'messianic secret'. If that sounds intriguing, all will be revealed in the section on Mark. John's Gospel is very different from the other three, as we will see.

For those in the process of considering how they might see Jesus apart from his imposed *alter ego* the 'Christ', it is important that they not fall into the 'proof text' trap. People do claim that "Jesus must be the Messiah; it says so in the gospels".

As you read into this section, you will be reminded that the reason the gospels portray Jesus as Messiah is quite simple. That messianic portrayal was the primary reason for which the gospels were written! Each gospel writer's aim was to present his case for Jesus as Messiah. The Australian biblical scholar Robert Crotty names the Jesus of the gospels the 'Literary Jesus',[48] which gathers up the fact that this Jesus is a literary creation, in which little attention is paid to the human Jesus who lived and died a Jew, in first century CE Palestine.

We can only be thankful that along with his messianic intention in creating a story of Jesus, Matthew the gospel writer included the priceless teachings we call 'the Sermon on the Mount' (to a lesser extent, Luke also), plus Jesus' authentic parables about the kingdom of heaven on earth. Without access to those teachings, the world would be unimaginably the poorer.

Jesus the Messiah in the Gospel of Mark

L ike the other synoptic gospel-writers, the author of Mark is looking back from his own perspective after the Jewish War (post-70 CE), to the time of Jesus' life at least forty years earlier. When Mark was writing, ideas about a Messiah had to be understood against the background of a Temple destroyed, along with much of the holy city, Jerusalem. In addition to the physical annihilation of the buildings the war also meant the destruction of the Temple priestly system and the redundancy of religious and scriptural ideas that supported it. This was a time of great turbulence and confusion among Jews in Judea, Galilee and the Jewish Diaspora.[49] Judaism was in a state of flux – a period of transition from a Temple-based understanding of the God to whom one offered sacrifices, to a Torah-based religion located in synagogue communities inside and outside Judea and Galilee. There are many sign-posts within the gospel that indicate Mark's backwards-looking perspective on all of this. Most important are the sign-posts that point to Mark's difficulties and challenges in portraying Jesus as Messiah.

Mark's intended readers

Most scholars regard Mark as the first of the canonical gospels, primarily because both Matthew and Luke use and interpret or expand Mark's material. For that reason we will examine Mark first, to see the developing messianic portrait of Jesus that continued to unfold in subsequent gospels. Mark has long been thought to have been written in Rome by an associate of Peter and Paul named John Mark, based on his conversations with the disciple Peter. There are legitimate questions about that, particularly because Mark portrays Peter as chronically uncomprehending of Jesus' messianic identity. Would Mark have presented Peter his teacher in such a way, if Peter had been the source of his writing? Peter's humility might be assumed, but to that extent?

If Rome is ruled out, there is nothing to stop Mark from being written by a Greek-speaking Jew (or group of Jews) in either the Diaspora or the Galilee. Its intended readership therefore probably includes both Hellenistic Jews and Gentiles. Even if not sourced from Peter, this gospel shows signs of originating from oral sayings traditions about or from Jesus. Because Paul's earlier writings do not include a 'story of Jesus', or at least some excerpts from Jesus' teaching, Mark's Gospel is the first New Testament story about Jesus. Its writer links and weaves sayings traditions most likely to have originated from Jesus into a narrative that serves as a messianic portrait of him. The oral sources Mark used probably included messianic ideas about Jesus that were developed and repeated during the forty years between the crucifixion and the writing of Mark's gospel.[50] If we rule out a 'Peter source' for Mark's Gospel, it leaves room for the possibility that Mark's messianic viewpoint carries a definitive Pauline (rather than Petrine) influence.

In any case, Mark has used scriptural paint of many colours for his messianic portrait of Jesus. These scriptural sources are used to place Jesus within Jewish salvation history as the one (described in several books of the Hebrew Scriptures) expected to restore Israel to favour with God. Mark's choice of scriptural quotations has the aim of 'proving' that Jesus fits a messianic interpretation of those scriptures. This represents internal proof-texting, by which Jesus' words and actions (as written by Mark in accordance with scripture) 'prove' that he conforms to scriptural expectations. It is a methodology used in different ways by all four canonical gospel writers. It was not an uncommon literary method in the Hellenistic world of that time, nor was it unheard of for a writer to place his own words in the mouths of biblical or other luminaries (such as Jesus). It is almost universally acknowledged among scholars that the gospel writers frequently did that, apparently with impunity. Yet the church has consistently remained tight-lipped about that.

John the Baptist in the Gospel of Mark

Mark's gospel begins with the words: *"The beginning of the good news of Jesus Christ, the Son of God."* With his use of the title *"Jesus Christ"*, Mark immediately shows his hand. The reader is left in no doubt that this piece of writing is about the Messiah, whom the writer will identify, albeit in a largely secretive fashion, as Jesus of Nazareth. Instead of beginning with a birth narrative as did the later gospels Matthew and Luke, Mark leaps immediately into setting out his messianic thesis concerning the adult Jesus. That in itself is interesting, probably indicating that Mark possessed no knowledge of the circumstances of Jesus' birth. If he did, he did not see it as important enough to include in his messianic portrait. If details of Jesus' birth were known to Mark, he may even have considered them inappropriate for inclusion in his story of the Messiah.

Initially, Mark makes use of the historically well-known figure John the Baptist, who was eventually executed by Herod Antipas. According to the Jewish first century historian Josephus, John was disposed of because many people were attracted to what he was doing. He was urging them to repent of their previous ways, treat others justly and behave with reverence toward God. Having reached a point of repentance of past misdeeds they were then to engage in ritual 'washing' in the Jordan, similar to ideas in the Jewish ritual of water purification called the *mikvah*. Josephus' understanding is also that John the Baptist called for a process of repentance involving God's forgiveness, after which came the ritual of purification in the Jordan River. All of it was in preparation for the time when God would intervene to free the repentant people of Israel from their suffering under the Romans and restore the covenant with them. Those who had repented would then escape the judgment of God on the expected *"Day of the LORD"*. Not unexpectedly, John's obviously political/theological agenda aroused the ire of the old collaborator with Rome, Herod Antipas.

I reiterate that the *"Day of the LORD"* is a time of

judgment at an End-time when evil will be defeated and repentant Israel restored, but it is not about the end of the world itself. One of the extra-canonical books written about the *"Day of the LORD"* and which includes references to the messianic Son of Man, is 1 Enoch.[51] The American biblical scholar James Charlesworth argues that 1 Enoch is composed of several parts. It is therefore possible, he says, that chapters 37-71, which contain Son of Man sayings, were added in the late second century BCE or even in the first century CE.[52] If that is so, the Son of Man sayings could refer either to Israel's oppression under the Greeks, two hundred years before Jesus, or to its suffering under the Romans. In either case, an apocalyptic scenario from 1 Enoch is quoted in the New Testament in Jude 1: 14-15:

> *It was also about these that Enoch, in the seventh generation from Adam, prophesied, saying, "See, the Lord is coming with ten thousands of his holy ones, to execute judgment on all, and to convict everyone of all the deeds of ungodliness that they have committed in such an ungodly way, and of all the harsh things that ungodly sinners have spoken against him."*

In Matthew, John the Baptist's scathing condemnation of the ruling elite who respond to his call to repent, highlights the nature of their expectations of a *"Day of the LORD"*:

> *"But when he saw many Pharisees and Sadducees coming for baptism, he said to them, "You brood of vipers! Who warned you to flee from the wrath to come?" (3:7).*

Naturally then, the crowds gathering around John came to be regarded by Herod Antipas the Jewish tetrarch of Galilee, (a puppet ruler under the Romans), as a threat to his own and religious authority. Mark emphasizes the size of the crowds with: *"And people from the whole Judean countryside and all the people of Jerusalem were going out to him ..."* (1:5). A later defeat of Herod's army by the Arab king Aretas was claimed by many Jews as God's punishment for Herod's execution of John the Baptist. Flavius Josephus describes it like this:

> *Now some of the Jews thought that the destruction of Herod's army came from God, and was a very just punishment for what he did against John called the Baptist [the dipper]. For Herod had him killed, although he was a good man and had urged the Jews to exert themselves to virtue, both as to justice toward one another and reverence towards God, and having done so join together in washing. For immersion in water, it was clear to him, could not be used for the forgiveness of sins, but as a sanctification of the body, and only if the soul was already thoroughly purified by right actions. And when others massed about him, for they were very greatly moved by his words, Herod, who feared that such strong influence over the people might carry to a revolt – for they seemed ready to do anything he should advise – believed it much better to move now than later have it raise a rebellion and engage him in actions he would regret. And so John, out of Herod's suspiciousness, was sent in chains to Machaerus, the fort previously mentioned, and there put to death; but it was the opinion of the Jews that out of retribution for John God willed the destruction of the army so as to afflict Herod.[53]*

Josephus' comments about John indicate that he approved of what John was doing and was well disposed toward him. That would have been highly unlikely if John actually had been promoting the coming of a Messiah. How do we know that? Because in all of his writings Josephus scrupulously avoids support for Messiah figures, and is vehemently opposed to messianic groups. These he understandably sees as big trouble for the Jewish people, especially given his post-Jewish War perspective toward the end of the first century, contemporaneous with the writing of the gospels.

Considering the dangerous political circumstances in

which Mark and his community lived, it is significant that through his story about Herod Antipas' scandalous family he neatly absolves Herod of guilt in the execution of John.

> 6:21-29: ... *an opportunity came when Herod on his birthday gave a banquet for his courtiers and officers and for the leaders of Galilee. When his daughter Herodias came in and danced, she pleased Herod and his guests; and the king said to the girl, "Ask me for whatever you wish, and I will give it." And he solemnly swore to her, "Whatever you ask me, I will give you, even half of my kingdom." She went out and said to her mother, "What should I ask for?" She replied, "The head of John the baptizer." Immediately she rushed back to the king and requested, "I want you to give me at once the head of John the Baptist on a platter." The king was deeply grieved; yet out of regard for his oaths and for the guests, he did not want to refuse her. Immediately the king sent a soldier of the guard with orders to bring John's head. He went and beheaded him in the prison, brought his head on a platter, and gave it to the girl. Then the girl gave it to her mother.*

This story (apparently unknown to Josephus) also appears mainly intact in Matthew, which adds weight to the theory that both Mark's and Matthew's gospels originate in Galilee, in the territory of Herod Agrippa II, Tetrarch of Tiberius and Galilee. Agrippa II was the last king of the Herodian dynasty and he died about 90CE. Luke simply has Herod state: "*John I beheaded*", with no attempt to place the blame elsewhere. That is hardly surprising, given that Luke's gospel was most likely written for people living after the end of the Herodian era. There were no more Herods left to fear.

The tradition of the 'returned Elijah'
At this point it is useful to consider in more detail a tradition used by Mark, Matthew and Luke to announce the messiahship of Jesus. The tradition concerns the return to earth of Elijah the

prophet. As I have noted in Section 2, this Elijah tradition was well known, particularly in the lower socio-economic Palestinian Jewish classes at the time of Jesus. The tradition says Elijah will return from heaven to call the people to repentance and prepare them for the apocalyptic Day of the LORD, when God will appear in the purified Temple (Malachi 3:1). This kind of apocalyptic belief occurs commonly among oppressed, powerless people, for whom there is no hope of escape from oppression other than through the direct intervention of God. Their own role is understood as repenting and waiting for the Day.

The idea of Elijah's return from heaven[54] was developed from the biblical tradition which has him escaping death by being taken up into heaven in a fiery chariot (2 Kings 2:11). Because he ascended alive to heaven, many believed that he could come back alive to earth. The 'returned Elijah' tradition had strong connections with the purification of the Temple and its officials, which places its origin prior to the 66-70 CE destruction of Jerusalem, including the Temple.

Oral and written traditions about Elijah had enormous significance for the gospel portrayal of John the Baptist, beginning with the Gospel of Mark. Mark includes the so-called 'transfiguration' (9:2-8), which portrays Elijah and Moses not only as predecessors of Jesus, but as subordinate to him. They represent the Prophets and the Law, but it is only Jesus whose clothes become "*dazzlingly white, such as no one on earth could bleach them*". Here Mark is allowing the disciples (and his readers) to imagine the shining glory that will surround Jesus at his second coming as Messiah.

The clearest sighting of Elijah traditions in the background of Mark occurs immediately following the 'transfiguration'. The usual question and answer scenario between Jesus and his disciples presents Mark's understanding of Elijah's role in the 'Day of the LORD' (or End Time). At that time Elijah will return to earth and God will intervene to defeat the Romans, restore Israel and send back Jesus the Messiah in all his glory. Peter, James and John ask:

9:9-13: *'Why do the scribes say that Elijah must come*

first?' He said to them, 'Elijah is indeed coming first to restore all things. How then is it written about the Son of Man, that he is to go through many sufferings and be treated with contempt? But I tell you that Elijah has come, and they did to him whatever they pleased, as it is written about him'."

Following as this does the story of John the Baptist's execution by Herod (6:17-29), Mark places words in Jesus' mouth here that identify John with Elijah. They also tackle the obviously vexing question at the time of Mark's writing: why has Jesus been crucified if he is the Messiah? (Mark expresses the messianic title here as Son of Man, the messianic figure in Daniel chapter 7). Jesus' words answer the question by saying that even someone as important as John the Baptist (aka Elijah the prophet/the Herald of the Messiah) was killed by the authorities.

Mark is the first gospel writer to depict John as an Elijah figure, including his clothing and his habitat in the wilderness:

1:6: *Now John was clothed with camel's hair, with a leather belt around his waist, and he ate locusts and wild honey.*

Mark's source for John's Elijian wardrobe is 2 Kings 1:8, which is copied by Matthew (3:4). Luke simply has John living in the desert (1:80), but otherwise does not identify him with Elijah. This likely indicates that Luke's readership is in the Hellenistic Jewish and Gentile Diaspora, where traditions about a returned Elijah were not well-known as they were in Judea and Galilee. In the exploration of Luke's Gospel we will see that Luke wants to dissociate Jesus altogether from Elijah traditions, except to claim that Jesus is superior to Elijah. John's gospel emphatically dissociates John the Baptist from traditions concerning Elijah, for reasons we will consider when looking at the Gospel of John. Each synoptic gospel writer deals in his own way with the popular oral tradition that associates John the Baptist with traditions about a returned Elijah at an End Time or 'Day of the LORD'.

Elijah in the Aramaic Targums

This oral tradition eventually came to be written into the Aramaic version of the Hebrew Scriptures (the Targums). The written Targums appeared from the second century CE onward. They include the Aramaic version of each verse of Hebrew Scripture, and commentary on that scripture. Targums offer a fascinating and unique glimpse of scriptural interpretation being offered at that time, probably first passed on orally from the 2nd century BCE to 1st century CE. Through the Targums we can take our places in first century CE synagogues and hear a local Aramaic-expressed interpretation of scripture that was being promoted in the time of Jesus.

The intriguing aspect of Targums is that they reveal a huge interest in Elijah as an End-time priestly figure. *Eliyahu kahana rabbah* (Elijah the High Priest) is mentioned in many of the Targums' Aramaic translations of books of the Hebrew Scriptures, and in commentary that follows many verses. This tells us that traditions about Elijah associated with expectations of the Day of the LORD (even though this means God, not Messiah), were well and truly 'in the air' in the first century CE. This argument is given excellent credence by the many references to the returning Elijah as herald of the Messiah in the first century CE gospels, Mark, Matthew and Luke. The gospels are a fascinating 'window' into Judaism in the first century CE.

I now offer my reader one of many references to Elijah in Targums. I first include Deuteronomy 30:4 in English from the NRSV version of the Hebrew scriptures, then in English from the Aramaic version in *Targum Pseudo-Jonathan to the Pentateuch*[55] (the Pentateuch being the first 5 books of the Bible):

- NRSV Deuteronomy 30:4: *Even if you are exiled to the ends of the world, from there the Lord your God will gather you, and from there he will bring you back.*
- Targum Pseudo-Jonathan of Deuteronomy 30:4: *Even if your outcasts are dispersed to the end of heaven, from there the Word of the Lord will gather you by the hand of Elijah the High Priest, and from there he will bring you near by the hand of the King Messiah.*[56]

There in the Targum we see where Mark and Matthew stand. For them (and the writer of *Targum Pseudo-Jonathan*) John the Baptist/Elijah is announcing not just the Day of the LORD, but the coming of the Messiah. John is depicted as the forerunner of the Messiah, who is identified by gospel writers as Jesus.[57] Mark and Matthew have linked John the Baptist with this kind of expectation.

Even so, this does not constitute proof that Jesus' original followers saw him as Messiah, or that he saw himself that way. It does link belief in John the Baptist as forerunner of the Messiah with later writings in the Targums about Elijah in that role. Those ideas were likely to have been circulating by the time of Mark's writing in the 70s CE. Luke does it differently. He associates John the Baptist with predictions in Isaiah about one who will *"prepare the way of the Lord"* (Luke 3:4-6). For Luke, *"the Lord"* is not God, but Jesus the Messiah. I will explain that more fully in my exploration of Luke.

The role of the returning Elijah in Malachi
The Book of Malachi's thinking about the expected role of the returned Elijah can be seen clearly in Mark's and Josephus's descriptions of John the Baptist. There are two primary elements to this role. Elijah is to challenge the officials of the Temple to purify the worship of the people:

> *"he will purify the descendants of Levi and refine them like gold and silver, until they present offerings to the Lord in righteousness."(3:1-4).*

In Mark's gospel Elijah's role is altered from the one who will purify the Temple to that of the forerunner of Messiah Jesus, who will himself carry out the 'cleansing of the Temple'. Identification of Jesus as the Messiah probably did not occur until after the crucifixion, when reports spread that he had appeared following his death. John the Baptist's self-identity was probably that of a restoration prophet; his aim being to restore Israel into covenant with God before the Day of the LORD, as per the Elijah tradition.

After John's arrest and execution by Herod, Jesus may have stepped into his shoes in a similar role. However, even if that were the case, Jesus differed fundamentally from John the Baptist. Rather than waiting for the Day of the LORD, when God would establish the kingdom of heaven on earth, Jesus developed teachings for his followers concerning the fulfilling of the Law of Moses. The teachings were given specifically to equip his followers to build the kingdom of heaven on earth. This is a crucial difference from the aim of John the Baptist.

What we have in Mark is his messianic interpretation of John the Baptist and of scripture concerning the *Day of the LORD*. This is the beginning point in Mark's portrait of Jesus as Messiah. Mark uses a quotation from Isaiah 40:3 to identify John as the one who will *"prepare the way of the Lord"*. In Mark's usage *"the Lord"* (lower case) is clearly not God, but Jesus the Messiah.[58]

Also in Malachi (4:5-6), Elijah is to call the people to repentance and to reconciliation with each other (and God) before *"the great and terrible day of the LORD comes."* In Mark's version, after the arrest of John the Baptist, Jesus carries on John's call to the people to repent. In doing so he re-states the Day of the LORD tradition as the coming of *"the kingdom of God"*, which he says has *"come near"* (1:15). Here is Mark's nod to the known real agenda of Jesus, albeit with added eschatological (End-time) interpretation. This 'kingdom' announcement by Jesus is followed by the calling of his disciples.

At this point in Mark and Matthew there are two groups following Elijah-styled leaders. One group is following John the 'returned Elijah' who is now also forerunner of the Messiah. The other group is following Jesus, who later continues John's Elijah role, but is seen by Mark and Matthew as the Messiah.

We cannot help but pick up the inconclusiveness of this where John the Baptist is concerned. On the one hand he explains that he is the forerunner:

"The one who is more powerful than I is coming after me; I am not worthy to stoop down and untie the thong of his sandals" (1:7).

On the other hand Mark does not have John specifically identify Jesus as *"the one … coming after me"*. Awkwardly, it is also clear that John's disciples continue to identify with him even after he has been arrested and put in prison. In Mark chapter 2 we see that the John the Baptist and Jesus groups are still separate:

> *"Now John's disciples and the Pharisees were fasting; and people came and said to him, "Why do John's disciples and the disciples of the Pharisees fast, but your disciples do not fast?" (2:18).*

If John the Baptist did not 'know' Jesus was the Messiah, Mark has chosen to resist putting words into John's mouth where he declares Jesus' messiahship. Matthew deals with this ambiguity by having John send his disciples to Jesus to ask if he is *"the one"*. Even then, Jesus does not give a straight answer. Instead he points to several sign-posts traditionally said to indicate the presence and activity of the Messiah in defeating evil and preparing the way for God's reign. Those sign-posts are also present in the Gospel of Mark.

Messianic 'sign-posts' in Mark:
1. The demons are defeated

5:1-13: They came to the other side of the sea, to the country of the Gerasenes. And when he had stepped out of the boat, immediately a man out of the tombs with an unclean spirit met him. He lived among the tombs; and no one could restrain him anymore, even with a chain; for he had often been restrained with shackles and chains, but the chains he wrenched apart, and the shackles he broke in pieces; and no one had the strength to subdue him. Night and day among the tombs and on the mountains he was always howling and bruising himself with stones. When he saw Jesus from a distance, he ran and bowed down before him; and he shouted at the top of his voice, "What have you to do with me, Jesus, Son of the Most High God? I adjure you by God, do not

torment me." For he had said to him, "come out of the man, you unclean spirit!"
Then Jesus asked him, "What is your name? He replied, "My name is Legion; for we are many." He begged him earnestly not to send them out of the country. Now there on the hillside a great herd of swine was feeding; and the unclean spirits begged him, "Send us into the swine; let us enter them." So he gave them permission. And the unclean spirits came out and entered the swine; and the herd, numbering about two thousand, rushed down the steep bank into the sea, and were drowned in the sea. (See also 1:21-28; 9:38-41; 16:17).

Exorcism of demons in first century Judaism was associated with belief in demon possession, for which 21st century medicine would offer other explanations such as schizophrenia or epilepsy. For Jesus and his contemporaries (we must treat Jesus as a first century man) the absence of medical knowledge led them to believe that a person who acted insanely must have been invaded by a representative of evil, a demon. The victim's possession was believed to be caused by personal sin, which had enabled the demon to enter him or her.

It was also believed by Jewish sects such as the Essenes and the Dead Sea Scrolls communities that the Messiah would appear as visible manifestation of God's intervention to defeat evil. Evil was personified in those times by the devil and his demons. Therefore, when Jesus is depicted exorcising someone's demons, for the gospel writers that is a sign-post pointing to him as Messiah. Mark says the demons *"knew him"* (1:34), probably meaning they knew him because as Messiah he was able to use the power of God to defeat them. Nonetheless, exorcism of demons was a common practice in the first century, not exclusively the preserve of the Messiah.[59]

2. The sick are healed

2: 1-12: *When he returned to Capernaum after some days, it was reported that he was at home. So many gathered around that there was no longer room for*

them, not even in front of the door; and he was speaking
the word to them. Then some people came, bringing to
him a paralyzed man, carried by four of them. And when
they could not bring him to Jesus because of the crowd,
they removed the roof above him; and after having dug
through it, they let down the mat on which the paralytic
lay. When Jesus saw their faith, he said to the paralytic,
"Son, your sins are forgiven." (See also 3:1-5; 7:31-35).

Illnesses not necessarily associated with demon possession were also believed to be the result of the sufferer's sin. It follows then, that Jesus tells the man lowered through the ceiling on a stretcher, *"Son, your sins are forgiven."* For Mark, this is the Messiah speaking as God's anointed representative on earth (which is the best definition of the Jewish word *mashiach* or 'messiah'), and therefore able to forgive sin in God's name. Yet this incident inadvertently presents a clear view of Jesus himself. In accordance with his own teaching, Jesus' response was compassion. He brought a compassionate response to people whose sense of failure in God's eyes blighted their life and health. His belief in a forgiving God would likely have led him to remind these people either that they were not blamed by God for their illness, or that God had already forgiven the repentant.

Although Mark wants to portray Jesus here as able to forgive sin, it does not follow from this story that Jesus thought he was divine and could forgive the paralysed man. In Luke's Gospel, at his crucifixion Jesus asks God to forgive the centurion (Luke 23:34).

Specific illnesses or disabilities healed by Jesus in Mark's gospel include deafness (and muteness), blindness and paralysis of limbs. It is no coincidence that healings of all of these are named in Isaiah (35) as evidence that the day of the LORD has come, where God has intervened, the enemy is defeated, the land is renewed and Israel is saved from evil into a new relationship with God. It is on such passages that first century Jewish messianism was based. These are the conditions that will ensue when the old world has passed and the new world has come. Because of that, Mark is at pains to cite those particular forms of healing.

There may therefore reasonably be some doubt about whether Jesus physically healed the blind, deaf and paralysed. It is plausible to argue that interpreters of the gospels who see these afflictions as examples of spiritual or psychological blindness, deafness and paralysis, may be closest to Mark's agenda here. Mark may have seen this kind of 'seeing', 'hearing' and rejuvenation as enabling the subjects of healing first to recognize Jesus as Messiah and then to follow him. An example is blind Bartimaeus.

> 10:46-52: *They came to Jericho. As he and his disciples and a large crowd were leaving Jericho, Bartimaeus son of Timaeus, a blind beggar, was sitting by the roadside. When he heard that it was Jesus of Nazareth, he began to shout out and say, "Jesus, Son of David, have mercy on me!" Many sternly ordered him to be quiet, but he cried out even more loudly, "Son of David, have mercy on me!" Jesus stood still and said, "Call him here." And they called the blind man, saying to him, "Take heart; get up, he is calling you." So throwing off his cloak, he sprang up and came to Jesus. Then Jesus said to him, "What do you want me to do for you?" The blind man said to him, "My teacher, let me see again." Jesus said to him, "Go; your faith has made you well." Immediately he regained his sight and followed him on the way."*

It is fortunate that the following centuries have seen countless numbers of Jesus' followers regard him literally as a healer and try to emulate him by working to alleviate physical suffering and find cures for all kinds of illness, including blindness. In Mark's time, a link between the 'cleansing' or purifying of the Temple and healings was the belief that offerings could not be made to God in the Temple by people (particularly by priests) who were blind, or lame or suffering from skin diseases such as leprosy (see Leviticus 21:16-24). Mark declares that by healing such people, Jesus the Messiah is demonstrating that he has defeated the evil that blinded or distorted them and has therefore also restored them into relationship with God.

Hence the notion of forgiveness linked with healing.

Mark uses Isaiah 56:7 to undergird his depiction of Jesus as the prophet/Messiah who will 'cleanse the Temple' and restore Israel to its right relationship with God. Mark's Jesus quotes Isaiah as he drives out money changers who have robbed the people:

> *"Is it not written, 'My house shall be called a house of prayer for all the nations'? But you have made it a den of robbers."* (56:7)

What of Jesus Healing Gentiles?

Within the context of another healing incident, Mark's gospel contains a very important instruction regarding the way Jewish readers of his gospel are to regard Gentiles. Being the first canonical gospel written, Mark is closest to the time of Paul, the self-appointed 'Apostle to the Gentiles'. Mark would have been very well aware of Paul and his emphasis, and in accordance with that he includes an encounter between Jesus and a Gentile woman. His intention is to add authority to Paul's aim of including the Gentiles in the salvation to be claimed in the second coming of the Messiah of Israel. The words he places in Jesus' mouth have been a continuing source of scandal, distress and incomprehension among Christians ever since. The centuries-later Greek-oriented depiction of Jesus as the second 'person' of the Holy Trinity (and therefore as perfect) has consistently been read back into gospel accounts in which Jesus is seen reflecting his own Jewish culture regarding Gentiles. Hence the confusion of later gospel readers.

> 7. 24-30: *From there he set out and went away to the region of Tyre. He entered a house and did not want anyone to know he was there. Yet he could not escape notice, but a woman whose little daughter had an unclean spirit immediately heard about him, and she came and bowed down at his feet. Now the woman was a Gentile, of Syrophoenician origin. She begged him to cast the demon out of her daughter. He said to her, "Let*

the children be fed first, for it is not fair to take the children's food and throw it to the dogs." But she answered him, "Sir, even the dogs under the table eat the children's crumbs." Then he said to her, "For saying that, you may go – the demon has left your daughter." So she went home, found the child lying on the bed, and the demon gone.

Mark evidently knows that Jesus' teaching was directed toward his own people, the Jews. Mark also knows that Jesus was a product of his Jewish environment, where Gentiles were regarded as inferior to Jews and not acceptable in the eyes of God. This incident therefore would have spoken volumes to Jews who were, in Mark's time, aware of Gentiles convinced that Jesus was the Jewish Messiah. Mark wants his readers to know that Gentiles, as well as Jews, are capable of great faith in the God of Israel and his Messiah Jesus. The message of Mark's story is that if Jesus could recognize that, as he does in this incident, then the gospel's Jewish readers could also feel free to welcome Gentiles into the community of believers in Jesus the Messiah.

3. The dead are raised

5:21-42: *When Jesus had crossed again in the boat to the other side, a great crowd gathered around him; and he was by the sea. Then one of the leaders of the synagogue named Jairus came and, when he saw him, fell at his feet and begged him repeatedly, "My little daughter is at the point of death. Come and lay your hands on her, so that she may be made well, and live." So he went with him.[60] While he was still speaking, some people came from the leader's house to say, "Your daughter is dead. Why trouble the teacher any further? But overhearing what they said, Jesus said to the leader of the synagogue, "Do not fear, only believe." He allowed no one to follow him except Peter, James, and John, the brother of James. When they came to the house of the leader of the synagogue, he saw a commotion, people weeping and wailing loudly. When he had entered, he said to them,*

"Why do you make a commotion and weep? The child is not dead but sleeping." And they laughed at him.
Then he put them all outside, and took the child's father and mother and those who were with him, and went in where the child was. He took her by the hand and said to her "Talitha, cum," which means, "Little girl, get up!" And immediately the girl got up and began to walk about (she was twelve years of age). At this they were overcome with amazement. He strictly ordered them that no one should know this, and told them to give her something to eat.

The raising of Jairus' daughter from death is a link with a messianic tradition held by the Pharisees. They believed that when the Day of the LORD came, the Messiah would appear and there would be a general resurrection of the dead. As I have noted already, this is based on the Book of Daniel, the second half of which reflects Jewish martyrdoms under the Greek emperor Antiochus Epiphanes (who reigned from 176 – 164 BCE). The scholarly interpreters of the Jewish Law known as Pharisees (meaning separated ones) had their beginnings at that time. Their idea concerning resurrection grew in response to the seeming futility of loyally following the Law of Moses, only to be tortured and killed by the Greek kings for such commitment to the Law. For the Pharisees, the reward for this martyrdom became associated with a rising to new life after death, at the *"time of the end"* (Daniel 12:4). The messianic figure in Daniel who would rise at the End-time and call on the righteous (read: martyrs for the Law) to rise with him, is called *"Michael the great prince, the protector of (the) people"* (12:1).

Yet the prophetic biblical tradition regards the raising of the dead as the act of a prophet. For example, in 1 Kings the prophet Elijah is depicted raising from death a widow's son:

1 Kings 17:17-24: *After this the son of the woman, the mistress of the house, became ill; his illness was so severe that there was no breath left in him. She then said to Elijah, "What have you against me, O man of God?*

You have come to me to bring my sin to remembrance, and to cause the death of my son!" But he said to her, "Give me your son." He took him from her bosom, carried him up into the upper chamber where he was lodging and laid him on his own bed.

He cried out to the LORD, "O LORD my God, have you brought calamity even upon the widow with whom I am staying, by killing her son?" Then he stretched himself upon the child three times, and cried out to the LORD, "O LORD my God, let this child's life come into him again." The LORD listened to the voice of Elijah; the life of the child came into him again, and he revived. Elijah took the child, brought him down from the upper chamber into the house, and gave him to his mother; then Elijah said, "See, your son is alive." So the woman said to Elijah, "Now I know that you are a man of God, and that the word of the LORD in your mouth is truth."

Given the similarities between this Elijah story and the story of Jairus' daughter, the inference can easily be made that Jesus is acting in a prophetic role like Elijah, not as 'Messiah'. It is impossible to know the choice of biblical sources that inspired Jesus' 'kingdom of heaven' vision, but his own context among the oppressed in the Galilee would see him likely to be influenced by traditions concerning the return of Elijah. He would also have known the visions of a renewed society set out in Isaiah. The messianic visions in Daniel are more strongly associated with the literate class – the Scribes and Pharisees.

Mark's difficulty with the ambiguity of this is expressed in a particular instance of the so-called 'messianic secret'. As in so many other Messiah-oriented occurrences, Mark's Jesus orders witnesses not to tell anyone he had raised Jairus' daughter from the dead, even though Mark's story says many knew she had died. Again it is plausible to say that for Mark the 'raising from death' represents an emergence from a kind of spiritual death, where the 'dead' person is awakened by Jesus to awareness that he is the Messiah. Scholars have long been divided over the reason Mark portrays Jesus trying to keep his messiahship a secret. Because of that a brief summary of scholarship relating to the so-called 'messianic secret' of Mark's Gospel may be found further on in this chapter.

Why the misunderstandings by the disciples?

> 8:14-21: *Now the disciples had forgotten to buy any bread; and they had only one loaf with them in the boat. And he cautioned them, saying, "Watch out – beware of the yeast of the Pharisees and the yeast of Herod." They said to one another, "It is because we have no bread." And becoming aware of it, Jesus said to them, "Why are you talking about having no bread? Do you still not perceive or understand? Are your hearts hardened? Do you have eyes, and fail to see? Do you have ears, and fail to hear? And do you not remember? When I broke the five loaves for the five thousand, how many baskets full of broken pieces did you collect?" They said to him, "Twelve." "And the seven for the four thousand, how many baskets full of broken pieces did you collect?" And they said to him, "Seven." Then he said to them, "Do you not yet understand?"* (See also 6:51-52; 9:30-32; 12:35-37; 16:14 for other examples of the disciples' inability to understand Jesus).

One of the literary methods Mark uses to inform the reader that Jesus is indeed the Messiah, is to portray the disciples as ignorant, in need of instruction about that. Let the reader of this book be in no doubt - it means Mark is instructing his readers! As I noted before, it is difficult to imagine the close ring of Jesus' disciples so uncomprehending of his messiahship, if in fact that was the self-understanding he was intent on making known. We can only conclude that the questions directed from the 'dim' disciples to Jesus about his puzzling words and actions are Mark's teaching device. These questions are presumed by Mark to be the questions of his readers.

Significantly, the questions the Markan disciples ask are almost entirely focussed on Jesus' identity, not on what he meant by the 'kingdom of God'. That was surely the most likely focus of questions from his followers, given Jesus' focus on proclaiming the kingdom. Mark's questions and answers 'reveal' Jesus as Messiah, even if he mostly denies it or evades the questions. Could this resort to portraying equivocation in Jesus' exchanges with his disciples stem from the difficult fact that he was not known actually to have claimed to be the Messiah?

Jesus' miracles

When is a miracle not a miracle? When it is one of Mark's sign-posts. I will cite here three 'miracles' of Jesus, and make a case for them not as miracles but as Markan sign-posts pointing to the Messiah.

- 6:41-44: *Taking the five loaves and two fish, he looked up to heaven, and blessed and broke the loaves, and gave them to his disciples to set before the people; and he divided the two fish among them all. And all ate and were filled; and they took up twelve baskets full of broken pieces and of the fish. Those who had eaten the loaves numbered five thousand men.*
- 8:5-9: *He asked them: "How many loaves do you have?" They said, "Seven." Then he ordered the crowd to sit down on the ground; and he took the seven loaves, and after giving thanks he broke them and gave them to his disciples to distribute; and they distributed them to the crowd. They had also a few small fish; and after blessing them, he ordered that these too should be distributed. They ate and were filled; and they took up the broken pieces left over, seven baskets full. Now there were about four thousand people. And he sent them away.* (See also 6:45-51; 8:1-9; 11:12-24).

The first miracle is two instances of feeding where Jesus takes the small amount of food the hungry hordes possess and turns it into plenty, so much that there is even more left over. Much is made by biblical scholars of a connection between this feeding and Moses' feeding of the Israelites with manna[61] in the desert. This link is particularly noticeable in the feeding story in the Gospel of Matthew, where Jesus is consistently given Moses-like characteristics.

There is another way of looking at it. As in all gospels, in Mark the two feeding stories point not to a 'miracle' that actually happened, but to conditions when the Messiah reappears to inaugurate the Kingdom of God and preside over the 'messianic banquet'. Both stories first indicate the hunger and distress of the people, then describe the provision of more than they can possibly eat.

The stories show clear signs of being based on Isaiah 24 and 25. Chapter 24 has a graphic description of the suffering, starving people, in need of repentance and forgiveness:

> *"The earth lies polluted under its inhabitants; for they have transgressed laws, violated the statutes, broken the everlasting covenant. Therefore a curse devours the earth, and its inhabitants suffer for their guilt; therefore the inhabitants of the earth dwindled, and few people are left. The wine dries up, the vine languishes, all the merry-hearted sigh."* (24:5-7).

Chapter 25 follows with God (not a Messiah) appearing on Mount Zion to make a feast for:

> *"all peoples, a feast of rich food, a feast of well-aged wines, of rich food filled with marrow,"* (25:6)

God will also destroy death forever:

> *And he will destroy on this mountain the shroud that is cast over all peoples, the sheet that is spread over all nations; he will swallow up death forever. (25:8)*

Mark's second miracle story comes directly after the first.

> 6:45-52: *Immediately he made his disciples get into the boat and go on ahead to the other side, to Bethsaida, while he dismissed the crowd. After saying farewell to them, he went up on the mountain to pray. When evening came, the boat was out on the sea, and he was alone on the land. When he saw that they were straining at the oars against an adverse wind, he came towards them early in the morning, walking on the sea. He intended to pass them by. But when they saw him*

walking on the sea, they thought it was a ghost and cried out: for they all saw him and were terrified. But immediately he spoke to them and said, "Take heart, it is I; do not be afraid." Then he got into the boat with them and the wind ceased. And they were utterly astounded, for they did not understand about the loaves, but their hearts were hardened.

This is the famous 'walking on water' incident, where Jesus not only walks on water, but his presence calms a strong wind. Mark's story has the disciples straining to row their boat against this strong wind. Jesus sees that and comes out toward them, walking on the waves. Could it be that here Mark looked for inspiration in the Book of Psalms?

Psalm 107:23-30: *Some went down to the sea in ships, doing business on the mighty waters; they saw the deeds of the LORD, his wondrous works in the deep. For he commanded and raised the stormy wind, which lifted up the waves of the sea. They mounted up to heaven, they went down to the depths; their courage melted away in their calamity; they reeled and staggered like drunkards, and were at their wits' end. Then they cried to the LORD in their trouble, and he brought them out of their distress; he made the storm be still, and the waves of the sea were hushed. Then they were glad because they had quiet, and he brought them to their desired haven.* (See also Psalms 77:16-20; 144:7-8).

The theme in those readings (as in Isaiah) is the physical suffering and moral struggle of the people, particularly under the hand of an occupying oppressor. This is regarded as a result of their own sinfulness and lack of loyalty to their God. The imagery has them in peril out on the stormy sea (the dangerous preserve of monsters in ancient lore), but finding that God comes to them even there, and stills the storms. In this they gain their salvation.

Mark clearly makes the point that Jesus' disciples did not understand the messianic significance of the feeding incident(s).

Nor did they understand that as Messiah Jesus was representing the saving God who walks on water and calms the waves. The story is written for Mark's readers, so they may 'hear' and understand the identity of Jesus, whom Mark believes is the Messiah, although not actually the divine Son of God (as the gospel writer John does).

Psalm 89, which does not understand David as divine Son of God, but as Messiah/son of God according to Jewish tradition (as also per Psalm 2:7), has God speaking about David in verses 24-25:

> *"My faithfulness and steadfast love shall be with him; and in my name his horn shall be exalted. I will set his hand on the sea and his right hand on the rivers."*

In Psalm 89 the Messiah/son of God is symbolically given power over the sea as God's representative, even though he is not literally, in his being, Son of God. In verse 26 David is instructed to call God *"my Father"*, as Jesus did (Mark 14:36). Again, this does not imply the actual 'divinity' of either David or Jesus.

- The third miracle story is the withering of the fig tree.
  11:12-14: *On the following day, when they came from Bethany, he was hungry. Seeing in the distance a fig tree in leaf, he went to see whether perhaps he would find anything on it. When he came to it, he found nothing but leaves, for it was not the season for figs. He said to it, "May no one ever eat fruit from you again." And his disciples heard it.*

Mark has placed this scene around the story of Jesus in Elijah mode, 'cleansing' the Temple. It is important then, to link the fig tree story with the Temple, as Mark clearly intends. Jesus probably did use a symbolic prophetic act to challenge the degradation of the Temple as a place of prayer. Mark is making a further accusation against the Temple through the symbol of a leafy, so apparently fruitful fig tree, which is actually barren. Mark knows very well what happened to the Temple. He knows that what looked to most of Jesus' contemporaries to be a strong and fruitful religious system based on the Temple did not, and after its destruction could not, 'feed' those who were hungry for spiritual nourishment. The fig tree, which represents the Temple, is therefore deceptive in its leafiness. To underline the symbolism of the barren fig tree, Mark reports that in another symbolic prophetic action, Jesus cursed the religious establishment represented by the Temple.

> 11:15-17: *Then they came to Jerusalem. And he entered the temple and began to drive out those who were selling and those who were buying in the temple, and he overturned the tables of the money changers and the seats of those who sold doves; and he would not allow anyone to carry anything through the temple. He was teaching and saying, "Is it not written, 'My house shall be called a house of prayer for all the nations'? But you have made it a den of robbers."*

Here the Elijah tradition (from Malachi) concerning the cleansing or 'purification' of the Temple is combined with a further quote from Isaiah. As Jesus challenges the financial corruption of the Temple's sacrificial system, he quotes Isaiah 56:7:

> *"Is it not written, 'My house shall be called a house of prayer for all the nations'? But you have made it a den of robbers."*

This is likely to be an instance of the historical Jesus' own Elijah-inspired prophetic agenda, which Mark has interwoven with the story of the fig tree.

The Temple story is written with the benefit of hindsight following the Temple's destruction. Looking back, Mark wants to portray Jesus' prophetic challenge to the Temple authorities as a messianic warning about the Temple's eventual destruction. His fig tree story underlines that. The fig tree story belongs post-Temple, so is not likely to originate with Jesus. Jesus' own agenda was most probably to purify the Temple of corrupt influences and restore it to a 'house of prayer'. In this he was fulfilling an Elijian restoration prophet role. Jesus may have wondered whether the Temple would survive Jewish opposition to the Roman occupation, but when he went to the Temple he knew no more than anyone else about its eventual fate around forty years after his death. To influence his readers, Mark here places into Jesus' mouth words that invest Jesus with the messianic ability to know the Temple's future.

Jesus' coming death and return as Son of Man

Mark's gospel contains many references from Jesus to the coming Kingdom of God, and to his role in its coming. For Mark, as for the other canonical gospel writers, belief in Jesus' understanding of himself as Messiah is the basic framework wherein the entire gospel portrait of Jesus is drawn. As we will see in the next section, Mark deals with historical ambiguity surrounding Jesus' own understanding of his role by portraying him either as denying or hushing up a messianic identity. While the literary methodology of the 'messianic secret' is implemented to deal with this ambiguity, Mark nonetheless uses messianic titles for Jesus that leave the reader in no doubt as to where he, as writer of the gospel, stands. Mark believes implicitly that Jesus is the Messiah.

He also believes in an apocalyptic coming kingdom of God, which will be established on earth when Jesus returns as Messiah/Son of Man. At the point of Mark's writing Jesus had been dead for approximately forty years, but hope for the second coming of the Son of Man as first taught by Paul to the Thessalonians, had by no means disappeared. A short survey of Mark's references to Jesus' death and resurrection appearances follows.

Predictions of Jesus' death and resurrection

An essential aspect of Mark's gospel is his portrayal of Jesus' messianic ability to predict his own rejection by the Jewish leadership, his suffering and death, and his resurrection after three days. Chapter 8:31 is the first of several examples that illustrate this:

"Then he began to teach them that the Son of Man must undergo great suffering, and be rejected by the elders, the chief priests, and the scribes, and be killed, and after three days rise again." (See also 9:9-9; 10:32-34; 13:1-8).

Mark's agenda can be seen through the scenarios in which Jesus makes those claims.

- They are set out in teaching episodes directed toward the learning of the reader. In all of the above references the context is Jesus answering questions from his disciples about his identity and destiny.
- They are presented as *private* teaching contexts, in which only the disciples are let into the 'messianic secret'. This serves to overcome the difficulty of explaining why Mark's community sees Jesus as Messiah, when it appears more than likely that the original pre-Easter followers did not. Mark wants to say that it was only the disciples who were told this, but they failed to 'get it'. By the time of Mark's writing they were most probably dead, and so unable to refute Mark's words.
- These episodes are very careful about how they place blame for Jesus' death. 8:31 (above) is pivotal. Here Jesus says he will be rejected by the leadership of his own people, the *"elders, the chief priests, and the scribes"*. The chief priests are, of course, the top tier of the Temple leadership. The elders and scribes include the Pharisees, who were leaders of Judaism in Mark's time, after the Temple and its priestly system were destroyed. The Pharisaic leaders in Mark's time were trying to reform Judaism around observance of the Torah in synagogue communities. The Pharisees were strongly opposed to messianic groups because such movements were often militant and the cause of Jewish deaths and suffering under the Romans. The Pharisees were therefore opponents of Mark's community of believers in Jesus the Messiah. This opposition to the Messiah Jesus movement was pivotal to the eventual parting of nascent Christianity from Judaism.

- The prediction episodes place no responsibility for Jesus' death at the feet of the Romans. It is often said that this is because it was dangerous to accuse the Romans of killing Messiah Jesus. That would have made his followers vulnerable to the threat of Roman attempts to stamp out rebellion. Such concerns were no doubt a part of Mark's agenda as he set out conversations between Jesus and his disciples about identity. Yet that was not the whole picture. It does not explain fully why the Romans get off so lightly. When Mark's Jesus explains the cause of his suffering the reason becomes clearer. Mark wants his readers to place the blame for Jesus' death squarely on the shoulders of the Jewish leadership. They will kill Jesus (even if not personally, but by requesting it of the Romans) because they regard his claim to be the Son of Man/Messiah as blasphemous. This is first an assertion that Jesus actually claimed to be the apocalyptic Son of Man (as per Daniel chapter 7). It also ignores the fact that the leaders of early first century Judaism did not regard messianic claims as blasphemous, although they did regard them as dangerous.
- Further, it does not take into account that it was the Romans who executed Jesus through the penalty reserved for insurrectionists, or traitors to the authority of Caesar. Most importantly, it does not allow for the strong possibility that the Jewish leadership thought it best that Jesus the prophetic teacher die instead of allowing him to continue stirring up the people, and (perhaps) have all of his followers wiped out by the Romans. This is a very different view of the Jewish leadership and obviously not one chosen by Mark. Historical verification of this is given substance by the fact that there is no Roman record of persecution of Jesus' original followers after his crucifixion.

- Mark 10:33 makes the boldest claim in the gospels that Jesus knew what would happen to him:

"See, we are going up to Jerusalem, and the Son of Man will be handed over to the chief priests and the scribes, and they will condemn him to death; then they will hand him over to the Gentiles; they will mock him, and spit upon him, and flog him, and kill him; and after three days he will rise again."

This is precisely the way Mark tells the story of Jesus' trial and crucifixion and resurrection. Mark's internal proof-texting (he has Jesus predict something or quote scripture and then describes it as actually happening) has convinced countless Christians that this gospel contains proof Jesus knew exactly how he would die. I will expand on this methodology of Mark's in the section on the trial and crucifixion.

Apocalyptic predictions from Jesus
Chapter 13 is the best known of the prediction passages, often referred to as the 'little apocalypse of Mark'.

13:24-27: *But in those days, after that suffering, the sun will be darkened, and the moon will not give its light, and the stars will be falling from heaven, and the powers in the heavens will be shaken. Then they will see 'the Son of Man coming in clouds' with great power and glory. Then he will send out the angels, and gather his elect from the four winds, from the ends of the earth to the ends of heaven."* (See also 14:61-62.)

Here Jesus 'predicts' the suffering of the people in the Jewish War against the Romans in 66-70 CE, when Jerusalem would be destroyed, including the Temple. This is Mark's point of view following the destruction, and it acts as reassurance for the reader that even though things look black, Jesus will soon reappear in an apocalyptic scenario as Son of Man, to herald the longed-for intervention of God. Significantly, Mark is at pains to say that when Jesus predicted the destruction of the Temple, his words were not public:

*When he was sitting on the Mount of Olives opposite the
temple, Peter, James, John and Andrew asked him
privately, "Tell us, when will this be, and what will be the
sign that all these things are about to be accomplished?"*
(13:3:3-4).

Again this indicates that Jesus' predictions in Mark are
not based on instances of public knowledge. Recognition that
this is Mark's own point of view also refutes the frequent claims
that the reason the Jewish leadership wanted Jesus dead was his
threats against the Temple. In fact he was a loyal Jew of his time,
who most likely wanted only to purify the Temple from its
corrupt financial practices to prepare for the coming of the
kingdom of God/heaven.

*Again the high priest asked him, "Are you the Messiah, the
Son of the Blessed One?" Jesus said, "I am; and 'you will
see the Son of Man seated at the right hand of the Power,'
and 'coming with the clouds of heaven'." (14:61-62).*

Here is a further prediction and confession from Jesus
that he is the Messiah, this time made to the high priest. Again,
a private context. Who was recording this conversation? The
charge the Temple leadership brings against Jesus is that he
threatened to destroy the Temple. This is another of Mark's
backward glances at the Jewish War. For Mark's readers the
charge that Jesus wished to destroy the Temple strengthens the
accompanying messianic claim; after all, the Temple was
destroyed, wasn't it? Surely this means Jesus had messianic
powers of foresight. Therefore he must be the Messiah. Mark
again uses the apocalyptic language of Daniel chapter 7,
concerning the *"one like a Son of Man coming with the clouds of
heaven"*. (7:13)

For my readers, the insertion of a quotation from Daniel
concerning the Son of Man is important here. Given that the
Greek-speaking Mark would have been working from the Greek
version of the Hebrew Scriptures, I have used an English
translation of that (the Greek 'Septuagint') for this quotation:

Daniel 7:13-14: *"I beheld in the night vision, and lo, one coming with the clouds of heaven as the Son of man, and he came on to the Ancient of days, and was brought near to him. And to him was given the dominion, and the honour, and the kingdom; and all nations, tribes, and languages, shall serve him: his dominion is an everlasting dominion, which shall not pass away, and his kingdom shall not be destroyed."*

A problem here for interpretation of the *"Son of man"* as Jesus, is that Jewish scholarship sees this apocalyptic figure as representing the people of Israel at the End-time Day of the LORD. A further problem, probably unknown to most of Mark's original readership, is that the *"Son of man"* in Daniel is going on *"the clouds of heaven"* from earth to heaven. He is not coming from heaven to earth, as one might expect if this represents what Mark sees as a prediction of Jesus' second coming as Messiah.

16:19: *So then the Lord Jesus, after he had spoken to them, was taken up into heaven and sat down at the right hand of God.*

In the 'ascension' scene at the end of Mark is the Son of Man in his place at God's right hand. Yet right up to the end of Jesus' time with the disciples, they had not understood his identity. Mark's portrayal of them as incapable of understanding Jesus' repeated efforts to reveal himself to them as Messiah, reaches its climax in 16:14. This is part of the so-called 'longer' resurrection narrative of Mark, most probably not written by Mark, where Jesus finally loses his patience with his dim followers. (We might also regard this scene as the writer of the longer ending's loss of patience with Mark's 'messianic secret'!) In this scenario Jesus gives the disciples a thorough dressing down for *"their lack of faith and stubbornness, because they had not believed those who saw him after he had risen."* (16:14).

Even so, Jesus is here revealing himself as Messiah to the few, not to the many.

The Messianic Secret Debated

Mark's methodology in declaring Jesus' messiahship without evidence that Jesus claimed it himself, has often been called 'the messianic secret' of Mark's gospel. As we have noted throughout Mark's Gospel, when Jesus is asked whether or not he is the Messiah, the question is asked by his small group of disciples and his answer is even then often evasive. Or he issues firm orders to bystanders not to tell anyone about something he has done which might be called 'messianic'. Or he commands demons who do identify him as Messiah, to be quiet. The following will set out some of the many scholarly attempts to understand why the writer of Mark, who obviously believed in Jesus as Messiah, portrayed Jesus' messiahship in such ambiguous terms.

It is now over a century since William Wrede first attempted to explain why Jesus is shown behaving in such an enigmatic manner concerning his messiahship, especially in the Gospel of Mark.[62] Wrede wrote in the context of a growing 'quest of the historical Jesus' which favoured a view of Jesus as a man of his place and time. It is not unimportant that Wrede's colleague early in his career was Julius Wellhausen, who denied that Jesus believed he was the Messiah, and argued in addition that Jesus did not believe in an End-time when God would intervene to save Israel.[63] Wellhausen advocated the position that messianism and eschatology (End-time ideas) were the beliefs of the early church, not of Jesus himself.

Wrede's primary position was that the 'messianic secret' is explained by the argument that messianic ideas about Jesus were not developed until after his death, and were therefore not those of Jesus himself. He also pointed to the disciples' inexplicable failure to understand Jesus' messianic identity, indicating his position that they did not know it because Jesus did not say it. Wrede summarizes his conclusions as:

> *The one is an idea about Jesus and it rests on the fact that Jesus became messiah – so far as the belief of his followers was concerned – with the Resurrection, and the other is an idea about the disciples which rests upon the*

fact that they acquire a new understanding of Jesus as a result of the Resurrection. But the starting-point manifests itself in the end to be one and the same. Both ideas rest upon the fact that the Resurrection is the decisive event for the messiahship and that Jesus' earthly life was not to begin with regarded as messianic.[64]

Wrede's conclusions were roundly attacked by some scholars, but supported by Albert Schweitzer, who saw Mark's Gospel as containing both 'natural' and 'supernatural' dogmatic representations of Jesus:

The complete want of connexion, with all its self-contradictions, is ultimately due to the fact that two representations of the life of Jesus, or, to speak more accurately, of His public ministry, are here crushed into one; a natural and a deliberately supernatural representation. A dogmatic element has intruded itself into the description of this Life – something which has no concern with the events which form the outward course of that Life. This dogmatic element is the Messianic secret of Jesus and all the secrets and concealments which go along with it.[65]

Even so, Schweitzer was not totally supportive; he criticized Wrede's theory that the 'messianic secret' is a literary device created by Mark. He also argued that the post-Easter Christ movement would have accepted Mark's claim that Jesus was the Messiah only if Jesus had actually claimed that himself. Other early 20th century German scholars such as Johannes Weiss preferred the idea that Jesus simply did not want to be known as Messiah, even though he did believe himself to be that.

Conservative scholars in the 1930s such as the German Julius Schniewind,[66] argued strongly against Wrede's belief that the messianic secret was a literary creation of Mark's. Instead Schniewind saw it as the unique way Jesus deliberately presented himself as fulfilment of Jewish expectations of the Messiah. On the other hand, the American scholar F. C. Grant was one of Wrede's most enthusiastic supporters. He argued that the gospels were not written to preserve the historical integrity of Jesus, but to give hope and support to the early Christ movement. Grant supported Wrede's position that Jesus never claimed to be the Messiah.

In contemporary scholarship the British scholar N. T. Wright argues that Jesus did think of himself as the Messiah, and that his followers also knew that. He told them to keep quiet about it because otherwise he would have been at risk from threatened authority figures such as King Herod, and also from militant insurrectionists who would have wanted him to accept military-style leadership. Even so, Wright concedes that Jesus, who he says knew he was the Messiah and had deliberately guarded the messianic secret, had also redefined the understanding of Messiah to include the prophetic role of 'cleansing' the Temple. [67]

This argument of Wright's is perilously close to traditional Christian understandings of Jesus as unique - unlike any other Jew - even in his messiahship. Another British scholar – Morna Hooker – sees Mark's literary methodology in creating the messianic secret as his way of proclaiming Jesus' particular (humble) brand of messiahship.[68]

None of the foregoing specifically spells out the most simple and therefore one of the most likely answers regarding Jesus as the 'secret' Messiah. It is surely that:
- Jesus never did claim messiahship.
- Some people asked him about it but he denied it.
- Word got around that he had appeared after his death to his friends.
- Pharisaic belief in the appearance of the Messiah before the general resurrection of the righteous dead became identified with belief in Jesus' resurrection.
- *Ipso facto*, he was the Messiah.

Belief that Jesus claimed to be the Messiah (or not) usually hinges on whether a person believes him to be the Christ of faith, or self-identifies as a follower of Jesus' teaching. My reader knows that I see the messiahship of Jesus as a post-resurrection development on the part of believers other than Jesus' own pre-Easter followers.

The events of Easter

We continue this exploration of Mark's messianic agenda into his narrative concerning the events of Easter. This is the climax of Mark's attempts to persuade his reader that Jesus is the Messiah, or in Greek, the Christ. His literary methods remain much the same, as we will see.

The messianic entry into Jerusalem

> 11:7-10: *Then they brought the colt to Jesus and threw their cloaks on it; and he sat on it. Many people spread their cloaks on the road, and others spread leafy branches that they had cut in the fields. Then those who went ahead and those who followed were shouting, "Hosanna! Blessed is the one who comes in the name of the Lord! Blessed is the coming kingdom of our ancestor David! Hosanna in the highest heaven!"*

Mark sets the scene for his Easter narratives with Jesus' triumphal entry into Jerusalem. Here it is not only the disciples who hail him as Messiah, but *"many people"* (11:8). Mark's intention is to persuade his readers that Jesus' messiahship was recognized by large numbers of the Jewish population. While it is impossible to know whether at that time 'many people' would have believed Jesus to be the Messiah, there are good reasons to argue that Mark has borrowed his imagery here from scripture concerning the Jewish Festival of Booths or *Sukkot*.[69] As in earlier times, in Jesus' day the people would have cut palm branches from trees and carried them up to the Temple to give thanks for the harvest, as per Leviticus 23:40-41:

> *On the first day you shall take the fruit of majestic trees, branches of palm trees, boughs of leafy trees, and willows of the brook; and you shall rejoice before the LORD your God for seven days. You shall keep it as a festival to the LORD seven days in the year.*

Of course, there are difficulties with the timing of the 'entrance into Jerusalem' if it coincides with Sukkot (autumn), rather than with Passover (springtime), but Mark is not going to let that get in the way of a good story! Psalm 118 is also an obvious source of inspiration for Mark, as in verses 26-27:

> *"Blessed is the one who comes in the name of the Lord. We bless you from the house of the Lord. The Lord is God, and he has given us light. Bind the festal procession with branches, up to the horns of the altar."*

Mark's use of those verses has a messianic purpose, but they place Jesus' arrival in Jerusalem in October (at *Sukkot*), rather than at the time of the Passover in March/April. This would probably have been of little account to early Greek-speaking Gentile readers of the gospel, firstly because their attention was focussed on Mark's revelation of Jesus as the Christ, and secondly, because many would have had little knowledge of Judaism and its scriptures.

The quotation from Psalm 118 is followed by a confirmation of Jesus' messiahship in the words of the people: *"Blessed is the coming kingdom of our ancestor David!"* (Mark 11:10). Here the people inform Mark's readers that Jesus conforms to Jewish expectations of a Davidic Messiah,[70] and that it is this Davidic Messiah who will inaugurate the kingdom of God on earth. This quotation is likely to have been included as counter to a common Jewish charge against the Christ movement. The charge was that Jesus did not conform to traditional Jewish expectations of a Messiah in the mould of David, the first Messiah.

Mark, however, endeavours to raise the messianic profile of Jesus to someone greater than David. In doing so he is also answering the difficult question of why in his time (post -70 CE) Jesus the Messiah has not come back to earth to establish the kingdom of God. This is his master stroke. In 12:35-36 he includes a quote from Psalm 110:1 in which David says:

> *"The Lord said to my Lord* [apparently meaning the

Messiah], *sit at my right hand, until I put your enemies under your feet."*

By using this quote, Mark implies that this is why Jesus has not yet returned to rule as Messiah; he is sitting at God's right hand until evil has been defeated![71]

The story in 11:1-7 about Jesus riding a donkey colt into Jerusalem creates a link with other Jewish writings of the time. In the Dead Sea Scrolls the Messiah was called the 'King Messiah'. He was also known in those writings as a priestly Messiah, or 'Messiah of Aaron'.[72] The imagery of Jesus riding into the city on a donkey is linked with kingship in Zechariah 9:9:

> *"Rejoice greatly, O daughter Zion! Shout aloud, O daughter Jerusalem! Lo, your king comes to you; triumphant and victorious is he, humble and riding on a donkey, on a colt, the foal of a donkey."*

Even if the words 'triumphant and victorious' seem at odds with the humble Jesus portrayed in the gospels, the donkey on which he rides tallies with a peaceful rather than a militaristic entry into the city. However, if a message that Jesus was regarded by some as King/Messiah had been communicated to Roman and Herodian authorities, that would have been sufficient for him to be charged by the Romans with insurrection, by Herod with treason, and by the High Priest with being a danger to the Jewish people. In any case, he would have been doomed to execution. Even if Jesus did not see himself as King Messiah, some people may well have wanted to see him that way, which ultimately sealed his fate.

The 'cleansing' of the Temple

11:15-18: *Then they came to Jerusalem. And he entered the temple and began to drive out those who were selling and those who were buying in the temple, and he overturned the tables of the money changers and the seats of those who sold doves; and he would not allow anyone to carry anything through the temple. He was teaching and saying, "Is it not written' My house shall be called a house of prayer for all the nations'? But you have made it a den of robbers." And when the chief priests and the scribes heard it, they kept looking for a way to kill him, for they were afraid of him, because the whole crowd was spellbound by his teaching.*

The 'cleansing' has a distinctly Elijian flavour. As we have noted, Elijah's role as per Malachi included the purification of the Temple and its authorities. Jesus probably did carry out a prophetic 'cleansing' of the Temple from its desecration by corrupt money changers and Temple apparatchiks. The point to note is that Mark quotes Isaiah 56:7b in full: *"for my house shall be called a house of prayer for all peoples."* Mark is in agreement with Paul that Jesus is Messiah/Christ for the Gentiles as well as the Jews. As we will see, Matthew does not regard it that way. Therefore he drops *"for all peoples"*.

Jesus as Messiah in the Last Supper, Trial, Crucifixion and Resurrection Narratives

Before recognizing the messianic sign-posts in the last supper, trial, crucifixion and resurrection narratives, it will be useful to name the scriptural sources used by the writer of Mark's Gospel to create them. They are Daniel 7:13; Psalm 22:1,7,18; Psalm 41:9; Psalm 69:21; Psalm 109:25; Isaiah 53:12; Exodus 24:8, Exodus 26:31-33; Jeremiah 31:31-34; Zechariah 13:7; Leviticus 24:16. There are also signs of Pauline influence from 1 Corinthians 11: 23-25. These sources will be identified and/or quoted in the following discussion of the narratives.

The Last Supper

14:17-25: When it was evening, he came with the twelve. And when they had taken their places and were eating, Jesus said, "Truly I tell you, one of you will betray me, one who is eating with me." They began to be distressed and to say to him one after another, "Surely, not I?" He said to them, "It is one of the twelve, one who is dipping bread into the bowl with me. For the Son of Man goes as it is written of him, but woe to that one by whom the Son of Man is betrayed! It would have been better for that one not to have been born." While they were eating, he took a loaf of bread, and after blessing it he broke it, gave it to them, and said, "Take; this is my body." Then he took a cup, and after giving thanks he gave it to them, and all of them drank from it. He said to them, "This is my blood of the covenant, which is poured out for many. Truly I tell you, I will never again drink of the fruit of the vine until that day when I drink it new in the kingdom of God."

During Mark's version of the gathering of Jesus and his disciples at the Passover Meal, Jesus makes cryptic references to his coming betrayal. Again this is Mark attributing predictive powers to Jesus concerning his own death. This was obviously very important for Mark in making his case for a predicted death of the Messiah. He needs to overcome the mainstream Jewish opposition that naturally insisted there was no tradition of a dead Messiah – let alone one executed as a rebel. As always, Mark is looking backwards with the clarity and knowledge of hindsight, from well beyond the events of Easter. It is likely though, that one aspect of Mark's story has historical correctness. It is possible that one of Jesus' group did betray him, hoping he would then be provoked into revealing himself as the expected (Davidic) Messiah.

Mark's institution of the Eucharist is often said to indicate signs of being sourced from 1 Corinthians 11: 23-25, where Paul speaks:

"For I received from the Lord what I also handed on to you, that the Lord Jesus on the night when he was betrayed took a loaf of bread, and when he had given thanks, he broke it and said, "This is my body that is for you. Do this in remembrance of me. In the same way he took the cup also, after supper, saying, "This cup is the new covenant in my blood. Do this, as often as you drink

it, in remembrance of me." For as often as you eat this bread and drink the cup, you proclaim the Lord's death until he comes."

There are definite similarities with Mark's version, but as James Crossley points out, it is possible that both Paul and Mark used an earlier tradition.[73] This makes sense when it is remembered that the post-Easter Messiah/Christ movement preceded Paul's conversion. The movement's existence obviously influenced Paul's thinking so much that he joined it! This is irrespective of the historicity of the Acts account of his encounter with a 'risen Christ'. In any case, if an early eucharistic tradition existed prior to Paul's first letter to Corinth (c.54CE), he (Paul) may have modified it in accordance with his own messianic expectations of Jesus. Mark's Eucharist may well have been based on a pre-Paul tradition being used by early hellenized Jewish followers of Messiah Jesus.

Regardless of the historical origin of this meal, Mark's outline begins with the traditional Jewish blessing of the bread and wine before the meal, which Mark is the first to tell us is a Passover meal. The Passover meal has always commemorated and celebrated the covenant of redemption between God and the Israelites who were rescued from Egypt. Accordingly, Mark 14:24 contains a reference to the Mosaic covenant that followed the Exodus: Jesus says:

"This is my blood of the covenant, which is poured out for many."

The background for that is Exodus 24:8, which describes Moses taking the blood of the sacrifices, throwing it over the people and saying:

"See the blood of the covenant that the Lord has made with you in accordance with all these words."

A non-messianic understanding of 'The Last Supper'
If Jesus did see himself as a prophetic teacher, dedicated to

calling Israel to repentance and restoring the people to their covenant relationship with God, it is surely likely that this was the understanding of his original followers. Their aim then would have been to remember him as prophet/teacher calling them to renew their covenant with God by following his teaching about the kingdom of God on earth. As orthodox Jews[74] they would never have associated drinking wine with drinking Jesus' blood. Jesus may have asked his friends to 'remember me' during his last meal with them, which led to the development of a ritual 'remembering' meal that may or may not have been associated with Passover.[75] Portraying the meal as a Passover meal was of great significance for Mark, as he wished to associate the death of the Messiah with the sacrifice of the Passover lamb. That was the best answer Mark could find for the puzzling death of Jesus the Messiah.

Yet for Jesus' original disciples his death would have been understood as the death of a prophet/teacher who challenged the Jewish and Roman leadership and was killed, as were Jeremiah and other prophets who challenged the monarchy. Jesus' twelve disciples were probably representative of a restored twelve tribes of Israel, reconciled with God. For that reason it makes sense that Jesus may actually have chosen to surround himself with twelve students (or disciples). A distinctive mark of an original ritual over against Paul and Mark's messianic Eucharist would be the absence of references to the wine as symbolic of Jesus' blood, or to a second coming. (In the following section we will see an example of that absence in the earliest known example of the Eucharist, in the late first century CE document called the *Didache*.)

A messianic understanding of the Eucharist

A shift in understanding of an original ritual 'remembering' meal is likely to have taken place with the early development of messianic beliefs about Jesus. In the fourth and fifth decades of the first century, followers of Jesus the Messiah/Christ were doubtless struggling to find meaning in the death of the man they believed to be the Messiah. That was not supposed to happen! While the Temple continued to exist, a possible answer would have been to see Jesus' death as ultimate atoning sacrifice for the redemption of Israel. As Messiah, he would have been the only one they could have imagined worthy to be that sacrifice. In accordance with that, an understanding of Jesus as Saviour of the Gentiles is totally absent from the pre-Paul speech before the high priest attributed to Stephen in Acts 7.

By the late 50s and 60s CE Paul had extended the salvific understanding of Jesus' death to the Gentiles, as per his words (attributed to Jesus) in 1 Corinthians 11: 23-25: *"this cup is the new covenant in my blood"*. Paul's understanding of himself as the *"apostle to the Gentiles"* (Romans 11:13) necessitates that they be included in a new or renewed covenant with God. For Paul the Jew, the issue was opening the door to the God of Israel for the Gentiles by means of this new covenant in the blood of Messiah Jesus. It is important to remember that the Jewish man Paul and his followers were developing understandings of Jesus the Messiah/Christ during the life of the Temple and its system of sacrifices. The Temple would have loomed very large in their attempts to place meaning around the death of the Messiah.

The biggest shift in understandings of Jesus' death occurred after the Temple was destroyed in 70CE. This is the beginning of the 'gospel era', when the canonical gospels were written. Paradoxically, the absence of the Temple by then did not mean the end of sacrificial ideas applied to Jesus' death. Instead it led to an understanding of Messiah Jesus as the perfect sacrificial lamb who transcended the sacrifices of the now-destroyed Temple:

> *"Here is the lamb of God, who takes away the sin of the world!"* (John 1:29).

The destruction of the Temple is now understood as the will of God. The Temple's demise fits with God's plan to declare it redundant after the once-for-all sacrifice of the 'lamb of God'.

For Mark, Jesus is not the prophet who dies trying to reconcile Israel with God; he is the Messiah who knows he is to become the redeeming sacrifice. Hence the many 'predictions' of his death attributed to Jesus. This development in christological thinking toward the end of the first century CE is instructive concerning the difficult social and religious context in which followers of Messiah Jesus were situated. It indicates their urgent need to find an answer to the strong objection aimed at the early believers. The objection insisted that nowhere is it written that the Messiah would die and rise after three days. The problem for the believers was that the objection was true; they had to find a way to over-rule it.

None of the foregoing necessitates that Jesus himself instituted a eucharistic ritual at his meal. There is a real problem with an understanding of wine as even symbolic of Jesus' blood, shed when he was crucified. This problem applies even if the blood merely symbolizes a Jewish understanding of the blood of the (renewed) covenant. The problem relates to the very strong prohibition on eating blood in Leviticus 17:10-11:

> *"If anyone of the house of Israel or of the aliens who reside among them eats any blood, I will set my face against that person who eats blood, and will cut that person off from the people. For the life of the flesh is in the blood; and I have given it to you for making atonement for your lives on the altar; for, as life, it is the blood that makes atonement."*

Although it is appropriate to shed blood *"for making atonement for your lives on the altar"*, it is not to be consumed. Eating or drinking blood is anathema to Jews both then and now, representing as it does the life of the person or animal, given by God. Yet Mark and Paul were both Jews. That indicates how important it became for messianic followers to understand why the Messiah died. They had to develop a reason that could explain such an unexpected and unthinkable development. Accordingly, a huge shift away from Jewish tradition became necessary for Paul's and Mark's communities. For them the eucharistic wine became symbolic of the blood of 'Christ' – of his willingness to become the atoning sacrifice for sin. Even though the wine was only symbolic of the blood, the problem was that the Eucharist still entailed drinking the symbol.

The Eucharist was therefore sometimes thought by Roman writers (particularly Tertullian) to entail an actual eating and drinking of human flesh and blood (Christians were sometimes called cannibals).[76] By the second century many Christians were martyred when that view of the eucharistic meal became public and for that reason they often met in secret to celebrate the Eucharist. Given the timing of Paul's first letter to the Corinthians (53-57 CE), it is likely that he developed his eucharistic ideas to incorporate a more explicit messianism than was included in earlier 'remembering' meals concerning Jesus. These he would likely have encountered when he first converted to the already existing movement.

Mark incorporated this Paul-inspired ritual into his gospel and linked his description of the last meal shared by Jesus and his disciples with an allusion to the messianic banquet *"in the kingdom of God"* (14:25). Mark and his readers are to remember Jesus in this way until the 'kingdom' comes, presumably on the resurrected Messiah's reappearance. Paul's ritual points to that; it concludes with a clear prediction of the return of Jesus the Messiah:

> 1 Cor. 11:26: *"For as often as you eat this bread and drink the cup, you proclaim the Lord's death until he comes."*

Demonstrating clearly that there were varied interpretations of the 'remembering meal' celebrated among followers of Jesus, the manuscript called the 'Didache'[77] carries a different understanding of the Eucharist from either Paul or the gospel writers. It makes no mention of Jesus' death and resurrection, or of the bread and wine as Jesus' body and blood. In the prayer of thanksgiving the wine represents *"the holy vine of David your servant, which you made known to us through Jesus your servant."* The bread represents *"the life and knowledge which you made known to us through Jesus your servant."* This looks like a celebration by a messianic Jewish community with traditional understandings of the Messiah and of Jesus as teacher; not one that worshipped Jesus as the risen Christ and divine Son of God. New Testament scholar Burton L.

Mack makes this comment:

> *Accustomed as we are to the memorial supper of the Christ cult and the stories of the last supper in the synoptic gospels, it has been very difficult to imagine early Christians taking meals together for any reason other than to celebrate the death of Jesus according to the Christ myth. But here in the Didache a very formalistic set of prayers is assigned to the cup and the breaking of bread without the slightest association with the death and resurrection of Jesus.*[78]

Scholarly datings for the Didache now include a late first century origin among Jewish rural dwellers in northern Palestine.[79] This is not a Gentile document; its reference to David requires a thoroughly Jewish setting among people for whom the reference to David the Messiah forms the background to their understanding of Jesus the Messiah. The Didache looks like a preserved understanding of the kind of 'remembering meal' likely to have been observed by Palestinian Jewish followers of Messiah Jesus. The writers of this document may not have been Jesus' original followers, but their traditional messianic ideas about him probably originate from well before those recorded in Paul's writings or in the gospels.

My understanding of the Eucharist

In addition to all the other scholarly speculation surrounding this subject, I want to give my reader a clear understanding of my own view of the Eucharist. First, I do not believe that Jesus instituted a Eucharist of any sort. He may have asked his friends to "remember me" at their meals when he sensed he was in danger from Roman authorities and the Temple leadership. It is perfectly reasonable to believe that they did remember him ritually as prophet and teacher of the kingdom of God. The belief that Jesus saw himself as a covenant sacrifice[80] to reconcile the people with God, actually entails human sacrifice (or human/divine sacrifice). As an observant Jew, Jesus would have regarded that as personally offensive and as an affront to God. As we have said, references to the *"blood of the covenant"* (Mark 14:24) are Mark's attempt to deal with the dilemma of a Messiah who dies. Yet because Jesus was a Jew, he would never have thought of himself as fully human and fully divine (a third to fourth century development). That understanding lent itself to the idea that it was 'God in Christ' who died on the cross for the salvation of humanity. In the story of Abraham and Isaac, God makes it perfectly clear to the Jews that human sacrifice is an abomination.

Yet for Paul, a hellenized Jew with universalist views of the significance of Jesus, he became the perfect sacrifice for the redemption all people. Jesus' death marked the beginning of the new covenant, sanctified by the shedding of his own blood. The fact that Mark associated Jesus' last meal with his disciples with the Passover meal enabled Christian writers and theologians to develop their sacrificial ideas about Jesus' death, which they incorporated in the Eucharist.[81] As we have noted, some early Palestinian Jewish followers (the writers of the Didache) did not have that understanding.

It is worth asking how Paul reconciled his view of the death of the Messiah with his Jewish background. Significantly for Paul's developing Christology, he had been part of the Temple administration before his conversion, which meant that his thinking would have been much influenced by the Temple's sacrificial theology, including the blood associated with the giving of the Mosaic covenant. He was also a Greek scholar, raised in the Diaspora among Greek ideas, including the sacrifice of 'sons of gods'. Need we say that Jesus did not have that kind of hellenized background?

Through Paul's entire lifetime the Temple existed; consequently it had an enormous influence on his thinking. He had even been an official of the Temple, charged with arresting messianic Jews who were stirring up trouble with the Romans. His change of heart was a huge leap from one side of the messianic conflict to the other. So it is hardly surprising that it was over against the Temple that a great many of his ideas were generated. For him the sacrifices in the Temple were now redundant; Jesus the Messiah had become the ultimate sacrifice for the redemption not only of Israel, but of all humanity. Naturally enough, this did not endear him to the Temple leadership.

Richard Horsley proposes a possible interpretation that Jesus' Palestinian (post-Easter) followers may have held. It entailed him dying as a martyr to the cause of renewing Israel under the rule of God (i.e. the kingdom of God on earth). Accordingly, those early followers may have regarded Jesus' death and resurrection (in whatever way they understood the resurrection) as catalyst for the expansion of his movement. That would have included belief that the martyred prophet Jesus, vindicated by God in his resurrection, would soon return to restore Israel.[82]

As a 21st century follower of Jesus, my instinct is that we eat bread and drink wine as our way of remembering that Jesus did this with his first followers as he followed the dangerous path of challenging Roman power.[83] For us the bread and wine become spiritual nourishment for our own sometimes difficult journey in following his Way. In the remembering, we recall that Jesus was brutally killed for the sake of his vision of the kingdom of God (or heaven) on earth. Our response is to rededicate ourselves to work together and implement his vision, certainly not to await an apocalyptic End-time in which God fixes the world for us. I reject any notions of the bread as symbol of Jesus' body and the wine as symbol of his blood. Those symbols are linked irrevocably to traditional atonement theory. They imply an unforgiving God who required that Jesus the Messiah submit to being sacrificed as atonement for the redemption of humanity. Jesus' teachings do not indicate that he believed ideas about God such as that. He did teach his followers to pray that they will 'hallow' (bring honour to) God's name.

The Trial

14:43-50: *Immediately, while he was still speaking, Judas, one of the twelve, arrived; and with him there was a crowd with swords and clubs, from the chief priests, the scribes, and the elders. Now the betrayer had given them a sign, saying, "The one I will kiss is the man;*

arrest him and lead him away under guard." So when he came, he went up to him at once and said, "Rabbi!" and kissed him. Then they laid hands on him and arrested him. But one of those who stood near drew his sword and struck the slave of the high priest, cutting off his ear. Then Jesus said to them, "Have you come out with swords and clubs to arrest me as though I were a bandit? Day after day I was with you in the temple teaching, and you did not arrest me. But let the scriptures be fulfilled." All of them deserted him and fled. (See also 14: 61-65).

Into his story of Jesus' arrest, Mark adds the mysterious betrayal by the disciple Judas Iscariot. Judas' name indicates that he may have been associated with the *Sicarii*, who had militant messianic expectations. The *Sicarii* were operating at the time of the Jewish War (66-70 CE), but had their beginnings in Jewish revolts against the Roman census conducted around the turn of the first century CE. The *Sicarii* were probably named by the Romans (*Sicarii* is a Latin name) after the dagger (*Sica*) they carried. Josephus called them Zealots.

Mark tells us that Jesus was delivered into the hands of the Temple (the High Priest), the Palace (Herod) and the Romans (Pilate) by someone called Judas Iscariot. Many have made the connection between Judas and the *Sicarii*, and if that were true, Judas may have been trying to persuade Jesus to lead an armed revolt. He may even have thought he would precipitate this by placing Jesus into the hands of the authorities. Now Jesus would reveal himself as Messiah and the Romans would be overthrown on the intervention of God.

Mark adds credence to the argument for Judas' *Sicarii* credentials when "*one of those who stood near*" drew a sword against the Temple officials who were arresting Jesus (14:47). These bystanders are not identified as members of the 'twelve', but their presence could indicate that insurrectionists were attracted to the scene of Jesus' arrest. Perhaps they were even summoned by Judas Iscariot. One of them makes an attempt to respond violently to the arrest, and cuts off the ear of the High

Priest's servant. Distancing himself from all of that, Jesus points out to the Temple police that they did not need to arrest him as though he were a violent insurrectionist; he has been peacefully available to them every day in the Temple.

Mark then has Jesus identify himself as the one scripture predicts will be handed over to suffering (Isaiah 53): *"But let the scriptures be fulfilled"* (14:49b). When the insurrectionists (or *Sicarii*) standing around see that he is not going to fulfil their hopes by adopting a Davidic messianic leadership role and leading them into an armed uprising against the Romans, they run away, presumably accompanied by Judas. It appears that the rest of the 'twelve' also flee. Judas appears no more in Mark's gospel.

Mark's version of the last meal and trial narrative necessitates the whole Sanhedrin being summoned in the middle of the night (after the Passover meal) on the Day of Preparation for the first Sabbath of the Festival of Unleavened Bread, when it is highly unlikely that any business of the Sanhedrin would have been conducted. They also reconvened at dawn to send Jesus to Pilate. Given the historical unlikelihood of this scenario, it may be seen as part of Mark's intentionally messianic trial and crucifixion narrative. For one thing, Mark wants his readers to see that Jesus was taken so seriously by the Temple leadership that they would break their own laws regarding the observance of Passover. It is decisive that the only time Mark has Jesus openly declare his messiahship, it is once again not in public; it is to the high priest (14:61-62).

The conversation between Jesus and the high priest is hardly likely to be a historical record, but Mark makes a case for its historicity by placing Peter within earshot:

14:54: *"Peter had followed him at a distance, right into the courtyard of the high priest; and he was sitting with the guards, warming himself at the fire."*

At the time he wrote his gospel (probably during the 70s or 80s CE), Mark's version of a conversation between Jesus and the high priest could no longer be challenged or corroborated by

Peter. Most scholars agree that Peter was executed during the reign of the emperor Nero, about 64CE. Mark has Jesus quote Daniel 7 to answer in the affirmative the High Priest's inquiry if he is:

> 14:62: *"the Messiah, the Son of the Blessed One". Jesus says, 'I am ... and you will see the Son of Man seated at the right hand of the Power and 'coming with the clouds of heaven.' "*

As I noted before, the one *"like a son of man"* in Daniel 7 is going from earth to heaven, not the other way around.

Then from the high priest comes the curious accusation of blasphemy. The charge of blasphemy in the Law of Moses is set out in Leviticus 24:16: *"One who blasphemes the name of the LORD shall be put to death; the whole congregation shall stone the blasphemer."* Yet there is no sense in which Mark's version of Jesus' reply deserves the charge of blasphemy. He had certainly not cursed the name of God. Even if he had claimed to be *"the Son of the Blessed One"*, Jesus would not have departed from messianic tradition. Psalm 2:7 identifies the first Messiah, King David, as son of God. David says: *"I will tell of the decree of the LORD: He said to me, "You are my son; today I have begotten you."* Claiming to be the Messiah was not a stoning offence in first century Judaism and others had claimed publicly to be the Messiah without accusation of blasphemy from the high priest.

In any case, it is significant that the Sanhedrin and high priest did not order and carry out the stoning for a blasphemer as per Leviticus 24:16. Religious stonings were allowed under the power-sharing agreement between Rome, the Herods and the Temple leadership. Even allowing for the unlikely historicity of Acts, it does describe the stoning of Stephen. This was carried out as a result of Stephen's speech to the high priest, which indicates that it is depicted as during the time before the destruction of the Temple (Acts 7:54-60). The likeliest explanation of why Jesus was not stoned to death for blasphemy is because he did not actually claim to be the Messiah, even if that were a stoning offence, which it is not.[84]

It is much more likely that Jesus' popularity meant he might attract militant insurrectionists and therefore be regarded as a threat to Roman secular authority and Jewish religious authority. On the basis of his prophetic action in the Temple, it is also possible that Jesus was charged with plotting to destroy the Temple:

> 13:2: *Then Jesus asked him, "Do you see these great buildings? Not one stone will be left here upon another; all will be thrown down."*

Even though that is one of the hindsight predictions of Mark's Jesus, there may have been an accusation of that sort made against Jesus. In any case, only the Romans had the power to carry out executions where the charge was political. For that reason the trial moved on to the palace of Pontius Pilate, the Roman Procurator. *Note well* that nowhere is it said in Mark's gospel that Herod Antipas was involved in Jesus' trial. Could it be that once again there is no criticism of Herod because Mark and his community of messianic Jesus followers lived during the 70s and 80s within Herod Agrippa II's jurisdiction of Tiberius and the Galilee?

> 15:2-11: *They bound Jesus, led him away, and handed him over to Pilate. Pilate asked him, "Are you the King of the Jews?" He answered him, "You say so." Then the chief priests accused him of many things. Pilate asked him again, "Have you no answer? See how many charges they bring against you." But Jesus made no further reply, so that Pilate was amazed.*

Pilate, it turns out, supplies the 'real' reason why the high priest has requested that the Romans crucify Jesus: the Temple leadership is *"jealous"* (15:10) of Jesus' popularity with the people. Pilate is portrayed as perfectly reasonable and reluctant to order Jesus' crucifixion, even offering to free him. It is then the Jewish crowds who take the brunt of the blame for forcing Pilate's hand and demanding execution of Jesus by crucifixion.

Whether or not Jesus claimed to be Messiah/King of the Jewish people, it is likely that this charge would have been laid because of Pilate's knowledge that there were people (possibly the Zealots/Sicarii) who were keen to take advantage of Jesus' popularity, declare him to be Messiah and follow him into a rebellion against the Romans. In accordance with that, Mark sets out a scenario whereby Roman soldiers dress Jesus as a king in a purple cloak, place a crown made of thorns on his head and mockingly pretend to acknowledge his kingship. This serves as additional confirmation for Mark's readers that Jesus actually did claim messianic kingship, albeit of a non-violent sort.

The Crucifixion
Mark's crucifixion scene includes a good deal of scriptural sourcing, what I have called internal proof-texting. Crucifixions of people charged with insurrection were often carried out by the side of a road, so the victims could be seen and therefore function as a deterrent to anyone else considering rebellion against Rome. Other scholars see the site of Jesus' crucifixion as on a rock in a disused nearby quarry. In either case it is unlikely that there would have been reliable eye-witnesses from among his followers standing by to record Jesus' utterances from the cross. It would have been too dangerous to be seen to be associated with someone crucified for treason against Rome. That would have applied even if Jesus had been able to articulate anything at all, other than expressions of agony.

What we have in describing the crucifixion is an interweaving of scriptural references, chosen to add weight to Mark's contention that Jesus was being executed because he had claimed to be the true Messiah/King of the Jews. The scriptural references begin in 15:24 where the crucified Jesus' clothes are taken by the soldiers, who cast lots to see who would take which parts of his garments.

> 15:24-39: *And they crucified him, and divided his clothes among them, casting lots to decide what each should take. It was nine o'clock in the morning when they crucified him. The inscription of the charge against him*

*read, "The King of the Jews." And with him they crucified
two bandits, one on his right and one on his left. Those
who passed by derided him, shaking their heads and
saying, "Aha! You who would destroy the temple and
build it in three days, save yourself, and come down
from the cross!" In the same way the chief priests, along
with the scribes, were also mocking him among
themselves and saying, "He saved others; he cannot save
himself. Let the Messiah, the King of Israel, come down
from the cross now, so that we may see and believe."
Those who were crucified with him also taunted him.
When it was noon, darkness came over the whole land
until three in the afternoon. At three o'clock Jesus cried
out with a loud voice, "Eloi, Eloi, lema sabachthani?"
which means, "My God, my God, why have you forsaken
me?" When some of the bystanders heard it, they said,
"Listen, he is calling for Elijah." And someone ran, filled
a sponge with sour wine, put it on a stick, and gave it to
him to drink, saying, "Wait, let us see whether Elijah will
come to take him down." Then Jesus gave a loud cry and
breathed his last. And the curtain of the temple was torn
in two, from top to bottom. Now when the centurion,
who stood facing him, saw that in this way he breathed
his last, he said, "Truly this man was God's Son!"*

This is a close match with Psalm 22:18, where the
suffering one is exposed to his adversaries, and "*they divide my
clothes among themselves, and for my clothing they cast lots.*"
The next reference is not found in the NRSV version of Mark, but
was included in an early version of the gospel as verse 28 (there
is no verse 28 in the NRSV). This verse is linked with Mark's
information that "*with him they crucified two bandits, one on
his right and one on his left.*" The missing verse 28 says, "*And
the scripture was fulfilled that says, "and he was counted
among the lawless.*" The original scriptural reference for this is
Isaiah 53:12b: " *... because he poured himself out to death, and
was numbered with the transgressors.*" (Luke added this quote
to his version of the crucifixion.) The hostile, jeering reaction of

bystanders in Mark's version of the crucifixion is based on Psalm 22:7, where the suffering figure says: *"All who see me mock at me: they make mouths at me, they shake their heads; ..."* Concerning Jesus, Mark has: *"Those who passed by derided him, shaking their heads and saying "... save yourself, and come down from the cross!"*

Mark includes only one instance of 'Words from the Cross'. In 15:34, Jesus cries out loudly (in Aramaic), *"Eloi, Eloi, lema sabachthani?"*[85] which means, "My God, my God, why have you forsaken me?" Mark acknowledges the Elijah consciousness of the people (as per Chapter 2 of this book) when he has them mistake Jesus' word *Eloi* (my God) for *Elia*, a shortened version of *Eliahu*, or Elijah. These words attributed to Jesus are the clearest instance of Mark's use of Psalm 22:1: *"My God, my God, why have you forsaken me? Why are you so far from helping me, from the words of my groaning?"*

This quotation attributed to Jesus has evoked three common scholarly responses:

- First is that it is hardly likely Jesus could have been capable of quoting a psalm while being crucified.
- Second is that he may have felt deep despair when God did not prevent the crucifixion and was expressing it this way.
- Third is that he knew the ending of Psalm 22.

According to this theory Jesus began to recite Psalm 22 expecting that verse 24 would come true: *"For he did not despise or abhor the affliction of the afflicted; he did not hide his face from me, but heard when I cried to him."* In any case, the quotation is Mark's further 'proof' that although Jesus died, he is the one predicted by scripture to suffer and then to be vindicated by God. For Mark, that explains the crucifixion.

The crucifixion scene ends with Mark simply saying that women were watching from a distance. Three of them are named, but Mark makes it clear that *"many other women"* (15:41) had followed Jesus from the Galilee. They had looked after him while he was travelling and teaching. Matthew and Luke include this scene in much the same way, but John's Gospel has a very different treatment of it, as we will see.

The Resurrection – the original ending

16:1-8: *When the Sabbath was over, Mary Magdalene, and Mary the mother of James, and Salome bought spices, so that they might go and anoint him. And very early on the first day of the week, when the sun had risen, they went to the tomb. They had been saying to one another, "Who will roll away the stone for us from the entrance to the tomb?" When they looked up, they saw that the stone, which was very large, had already been rolled back. As they entered the tomb, they saw a young man, dressed in a white robe, sitting on the right side; and they were alarmed. But he said to them, "Do not be alarmed; you are looking for Jesus of Nazareth, who was crucified. He has been raised; he is not here. Look, there is the place they laid him. But go, tell his disciples and Peter that he is going ahead of you to Galilee; there you will see him, just as he told you." So they went out and fled from the tomb, for terror and amazement had seized them; and they said nothing to anyone, for they were afraid.*

Mark's resurrection narrative in chapter 16 has been the subject of a great deal of scholarly debate. There is a consensus that the so-called 'shorter ending' (between verses 8 and 9) was added by someone other than Mark, as were verses 9-20, the so-called 'longer ending'. This consensus includes the argument that it seems unlikely for Mark to have ended his gospel with the disciples fleeing from the empty tomb in terror and amazement, and saying nothing about it to anyone. It follows then (according to this consensus), that the original gospel's last page or pages, must at some early stage, have been considered lost. That meant it was up to others to supply an 'appropriate' ending. There is little doubt that those who wrote the 'longer ending' were consulting the gospels of Matthew, Luke, and even John. The editing was undertaken because the manuscript of Mark available at the time ended before it set out more fully the messianic implications of Jesus' resurrection as per the 'longer ending'.

16:6-7: *"Do not be alarmed; you are looking for Jesus of Nazareth, who was crucified. He has been raised; he is not here. Look, there is the place they laid him. But go, tell his disciples and Peter that he is going ahead of you to Galilee; there you will see him, just as he told you."*

In the original ending Jesus does not appear personally to the two women. In accordance with Mark's messianic secret, his resurrection is still not attested by his followers; it is proclaimed by the *"young man dressed in a white robe"*. He is possibly meant to be an angel, a messenger from God, but Mark may have meant his reader to understand that this was the same young man who was nearby at Jesus' trial, but ran off when the temple police tried to arrest him (14:51). Some scholars think he is Lazarus, the brother of Mary and Martha. Others think he is Mark, the author of the gospel, claiming the credibility of his gospel from an eye-witness point of view. In any case the young man is not one of the twelve. His proclamation of Jesus' resurrection does not involve the original followers, who remain 'in the dark', terrified and amazed.

There is almost no credible argument that either the shorter ending (inserted between verses 8 and 9) or the longer ending (9–20) of chapter 16 can be attributed to Markan authorship. Bruce Metzger summarises findings about the longer and shorter endings:

> *The last twelve verses of the commonly received text of Mark are absent from the two oldest Greek manuscripts, from the Old Latin codex Bobiensis, the Sinaitic Syriac manuscript, about one hundred Armenian manuscripts, and the two oldest Georgian manuscripts (written A.D. 897 and A.D. 913). Clement of Alexandria and Origen show no knowledge of the existence of these verses; furthermore Eusebius and Jerome attest that the passage was absent from almost all Greek copies of Mark known to them.*[86]

Significantly, the earliest quote from the long ending

appears in the writing of the 'church father' Irenaeus,[87] during the last half of the second century CE. By then there had been about a hundred years of development applied to Paul's messianic Christology. The longer ending reflects that.

I now want to propose to my readers a different understanding of these endings. Most certainly the shorter and longer endings are attempts to give Mark's gospel an unambiguously messianic flavour in its final chapter. As I noted, the writers of these additional verses have gleaned their thoughts from the other more overtly messianic gospels. None of that need rule out the argument that Mark actually intended his gospel to end at 16:8:

> *"So they went out and fled from the tomb, for terror and amazement had seized them; and they said nothing to anyone, for they were afraid."*

We have noted all along that Mark is dealing with a huge challenge as he creates his portrait of Jesus the Messiah. Nowhere in any of the sources from the earliest followers, written or oral, is there a claim from Jesus himself that he was the Messiah. Mark has dealt with this by depicting Jesus making messianic claims only in private – mostly to his small group of followers. Where anyone else makes that claim, Jesus tells them to be quiet about it. By these means Mark hopes to convince his readers that Jesus was in fact the Messiah, and claimed to be the Messiah, but that this was known only to a select few. But why did the 'few' not pass it on?

The answer from Mark is that they did not understand. They did not 'get it'. Only one made a specific claim about Jesus' messiahship; Peter proclaimed Jesus to be the Messiah:

> *"Peter answered him, "You are the Messiah". (8:29). But even then, "... he sternly ordered them not to tell anyone about him." (8:30).*

Given Mark's consistency in presenting Jesus' messiahship as a secret, hidden even from most of his closest

followers, the original ending begins to make more and more
sense. When Jesus' body is placed in a tomb belonging to the
Pharisee Joseph of Arimathea, the women, *"Mary Magdalene
and Mary the mother of Joses"* (15:47) are watching. On the first
day of the week they go to the tomb with spices to anoint Jesus'
body. Mark's story does not deal with the problem of how two
women will roll away a tombstone (although they were
concerned about it – 16:3). Instead it says that the stone which
had sealed the tomb had already been rolled away, and instead
of Jesus' body, the tomb contained a young man dressed in
white. Are we to assume that he is an angel – a messenger from
God? (Matthew certainly thinks so: 28:2). The man in white
says:

> 16:6-7: *"Do not be alarmed: you are looking for Jesus of
> Nazareth who was crucified. He has been raised; he is
> not here. Look, there is the place they laid him. But go,
> tell his disciples and Peter that he is going ahead of you
> to Galilee; there you will see him, just as he told you."*

This ought to have been exactly the kind of news the
disciples were expecting. If Mark was right and Jesus did claim
to be the Messiah, and had actually told his close followers, albeit
privately, at this point the penny should well and truly have
'dropped'. They should all have been waiting for exactly this,
both the men and the women. They should have been full of
excitement because they had been told to expect Jesus to rise
from death as the Messiah. They should have been there to
witness his resurrection. They were not there. The women were
there merely to perform their duty and anoint his dead body with
oils. The men were nowhere to be seen. The implication is that
they were lying low, devastated, afraid and hopeless. Mark says
the women were taken completely by surprise at the empty tomb
and the message of the man in white. They were so *"seized"* with
"terror and amazement" that they did not carry out the
assignment he gave them. They said nothing to anyone! Mark
claims that this happened because *"they were afraid"*. This is his
last explanation as to why the original group did not proclaim

Jesus as Messiah. Even after the resurrection, they still did not understood who he was. Mark, on the other hand, did understand.

There are several points to be made about the original ending of Mark:

- The original ending is entirely congruent with everything that comes before it about Jesus as Messiah.
- The lack of a resurrection appearance by Jesus indicates that there were no such 'appearances' in the sources used by Mark.
- The women's terror and amazement indicate that they had no expectation of Jesus' resurrection. Surely joy and excitement would have been the appropriate responses.
- The women say nothing about this encounter with an angel, who tells them exciting news. This is consistent with the 'messianic secret' reiterated throughout Mark's gospel.
- The reason given for them saying nothing is that they were afraid. That would certainly ring bells with Mark's original readers, in their own dangerous political context. Proclaiming a Messiah was very risky in the time of Mark and his readers.
- Mark has nonetheless proclaimed Jesus as the resurrected Messiah, but there is no human witness who can confirm that. It is the angel (i.e. messenger of God) who makes the claim and obviously cannot be consulted for verification. So the 'messianic secret' is kept until the end of the gospel. Mark's inclusion of the angel is his final and irrevocable proclamation of Jesus as Messiah.
- The implication and message of Mark's resurrection story is that eventually the followers (readers of Mark's gospel) will see him when he reappears as Messiah. Mark's community lives in Galilee, and there they will see him. Mark is offering hope to the readers of his gospel, who are waiting for Jesus to return in triumph.

The 'shorter' ending of Mark:

[["And all that had been commanded them they told briefly to those around Peter. And afterward Jesus himself sent out through them, from east to west, the sacred and imperishable proclamation of eternal salvation."]]

- The 'shorter' ending has the women telling Peter and the others what the angel had said. The implication is that from here on the original disciples did come to understand Jesus as Messiah.
- Jesus himself then appears, to send them out to proclaim *"eternal salvation"*. There is no explanation of 'eternal salvation', but it probably means the resurrection to eternal life of the 'righteous', that is, all who believe in Jesus the Messiah/Christ.
- This is a universal perspective, formulated long after the time of Jesus and from a Hellenistic Jewish/Gentile perspective.
- It makes no mention of passing on Jesus' teachings concerning the Kingdom of God.

The longer ending of Mark:

16:9-20: [[Now after he rose early on the first day of the week, he appeared first to Mary Magdalene, from whom he had cast out seven demons. She went out and told those who had been with him, while they were mourning and weeping. But when they heard that he was alive and had been seen by her, they would not believe it. After this he appeared in another form to two of them, as they were walking into the country. And they went back and told the rest, but they did not believe them. Later he appeared to the eleven themselves as they were sitting at the table; and he upbraided them for their lack of faith and stubbornness, because they had not believed those who saw him after he had risen. And he said to them, "Go into all the world and proclaim the good news to the whole creation. The one who believes and is baptized will be saved; but the one who does not believe will be condemned. And these signs will accompany those who believe; by using my name they will cast out demons; they will speak in new tongues; they will pick up snakes in their hands, and if they drink any deadly thing, it will not hurt them; they will lay their hands on the sick, and they will recover."

So then the Lord Jesus, after he had spoken to them, was taken up into heaven and sat down at the right hand of God. And they went out and proclaimed the good news everywhere, while the Lord worked with them and confirmed the message by the signs that accompanied it.]]

These verses deal with several 'problems' the writers of this longer ending found in Mark's gospel.

- There was no actual resurrection appearance by Jesus.
- Jesus now 'appears' to different disciples in different places (as in the gospels of Matthew, Luke and John), but the rest do not believe them. This perhaps reflects a historical situation in which some (perhaps women) had an experience of Jesus after his death, but were not believed.
- Jesus is angry with the disciples who did not believe people who claimed to have seen him after he had risen (even though this does not appear in the original ending).
- There is a universal perspective in the 'commission' to "*go into all the world*". The writers of the 'longer ending' apparently do not feel represented in Mark's gospel and are addressing Gentiles and Jews in the Diaspora. (This kind of 'commission' was also added to Matthew's Gospel).
- Those who believe will be able to do miracles. This is a major 'corrective'. There are no examples of followers acting in Jesus' name in Mark's gospel. They are merely (uncomprehending) students of his teaching.
- Because there are no resurrection appearances in the original ending, there is also no 'ascension' of Jesus into heaven. The longer ending supplies that, based on the ascension stories in Luke/Acts.

It is entirely plausible to say that Mark's 'messianic secret' literary methodology emerged from his genuine challenge to proclaim as Messiah a man who never thought that of himself, and never said it. The original, shorter, and longer endings are all attempts to deal with that, in different ways. The added endings, probably mid to late second century CE, are entirely unambiguous and explicit in their messianic proclamation, as Mark's ending never was.

Jesus the Messiah in the Gospel of Matthew

Matthew is probably the second of the canonical gospels, chronologically speaking. It makes sense to say that Matthew knew Mark and other oral or written sources containing Jesus' teaching (known as Q) and was not dependent on Luke, which was written later. As we have noted, John's Gospel is very different, being an interpretation of the synoptic gospels but departing from them in many literary and theological aspects. The name Matthew (*Matityahu* in Hebrew) means 'gift of God'. We do not know who actually wrote the gospel, but he apparently wanted the reader to regard his writing as a word from God, so he chose the 'pen' name Matthew. The jury is out as to whether Matthew was written first in Hebrew or in Aramaic and then translated into Greek, or was originally written in Greek. I do not see this issue as crucial to an understanding of the theological and social context of Matthew's Gospel.

The writer of Matthew does not labour so much under the historical challenges that led Mark to write in accordance with a 'messianic secret'. There is one instance only in Matthew where we find the writer's nod to lack of evidence for a messianic group that followed Jesus during his lifetime. This is where (16:20) *"Jesus sternly ordered the disciples not to tell anyone that he was the Messiah."* Matthew's gospel unambiguously proclaims Jesus as Messiah from its first verse, which introduces a thoroughly Jewish genealogy of Jesus: *"An account of the genealogy of Jesus the Messiah, the son of David, the son of Abraham."*

Matthew's aim, in contrast with Mark's, is to place Jesus as Messiah within Jewish messianic tradition, as its fulfilment. Jesus' teaching in Matthew is presented as fulfilment of the Law of Moses. For that reason Matthew's gospel may be understood as a Jewish response to the universalizing message about Jesus as the Messiah/Anointed One from the 'Apostle to the Gentiles', Paul. Paul's messianic teaching for both Jews and Gentiles had been established for about thirty years before Matthew's gospel was written.

Many scholars have nominated the place of origin of Matthew's gospel as Antioch in Syria, but there is good reason to place it within a Palestinian Jewish context. Like Mark's, this gospel's resurrection narrative directs Jesus' followers to meet him in Galilee, which surely indicates the location of the writer and his community. Given Matthew's anti-Pharisaic standpoint, his gospel is likely to originate in Palestine, the home territory of the Pharisees. Matthew also shows clear signs of a retrospective or backwards-looking view of the destruction of Jerusalem and its Temple in 66-70CE. Accordingly, the gospel is replete with Jesus' 'predictions' of the coming destruction. In addition, it indicates that there has been sufficient time for the Pharisees to assume the leadership of a reformed Judaism after the demise of Temple and priesthood. Because of this, the most likely dating places Matthew in an 80s – 90s time frame.

As in Mark, Matthew links predictions about Jerusalem and the Temple to an apocalyptic understanding of when Jesus' teachings about the kingdom of heaven will be fulfilled on earth. Matthew's gospel forges the clearest link between the return of Jesus the Messiah and Jesus' teachings about the kingdom of heaven on earth. Matthew apparently believes that as the new Torah, Jesus' teachings are examples of the coming kingdom of heaven that will be inaugurated on earth only at the 'second coming'. Matthew's use of apocalyptic imagery indicates that he did not believe Jesus' followers were capable of bringing the divine kingdom to fulfilment on earth through following the teachings.

With that background we will explore Matthew for sign-posts, including apocalyptic neon lights, that the writer uses to point to messianic understandings of Jesus. We will also be watching for instances of the 'internal proof texting' we discovered in the Gospel of Mark. Like Mark, Matthew bases his portrait of Jesus the Messiah squarely on the Hebrew Scriptures. His aim is to convince fellow Jews who read his gospel that Jesus of Nazareth was the Messiah for whom they were waiting. For that reason Matthew is often called the 'Jewish gospel'. There is a lot more to it than that.

Matthew's intended readers
Is this the Gospel to the Pharisees? I will argue in this chapter that the readers Matthew had in mind were a particular group of Jews. There are many reasons to see this gospel as written primarily for the Pharisees. Matthew's Messiah Jesus group is in a situation of rivalry, even hostility, with leaders of the reformed Judaism taking shape in the 80s CE after the destruction of the Temple and its priestly system of ritual and sacrifices. The foundational new leaders were the Pharisees, the precursors of the Rabbis who took Judaism into a new and highly successful reformation. This reformed Judaism was based on observance of Torah and situated in synagogue communities throughout the land of Israel/Palestine and in the Jewish Diaspora.

It is helpful to remember that Matthew was a convert to belief in Jesus as Messiah. The same could be said for all gospel writers and their communities, but Matthew is in a particularly fraught situation. In order for his own people to be reconciled with God through Jesus the Messiah, he apparently believed he needed to convince Pharisaic leaders to recognise Jesus' messiahship. It is very likely that the writer of Matthew was a Pharisee himself, who converted to belief in Jesus as Messiah. If not a Pharisee, Matthew was a highly educated Jew with a thorough knowledge of the Hebrew scriptures and oral traditions concerning the Torah/Law of Moses. For that reason he was profoundly disappointed that the vast majority of Pharisees did not agree with him about Jesus. Disappointment often leads to anger, which will be seen most clearly in Matthew Chapter 23.

As a possible Pharisee himself, Matthew exhibits the

characteristics of a teacher, especially in his emphasis on Jesus'
teachings as a renewed Torah. By setting these out he intends to
convince the Pharisees that Jesus is the Messiah for whom they
have waited. Matthew's gospel is his response to the
development of a reformed Judaism (sans Messiah) that took
place following the Temple's destruction in 70 CE. His main
rivals for leadership of the people are the Pharisees, who refute
claims that Jesus is Messiah and establish synagogues from
which the followers of Jesus the Messiah are evicted, even
violently:

> 10:17, 23: *"Beware of them, for they will hand you over
> to councils and flog you in their synagogues; and you
> will be dragged before governors and kings because of
> me, as a testimony to them and the Gentiles ... When they
> persecute you in one town, flee to the next; for truly I tell
> you, you will not have gone through all the towns of
> Israel before the Son of Man comes."*

Watch for sign-posts along the way that point to a
Pharisaic understanding of the Messiah. I will explain them as
we go.

The Genealogy

> 1:1-17: *An account of the genealogy of Jesus the Messiah,
> the son of David, the son of Abraham.*
> *Abraham was the father of Isaac, and Isaac the father of
> Jacob, and Jacob the father of Judah and his brothers,
> and Judah the father of Perez and Zerah by Tamar, and
> Perez the father of Hezron, and Hezron the father of
> Aram, and Aram the father of Aminadab, and Aminadab
> the father of Nahshon, and Nahshon the father of
> Salmon, and Salmon the father of Boaz by Rahab, and
> Boaz the father of Obed by Ruth, and Obed the father of
> Jesse, and Jesse the father of King David.*
> *And David was the father of Solomon by the wife of
> Uriah, and Solomon the father of Rehoboam, and
> Rehoboam the father of Abijah, and Abijah the father of*

Asaph, and Asaph the father of Jehoshaphat, and Jehoshaphat the father of Joram, and Joram the father of Uzziah, and Uzziah the father of Jotham, and Jotham the father of Ahaz, and Ahaz the father of Hezekiah and Hezekiah the father of Manasseh, and Manasseh the father of Amos, and Amos the father of Josiah, and Josiah the father of Jechoniah and his brothers, at the time of the deportation to Babylon.

And after the deportation to Babylon: Jechoniah was the father of Salathiel, and Salathiel the father of Zerubbabel, and Zerubbabel the father of Abiud, and Abiud the father of Eliakim, and Eliakim the father of Azor, and Azor the father of Zadok, and Zadok the father of Achim, and Achim the father of Eliud, and Eliud the father of Eleazar, and Eleazar the father of Matthan, and Matthan the father of Jacob, and Jacob the father of Joseph the husband of Mary, of whom Jesus was born, who is called the Messiah.

So all the generations from Abraham to David are fourteen generations; and from David to the deportation to Babylon, fourteen generations; and from the deportation to Babylon to the Messiah, fourteen generations.

Unlike the beginning of Mark, Matthew's gospel first places Jesus within an exhaustive (and exhausting!) genealogy of Israel's patriarchs and kings, including David, the first Messiah/King. Given that he was to claim messiahship for Jesus, Matthew needed first to establish Jesus' credentials in Hebrew tradition. The intention of the genealogy is to argue that Jesus is the culmination of a direct line of descent from Abraham through David to Joseph, the husband of Mary his mother. It is apparent that there is something else going on here, given that the genealogy does not in fact allow for Joseph's fatherhood of Jesus! If the reader is unclear about that from reading the genealogy, verse 25 of chapter 1 makes it unavoidable with *"(Joseph) had no marital relations with her until she had borne a son; and he named him Jesus."*

As part of a messianic purpose, might it be that the aim of the genealogy is to deal with irregularities surrounding the historical Jesus' actual birth? Perhaps there was scandal, arising from a rumour that Joseph was not Jesus' father. The genealogy may have been formulated to point to scandal surrounding Mary as similar to that surrounding the mothers of other luminaries in Hebrew history. For that reason it takes the unusual step of including women in a Jewish genealogy of that time. As well as Mary, four other women are mentioned – Tamar, Rahab, Ruth and Bathsheba.

Tamar was Judah's daughter-in-law, and also (scandalously) the mother of his twins Perez and Terah. Tamar also appears in a genealogical list in I Chronicles. Rahab is an Amorite described as a prostitute, who hid the spies Joshua sent out into the 'promised land'. Eventually she married one of the spies (Salmon) and became the ancestor (great, great grandmother) of King David. Ruth was a Moabite woman, whose unorthodox method of seducing Boaz led to her marrying him, and becoming the great grandmother of King David. Bathsheba was a Hittite woman who was seduced by King David and became the mother of King Solomon.

Catholic scholar Raymond E. Brown, in his *The Birth of the Messiah*,[88] offers three proposals for explaining the inclusion of these four women in Matthew's genealogy:

- The first is that they are all sinners, included in the genealogy of one who will be understood as the Saviour of sinners. If there was scandal about Jesus' birth, through this proposal Mary is not just vindicated, but included in God's mysterious way of bringing to birth the great figures of Hebrew history, including its Messiah.
- Secondly, Brown lists a commonly held proposal that given the four women from the Hebrew scriptures were all foreigners, this foreshadows the inclusion of the Gentiles in the messianic salvation. But, as Brown acknowledges, this falls down because Mary is clearly not a 'foreigner' herself.
- Brown's third proposal is that there is something

extraordinary in these women's unions with their partners. Through those extraordinary unions, the lineage of the Messiah was continued. The women concerned actually took initiatives to achieve this, including Mary, who agreed to give birth to 'God's son' by the extraordinary means described in chapter 1.

Then follows Matthew's narrative of Jesus' birth:

1:18-25: *Now the birth of Jesus the Messiah took place in this way. When his mother Mary had been engaged to Joseph, but before they lived together, she was found to be with child from the Holy Spirit. Her husband Joseph, being a righteous man and unwilling to expose her to public disgrace, planned to dismiss her quietly. But just when he had resolved to do this, an angel of the Lord appeared to him in a dream and said, "Joseph, son of David, do not be afraid to take Mary as your wife, for the child conceived in her is from the Holy Spirit. She will bear a son, and you are to name him Jesus, for he will save his people from their sins." All this took place to fulfil what had been spoken by the Lord through the prophet: "Look, the virgin shall conceive and bear a son, and they shall name him Emmanuel," which means, "God is with us." When Joseph awoke from sleep, he did as the angel of the Lord commanded him; he took her as his wife, but had no marital relations with her until she had borne a son; and he named him Jesus.*

The birth narrative is based on Isaiah 7:14:

"Therefore the Lord himself shall give you a sign; behold a virgin shall conceive in the womb, and shall bring forth a son, and thou shalt call his name Emmanuel."

This is a quotation from the Greek version of Isaiah. The Hebrew version does not say 'virgin', but merely 'young woman'. It could therefore be said that whoever wrote the birth narrative deliberately made use of the Greek (mis)translation to rescue

Mary (and Jesus) further from the possibility that Jesus' birth had been regarded by his community as scandalous. In any case, there is the irreconcilable inclusion of Joseph in Jesus' genealogy with the declaration (1:25) that Joseph and Mary did not have marital relations until after Jesus' birth. That surely renders the Davidic genealogical line from Abraham to Joseph, irrelevant. I have expressed the following in italics to emphasise its importance.

The difficulty with these discontinuities may be explained if the genealogy was written by an author who knew nothing of any 'birth narrative'. In that case he would not be aware of virgin birth aspects of the birth narrative that would later be included in Matthew's gospel. That would add weight to the possibility that the genealogy (1:1-17) and the birth narrative (1:18 – 2:23) are from different sources, added at later stages to Matthew's original gospel. The birth narrative itself may well be composed of various sections from different sources.

Given the widely held consensus that Matthew had Mark at his disposal when writing, it would make sense to argue that Matthew's gospel originally began at Chapter 3, with the appearance of John the Baptist (as does Mark's). Some scholars have argued against this, on the grounds that there is a similarity of style between the first 2 chapters and the rest of the gospel. That could be explained in three ways:

- First, Matthew rewrote/edited the genealogy and infancy story in his own style.
- Second, the translation of the whole gospel from an original Hebrew or Aramaic Matthew (complete with genealogy and infancy narrative) into Greek, by another scribe.
- Third, the copying of the whole gospel from Greek to Greek by a single scribe, thus ensuring continuity of the Greek style.

A good argument that the infancy chapters are 'add-ons' by someone other than Matthew is the fact that no one in the subsequent gospel knows anything about the extraordinary birth of Jesus the Messiah as outlined in the birth story. No one mentions it! That discontinuity militates against the argument that chapters 1 and 2 had been Matthew's original starting point.[89] The infancy narrative does reinforce Matthew's portrayal of Jesus as the 'prophet like Moses' (Deuteronomy 18:15) who will arise from among his own people. That does not rule out its having been written by another author, as Jesus was probably widely seen by messianic Jewish followers as Messiah in the mould of a 'new Moses'. We will see how Jesus' story resembles that of Moses in various places in the gospel, beginning with the infancy narrative.

The Infancy Narrative (1:18 – 2:23)

Regardless of authorship, the infancy narrative was written specifically to proclaim Jesus as the expected Jewish Messiah, anointed by God for this role from his birth. The claim of a virgin birth supports this proclamation, which announces the appearance of someone who transcends all of the prophets and holy men who preceded Jesus (as in the genealogy). The writer argues that Jesus is the one to whom they all had pointed. The infancy narrative sets out to make this extraordinary claim by announcing that although Jesus was brought to birth by Mary, he is *"from the Holy Spirit"*. This claim should immediately grab our attention. It indicates a high probability that the birth narrative has a later origin than the first century. It appears to point to a more developed Christology concerning the 'divinity' of Jesus Christ, possibly even from the third or fourth century.

As I pointed out in the chapter on Mark's gospel, in Hebrew tradition 'son of God' did not mean a biological relationship between a human being and God. Psalm 2:7 clearly states that God called David the first Messiah "son": *"I will tell of the decree of the Lord: He said to me, 'you are my son; today I have begotten you'."* This is a reference to David's anointing as Messiah, not to his birth as a divine/human being. The birth narrative in Matthew intends the reader to see a literal understanding of Jesus as conceived *"from the Holy Spirit"*, in other words, as Son of God. As a probable Pharisee, the writer of the gospel itself would have been most unlikely to have regarded Jesus in that way.

In the early centuries of the Common Era a woman's genetic contribution to a foetus (her ovum) was unheard of, which made it easier to claim that Jesus was God's son, merely implanted by the Holy Spirit in Mary's womb to grow until birth. Early church theologians made much of this in their development of the doctrine of incarnation. They had little problem with this argument because they were ignorant of the biology of human reproduction. In fact the human ovum was not actually discovered microscopically until 1925, although speculation about it had existed from the 17th century.

In the birth narrative we find the first instance of the kind of internal proof texting we noted in Mark. It occurs in 1:23, with that (Greek) quotation from Isaiah: *"Look, the virgin shall conceive"* (Is.7:14). If Matthew were a Pharisee, he would almost certainly have consulted the scriptures in Hebrew. He would not have made the mistake of reading the Hebrew word *almah* (young woman of marriageable age) as 'virgin'. The Hebrew word for virgin is *b'tulah*, meaning a mature girl who has 'not known a man'.[90] The Son of God and virgin references are good reasons to argue that Matthew's messianic proclamation may not originally have included an infancy narrative containing the idea that Jesus was born of the Holy Spirit through a 'virgin birth'.

On the other hand, although a virgin birth sounds preposterous to 21st century ears, it was not an unusual idea in antiquity. In the first century CE the Greek Platonist philosopher Plutarch penned his *Parallel Lives*. In his volume on Numa Pompilius, the legendary second king of Rome after Romulus, Plutarch refers to virgin births:

> *It is difficult to believe that a god or phantom would take carnal pleasure in a human body in its beauty. Nevertheless the Egyptians make a plausible distinction in such a matter. A woman can be made pregnant by a*

spirit (pneuma) of a god, but for a human there is no physical intercourse with a god.[91]

This tells us that in the first century Mediterranean region it was not impossible to think of a miraculous or virginal conception of a notable person. Plato himself was thought to have been the son of the god Apollo. It would have been no surprise for Greek-educated people to hear that Jesus the Messiah was born of a virgin via the (holy) 'spirit'. That gives further weight to an argument that this part of the infancy narrative was written by a hellenized Jew, not by the Palestinian Jewish gospel writer Matthew.

The announcement of Jesus' birth in the Matthean infancy story contains no descriptive narrative (like Luke's); Jesus is simply born and named 'Jesus'. Jesus' name, which in Hebrew is *Yeshua*, means 'God saves'. Verse 22 of chapter 2 explains why he is called *Yeshua* – "*he will save his people from their sins.*" The reason for the lack of detail about the birth itself is most likely because any such details were unknown to the writer of the Matthean infancy narrative. That posed no problem; his purpose in writing was to propose a scenario for the extraordinary birth of Jesus the Messiah, not to write a biography of Jesus of Nazareth.

2:1-15: *In the time of King Herod, after Jesus was born in Bethlehem of Judea, wise men from the East came to Jerusalem, asking, "Where is the child who has been born king of the Jews? For we observed his star at its rising, and have come to pay him homage." When King Herod heard this, he was frightened, and all Jerusalem with him; and calling together all the chief priests and scribes of the people, he inquired of them where the Messiah was to be born. They told him, "In Bethlehem of Judea; for so it has been written by the prophet: 'And you, Bethlehem, in the land of Judah, are by no means least among the rulers of Judah; for from you shall come a ruler who is to shepherd my people Israel.' " Then Herod secretly called for the wise men and learned from*

*them the exact time when the star had appeared. Then he
sent them to Bethlehem, saying, "Go and search
diligently for the child; and when you have found him,
bring me word so that I may also go and pay him
homage." When they had heard the king, they set out;
and there, ahead of them, went the star that they had
seen at its rising, until it stopped over the place where
the child was. When they saw that the star had stopped,
they were overwhelmed with joy. On entering the house,
they saw the child with Mary his mother; and they knelt
down and paid him homage. Then, opening their
treasure chests, they offered him gifts of gold,
frankincense, and myrrh. And having been warned in a
dream not to return to Herod, they left for their own
country by another road.*

The beginning of chapter 2 marks another distinctively
different section in the infancy narrative. Time has moved on to
a period following Jesus' birth. There is no indication of whether
it is days, weeks or even two years following the birth, but for the
first time we note that Jesus was born in *"Bethlehem of Judea"*
(with no mention of Nazareth). We learn why the location is
Bethlehem in 2:6, which is a quotation from Micah 5:2. To help
understand the mind of the infancy narrative writer, I will quote
Micah first from the Hebrew version and then from the Greek
translation of the Hebrew.

- First the Hebrew version:
  *"But you, O Bethlehem of Ephrathah, who are one of the
  little clans of Judah, from you shall come forth for me
  one who is to rule in Israel, whose origin is from of old,
  from ancient days."*
- Contrast that with the Greek version:
  *"And thou Bethleem, house of Ephratha, art few in
  number to be reckoned among the thousands of Juda;
  yet out of thee shall one come forth to me, to be a ruler of
  Israel; and his goings forth were from the beginning,
  even from eternity."*[92]

The second version is an example of messianic ideas incorporated in the Greek translation of Micah. It could be understood as saying that the Messiah is a divine/human entity who has come from God, where he has been since the beginning of time. It contrasts with the idea in the Hebrew version that the ruler will be a human being who has an ancient pedigree but probably pointing back only to David, the first Messiah. In summary: the Greek version of Micah 5:2, while it would have influenced those who wrote and read the infancy narrative in Greek, may not have been the version of Micah consulted by the Jewish writer Matthew.

This section of the infancy narrative (from 2:1) introduces *"wise men from the East"*, who arrive in Jerusalem. Their query matches Matthew's messianic understanding of Jesus as a King (or Davidic) Messiah: *"Where is the child who has been born king of the Jews?"* We learn here that King Herod is jealous or apprehensive that this new-born 'king' might commandeer his throne. Herod knows that his kingship was conferred by the Romans, whereas the king Messiah's authority would be conferred by God. The wise men then find Jesus living in a "house", his parents having made no apparent move to go to Nazareth. The impression is given that they had been living in Bethlehem all along, and were not just visiting.

The wise men's gifts are significant for the infancy narrative writer's interpretation of Jesus. Gold represents Jesus as a kingly Messiah; frankincense represents Jesus as a priestly Messiah (two Messiahs – kingly and priestly - feature in the Dead Sea Scrolls); myrrh indicates that the Messiah will die. For readers of the story post-70CE, this forecast of Jesus the Messiah's death would be seen as vindicated in Matthew's description of the historical event of the crucifixion. The star followed by the wise men fits within astrological belief held in countries surrounding Palestine in those days. Astrology was not followed or encouraged by Jews, but Syrian astrologers did 'read the stars' for signs of important events or the birth of important people. The author of the infancy narrative is using intellectual, religious, cultural and scientific developments in the middle-eastern worldview of that time, to proclaim the Messiah.

This astrological prediction of the birth of the Messiah points to an origin for the infancy narrative outside of the land of Palestine. It possibly originated among Gentiles who had converted to belief in Jesus as Messiah, or was written by hellenized Jewish converts to Jesus' messiahship, who lived outside Palestine. In any case it affirms the wisdom of Gentiles in recognizing Jesus' messiahship, another reason to see this narrative as originating from a period later than the Gospel of Matthew itself. As we will see, Matthew's Jesus focussed solely on "the lost sheep of the house of Israel." (10:6)

> 2:13-18: *Now after they had left, an angel of the Lord appeared to Joseph in a dream and said, "Get up, take the child and his mother, and flee to Egypt, and remain there until I tell you; for Herod is about to search for the child, to destroy him." Then Joseph got up, took the child and his mother by night, and went to Egypt, and remained there until the death of Herod. This was to fulfil what had been spoken by the Lord through the prophet, "Out of Egypt I have called my son." When Herod saw that he had been tricked by the wise men, he was infuriated, and he sent and killed all the children in and around Bethlehem who were two years old or under, according to the time that he had learned from the wise men. Then was fulfilled what had been spoken through the prophet Jeremiah: "A voice was heard in Ramah, wailing and loud lamentation, Rachel weeping for her children; she refused to be consoled, because they are no more."*

The remainder of the infancy narrative includes substantial reliance on the Hebrew scriptures for messianic references that 'fit' Jesus. Some of the biblical references work better than others. Verse 13 begins the story of 'the escape to Egypt'. When the wise men alert Herod (the Great) to the birth of the king Messiah, the story says Herod sets out to destroy the child. He orders all Jewish boys aged two and under to be slaughtered, in order to catch the king Messiah in his murderous net. But reminiscent of the story of Joseph in the Hebrew Scriptures, the New Testament Joseph is told in a dream to escape from Herod's clutches to Egypt. The historical timing is faulty; Herod had already died by the time Jesus was born. But there is a loose fit with the story of the Egyptian Pharaoh slaughtering all the little Hebrew boys (Exodus 1 – 2). He misses Moses, who is taken out of harm's way and comes out of Egypt to become deliverer of the Torah to his people. Herod misses Jesus, who is taken out of harm's way to (surprise, surprise) Egypt. He also comes 'out of Egypt' to become the deliverer of a new Torah to his people. This section of the story claims biblical precedent and authority with:

> *"This was to fulfil what had been spoken by the Lord through the prophet, "Out of Egypt I have called my son."*

That is a quote from Hosea (11:1), which cannot be said to contain any specifically messianic references. In fact, its context indicates that *"my son"* refers to the Israelite people, whom God cares for tenderly, as for a beloved child. Is the author of the infancy narrative relying on his readers being less than authorities on the Hebrew scriptures? In fact there is no historical evidence for a slaughter of young children by Herod the Great.

The next proof text comes from Jeremiah 31:15:

> *"A voice was heard in Ramah, wailing and loud lamentation, Rachel weeping for her children; she refused to be consoled, because they are no more."*

The author of the infancy narrative here displays signs of desperation in his search for proof texts. He wishes his reader to understand that this text about the slaughter of children on the invasion of Judah by Nebuchadnezzar II in 587 BCE, is a prediction of events in Jesus' infancy. He is claiming that Jesus' story is somehow a fulfilment of the prediction in the Jeremiah story. He is hoping this will add weight to his case for Jesus as Messiah.

> *2:19-23: When Herod died, an angel of the Lord suddenly appeared in a dream to Joseph in Egypt and said, "Get up, take the child and his mother, and go to the land of Israel, for those who were seeking the child's life are dead. Then Joseph got up, took the child and his mother, and went to the land of Israel. But when he heard that Archelaus was ruling over Judea in place of his father Herod, he was afraid to go there. And after being warned in a dream, he went away to the district of Galilee. There he made his home in a town called Nazareth, so that what had been spoken through the prophets might be fulfilled, "He will be called a Nazorean."*

The story moves on to Egypt, where the new family is evidently living. A not-so-subtle allusion to the story of the dreams interpreter Joseph, son of Jacob, has Joseph *"the husband of Mary"* receiving instructions from God via a dream. Joseph dreams that God tells him Herod is now dead and the family should return to Israel. The author then explains why they do not go back to Bethlehem, from where (he says) they came. The reason given is that although Herod is dead, his son Archelaus is now ruling in the province of Judea, which includes Bethlehem. By that means the author of this section of the infancy narrative places Jesus' birth in Bethlehem the 'city of David', as appropriate for the new Messiah, but then moves him to Nazareth, from where he was actually known to come. (Luke has other ideas about how to place Jesus in Bethlehem for his birth, as we will see).

The last gasp of the infancy narrative author is another internal proof text. This is probably the most tenuous of all:

> *2:23: "There he made his home in a town called Nazareth, so that what had been spoken through the prophets might be fulfilled, 'He will be called a Nazorean'."*

This may refer to the story of Samuel, who was dedicated to God from birth as a *Nazirite*, but given the reference to the place where Jesus grew up (and most probably was born), it most likely means Nazareth. In any case, there is no corresponding saying in scripture. The author of the infancy story may have known of such a saying, but it does not appear in any of the canonical books.

In summary, the infancy narrative(s) in Matthew contain indications of being written by a person or persons other than the writer of the gospel itself. Accordingly, 'Matthew' himself wrote from what came to be called chapter 3, onwards. The infancy narrative(s) have been added first in order to include a later understanding of Jesus as *"from the Holy Spirit"*. From chapter 3 onwards Matthew's gospel gives no indication that its writer saw Jesus in terms other than as the expected Anointed One, the human Jewish Messiah or Son of David, also called Son of God.

John the Baptist in Matthew

As noted before, there is good reason to contend that chapter 3 is the beginning of the original Gospel of Matthew. Matthew probably had Mark's Gospel to hand when he wrote his own and the following are three instances where John the Baptist makes significant appearances in Matthew:

- Mark's Gospel begins with the appearance of John the Baptist, as does Matthew chapter 3.

Here we have a re-stating of Mark's description of the Elijah-like John, calling the people to repent before the coming *"kingdom of heaven"*. This is a reference to the Day of the LORD, which verses 7-12 say will be a time of God's fiery vengeance against anyone who has not undergone John's baptism of repentance. Matthew gives the reader Mark's internal proof text to describe what John is doing:

"This is the one of whom the prophet Isaiah spoke when he said, 'The voice of one crying out in the wilderness:

'Prepare the way of the Lord, make his paths straight'."

The reference is to the repatriation of the Judean exiles from Babylon back to Jerusalem where God will appear, but Matthew uses it to announce the coming of someone who will herald *"the kingdom of heaven"* (on earth).

Unlike Mark, through the words of John the Baptist Matthew signals clearly (for the first time in verses 7-12) his fierce rivalry with the leaders of a nascent reformed Judaism, the Pharisees:

> *"But when he saw many Pharisees and Sadducees coming for baptism, he said to them, "You brood of vipers! Who warned you to flee from the wrath to come? Bear fruit worthy of repentance. Do not presume to say to yourselves, 'We have Abraham as our ancestor'; for I tell you, God is able from these stones to raise up children to Abraham. Even now the axe is lying at the root of the trees; every tree therefore that does not bear good fruit is cut down and thrown into the fire."* (3:7-10).

By the time Matthew was writing in the 80s the Temple had been destroyed and the Sadducees had lost their power base and their influence. Matthew knows they were still in power when John the Baptist was alive, so looking back, he includes them in John's condemnation. The focus of rivalry between Messiah Jesus followers such as Matthew's community and the mainstream of Judaism led by the Pharisees, was the Pharisaic denial that Jesus was the awaited Jewish Messiah. Most of the Jewish people did not believe that either, simply because Jesus did not measure up to traditional messianic expectations. (Refer back to Chapter 2 for more detail about messianic traditions in the first century).

The baptism of Jesus in Matthew is the first of gospel side-steps away from Jesus' need to be baptised. Mark baldly states: *"In those days Jesus came from Nazareth of Galilee and was baptised by John in the Jordan."* (1:9). Matthew's gospel reveals some difficulty with the notion that Jesus the Messiah needed to undergo a baptism of repentance at all. So Matthew has John the Baptist trying to prevent Jesus from being baptised. John says (3:14) *"I need to be baptised by you, and do you come to me?"*. But Jesus insists, because it is 'right' for that to happen.

Like Mark, Matthew then has the Spirit of God appear as a dove, and a voice from heaven, obviously meant as God's, calls Jesus *"my beloved Son"* (3:17). We have already noted the instance in Psalm 2:7 where God speaks to David the anointed one (Messiah) as "my son". By means of the voice Mark and Matthew identify Jesus as the Jewish Messiah, pointing to Psalm 2:7. In biblical usage the dove is a symbol of gentleness, peace and divine guidance.[93] It has also symbolized the wisdom of Sophia, the female manifestation of divine wisdom.[94] Given Matthew's consistent use of the Hebrew Scriptures, plus his dedication to convincing the Pharisees that Jesus conforms to traditional Palestinian Jewish expectations of the Messiah, it is more likely that for him the symbolism of the dove relates to other biblical sources such as the story of Noah. The appearance of a dove to Noah on his ark is God's sign that there is to be a new start for humanity after the great flood.

Throughout his gospel Matthew continues to identify Jesus as son of God. Instead of indicating Greek ideas about Jesus as 'Son of God' (in substance, as per later theological developments), Matthew is most likely alluding to the identification of the first Messiah David as 'son of God' through his anointing (Psalm 2:7). The baptism becomes, in effect, Jesus' (traditional Jewish) anointing as Messiah/Son of God. My reader will see here the difference between the author Matthew's Jewish way of seeing Jesus as Messiah and the view of the writer of the infancy narrative(s) (and of Mark).

In this respect the late Robert Anderson, Professor of Old Testament at the Uniting Church's Theological Hall from 1977-1993, argued that:

> *The whole issue of the church's claims about Jesus and its bolstering of those claims by the use of texts from the Hebrew Scriptures could be laid to rest once and for all if the word that is usually translated as 'messiah',*

namely mashiach, were simply translated as 'an anointed one', or 'an anointed person'. In this sense it may be said that Jesus is mashiach, an anointed one, but not – definitely not – the Messiah who is divine.[95]

Almost immediately after Jesus is baptized and then tempted in the wilderness (see section below), Matthew has John disappear off the scene, under arrest. Jesus immediately 'withdraws' to Galilee. He does not go back to Nazareth, but takes up residence in Capernaum *"in the territory of Zebulun and Naphtali".* (4:12-13). Here Matthew manages to find meaning in scripture for the fact that Jesus was known as living by the Sea of Galilee at Capernaum. He adds a proof text from Isaiah:

Isaiah 9:1-2: *"Land of Zebulun, land of Naphtali, on the road by the sea, across the Jordan, Galilee of the Gentiles – the people who sat in darkness have seen a great light."*

Given that it was Herod Antipas of Judea who arrested John, Matthew possibly means that as Jesus was going to take up John's role of proclaiming the coming of the kingdom of heaven, he needed to get away from Judea. He needed safety and seclusion to prepare himself and select his band of helpers. He finds the first five of them fishing in the Sea of Galilee.

- 11:2-19: *When John heard in prison what the Messiah was doing, he sent word by his disciples and said to him, "Are you the one who is to come, or are we to wait for another?" Jesus answered them, "Go and tell John what you hear and see; the blind receive their sight, the lame walk, the lepers are cleansed, the deaf hear, the dead are raised, and the poor have good news brought to them. And blessed is anyone who takes no offense at me."*

Chapter 11 finds Jesus well into his proclamation of the kingdom of heaven. At this point John the Baptist hears from prison about Jesus' activities and teachings. Significantly, he sends his "disciples" (students/followers) to see if Jesus is the Messiah he has been awaiting. From this it is obvious that Matthew knew John did not recognize Jesus as Messiah at his baptism; otherwise why would he include this scene in his gospel? Self-evidently, if John had seen Jesus as Messiah, he would not have needed to send his disciples to ask the question.

Until John's arrest by Herod, the historical scenario had him continuing to proclaim the coming of the kingdom of heaven, but according to Matthew he was not relating it to Jesus as Messiah. The underlying messianic apologetic in Mark's and Matthew's John the Baptist/Jesus story-line is revealed here, through the cracks. Matthew is using John the Baptist's question as a 'Dorothy Dixer' so Jesus can answer in accordance with prophetic statements in Isaiah 29, 35 and 61. These concern the good news and healings that will be brought by *the one who is to come*".

That is followed (11:7-15) by Matthew's rebuff to Pharisees who had not respected John as the Elijah figure pointing to the Messiah, now revealed as Jesus: "*And if you are willing to accept it, he is Elijah who is to come. Let anyone with ears listen!*"

Matthew is on a roll here; his words are dripping with sarcasm. In verse 25 he has Jesus thank God for hiding his messiahship from the "*wise and intelligent*" (read 'Pharisees') and revealing it to infants (read 'the ordinary people' of his own community). He caps it off by equating Jesus the Son of God with sacred wisdom through an allusion to Ecclesiasticus (Ben Sira) 51:26 concerning the 'yoke' of wisdom: "*Put your neck under her yoke, and let your souls receive instruction.*" The yoke (or teaching) of the Pharisees, on the other hand, is what Matthew calls a "*heavy burden*" (11:28).

- Matthew's John the Baptist story ends in chapter 14 with John's death by beheading.

Matthew's main point is that contrary to the Pharisees, "*the crowd*" saw John as a prophet predicting the coming of the Messiah. Herod is portrayed as being in two minds about executing John because he feared the popular recognition of John as a prophet. As in Mark, Herod is let off the hook when Herodias' daughter asks for the beheading. Before he dies, Matthew's John the Baptist has been persuaded that the Messiah is Jesus. This may or may not indicate that Jesus was a disciple of John before he began his own teaching. I am not persuaded that Jesus was a follower of John; only that he knew about John.

The Temptations of Jesus

4:1-11: *Then Jesus was led up by the Spirit into the wilderness to be tempted by the devil. He fasted forty days and forty nights, and afterwards he was famished. The tempter came and said to him, "If you are the Son of God, command these stones to become loaves of bread." But he answered, "It is written, 'One does not live by bread alone, but by every word that comes from the mouth of God.' " Then the devil took him to the holy city and placed him on the pinnacle of the temple, saying to him, "If you are the Son of God, throw yourself down; for it is written, 'He will command his angels concerning you.' And 'On their hands they will bear you up, so that you will not dash your foot against a stone.' " Jesus said to him, "Again it is written, 'Do not put the Lord your God to the test.' " Again, the devil took him to a very high mountain and showed him all the kingdoms of the world and their splendour; and he said to him, "All these I will give you, if you will fall down and worship me." Jesus said to him, "Away with you, Satan! For it is written, 'Worship the Lord your God, and serve only him.' " Then the devil left him, and suddenly angels came and waited on him.*

Mark wrote a very small reference to Jesus being sent off by God on a forty-day retreat in the wilderness. In just thirty three words Jesus goes to the wilderness, is tempted by Satan, lives with wild animals and is fed by angels. Matthew is hardly satisfied with that; he expands Mark's little story into three hundred and four words. His agenda quickly becomes clear when the story's expansion argues that Jesus conformed to a traditional Jewish version of Messiah. None of the synoptic gospel writers craft their Messiah Jesus portraits in a vacuum. All use the traditions at hand, including clearly prophetic proclamations, as well as more ambiguous references to "*one who is to come*".

Accordingly, Matthew's temptation story functions as introduction to his depictions of Jesus as a 'greater Moses'. The wilderness into which Jesus is driven for forty days and nights reflects the wilderness in which Moses led the Israelites for forty years. This is also the first instance where Matthew claims that Jesus had a Pharisaic level of knowledge and understanding of scripture. Matthew's agenda here is to persuade the Pharisees that Jesus was acting in accordance with scripture, which is their ultimate criterion for Jewish leadership, including that of the Messiah/anointed Son of God.

The temptations story first disproves any expectation that Messiah Jesus would be a miracle-worker who would turn stones into bread. Instead it turns the mind of a biblically knowledgeable reader to the story of Moses:

- First, it points to the time the Israelites wanted real bread and other food in the wilderness, rather than putting their trust in the word of God. Moses-like, Jesus passes the test by quoting Deut. 8:3: " ... *one does not live by bread alone, but by every word that comes from the mouth of the Lord.*" He fasts for the forty days, as did Moses (Deuteronomy 9:18).
- Second, Jesus resists the temptation to test God as the Israelites did at Massah (Exodus 17: 1-7) by quoting Deut 6:16: "*Do not put the Lord your God to the test.*"
- Third, Jesus tells Satan to go away when he is tempted to be ruler of the world if only he will worship Satan. Again there is a reference to scripture in Jesus' answer (Deut 6:13): "*Worship the Lord your God, and serve only him.*"

Matthew is presenting Jesus as the new and greater Moses who is also the teacher of Torah, quoting scripture in Pharisaic fashion. The Pharisees are meant to take note!

To whom is Jesus' teaching directed?

Chapter 10 contains a statement regarding Jesus' intended audience. Possibly in response to Pharisaic criticism of Paul for including Gentiles in the Messiah Jesus movement, Matthew here unequivocally claims that Jesus the Messiah is focussed only on the house of Israel. Jesus' instructions to his disciples in Chapter 10 are unambiguous:

> 10:5-6: *"Go nowhere among the Gentiles, and enter no town of the Samaritans, but go rather to the lost sheep of the house of Israel."*

Pharisees reading about "the lost sheep" would have been left in no doubt that Matthew was criticising their leadership of the Jewish people. This does not mean Matthew's gospel does not contain a good word for Gentiles; it simply was not written for them. References to violent interactions between followers of Jesus the Messiah and others, even between members of the same family, are likely to reflect the divisive situation post-Easter between messianic followers (such as those in Matthew's community) and other Jews.

> 10:34-39: *Do not think that I have come to bring peace to the earth; I have not come to bring peace, but a sword. For I have come to set a man against his father, and a daughter against her mother, and a daughter-in-law against her mother-in-law; and one's foes will be members of one's own household. Whoever loves father or mother more than me is not worthy of me; and whoever loves son or daughter more than me is not worthy of me; and whoever does not take up the cross and follow me is not worthy of me. Those who find their life will lose it, and those who lose their life for my sake will find it.*

Already here there are signs that Jesus' subversive teachings about non-violence are being sidelined by those determined first and foremost to declare him Messiah/Son of God.

Teachings about the Torah (12:1-8; 15:1-9)

- The first concerns teaching about the observance of the Sabbath.

  12:1-8: *At that time Jesus went through the grain fields on the Sabbath; his disciples were hungry, and they began to pluck heads of grain and to eat. When the Pharisees saw it, they said to him, "Look, your disciples are doing what is not lawful to do on the Sabbath." He said to them, "Have you not read what David did when he and his companions were hungry? He entered the house of God and ate the bread of the Presence, which it was not lawful for him or his companions to eat, but only for the priests. Or have you not read in the law that on the Sabbath the priests in the temple break the Sabbath and yet are guiltless? I tell you, something greater than the temple is here. But if you had known what this means 'I desire mercy and not sacrifice,' you would not have condemned the guiltless. For the Son of Man is lord of the Sabbath."*

Matthew has set out to prove to the Pharisees that the one they rejected is in fact the Jewish Messiah. In chapter 12 he produces examples of specific teachings from the Torah which are likely to have been humanely interpreted by Jesus himself. The first concerns the commonsense argument that if a person is hungry on the Sabbath, then the right thing to do is to prepare food and eat it. This was in opposition to the Pharisees' strict observance of the Torah which said:

> Exodus 20:10: *"The seventh day is a Sabbath to the Lord your God; you shall not do any work – you, your son or your daughter, your male or female slave, your livestock, or the alien resident in your towns."*

The Pharisees are represented as opposed to Jesus' interpretation. Matthew then has Jesus cite two examples of important people who broke the Sabbath and did not incur the wrath of God. They were David the first Messiah and priests in the Temple. How could the Pharisees complain about that? Matthew's post-Temple perspective follows: "*Something greater than the Temple is here.*" (12:6).

- The second example concerns a healing on the Sabbath. This takes place in a synagogue with Pharisees present, plus a man with a "*withered hand*" who is looking for healing. Jesus asks a question about Sabbath observance:

  12:9-14: "*Suppose one of you has only one sheep and it falls into a pit on the Sabbath; will you not lay hold of it and lift it out? How much more valuable is a human being than a sheep! So it is lawful to do good on the Sabbath.*"

You can almost hear the 'boom boom!' The man is then healed. Matthew's Pharisees cannot agree with that from their strict observance of Torah and they begin to plot Jesus' destruction. Here Matthew is using Jesus' discerning interpretation of Torah as a means of proving to the Pharisees that he is the expected Jewish Messiah. Wherever examples of Jesus interpreting the Torah occur in the gospel they have the same purpose: to prove that Jesus' liberal Torah scholarship is superior to that of the Pharisees. That will underline Matthew's claim that Jesus is the legitimate Jewish Messiah. Moses-like, Jesus brings a renewed Torah to the people.

- The third example concerns laws regarding purification. 15:1-9: *Then Pharisees and scribes came to Jesus from Jerusalem and said, "Why do your disciples break the tradition of the elders? For they do not wash their hands before they eat." He answered them, "And why do you break the commandment of God for the sake of your tradition? For God said, 'Honour your father and your mother,' and, 'Whoever speaks evil of father or mother must surely die.' But you say that whoever tells father or mother, 'Whatever support you might have had from me is given to God, then that person need not honour the father. So, for the sake of your tradition, you make void the word of God. You hypocrites! Isaiah prophesied rightly about you when he said: 'This people honours me with their lips, but their hearts are far from me; in vain do they worship me, teaching human precepts as doctrines.' "*

Chapter 15 contains more instances where Jesus rebuts criticism that he and his disciples do not observe Torah (Law of Moses) regarding purification laws, with his counter-claim that the Pharisees are guilty of much worse transgressions of Torah. Through their interpretations they regard it as legitimate to break one of the ten basic commandments – regarding the honouring of parents.

Verses 10 – 20 continue criticism of the manner in which Pharisees carry out the law. Jesus tells his disciples here that the Pharisees are *"blind guides of the blind"*. It is impossible to tell whether these encounters with Pharisees were known to have involved Jesus himself, or whether Matthew included in his gospel his own issues with Pharisees. The latter is possible, given Matthew's hostility toward a leadership group that will not recognise Jesus as Messiah. It is more than possible if in fact Matthew was written intentionally as the 'gospel to the Pharisees'.

Healing miracles

4:23-24: *Jesus went throughout Galilee, teaching in their synagogues and proclaiming the good news of the kingdom and curing every disease and every sickness among the people. So his fame spread throughout all Syria, and they brought to him all the sick, those who were afflicted with various diseases and pains, demoniacs, epileptics, and paralytics, and he cured them.*

Like Mark, Matthew depicts Jesus the Messiah/son of God as a healer. Also like Mark, Matthew lists diseases and afflictions that Jesus healed, mainly diseases of the mind or brain, such as epilepsy. "Demoniacs" were most likely people who suffered epileptic fits and were considered to be possessed by evil demons. Others were *"paralytics"*, possibly people immobilised by feelings of guilt and hopelessness. They were sometimes described as 'healed' after being told they were forgiven. Apart from that the description is vague – *"Various diseases and pains"* (4:24). The gospel goes on to describe more healings, including of a woman whose menstrual blood had 'polluted' her for twelve years (9:20-22). Her condition, plus diseases of the brain (or mind) and skin, alienated sufferers from their community and from the 'people of God'. Jesus is depicted sending healed lepers to the priest so they can be accepted back into the religious life of the community. As already noted, the problem with this is that in scripture, healing is traditionally the work of a prophet (such as Elijah), not of the Messiah.

My own approach to Jesus' healings is that rather than miraculous restoration of sight, hearing or mobility (all messianic gospel sign-posts and to be treated with appropriate caution), Jesus most probably focussed on the forgiveness of a loving God - as opposed to God's condemnation. In his time God's condemnation of sin was associated with illness of various kinds. His declaration that God is forgiving apparently enabled the restoration of the sufferer to family and community, through his or her renewed understanding of, and faith in, God. That does not completely rule out physical healings, but it certainly points to spiritual healing that can lead to wholeness of body as well as of the mind. This is increasingly recognized in modern medicine. In 2004 it was reported in the Journal of the American Medical Association that:

> *In 1994, only 17 of the 126 accredited US medical schools offered courses in spirituality in medicine. By 1998, this number had increased to 39, and by 2004, to 84 schools.*[96]

By 2010 the International Journal of Psychiatry in Medicine had reported that 90% of medical schools have courses or content on spirituality and health.

Through his descriptions of Jesus as healer, Matthew

expects that the readers of his gospel, whether Pharisees or others, will see that Jesus is both prophet (traditionally associated with healing) and Jewish Messiah/son of God. Significantly for Matthew's messianic proclamation, two blind men are healed when they recognize Jesus as Davidic Messiah ("*Son of David*" 9:27). In contrast, Matthew has the Pharisees associating Jesus not with God, but with Satan, in the nonsensical statement: "*By the ruler of the demons he casts out the demons.*" (9:34).

It is also important for Matthew to declare that the Pharisees are out of step with the people when they reject Jesus' messiahship. At several points in his gospel he emphasises that Jesus (the Messiah) had a great following among the Jewish people, from all over the land of Israel and even beyond into Gentile territory (e.g. 8:1; 8:18). On the other hand, the people in the towns and villages visited by Jesus were suffering from lack of leadership and confusion about the future. They were "*like sheep without a shepherd*" (9:36). This is actually the scenario after the Temple had been destroyed, when the Pharisees were still in the process of claiming leadership of the people. Matthew is again in effect calling the Pharisaic leaders bad shepherds.

The Dead are Raised
- 9:23-26: *But when the crowd had been put outside, he went in and took her by the hand, and the girl got up. And the report of this spread throughout the district.*

Matthew's intention to portray Jesus the Messiah with the characteristics of a Teacher, Prophet and Lawgiver stand behind his decision to include the Markan story of the raising of the synagogue leader's daughter. As we have noted in comments on this in Mark, the biblical background is the activities of the prophet Elijah. Whereas Mark's Jesus orders people who witness the raising of the girl to keep quiet about it, Matthew says word of it spread quickly all around the district. Matthew's portrait of Jesus is more explicitly messianic and does not have Mark's hesitancy in claiming that Jesus saw himself that way.

- 27:52: *The tombs also were opened, and many bodies of the saints who had fallen asleep were raised.*

Here is a scenario plainly addressed to the Pharisees. After the crucifixion and death of Jesus, whom Matthew believes is the Messiah, the dead 'saints' are brought back to life. This is a clear claim that the Pharisees' own belief in the resurrection of the righteous dead at the appearance of the Messiah had been fulfilled in the crucified and resurrected Jesus. Is it not curious that such a momentous event is not recorded in Mark, Luke or John ... ?

The Sermon on the Mount (Chapters 5, 6, 7)

The large gathering of people around Jesus as reported by Matthew forms the setting for the Sermon on the Mount, which is sometimes called the 'Discourse on Ethics', the first of five discourses. Jesus is addressing the crowds, but through that scenario Matthew is addressing the Jewish scripture scholars of his time, the Pharisees. Matthew makes it as plain as he can. Here is the new Moses: Jesus the prophet and Messiah handing down the 'new Torah' to the people gathered below him on the mountain.

The Beatitudes and other teachings in the 'Sermon on the Mount' are Matthew's compilation of Jesus' ethical teachings and sayings. These were most likely circulating as oral versions (singly or in groups) since Jesus' lifetime 50 years beforehand. For his own reasons, which are now impossible to retrieve, Matthew is more eager than Mark to preserve Jesus' teachings as set out in the Sermon on the Mount (in Luke, the 'Sermon on the Plain). For that we can only be eternally grateful. Matthew's intention is to show that Jesus was not teaching against Pharisaic interpretations of scripture, but was actually teaching an expanded (or fulfilled) interpretation of Torah. Jesus was not diminishing the Torah and certainly not abolishing it, but actually promoting it. In the other four teaching discourses in the gospel, Matthew's messianic agenda can be seen overtly and between the lines, but the Sermon on the Mount does not further that agenda. This is an important reason to regard the sayings in the Sermon on the Mount as originating with the historical Jesus.

Although the Beatitudes, which encapsulate in principle the teachings in the Sermon on the Mount, have been compiled into their order by Matthew, there is every reason to see almost all of them as originating from Jesus. One reason is that they relate strongly to each other, to other sayings in the Sermon on the Mount, and to many (although not all) parables that can be attributed to Jesus. The Sermon on the Mount contains the essence of Jesus' understanding of the 'kingdom of heaven' on earth.[97] Regardless of messianic motives, the fact that Matthew the teacher included in his gospel Jesus' ethical teachings, ensured that they have been preserved for all generations up until now and yet to come.[98] Matthew knew those teachings were from Jesus and included them in a gospel about Jesus the teacher/prophet/Messiah, interpreting anew the precepts of Torah. That certainly underlines Matthew's view of a Moses-like Messiah, delivering a fulfilled Torah. *However, one of the major arguments against Jesus' self-identity as Messiah is the complete lack of messianic/christological allusions in the Sermon on the Mount teachings.*

Matthew caps off his account of Jesus' teachings 'on the mount' with his in-your-face claim to his readers:

> 7:28-29 *"the crowds were astounded at his teaching, for he taught them as one having authority, and not as their scribes."*

Many of the 'scribes' were Pharisees!

The Other Four Discourses (10, 13, 18, 22-25)
- Chapter 10. The 'Discourse on Mission'.

> 10:1-14: *These twelve Jesus sent out with the following instructions: "Go nowhere among the Gentiles, and enter no town of the Samaritans, but go rather to the lost sheep of the house of Israel. As you go, proclaim the good news, 'The kingdom of heaven has come near.' Cure the*

sick, raise the dead, cleanse the lepers, cast out demons.
You received without payment; give without payment.
Take no gold, or silver, or copper in your belts, no bag
for your journey, or two tunics, or sandals, or a staff; for
labourers deserve their food. Whatever town or village
you enter, find out who in it is worthy, and stay there
until you leave. As you enter the house, greet it. If the
house is worthy, let your peace come upon it; but if it is
not worthy, let your peace return to you. If anyone will
not welcome you or listen to your words, shake off the
dust from your feet as you leave that house or town.

In contrast with the Discourse on Ethics, this one is
unreservedly messianic, including instructions from Jesus to his
followers to heal the sick, cast out demons and raise the dead in
his name. These are, as we have noted, messianic sign-posts.
There are specific instructions about staying away from Gentiles
and Samaritans and going only to "*the lost sheep of the house of*
Israel" (10:6). This is Matthew's assurance to the Pharisees that
Jesus really is the expected Jewish Messiah. He does not fit the
universalist idea of the Messiah/Christ expounded by Paul. In
accordance with Matthew's expectation of Jesus' return as
Messiah, the disciples are to give the Jewish people the
apocalyptic message that "*the kingdom of heaven has come*
near." The mission is therefore urgent, and the disciples are to
take no excess luggage, and waste no time on people who will not
listen to their message.

Verses 21-23 are a clear view of the circumstances faced
by members of Matthew's community as they try to convince
their fellow Jews that Jesus is Messiah:

10:21-23: *Brother will betray brother to death, and a*
father his child, and children will rise against parents
and have them put to death; and you will be hated by all
because of my name. But the one who endures to the end
will be saved. When they persecute you in one town, flee
to the next ...

In verse 32 Matthew adds the fear of hell to those who choose not to believe Jesus is the long-awaited Jewish Messiah. Jewish authorities in the 80s were apparently arresting members of Matthew's community and sentencing them to punishment. Matthew believes that when they die, Jesus will commend the believers to God and condemn the non-believers. It is clear here that Matthew's community's belief in Jesus as Messiah has already caused division and suffering among the Jewish people. In the final chapter of this book I will discuss some of the negative outcomes of christological beliefs throughout the history of Christianity.

- Chapter 13. The Discourse on the Kingdom.

This one is full of parables. Let my reader be aware that not all parables in the synoptic gospels (there are none in John) come from Jesus. There are clues about which come from Jesus and which from Matthew. Jesus' *modus operandi* was to give his hearers a story or a saying. As a good teacher, he would then have allowed them to make of the stories what they thought appropriate, without his further explanation. Primarily, his purpose was to help his hearers imagine what the world would be like if God (not Caesar) were king. Given that, Matthew's *explanation* of the Parable of the Sower (13:18-23) is a dead giveaway. This is not Jesus speaking; this is Matthew explaining to readers of his gospel who are 'in mission' why not everyone believes what they say about Jesus, or why some believe it at first and then lose their enthusiasm.

Matthew also *explains* the Parable of the Weeds (13:27-30) in apocalyptic terms, including the judgment of all (the weeds) who do not believe in Messiah Jesus. Jesus' authentic parables about the kingdom of heaven on earth are simply-stated invitations to imagine a new God-centred world, with no further explanation. They do not include apocalyptically-oriented threats.

Chapter 13 contains 5 parables that are not found in Mark. Of these, the parables of the mustard seed (13:31-32) and the yeast (13:33) are compatible with the ethical sayings in the

Sermon on the Mount in that they point to the slow but steady growth of the kingdom of heaven among Jesus' followers

> 13:31-32: *"He put before them another parable; "The kingdom of heaven is like a mustard seed that someone took and sowed in his field; it is the smallest of all the seeds, but when it has grown it is the greatest of shrubs and becomes a tree, so that the birds of the air come and make nests in its branches."*

The mustard bush is regarded as a noxious weed, that spreads everywhere. It does not "*become a tree, so that the birds of the air come and make nests in its branches.*" B. Brandon Scott regards this as an allusion to the 'cedars of Lebanon' in Ezekiel 17: 22-23; 31: 2-6 and Daniel 4: 10-12, which are associated with mighty earthly empires. The lowly mustard bush, on the other hand, is associated with the kingdom of heaven on earth, where the 'last' becomes the first, and yet all are able to find 'shelter' in it.[99]

> 13:33: *He told them another parable: "The kingdom of heaven is like yeast that a woman took and mixed in with three measures of flour until all of it was leavened."*

Here used as a metaphor, leaven or yeast is regarded as a corrupting influence. Scott sees this as representing the teachings of Jesus about the kingdom of heaven on earth, which 'corrupt' the status quo and change all of society, as yeast causes profound changes in flour.[100]

The parable of the net and the fish (13:47-50) does not look like a parable of Jesus. It reflects the difficult situation faced by the followers of Jesus the Messiah in the time of Matthew. It also illustrates Matthew's belief that those who choose not to believe in Jesus' messiahship will meet a dreadful punishment "*at the end of the age*" (13:49). Where parables describe the violent fate of unbelievers they are profoundly at odds with the 'love imperative' (including the teaching about loving enemies) that undergirds the Sermon on the Mount.

In the midst of the parables in Chapter 13 (34-43), Matthew follows Mark in stating that Jesus taught the crowds only in parables, but that in private, he explained them to the disciples. This is Matthew giving himself permission to include his own explanations of parables in his gospel, emphasizing the apocalyptic return of the Son of Man (a reference to Daniel 7:13-14) and the exclusion of the unbelievers.

Regardless of the authenticity of some of Matthew's parables, the final parable (of the 'storeroom') is justification of Matthew's use of the 'old' (the Hebrew Scriptures) and his promotion of the 'new' – the teaching of Jesus as giver of the new Torah:

> 13:51-53: *And he said to them, ("Therefore) every scribe who has been trained for the kingdom of heaven is like the master of a household who brings out of his treasure what is new and what is old."*

The difficulty of persuading the 'house of Israel' to believe in Jesus' messiahship is illustrated in verses 54-58, where Matthew says that even Jesus' own neighbours in Nazareth did not believe he was the Messiah:

> 13: 54-58: *He came to his hometown and began to teach the people in their synagogue, so that they were astounded and said, "Where did this man get this wisdom and these deeds of power? Is not this the carpenter's son? Is not his mother called Mary? And are not his brothers James and Joseph and Simon and Judas? And are not all his sisters with us? Where then did this man get all this?" And they took offense at him. But Jesus said to them, "Prophets are not without honour except in their own country and in their own house." And he did not do many deeds of power there, because of their unbelief.*

- *Chapter 18. The Discourse on Community Life.*

This is directed to the followers in Matthew's time, to add to their sense of urgency in preaching Jesus the Messiah. The chapter begins with what looks like a teaching from Jesus about the humble being able to build and enter the kingdom of heaven. That fits with the first Beatitude: *"Blessed are the poor in spirit* (read 'humble-minded') *for theirs is the kingdom of heaven"*. Then there is a series of warnings about the penalty for putting *"stumbling blocks"* in front of the humble believers. If members of Matthew's community of believers have differences, this instruction says they must resolve them, or be treated as Gentiles or tax collectors (i.e. with contempt and exclusion). This looks like an attempt to create and/or preserve unity among the Matthean community through instilling fear of God's judgment.

Chapter 18 has two parables not included in Mark. They are first the parable of the lost sheep:

> 18: 10-14: *Take care that you do not despise one of these little ones; for, I tell you, in heaven their angels continually see the face of my Father in heaven. What do you think? If a shepherd has a hundred sheep, and one of them has gone astray, does he not leave the ninety-nine on the mountains and go in search of the one that went astray? And if he finds it, truly I tell you, he rejoices over it more than over the ninety-nine that never went astray. So it is not the will of your Father in heaven that one of these little ones should be lost.*

This looks like a warning to people who are not willing to include those Matthew describes as *"these little ones"* (perhaps the poor or 'sinners' such as former tax collectors), as members of the Matthean community. This also looks designed to appeal to the strong Pharisaic belief in angels. Matthew is perhaps intent here on reminding those (probably Pharisees) who 'despise' *"these little ones"* that there are angels watching over them.

The second parable in Chapter 18 concerns the

unforgiving servant:

> 18:23-25: *For this reason the kingdom of heaven may be compared to a king who wished to settle accounts with his slaves. When he began the reckoning, one who owed him ten thousand talents was brought to him; and, as he could not pay, his lord ordered him to be sold, together with his wife and children and all his possessions, and payment to be made. So the slave fell on his knees before him, saying, 'Have patience with me, and I will pay you everything.' And out of pity for him, the lord of that slave released him and forgave him the debt. But that same slave, as he went out, came upon one of his fellow slaves who owed him a hundred denarii; and seizing him by the throat, he said, 'Pay what you owe.' Then his fellow slave fell down and pleaded with him, 'Have patience with me, and I will pay you.' But he refused; then he went and threw him into prison until he would pay the debt. When his fellow slaves saw what had happened, they were greatly distressed, and they went and reported to their lord all that had taken place. Then his lord summoned him and said to him, 'You wicked slave! I forgave you all that debt because you pleaded with me. Should you not have had mercy on your fellow slave, as I had mercy on you?' And in anger his lord handed him over to be tortured until he would pay his entire debt. So my heavenly Father will also do to every one of you, if you do not forgive your brother or sister from your heart.'*

This judgmental God looks like a clear contradiction of teaching attributed to Jesus in the previous verses (21-22). When asked there how many times to forgive, Jesus says, "*Not seven times, but, I tell you, seventy-seven times.*" That is often translated as 'seventy times seven', in either case symbolizing an unlimited number.

Yet the unforgiving servant is sent off by the king/God to be tortured until he repays the debt. Matthew warns that God will do that to everyone who does not forgive from the "*heart*".

The ending of this parable does not accord with Jesus' ethical teachings in the Beatitudes about mercy/compassion. It does indicate that 50 years after the crucifixion a strongly apocalyptic and judgmental overlay was beginning to cover Jesus' ethical teachings about the kingdom of heaven. This adds credence to the idea that Matthew himself may have been a Pharisee, with a Pharisaic view of the resurrection as only of the righteous dead.

The historian Josephus described that Pharisaic belief as follows:

> *Pharisees taught that "every soul is imperishable, but that only those of the righteous pass into another body, while those of the wicked are, on the contrary, punished with eternal torment."*[101]

I would argue that where parables are attributed to Jesus and end with apocalyptic judgment, they are either parables from a source other than Jesus, or they are originally from Jesus and have had apocalyptic endings added to them.

For Matthew, it is only believers in Jesus as Messiah who are 'righteous'. That view is contradictory to Jesus' teachings about mercy and forgiveness, and it is typical of apocalyptic and judgmental warnings added to Jesus' teaching. The parable of the unforgiving servant is an example of contradictory messages in the gospels that have been given to Christians over millennia. It is not surprising that so many Christians have given it all up as nonsense.

There is another parable not in Mark but most probably from Jesus, because it overturns the status quo of human society in his age or any age. It is the parable of the workers in the vineyard:

> 20:1-16: *For the kingdom of heaven is like a landowner who went out early in the morning to hire labourers for his vineyard. After agreeing with the labourers for the usual daily wage, he sent them into his vineyard. When he went out about nine o'clock, he saw others standing*

*idle in the marketplace; and he said to them, 'You also go
into the vineyard, and I will pay you whatever is right.'
So they went. When he went out again about noon and
about three o'clock, he did the same. And about five
o'clock he went out and found others standing around;
and he said to them, 'Why are you standing here idle all
day?' They said to him, 'Because no one has hired us.' He
said to them, 'You also go into the vineyard.' When
evening came, the owner of the vineyard said to his
manager, 'Call the labourers and give them their pay,
beginning with the last and then going to the first.' When
those hired about five o'clock came, each of them
received the usual daily wage.*

*Now when the first came, they thought they would
receive more; but each of them also received the usual
daily wage. And when they received it, they grumbled
against the landowner, saying, 'These last worked only
one hour, and you have made them equal to us who have
borne the burden of the day and the scorching heat.' But
he replied to one of them, 'Friend, I am doing you no
wrong; did you not agree with me for the usual daily
wage? Take what belongs to you and go; I choose to give
to this last the same as I give to you. Am I not allowed to
do what I choose with what belongs to me? Or are you
envious because I am generous?' So the last will be first,
and the first will be last."*

No matter when they come and ask to 'work in the
vineyard' (meaning to follow the teaching of Jesus) they will be
treated the same as all other workers. Even those who arrive
today will be equal to others who have worked in the community
for years. Here is Jesus giving his hearers an exercise in
imagining a mind-blowing scenario – what the world would look
like if God were in charge. Accordingly, people who object to this
and claim seniority or privilege will be 'last' in the kingdom of
heaven. This is one of the parables from Jesus that stands
alongside and illustrates the ethical teachings in the Sermon on
the Mount.

- *Chapters 22 – 25 – The Discourse on Judgment.*

Matthew is here approaching his description of the trial and crucifixion of Jesus. He wants to place the blame for this on the Jews who have not responded to his community's proclamation of Jesus the Messiah. Chapter 22 therefore contains Jesus' teaching on some of the hard questions that exercise the skill of the Pharisees. They include the dilemma of paying taxes to Caesar (who regarded himself as a god) while maintaining loyalty to the God of Israel; problems associated with divorce when the general resurrection of the dead occurs (who will be married to whom?); the greatest commandment; and how is the Messiah to be related to the first Messiah, David?

Chapter 22 also contains what might be called the 'definitive' parable for Matthew. It is not in Mark and shows signs of being written by Matthew himself:

> 22:1-14: *The kingdom of heaven may be compared to a king who gave a wedding banquet for his son. He sent his slaves to call those who had been invited to the wedding banquet, but they would not come. Again he sent other slaves, saying, 'Tell those who have been invited: Look, I have prepared my dinner, my oxen and my fat calves have been slaughtered, and everything is ready; come to the wedding banquet.' But they made light of it and went away, one to his farm, another to his business, while the rest seized his slaves, mistreated them, and killed them. The king was enraged. He sent his troops, destroyed those murderers, and burned their city. Then he said to his slaves, 'The wedding is ready, but those invited were not worthy. Go therefore into the main streets, and invite everyone you find to the wedding banquet.' Those slaves went out into the streets and gathered all whom they found, both good and bad; so the wedding hall was filled with guests. But when the king came in to see the guests, he noticed a man there who was not wearing a wedding robe, and he said to him, 'Friend, how did you get in here without a wedding*

robe?' And he was speechless. Then the king said to the attendants, 'Bind him hand and foot, and throw him into the outer darkness, where there will be weeping and gnashing of teeth.' For many are called, but few are chosen."

The parable of the wedding feast appears to be addressed to those Jews who have not accepted Jesus as Messiah. It looks as if the audience Matthew has in mind is primarily the Pharisees. The wedding feast represents the 'messianic banquet', where some of *"those who have been invited"* (read, the Jews/Pharisees) refuse to come. In fact, they mistreat the king's slaves (the king/God's servants in the Matthean community), even killing some.

Surely we can read here historical circumstances surrounding Matthew's mission to his own Jewish people, where sometimes the reaction is extremely hostile. The parable says the king/God is angry with these 'invited ones' who have rejected the invitation to the messianic feast. He sends troops to destroy their city. Remember that Matthew was written after Jerusalem, including the Temple of the priests and Pharisees, was destroyed. After they refuse the invitation, the king's servants find anyone who will come – both good and bad – and invite them to the feast. They come. Apparently they are each given a wedding robe before they enter the hall. This identifies them as those who have accepted the invitation.

The story says one person is there without a robe. Could he be someone who refused the invitation but has now changed his mind? If so, Matthew is saying that the time to accept the invitation is now; delay will mean being excluded from the kingdom of heaven. In any case, the fate of the one without a wedding robe is to be excluded from the messianic feast. There he weeps in pain and remorse that he had not responded immediately to the invitation. Those who eagerly accepted the invitation are now called the 'chosen'.

In Chapter 23 comes Matthew's most savage, scornful and relentless attack on the Pharisees. He is not criticising what they teach; he is criticising them for what he says is the flawed way they carry out their own teaching. One example will suffice:

> 23:2-4: *"The scribes and the Pharisees sit on Moses' seat,*
> *therefore, do whatever they teach you and follow it; but*
> *do not do as they do, for they do not practice what they*
> *teach. They tie up heavy burdens, hard to bear, and lay*
> *them on the shoulders of others; but they themselves are*
> *unwilling to lift a finger to move them."*

If, as I believe, Matthew was himself a Pharisee, he knows Pharisees have the role of teaching and interpreting the Law of Moses. He is not saying that what they teach is in any way incorrect. He is saying that they themselves do not place the Law first in their own lives. It is always important to remember that Matthew is a convert to belief in Jesus as Messiah. Converts are often very angry or frustrated with others who will not agree with their reasons for conversion. Partly to allay their own insecurity, they try to convince others to convert and if that is unsuccessful there can be first disappointment, followed by anger and a desire to discredit the 'unconverted'. It is possible to see all of those background feelings on reading chapter 23.

To add weight to his points, Matthew places all of his invective in the mouth of Jesus (the Messiah), including the accusation that the Pharisees are descendants of those who murdered prophets. Matthew's Jesus describes the Pharisees as hypocrites because they will kill those he is sending to them. Matthew's anger at his community's and Jesus' treatment by Pharisees pours out in his final proclamation of their guilt:

> 23:35-36: *"... upon you may come all the righteous blood*
> *shed on earth, from the blood of righteous Abel to the*
> *blood of Zechariah son of Barachiah, whom you*
> *murdered between the sanctuary and the altar. Truly I*
> *tell you, all this will come upon this generation."*

Verse 38 is Matthew's backward glance at Jerusalem destroyed. His righteous but gleeful anger is couched in another 'prediction from Jesus': *"See, your house is left to you, desolate."*

Chapter 24 is primarily warnings about being watchful and ready for when Jesus returns to establish the kingdom of heaven on earth. This is an apocalyptic expectation that actually has the effect of rendering the do-it-yourself teachings ineffectual! The Sermon on the Mount is surely about each follower taking responsibility for building the kingdom of heaven on earth through his or her own work and witness in love for the other. Apocalyptic interpretations that assume a return of Jesus the Messiah when God intervenes to establish the kingdom, are disenfranchising and disempowering of those who wish to follow Jesus' teachings. Why should we bother? Jesus/God will 'fix it'. Jesus' teachings do not assume an interventionist and domineering God. They are in themselves the clearest refutation of any claim that Jesus thought of himself as the Messiah who will return to earth for an apocalyptic fulfilment of all things.

Chapter 25 continues in this apocalyptic vein, culminating in the teaching (sometimes called the parable of the sheep and the goats) about how Jesus would recognise his own followers through their care of others: *"Truly I tell you, just as you did it to one of the least of these who are members of my family, you did it to me."* As such this is congruent with Jesus' teachings, but only up to and including verse 40. Verses 41-46 are Matthew's additions to this teaching:

25:41-46: *Then he will say to those at his left hand, 'You that are accursed, depart from me into the eternal fire prepared for the devil and his angels; for I was hungry and you gave me no food, I was thirsty and you gave me nothing to drink, I was a stranger and you did not welcome me, naked and you did not give me clothing, sick and in prison and you did not visit me.'*
Then they also will answer, 'Lord when was it that we saw you hungry or thirsty or a stranger or naked or sick or in prison, and did not take care of you?' Then he will answer them, 'Truly I tell you, just as you did not do it to one of the least of these, you did not do it to me.' And these will go away into eternal punishment, but the righteous into eternal life."

These verses incorporate the most overtly messianic of the teachings attributed to Jesus in Matthew, including the End-time scenario where Jesus returns to judge humanity as the Son of Man/Messiah and the punishment for those who did not follow Jesus the Messiah: *"And these will go away into eternal punishment, but the righteous into eternal life."* (46). We can hear Jesus saying: "Not in my name!"

Jesus as greater than Moses

Given Matthew's emphasis on Jesus as teacher of a new interpretation of Torah, it is not surprising that there are Mosaic understandings of Jesus scattered throughout his gospel.

- 4:1-11. Just as Moses fasted forty days and forty nights while he received the Law from God, Jesus is in the wilderness forty days and forty nights, receiving the 'new Law' from God.

- 5:1ff. Like Moses ascending a mountain to give the Law to the people, Jesus ascends a mountain to give the new Law – the Sermon on the Mount.

- 5-7, 10, 13, 18, 22-25. Moses is sometimes still regarded by those who read scripture literally, as having written the first five books of the Hebrew Scriptures. As we have already noted, Matthew divides Jesus' teachings into five speeches.

- 14:13-21. An obvious Mosaic example is the feeding of the five thousand, where Jesus' feeding far exceeds Moses' feeding of the people in the wilderness (20-21):

  "Jesus said to them, "They need not go away; you give them something to eat." They replied, "We have nothing here but five loaves and two fish." And he said, "Bring them here to me." Then he ordered the crowds to sit down on the grass. Taking the five loaves and the two fish, he looked up to heaven, and blessed and broke the

loaves, and gave them to the disciples, and the disciples gave them to the crowds. And all ate and were filled; and they took up what was left over of the broken pieces, twelve baskets full. And those who ate were about five thousand men, besides women and children."

Matthew represents here the abundance of the messianic banquet in the kingdom of heaven, to be presided over by the Messiah. This is also a glance forward to the Last Supper when Jesus declares that he will drink wine again with his disciples in *"my Father's kingdom"* (26:29). Again, Jesus acts within Jewish tradition by breaking the bread and asking God's blessing on it before the meal. The twelve baskets full of leftovers imply that Matthew is reminding his readers how Jesus the Messiah has come to 'feed' all of the people, from all twelve tribes of Israel. This is a further signal to his co-religionists and their leaders that Jesus is the expected Messiah of Israel.

- 15:32-39: *"Jesus asked them: "How many loaves have you?" They said, "Seven, and a few small fish." Then ordering the crowd to sit on the ground, he took the seven loaves and the fish; and after giving thanks he broke them and gave them to the disciples, and the disciples gave them to the crowds. And all of them ate and were filled; and they took up the broken pieces left over, seven baskets full. Those who had eaten were four thousand men, besides women and children."*

Why another feeding scene? The second contains very similar elements to the first. Matthew is following Mark in including a second feeding, but with important differences. Mark has the second feeding occur in Gentile territory, where Jesus is placed in the Decapolis, beyond the Sea of Galilee (Mark 7:31). Mark's gospel does not have Matthew's difficulty with having Jesus address Gentiles. As we have noted, Matthew's gospel is focussed overtly on the Jews and their post-Temple leaders. Therefore, although Matthew places Jesus and his disciples in the same general area, it is not named specifically as Gentile territory.

As with Mark, in Matthew's account of the second feeding there are seven baskets of leftovers, not twelve as in the first. The significance here is that the number seven is traditionally said to refer to the seventy nations who were descended from the seventy grandsons of Noah. Unless this second feeding episode has been added to Matthew by later universalist messianic editors, it appears that Matthew wants to include this reference to Jesus feeding Gentiles (the seventy nations). But as in Mark, that happens after the Israelites have already been fed.

In both Mark's and Matthew's second feeding, Jesus breaks the bread and gives thanks (in the first feeding he asks a traditional Jewish blessing). This thanksgiving at the second feeding is regarded by some scholars as an allusion to the Eucharist, which by the time of Matthew's gospel was being practised more among Gentiles than among Jews. In any case, more explicitly in Mark than in Matthew, the feeding stories are 'signs' that Jesus the Messiah has come for all people. He is therefore of greater significance than Moses.

On the other hand, the second feeding story in Matthew may be the work of a later editor with a universalist view of Jesus' messiahship. In case my reader may think there is only a slim chance of this happening, the fact is that there are no original manuscripts of the canonical gospels in existence. Because of that we have no way of knowing the real extent of editorialising undertaken during the second to the third centuries, when christological harmonizing of the New Testament canon appears to have taken place.

- 17:1-13: *Six days later, Jesus took with him Peter and James and his brother John and led them up a high mountain, by themselves. And he was transfigured before them, and his face shone like the sun, and his clothes became dazzling white. Suddenly there appeared to them Moses and Elijah, talking with him. Then Peter said to Jesus, "Lord, it is good for us to be here; if you wish, I will make three dwellings here, one for you, one for Moses, and one for Elijah." While he was still speaking, suddenly a bright cloud overshadowed them, and from the cloud a voice said, "This is my Son, the Beloved; with him I am well pleased; listen to him!" When the disciples heard this, they fell to the ground and were overcome by fear. But Jesus came and touched them, saying, "Get up and do not be afraid." And when they looked up, they saw no one except Jesus himself alone.*

In his version of the transfiguration Matthew changes Mark's order of Elijah and Moses; he naturally places the giver of the Law first. Matthew wants his readers to see that Moses the Lawgiver acknowledges Jesus here as giver of the ultimate interpretation (or fulfilment) of the Law. He has Jesus' face shine *"like the sun"*, an allusion to Moses' shining face after he received the Law from God (Exodus 34: 29-35). Peter addresses Jesus with a title ('Lord') which is more messianic than the 'Rabbi' (teacher) used by Mark. For Jews, Moses is considered the paramount teacher, prophet and lawgiver. Elijah is the one who will announce the coming of the Messiah, but for Matthew, Jesus is the teacher, prophet and lawgiver even greater than Moses; he is therefore the Messiah.

- The 'Institution of the Lord's Supper':
  26:26-29: *While they were eating, Jesus took a loaf of bread, and after blessing it he broke it, gave it to the disciples, and said, "Take, eat; this is my body." Then he took a cup, and after giving thanks he gave it to them, saying, "Drink from it, all of you; for this is my blood of the covenant, which is poured out for many for the forgiveness of sins. I tell you, I will never again drink of this fruit of the vine until that day when I drink it new with you in my Father's kingdom."*

Matthew has Moses in the background here, as the broker of the covenant between God and the people. That follows the giving of the Law: *"Moses took the blood and dashed it on the people, and said, "See the blood of the covenant that the LORD has made with you in accordance with all these words."*

(Exodus 24:8). After Jesus has given the 'new Law', ending in chapter 25, he then institutes the 'new covenant', which will be sealed through the shedding of his own blood (26:28). This is Matthew's Mosaic take on the meaning of Jesus' crucifixion.

The 'cleansing' of the Temple

21:12-17: *Then Jesus entered the temple and drove out all who were selling and buying in the temple, and he overturned the tables of the money changers and the seats of those who sold doves. He said to them, "It is written, 'My house shall be called a house of prayer'; but you are making it a den of robbers."*

Like Mark's, Matthew's version of this story is placed in Jesus' final week to accentuate the idea that Jesus' death was brought about because of his opposition to the Temple and its authorities, including the Pharisees. In Matthew this serves to heighten the general anti-Pharisaic focus, along with the explicit claim of the people at Jesus' trial that the Jews were Jesus' executioners, albeit via a Roman cross (27:25: *Then the people as a whole answered, "His blood be on us and on our children!"*). What distinguishes the Isaiah quotation in Matthew from Mark's version of the temple 'cleansing' (*"for my house shall be called a house of prayer for all peoples"*) is the omission of the words *"for all peoples"*. Matthew's Messiah Jesus has come for the *"lost sheep of the house of Israel"* (10:6), not for the Gentiles.

Jesus as Messiah in the Last Supper, Trial, Crucifixion and Resurrection Narratives

The Last Supper

26:17-19: *On the first day of Unleavened Bread the disciples came to Jesus, saying, "Where do you want us to make the preparations for you to eat the Passover?" He said, "Go into the city to a certain man, and say to him, 'The Teacher says, My time is near; I will keep the Passover at your house with my disciples.'" So the disciples did as Jesus had directed them, and they prepared the Passover meal.*

It is important to look at the timing of the meal Jesus had with his disciples in Matthew's Gospel. It is called the Passover meal. Given that Jesus was crucified on the day of Preparation for the first Sabbath of the Festival of Unleavened Bread, that means the Passover meal was eaten the day before, on what we would call Thursday. That makes sense of Jesus' words: *"My time is near; I will keep the Passover at your house with my disciples."* Yet this is by no means proof that Jesus' last meal was in fact the Passover meal. As I have pointed out in the chapter on Mark, that timing of the meal meant gospel writers could draw inferences from the Passover regarding Jesus' death as sacrifice. There are more implications of this timing, as we will see in the section concerning the resurrection.

During the meal (26:26-29) Matthew's Jesus tells his disciples that he is to be the sacrifice of the 'new covenant', by which Matthew means the new understanding of Torah now mediated by Messiah Jesus. Although this is often read by Christians as referring to God's 'new covenant' with the church, nothing could have been further from the mind of Matthew (or Jesus). Jesus the teacher of the Law from Nazareth would not have wanted to imagine a new religion established in his name. He tells the disciples during his last meal with them that he will see them again at the messianic banquet, when they are all reunited in the kingdom of heaven. The implication there is that he will return to inaugurate the kingdom of heaven on earth on the apocalyptic Day of the LORD. This is the expectation through which Matthew has become reconciled with the unexpected and shocking reality of the death of the Messiah.

In support of this prospect, Matthew's portrayal of Jesus includes his ability to predict the coming trial and execution. While on the way to Jerusalem, Jesus tries to make his disciples understand what will happen there. With the benefit of hindsight, Matthew has Jesus say:

20:18-19: *"See, we are going up to Jerusalem, and the*

Son of Man will be handed over to the chief priests and scribes, and they will condemn him to death; then they will hand him over to the Gentiles to be mocked and flogged and crucified; and on the third day he will be raised."

Of course Matthew then proceeds to describe those events in accordance with that 'prediction'. To deal with the inexplicable desertion of Jesus by his disciples during the night to follow, Matthew gives Jesus another prediction, this time from Zechariah:

13:7: *"Then Jesus said to them, 'You will all become deserters because of me this night; for it is written, I will strike the shepherd, and the sheep of the flock will be scattered'."*

The desertion is therefore vindicated; the followers were destined to act that way in accordance with scriptural prediction!

The Garden, the Betrayal and Trial

26:36-42: *Then Jesus went with them to a place called Gethsemane; and he said to his disciples, "Sit here while I go over there and pray." He took with him Peter and the two sons of Zebedee and began to be grieved and agitated. Then he said to them, "I am deeply grieved, even to death; remain here, and stay awake with me." And going a little farther, he threw himself on the ground and prayed, "My Father, if it is possible, let this cup pass from me; yet not what I want but what you want." Then he came to the disciples and found them sleeping; and he said to Peter, "So, could you not stay awake with me one hour? Stay awake and pray that you may not come into the time of trial; the spirit indeed is willing, but the flesh is weak." Again he went away for the second time and prayed, "My Father, if this cannot pass unless I drink it, your will be done."*

Matthew lifts the scene in the Garden of Gethsemane

almost intact from Mark. Apart from a small number of different words, the meaning is the same. Jesus prays that he will not have to go through the crucifixion, but agrees to do so because it is 'God's will': *"My Father, if this cannot pass unless I drink it, your will be done."* (26:42). No one knows what Jesus actually thought or prayed when he knew he was in imminent danger of arrest, but his words in Mark and Matthew during the night in Gethsemane fit the gospel writers' portrayal of him as the understandably reluctant, but ultimately willing, sacrifice. As in Mark, the disciples themselves don't 'get it'. They can't help going to sleep.

> 26:43-46: *So leaving them again, he went away and prayed for the third time, saying the same words. Then he came to the disciples and said to them, "Are you still sleeping and taking your rest? See, the hour is at hand, and the Son of Man is betrayed into the hands of sinners. Get up, let us be going. See, my betrayer is at hand."*

Matthew continues to follow Mark in the description of Judas' betrayal of Jesus, except for one important difference. After a man who was (according to Matthew) *"with Jesus"* draws his sword to attack the arresting party from the Temple and cuts off the ear of a slave of the High Priest, Jesus tells him to put his sword away. Matthew does not regard Mark's description as sufficient reaction from Jesus at that point. He therefore has Jesus 'prove' his messianic identity with the following:

> 26:53-54: *"Do you think that I cannot appeal to my Father, and he will at once send me more than twelve legions of angels? But how then would the scriptures be fulfilled, which say it must happen in this way?"*

Here Matthew echoes apocalyptic writings of the time such as the Dead Sea Scrolls, in particular the *War Scroll* in its depiction of a final End-time battle of good against evil: *For the angels of holiness shall accompany their armies* (1QM 7:6).

Matthew then has Jesus say that his arrest is happening

to fulfil the scriptures. Certainly this fits with Matthew's (and Mark's) understanding of Jesus as Messiah, but it also fits with their descriptions of this event – hardly surprising, given that their stories are both sourced from scripture. Mark and Matthew say that at this point the disciples deserted Jesus and fled. Still these followers do not understand that Jesus is the Messiah and that he has to die to fulfil a quote from scripture, even if that quote cannot be found in scripture!

> 26:57-58: *Those who had arrested Jesus took him to Caiaphas the high priest, in whose house the scribes and the elders had gathered. But Peter was following him at a distance, as far as the courtyard of the high priest; and going inside, he sat with the guards in order to see how this would end.*

Mark and Matthew both place Peter in the courtyard of the High Priest as Jesus is being brought to trial. Matthew gives Peter's presence extra meaning. By deliberately placing him close to the trial scene, the implication is that Peter is then able to report accurately what Jesus says to the High Priest and the Pharisees. Like Mark, Matthew says the charge against Jesus is that he is a threat to the Temple. In both gospels this charge is based on what happened when Jesus was leaving the Temple. He looked at the buildings and said:

> 24:1-2: *"You see all these, do you not? Truly I tell you, not one stone will be left here upon another; all will be thrown down."*

This is another of Jesus' Matthean 'predictions', placed before the arrest and trial so as to make sense of the High Priest's accusation.

In the arrest and trial scenes two things are being emphasised. First is that true to his teachings, Jesus is depicted as against the use of violence. Second is that following Mark, Matthew is presenting a case against the Jewish leadership of the Temple, including Pharisees (*"scribes and elders"*). That case will place blame for the death of the Messiah squarely on their shoulders and on the shoulders of their Jewish supporters. Matthew's description of the trial scene at the house of Caiaphas the high priest is also taken almost completely from Mark. Matthew uses it as his charge against the Temple leadership that they were responsible for Jesus' death. In so doing he moves responsibility for Jesus' crucifixion from the Romans to the leaders of the Jews. This is a crucial issue of security for the ongoing followers of Jesus the Messiah. It cannot be overstated that Matthew had no way of knowing how ominous for the Jewish people would be the historical consequences of this line of argument. (See the final chapter of this book for a fuller explanation.)

Jesus is then taken to appear before the "whole council":

26:59-64: *Now the chief priests and the whole council were looking for false testimony against Jesus so that they might put him to death, but they found none, though many false witnesses came forward. At last two came forward and said, "This fellow said, 'I am able to destroy the temple of God and to build it in three days.'" The high priest stood up and said, "Have you no answer? What is it that they testify against you?" But Jesus was silent. Then the high priest said to him, "I put you under oath before the living God, tell us if you are the Messiah, the Son of God." Jesus said to him, "You have said so. But I tell you, from now on you will see the Son of Man seated at the right hand of Power and coming on the clouds of heaven."*

At the house of Caiaphas the High Priest, (where Peter slips in among the guards) *"scribes and elders"* are trying to press home charges against Jesus of insurrection. According to Matthew this is all happening on the Day of Preparation for the first Sabbath of the Festival of Unleavened Bread. It is extraordinary that matters such as these are being dealt with by the Temple leadership (including priests) so close to the high holy Sabbath. Yet given Matthew's Jewish identity and the intended Jewish readership of his gospel, there may be room to suppose that such a thing could happen in exceptional circumstances.

Those exceptional circumstances might be occasioned by the huge crowds thronging Jerusalem for the Passover and the alertness of the Prefect Pontius Pilate and his soldiers to the slightest sign of trouble. In that scenario the "*scribes and elders*" might want to get rid of Jesus before there is a crackdown on the people by the Romans. They might also want it all over and done with before the first Sabbath of the Festival of Unleavened Bread.

The Jewish leaders therefore quickly find people willing to testify falsely that Jesus was plotting against the Temple. According to Matthew the Temple leadership sees Jesus as a popular prophetic teacher (probably involved with insurrectionists) accusing them of corruption in Temple practice and collaboration with Rome. They know that two witnesses (even false witnesses) are needed if a death sentence is to be imposed by the Romans for insurrection. Yet Matthew says that even the false witnesses cannot offer a plausible reason to condemn Jesus.

So the High Priest tries again. This time he asks Jesus explicitly if he is the Messiah. Jesus simply says, "*You have said so,*" but like Mark, Matthew then has him quote from the Book of Daniel concerning "*the Son of Man seated at the right hand of Power and coming on the clouds of heaven*" (64). This is an apocalyptic End-time image, very different from a traditional description of the Davidic Messiah, who is an earthly figure, anointed by God to lead Israel to victory against its enemies. As I have noted previously, the biblical scenario in Daniel has the Son of Man going from earth to heaven, not from heaven to earth, as would be expected of a returning Messiah Jesus. However, Matthew considers this quote a suitable means whereby Jesus can admit to messiahship.

There are good reasons for this choice of scripture. It gives Matthew and Mark a way to hold the Temple leadership primarily responsible for the death of Jesus. This is where the gospel writers depart from traditional scriptural understandings of Messiah and identify Jesus with apocalyptic ideas that will see him die, rise from death and return to earth according to what they find in scripture about the 'Day of the LORD'. Mark's and Matthew's argument for this version of Jesus as Messiah is based on their knowledge that Jesus was in fact crucified, and believed by some to have risen from death. Their storyline is at least partially congruent with Pharisaic understandings of a Messiah who will appear at the general resurrection of the righteous dead.

At this point the charge of blasphemy is made against Jesus:

> 26:65-68. *Then the high priest tore his clothes and said, "He has blasphemed! Why do we still need witnesses? You have now heard his blasphemy. What is your verdict?" They answered, "He deserves death." Then they spat in his face and struck him; and some slapped him, saying, "Prophesy to us, you Messiah! Who is it that struck you?"*

Matthew's (and Mark's) scenario of the Temple leadership looking for a reason to request the Romans to execute Jesus is further advanced when the High Priest makes the extraordinary claim that by his admission of messiahship, Jesus is blaspheming. Yet there appears to be nothing blasphemous in a Jewish man claiming he was the Messiah; plenty of others had done the same. The only sense in which a claim of messiahship would have been blasphemous was if in so doing, the claimant invoked the divine name falsely to promote his own cause, an offence punishable by stoning to death.

Very important in this scenario is the use of the word 'Power', as in *"From now on you will see the Son of Man seated on the right hand of Power."* The capital letter in the NRSV indicates that the translators regard this word as representing God. 'Power' is a substitution for other divine names in both the Hebrew Scriptures and the New Testament. Matthew and Mark are written in Greek and both quote extensively from the Hebrew Scriptures (Greek version) in which the Greek word *dunameos* refers explicitly to God's power. In 2 Timothy 1:7 the Holy Spirit is called "the Spirit of Power" (in Greek, *pneuma dunameos*).

In Hebrew the word for power is *gibbor*. It is associated with God in Isaiah 10:21, where God is called "*mighty*" (or powerful); in Isaiah 9:6: "*For a child has been born for us, a son given to us; authority rests upon his shoulders; and he is named Wonderful Counsellor, Mighty God, Everlasting Father, Prince of Peace*"; and with the King Messiah (meaning Son of David) who will come to represent God. To say that someone would be sitting on the right hand of Power was to say this person would be sitting on the right hand of God in heaven. That imagery is a significant departure from the traditional Jewish understanding of Messiah – as a human kingly figure 'anointed' by God to be divine representative on earth.

The use of scriptural imagery to depict Jesus sitting on the right hand of God was sufficient background for Matthew to set out the high priest's likely reaction. Caiaphas could now regard Jesus as misusing God's name (blaspheming) by claiming to be a Messiah who sits on the 'right hand' of God. According to Matthew and Mark, this became the high priest's warrant to have Jesus put to death. Clearly though, the words of Jesus here and the high priest's reaction are the work of Mark and Matthew. The words have two aims. First, they explain for the gospels' readers the otherwise inexplicable death of the Messiah. Second, they place the blame for the Messiah's death on the shoulders of the Jewish leadership.

The next morning (still the Day of Preparation for the Sabbath) the chief priests and the "*elders*" of the people (read Pharisees) hand Jesus to Pilate[102], ostensibly on the grounds that Jesus is a blaspheming trouble-making King/Messiah claimant who is a threat to both the Temple and Rome. Pilate naturally questions Jesus about that:

> 27:11-14: *Now Jesus stood before the governor; and the governor asked him, "Are you the King of the Jews?" Jesus said, "You say so." But when he was accused by the*

chief priests and elders, he did not answer. Then Pilate said to him, "Do you not hear how many accusations they make against you?" But he gave him no answer, not even to a single charge, so that the governor was greatly amazed.

There is good reason to see that this aspect of the trial is based on the description of the 'suffering servant' in Isaiah 53:7, where: *"He was oppressed, and he was afflicted, yet he did not open his mouth; like a lamb that is led to the slaughter, and like a sheep that before its shearers is silent, so he did not open his mouth"*. Pilate's even-handed, even generous attitude toward Jesus is further illustrated by his willingness to release him. This is explained in Matthew by two things. First, Pilate sees the Jewish leadership as *"jealous"* of Jesus' popularity (27:18). Second, Pilate's wife has had a dream about Jesus as an *"innocent man"* (27:19). Yet the crowd chooses Barabbas for release instead of Jesus. Barabbas is apparently a popular Jewish insurrectionist leader who used violent means to resist the Romans.

Matters are getting out of hand by this time, so Pilate washes his hands of the whole thing. Then follows some of the most dangerous words ever committed to parchment: *"Then the people as a whole answered, "His blood be on us and on our children!"* (27:25).[103] It is the leaders of the Temple and the Pharisees who *"persuade the crowds"* to ask for Barabbas to be freed and for Jesus to be killed. Yet given the anti-Pharisaic nature of Matthew's Gospel, there is good reason to see that Matthew is actually pointing to the Temple leadership (including the Pharisees) and their supporters when he has *"the people as a whole"* accept responsibility for Jesus' crucifixion (27:25).

Given that Jesus was a popular prophet/teacher, the implication that *"the people as a whole"* (meaning all Jews) wanted him crucified is misleading, to say the least. Yet tragically, this verse has been read in the church in this way as literal truth for centuries, leading to extremely hostile antisemitic Christian views of Jews. The Roman soldiers then proceed to treat Jesus as a failed Messiah; a false 'King of the Jews'. Accordingly, they torment him with mock obeisance.

In short, the trial scenes in Matthew were designed to blame not only the Jewish leaders (including the Pharisees) for the crucifixion, but also the Jewish people who supported them and rejected Messiah Jesus. This applied even though the crucifixion itself was carried out by the Romans. Pilate is portrayed throughout as a reasonable man, an unwilling agent of the execution, pressured by the Temple leadership.

The extent to which the gospel writers wanted to placate Pontius Pilate and other Roman authorities by portraying Pilate as a decent man, can be seen by comparing their depiction of him with historical records. The description of him by the Jewish philosopher Philo of Alexandria will give the reader some idea of the real Pilate. According to Philo, Pilate was in the habit of deliberately annoying and stirring up the Jewish people under his control. Philo describes him as:

> *A man of inflexible, stubborn and cruel disposition, a spiteful and angry person.* Philo specifies in detail: *his venality, his violence, his thefts, his assaults, his abusive behaviour, his frequent executions of untried prisoners, and his endless savage ferocity.*[104]

Pilate's savagery culminated in him being recalled from his post by the Emperor Tiberias, the first instance of that in the Roman Empire. It is no wonder that the gospel writers thought it prudent to whitewash him!

The Crucifixion

> 27:33-44: *And when they came to a place called Golgotha (which means Place of a Skull), they offered him wine to drink, mixed with gall; but when he tasted it, he would not drink it. And when they had crucified him, they divided his clothes among themselves by casting lots; then they sat down there and kept watch over him. Over his head they put the charge against him, which read, "This is Jesus, the King of the Jews." Then two bandits were crucified with him, one on his right and one on his left. Those who passed by derided him, shaking their heads and saying, "You who*

would destroy the temple and build it in three days, save yourself! If you are the Son of God, come down from the cross." In the same way the chief priests also, along with the scribes and elders, were mocking him, saying, "He saved others; he cannot save himself. He is the King of Israel; let him come down from the cross now, and we will believe in him. He trusts in God; let God deliver him now, if he wants to; for he said, 'I am God's Son.' " The bandits who were crucified with him also taunted him in the same way.

In accordance with Roman procedure, a sign was placed on the cross stating the crime of the crucified 'criminal'. According to Matthew, the sign on Jesus' cross read: *"This is Jesus, the King of the Jews."* (27:37). If this is historical fact, it supports the argument that Jesus was condemned for plotting against Rome. Two men described as *"bandits"* were crucified with Jesus. They would have been Jewish nationalist rebels, crucifixion being the punishment for treason or insurrection against Rome. Two internal proof texts from Psalm 22 are employed here. The first is 22:1: *"My God, my God, why have you forsaken me?"* The second is 22:17-18: *"They stare and gloat over me; they divide my clothes among themselves, and for my clothing they cast lots."* Matthew includes the highly unlikely scenario of the chief priests and the whole Sanhedrin attending a crucifixion so close to Passover, when they needed to avoid the pollution of close proximity to dead bodies.

For Matthew's purpose, their taunts to Jesus about saving himself are turned back on themselves by the earth-shattering events that follow the crucifixion:

27:51-53: *At that moment the curtain of the temple was torn in two, from top to bottom. The earth shook, and the rocks were split. The tombs also were opened, and many bodies of the saints who had fallen asleep were raised. After his resurrection they came out of the tombs and entered the holy city and appeared to many.*

The holy place venerated by the Temple leadership is violated when the curtain veiling the 'holy of holies' is split from top to bottom. The symbolism is that with his death Jesus the Messiah has taken over the role of the high priest and is now the only person worthy to go into the presence of God. In this regard it is worth remembering that Matthew's and Mark's gospels were read first by people who may have been able to remember the destruction of the Temple.

Matthew then takes the story further than Mark's version. He wants to make here his strongest case to the Pharisees that Jesus is the Messiah. He claims that on Jesus' death there is an earthquake; tombs are opened and the dead are raised. He states that after Jesus is resurrected, the dead walk the streets of Jerusalem. This is meant as undeniable vindication of Matthew's claim that Jesus is the Messiah. It is a message to the Pharisees that they should wake up and realise what has happened. Jesus' resurrection heralds what they had been waiting for all along when the Messiah appeared; the general resurrection of the righteous dead.

Matthew is likely to be relying for credibility on the time elapsed between the crucifixion and the date of his writing, which was most probably over 50 years. By the 80s CE the Pharisees would not have been able to ask eye-witnesses whether Matthew's claims were true. It is curious, to say the least, that if this were true, no one else documented such an astounding event occurring at the time of the crucifixion. Touching on an important safety issue for Matthew's community, here Matthew gives the Romans yet another pardon from their action in carrying out Jesus' crucifixion. The soldiers who crucified him witness the earthquake and the graves being opened. In response they are the first Gentiles to proclaim that *"Truly this man was God's Son!"* (27:54). This is Matthew saying that the Romans 'got it', but the 'blind' Pharisees did not.

The Resurrection

27:57-61: *When it was evening, there came a rich man from Arimathea, named Joseph, who was also a disciple of Jesus. He went to Pilate and asked for the body of*

Jesus; then Pilate ordered it to be given to him. So Joseph took the body and wrapped it in a clean linen cloth and laid it in his own new tomb, which he had hewn in the rock. He then rolled a great stone to the door of the tomb and went away. Mary Magdalene and the other Mary were there, sitting opposite the tomb.

Like Mark, Matthew has a man called Joseph of Arimathea claim the body of Jesus. Mark says Joseph is a Pharisee waiting for the kingdom of God, meaning he is a follower of Jesus the Messiah. Matthew differs from that. For him Joseph is simply a rich man from Arimathea, through whom Matthew is again pointing to the description of the 'suffering servant' of Isaiah 53; *"They made his grave with the wicked and his tomb with the rich, although he had done no violence and there was no deceit in his mouth."* For his Jewish readership, Matthew is keen to press into service as many biblical quotes as possible. However, there is no place that has been identified as 'Arimathea', and no historical records exist of 'Joseph of Arimathea', only legends that have him visiting England with a young Jesus. Hence the hymn: "And did those feet in ancient time, walk upon England's mountains green?"

The following day we see a preposterously unlikely scenario:

27:62-66: *The next day, that is, after the day of Preparation, the chief priests and the Pharisees gathered before Pilate and said, "Sir, we remember what that impostor said while he was still alive, 'After three days I will rise again.' Therefore command the tomb to be made secure until the third day; otherwise his disciples may go and steal him away, and tell the people, 'He has been raised from the dead,' and the last deception would be worse than the first." Pilate said to them, "You have a guard of soldiers; go, make it as secure as you can." So they went with the guard and made the tomb secure by sealing the stone.*

This is the moment for my reader to sit up and take notice. Matthew is about to deal with people in his time who rejected his claim that Jesus 'rose from the dead'. His explanation begins at 27:62. The very people (the chief priests and Pharisees) who do not believe for a moment that Jesus is the Messiah, have gathered on the day following the Day of Preparation (none other than this highly significant Sabbath Day!) in the polluted territory of Pilate's headquarters. Nothing could be further from the reality of religious life for Temple leadership in Jesus' time. The requirements of Sabbath, including purity laws governing contact with Gentile territory, would rule out completely what Matthew is saying.

But Matthew was writing in the 80s when the Temple and its officials were no longer a factor in Jewish life. That may have given him more freedom to write his story. Matthew may also have been trying to convince his readers that the death of Jesus was recognized by the Temple to have greater importance than the purity laws surrounding observance of religious festivals. In any case, what we see in this story about the Pharisees and Pilate is Matthew trying to refute rumours in his own time that Jesus did not rise from death; that instead his body was stolen by his followers.

In Matthew's unlikely scenario, Pilate is either convinced that Jesus might rise from the dead (Pilate as convert to messianic ideas), or he is keen to avoid the spread of rumours that it was in fact the Messiah who was crucified. To deal with either case, he sends soldiers to 'seal the tomb' and keep guard over it until the third day. The message for the readers of the gospel (for whom this was written) is clear: Jesus' followers could not possibly have taken his body away. That rules out one apparent explanation for the resurrection that evidently was circulating at the time Matthew wrote his gospel.

Unlike Mark's story of the resurrection, at the moment Mary Magdalene and "*the other Mary*" arrive at the tomb, Matthew introduces another earthquake:

28:1-10: *After the Sabbath as the first day of the week was dawning, Mary Magdalene and the other Mary went to see the tomb. And suddenly there was a great earthquake; for an angel of the Lord, descending from heaven, came and rolled back the stone and sat on it. His appearance was like lightning, and his clothing white as snow. For fear of him the guards shook and became like dead men. But the angel said to the women, "Do not be afraid; I know that you are looking for Jesus who was crucified. He is not here; for he has been raised, as he said. Come, see the place where he lay. Then go quickly and tell his disciples, 'He has been raised from the dead, and indeed he is going ahead of you to Galilee; there you will see him.' This is my message for you." So they left the tomb quickly with fear and great joy, and ran to tell his disciples. Suddenly Jesus met them and said, "Greetings!" And they came to him, took hold of his feet, and worshipped him. Then Jesus said to them, "Do not be afraid; go and tell my brothers to go to Galilee; there they will see me."*

Instead of finding an empty tomb as per Mark, the women witness an angel arriving from heaven accompanied by an earthquake. He rolls back the stone from the still-sealed tomb. The Roman guards are naturally enough terrified, and being immobilized "*like dead men*" (i.e. they fainted) are unable to prevent the angel from opening the tomb. The angel tells the women to look into the empty tomb and then go and tell the disciples. On their way to do that, Jesus appears and greets them. They are able to touch him, indicating that Matthew is promoting a bodily resurrection for the Messiah.

Meanwhile, the guards have regained consciousness and decided to report all of this to the authorities:

28:11-15: *some of the guard went into the city and told the chief priests everything that had happened. After the priests had assembled with the elders, they devised a plan to give a large sum of money to the soldiers, telling*

*them, "You must say, 'His disciples came by night and
stole him away while we were asleep.' If this comes to the
governor's ears, we will satisfy him and keep you out of
trouble." So they took the money and did as they were
directed. And this story is still told among the Jews to
this day.*

Here is what Matthew wants his readers to believe.
When the soldiers run to the chief priests and tell them about
the angel and that Jesus' body has disappeared from the tomb,
the priests now clearly believe Jesus must be the Messiah. Only
that would be responsible for such a momentous event. To
cover their involvement in the death of the Messiah, they are
now faced with concocting a story for the general public. To
protect themselves from accusations that they killed the
Messiah, they pay off the soldiers to tell everyone that Jesus'
followers stole his body during the night while they were
sleeping outside the tomb. Matthew then adds that this story is
still being told among the Jews at the time he is writing his
gospel. That is the 'reason' the people did not believe that Jesus
was the Messiah.

What may well have been a personal experience of Jesus
by some of his followers after his death has been developed out
of sight in accordance with messianic expectation. It is no
wonder that in its reworked version it held no credibility for
most Jews. This story about the leaders and the soldiers is
Matthew's heroic attempt to explain how the amazing news
that a man had come bodily back to life from the dead had not
been believed by most Jews. His story may have convinced
some of his early readers. It does not explain why the people
Matthew says actually saw the dead rise from their graves
when Jesus died, were not proclaiming such stupendous news
to the world.

The farewell
28:16-20: *Now the eleven disciples went to Galilee, to the
mountain to which Jesus had directed them. When they
saw him, they worshipped him, but some doubted. And*

Jesus came and said to them, "All authority in heaven and on earth has been given to me. Go therefore and make disciples of all nations, baptizing them in the name of the Father and of the Son and of the Holy Spirit, and teaching them to obey everything that I have commanded you. And remember, I am with you always, to the end of the age."

Matthew's gospel does not include an 'ascension' of Jesus. That idea comes later from Luke. Matthew concludes with a farewell scene where eleven disciples (Judas having died) meet him on a mountain in Galilee. They worship him, all except for some, who doubt him. We can only suppose from this that Matthew knows some of Jesus' friends had an experience of him after he died, perhaps even 'seeing' him, but that others did not.

Then follows the so-called 'missionary imperative' (or Great Commission). Aspects of Jesus' farewell message point to it being an interpolation into Matthew's gospel from a later period of Christian theological development. Several features of the text point to a much later dating. Jesus is now seen as the Lord of the Gentiles, as well as of the Jews. Inconsistently with the rest of Matthew's Gospel, his followers are now to go to *"all nations"*, not just to the *"house of the lost sheep of Israel"* (ch.10). Most telling is the trinitarian formula by which the followers are to baptize people from all nations. Although 'Father', 'Son' and 'Holy Spirit' are all mentioned in the New Testament, their relationship in a trinitarian doctrine or even a trinitarian formula was not developed until the late third and early fourth centuries. To state the obvious, Jesus the Jew is unlikely to have referred to himself as the second person of a three-person 'triune God'.

To be consistent, Matthew's gospel is much more likely to have ended with Jesus saying: "Go and make disciples in my name, teaching them to obey everything I have commanded you." Christian baptism (meaning baptism into 'Christ's' death and resurrection) is obviously ruled out of Jesus' own discourse. The final sentence presupposes that Jesus saw himself as returning at *"the end of the age"*. I contend through this book that Jesus' teachings inherently rule out any such End-time belief held by him or by his original followers.

Jesus the Messiah in the Gospel of Luke

L uke's gospel is logically the third of the synoptic gospels, both in chronological reckoning and in the development of messianic thought. Luke was probably written much later than Mark and Matthew. New Testament scholar James Charlesworth acknowledges changes in the scholarly dating of Luke:

> *The composition of Luke-Acts is usually dated around 80 – 90, though some experts now suggest perhaps between 90 and 110.*[105]

We have noted that Matthew's gospel appears to have been largely concerned with persuading Jewish leaders in Jerusalem that Jesus was the genuine Messiah as per traditional Jewish expectations. Luke's audience appears to be primarily Gentiles and hellenized (Greek speaking) Jews. However, on reading Luke's arguments about Jesus as Messiah it also becomes clear that he is appealing to Palestinian Jews to turn away from traditions that link the Messiah with the prophet Elijah. Given the various positive references to Samaritans in his gospel, it is evident that Luke is also reaching out to them. Luke the gospel writer is so thoroughly conversant with Jewish tradition that it is neither necessary nor sensible to regard him as a Gentile. He is most likely to have been a Jew living in the Diaspora in a hellenized Greek-speaking context.

Regarding the date of Luke's writing, the scholars of The Acts Seminar[106] state that: "*Acts was written in the early decades of the second century"*. Given widespread scholarly opinion that Acts is the second part of a Luke-Acts literary work, that also places the Gospel of Luke in that early second century time frame, at least two decades later than a common dating of Luke in the 80s CE. Luke's gospel follows the structure of Mark's gospel, in which Jesus fulfils a messianic theological purpose in his determination to make his way to Jerusalem.

Luke's intended readers: the superscription[107]

1:1-4: Since many have undertaken to set down an orderly account of the events that have been fulfilled among us, just as they were handed on to us by those who from the beginning were eyewitnesses and servants of the word, I too decided, after investigating everything carefully from the very first, to write an orderly account for you, most excellent Theophilus, so that you may know the truth concerning the things about which you have been instructed.

Luke's gospel begins with a thinly disguised signal that he intends to correct the records of previous writers concerning *"the events that have been fulfilled among us"*. Luke notes that *"many"* have set down *"orderly"* accounts of Jesus' life, death and resurrection. He, on the other hand, has first investigated everything carefully, from the beginning. Through his writing, his addressee Theophilus will finally know *"the truth"* about these things. Theophilus is perhaps a Gentile (maybe Roman) nobleman who converted to belief in Jesus as Messiah/Son of God. The implication is that Theophilus has not yet been given the truth as Luke understands it. Luke's purpose is to set out his story of Jesus according to eye-witness reports so that Theophilus *"may know the truth"*. As with Matthew's, Luke's writing is naturally influenced by his audience, presumably not confined to one reader, Theophilus. Given the meaning of the name ('lover of God'), the gospel may have been addressed to anyone who 'loves God'! The fact that the Book of Acts is also addressed to 'Theophilus' is often cited as proof that Luke wrote both the gospel and Acts.

The Infancy Narratives (1:5 – 2:52)

Again we are faced with questions about the original beginning of a gospel:

- As with Mark and Matthew, could the Gospel of Luke have originally begun with the appearance of John the Baptist?
- Might Luke have decided to add 'infancy narratives' to illustrate his different view of John the Baptist and of John's relationship to Jesus?
- Might they have been added by someone else, or written by others and added by Luke?

The scholarly work on these questions is considerable, but I offer the reader a brief glimpse:

- The infancy narrative in Luke is written in a style of Greek different from the rest of the gospel. Nonetheless (some scholars say) it may have been written by Luke in conscious imitation of the Greek in the Greek translation of the Hebrew Scriptures.
- The infancy narrative may also have been Luke's translation of Hebrew/Aramaic written Jewish sources about the birth of the Messiah.
- It may have been written and added to Luke's Gospel by a third person or group.
- In any case Luke possibly had two sources to work with. The material about the birth of John the Baptist looks like an earlier Jewish oral or written tradition originating with followers of John. The hymns (*Magnificat, Benedictus* and *Nunc Dimittis*) are likely to have come from a Jewish messianic source (Jews convinced that Jesus was the Messiah) close to the time of Luke's writing in the late first century CE.

It must be said that all of these theories are conjecture; there is no scholarly consensus about the source of the infancy narrative(s). As in Matthew, references to a 'virgin birth' in Luke are not mentioned again in the rest of the gospel. That fact alone raises the question of whether Luke (or Matthew) knew about 'infancy narratives', which may have been added by a later editor, perhaps the same editor who added a superscription to both Luke and Acts.

The earliest surviving full copies of Luke chapters 1 and 2 are the so-called Codex Vaticanus and Codex Sinaiticus, produced in the middle of the fourth century. None of the pre-fourth century fragments of Luke contain the 'virgin birth' narrative. Given concerted third and fourth century efforts to ascribe divinity to Jesus, the infancy narratives about the angelic announcement to Mary in chapter 1 and the 'virgin birth' story in chapter 2, look remarkably like additions from a later era. The material about the birth of John the Baptist in chapter 1 may have been added by Luke to his original (chapter 3) starting point with John's ministry. Or it may have been added by a later editor intent on 'harmonizing' gospel depictions of Jesus as Messiah.

The Prediction and Birth of John the Baptist

Luke's gospel was evidently written for Gentiles as well as for hellenized Jews who could read Greek. For that reason it needs to explain the Jewish background of the Messiah. Chapter 1: 1-25 grounds its story of Jesus the Messiah in Israel's salvation history:

> 1:5-25: *In the days of King Herod of Judea, there was a priest named Zechariah, who belonged to the priestly order of Abijah. His wife was a descendant of Aaron, and her name was Elizabeth. Both of them were righteous before God, living blamelessly according to all the commandments and regulations of the Lord. But they had no children, because Elizabeth was barren, and both were getting on in years. Once when he was serving as priest before God and his section was on duty, he was chosen by lot, according to the custom of the priesthood, to enter the sanctuary of the Lord and offer incense. Now at the time of the incense offering, the whole assembly of the people was praying outside. Then there appeared to him an angel of the Lord, standing at the right side of the altar of incense. When Zechariah saw him, he was terrified; and fear overwhelmed him. But the angel said*

to him, "Do not be afraid, Zechariah, for your prayer has been heard. Your wife Elizabeth will bear you a son, and you will name him John. You will have joy and gladness, and many will rejoice at his birth, for he will be great in the sight of the Lord. He must never drink wine or strong drink; even before his birth he will be filled with the Holy Spirit. He will turn many of the people of Israel to the Lord their God. With the spirit and power of Elijah he will go before him, to turn the hearts of parents to their children, and the disobedient to the wisdom of the righteous, to make ready a people prepared for the Lord."

Zechariah said to the angel, "How will I know that this is so? For I am an old man, and my wife is getting on in years." The angel replied, "I am Gabriel. I stand in the presence of God, and I have been sent to speak to you and to bring you this good news. But now, because you did not believe my words, which will be fulfilled in their time, you will become mute, unable to speak, until the day these things occur." Meanwhile the people were waiting for Zechariah, and wondered at his delay in the sanctuary. When he did come out, he could not speak to them, and they realised that he had seen a vision in the sanctuary. He kept motioning to them and remained unable to speak. When his time of service was ended, he went to his home.

After those days his wife Elizabeth conceived, and for five months she remained in seclusion. She said, "This is what the Lord has done for me when he looked favourably on me and took away the disgrace I have endured among my people."

This narrative is based firmly on the story of Samuel, who was forerunner of the first Messiah, King David. Like Samuel, John the Baptist is to be born to an older woman who has long been unable to conceive. Like Hannah, Elizabeth is portrayed as a righteous person, as is her husband Zechariah, a priest of the Temple. Very importantly, the narrative says Elizabeth is a descendant of Aaron, the first high priest. We will discover the significance of that later in the narrative. Zechariah's vision concerning the birth of John occurs in a place that further anchors him, John, Mary and Jesus, firmly in Israel's messianic and religious traditions. It is when Zechariah is offering incense in the 'holy of holies' in the Temple that he is told by an angel about the coming birth of John. Like Samuel, John is never to drink alcohol, and is to be dedicated to God.

The story then proceeds to an identification of John with the prophet Elijah. It borrows ideas from Malachi about Elijah's return to earth:

> 4:5-6: *Lo, I will send you the prophet Elijah before the great and terrible day of the Lord comes. He will turn the hearts of parents to the children and the hearts of children to their parents, so that I will not come and strike the land with a curse. Malachi says Elijah is to prepare the people for the "great and terrible day of the LORD".*

Luke's John the Baptist story leaves that out in favour of a more explicitly messianic treatment of Malachi. It simply says that John, "*with the spirit and power of Elijah*" will prepare the people for "*the Lord.*" 'Lord' refers here not to God as in Malachi, but to Jesus the Messiah/Son of God, whose own birth is shortly to be predicted. The writer of the John the Baptist section of the infancy narrative does not subscribe to the Jewish 'returning Elijah' tradition, which is related explicitly to the restoration of Israel's relationship with God. The writer has his eye on a bigger picture. Luke's gospel will also address the Gentile world.

Given that the narrative surrounding the birth of John the Baptist is a mythical story, probably originating from a John the Baptist oral or written source, the angelic prediction of the birth of the forerunner of the Messiah was understandably not known to the Jewish general public. The story endeavours to get over that awkwardness by having the angel strike Zechariah dumb until John is born (for not believing it will happen!). Elizabeth soon conceives, and Luke says she sees it as arranged by God.

The birth of Jesus is predicted

1:26-38: *In the sixth month the angel Gabriel was sent by God to a town in Galilee called Nazareth, to a virgin engaged to a man whose name was Joseph, of the house of David. The virgin's name was Mary. And he came to her and said, "Greetings, favoured one! The Lord is with you." But she was much perplexed by his words and pondered what sort of greeting this might be. The angel said to her, "Do not be afraid, Mary, for you have found favour with God. And now, you will conceive in your womb and bear a son, and you will name him Jesus. He will be great, and will be called the Son of the Most High, and the Lord God will give to him the throne of his ancestor David. He will reign over the house of Jacob forever, and of his kingdom there will be no end." Mary said to the angel, "How can this be, since I am a virgin?" The angel said to her, "The Holy Spirit will come upon you, and the power of the Most High will overshadow you; therefore the child to be born will be holy; he will be called Son of God. And now, your relative Elizabeth in her old age has also conceived a son; and this is the sixth month for her who was said to be barren. For nothing will be impossible with God." Then Mary said, "Here am I, the servant of the Lord; let it be with me according to your word." Then the angel departed from her.*

Here the birth stories of John and Jesus are linked. There are several parallels between John the Baptist and Jesus, but the annunciations are the most obvious. Even so, there are differences in one of them that are more appropriate for the announcement of the birth of the Messiah. Unlike the infancy story in Matthew, where an angel visits Joseph in a dream, in Luke's version the angel Gabriel (known as God's most senior messenger) goes directly to Mary to tell her she will conceive a son by the "*Holy Spirit*". Then follows the proclamation of Jesus as Messiah/Son of God:

"He will be great and will be called the Son of the Most

High, and the Lord God will give to him the throne of his ancestor David."

Not only is Jesus the expected Messiah, he is also divine. The divinity is explained through Gabriel's message:

"The Holy Spirit will come upon you, and the power of the Most High will overshadow you; therefore the child to be born will be holy; he will be called Son of God."

In Jewish tradition 'Son of God' is a messianic title related to David the first Messiah. It does not mean that the person concerned is in his own being 'divine'. He is simply the 'chosen' or Anointed One, divinely appointed to represent God on earth.

However, in the context of the story of the annunciation, the implication from Gabriel's message is that the child will be physically the 'Son of God'. It is important to note here again that the Lucan infancy narratives may well have been written in the late second or third centuries, at a stage when Jesus 'Christ' was beginning to be regarded as both human and divine. Without the influence of those developing ideas, there probably would have been no 'virgin birth' concept in the infancy narratives of Luke and Matthew. Following Gabriel's astonishing message to Mary, he assures Mary that *"nothing will be impossible with God"* by announcing that her elderly (supposedly infertile) relative Elizabeth is now pregnant. Mary decides to visit Elizabeth:

1:39-45: *In those days Mary set out and went with haste to a Judean town in the hill country, where she entered the house of Zechariah and greeted Elizabeth. When Elizabeth heard Mary's greeting, the child leaped in her womb. And Elizabeth was filled with the Holy Spirit and exclaimed with a loud cry, "Blessed are you among women, and blessed is the fruit of your womb. And why has this happened to me, that the mother of my Lord comes to me? For as soon as I heard the sound of your greeting, the child in my womb leaped for joy. And blessed is she who believed that there would be a fulfilment of what was spoken to her by the Lord."*

Mary visits her *"relative"* Elizabeth in a *"Judean town in the hill country"*, possibly meaning the village of *Ein Kerem* near Jerusalem in Judea, where tradition says John the Baptist was born. Elizabeth's unborn child recognizes the child in Mary's womb as his *"Lord"* (meaning Messiah/Son of God) and with that John's destiny as forerunner has already begun. Elizabeth's greeting, *"Blessed are you among women and blessed is the fruit of your womb"*, shows signs of belonging to an established tradition, poetic or hymnic in character. It is clearly the basis for the 'Hail Mary' Roman Catholic prayer tradition, developed after the fourth century.

> 1:46-55: *And Mary said, "My soul magnifies the Lord, and my spirit rejoices in God my Saviour; for he has looked with favour on the lowliness of his servant. Surely, from now on all generations will call me blessed; for the Mighty One has done great things for me, and holy is his name. His mercy is for those who fear him from generation to generation. He has shown strength with his arm; he has scattered the proud in the thoughts of their hearts. He has brought down the powerful from their thrones, and lifted up the lowly; he has filled the hungry with good things, and sent the rich away empty. He has helped his servant Israel, in remembrance of his mercy, according to the promise he made to our ancestors, to Abraham and to his descendants forever."*

The story of Mary's visit is interrupted by the insertion of the canticle known as the *'Magnificat'*. This is another allusion to the story of Samuel where Hannah praises God for rescuing her from her barrenness. The *Magnificat* speaks of the salvation of the humble poor, precisely those to whom the angels will announce Jesus' birth. It expresses belief that Jesus has fulfilled Israel's longing that God will keep the covenant by bringing salvation to the humble poor. However, the awkwardness of its place in the text appears to identify it as a later addition to the birth narrative. The story of Mary's visit then resumes, noting that Mary stayed with Elizabeth for three months before going back to Nazareth.

The birth of John the Baptist

1:67-79: Blessed be the Lord God of Israel, for he has looked favourably on his people and redeemed them. He has raised up a mighty saviour for us in the house of his servant David, as he spoke through the mouth of his holy prophets from of old, that we would be saved from our enemies and from the hand of all who hate us. Thus he has shown the mercy promised to our ancestors, and has remembered his holy covenant, the oath that he swore to our ancestor Abraham, to grant us that we, being rescued from the hands of our enemies, might serve him without fear, in holiness and righteousness before him all our days. And you, child, will be called the prophet of the Most High; for you will go before the Lord to prepare his ways, to give knowledge of salvation to his people by the forgiveness of their sins. By the tender mercy of our God, the dawn from on high will break upon us, to give light to those who sit in darkness and in the shadow of death, to guide our feet into the way of peace.

When John is born Zechariah's voice returns and again the narrative is interrupted as he speaks another canticle, traditionally known as 'The Benedictus'. It first predicts the birth of a "*mighty saviour for us in the house of his servant David*", an obvious reference to Jesus. From verse 76 the focus turns to John, who is to "*go before the Lord to prepare his ways*". This ostensibly refers to Isaiah 9:2, where the reference is to the coming of the LORD: "*The people who walked in darkness have seen a great light; those who lived in a land of deep darkness – on them light has shined*". This is about God coming to reverse the darkness in which the people have lived. As the canticle uses it, "The Lord" (lower case version) refers to Jesus the Messiah. The reference (Isaiah verses 6-7) to a child to be born is to a king in the line of David, who will "*guide our feet into the way of peace*". The canticle does not include that. It is selective of biblical text, to say the least.

Luke later (chapter 4) has Jesus quoting from Isaiah (61:1-2) as evidence for his messiahship. Luke's aim there is to have Jesus allude personally to messianic credentials, even though Isaiah 61 does not refer to a messiah. Isaiah is speaking of himself, and of a spirit of prophecy that God has placed on him. The Hebrew word *Mashiach*, translated as 'anointed' in Isaiah 61:1 and in Luke 4:18, has two meanings. It most often means 'Messiah', but it also means 'appointed'. In the case of the anointing of Saul to be king (1 Samuel 10:1) the meaning is not that Saul is to be the Messiah; he is 'appointed' by God as king. The first Messiah of Israel was David, who succeeded Saul as king.

At 1:80 the birth narrative resumes, where John grows up and lives in the "*wilderness*" until he begins his role as herald of the Messiah, in parallel with Jesus' time in the wilderness before beginning his teaching about the kingdom of God.

The birth of Jesus

2:1-7: *In those days a decree went out from Emperor Augustus that all the world should be registered. This was the first registration and was taken while Quirinius was governor of Syria. All went to their own towns to be registered. Joseph also went from the town of Nazareth in Galilee to Judea, to the city of David called Bethlehem, because he was descended from the house and family of David. He went to be registered with Mary, to whom he was engaged and who was expecting a child. While they were there, the time came for her to deliver her child. And she gave birth to her firstborn son and wrapped him in bands of cloth, and laid him in a manger, because there was no place for them in the inn.*

Unlike Matthew's version, the birth narrative in Luke locates Jesus' parents in Nazareth until shortly before the child is to be born. It says Jesus' birth coincides with a Roman requirement that Jewish males go to the town of their ancestral tribe to be counted. Luke and Matthew both name Joseph as "*of the house and lineage of David*", which necessitates that he and Mary be in Bethlehem, the 'house of David', for Jesus' birth. The sole documented census in the early first century CE was of Judean residents only, but for his messianic agenda the writer of the infancy narrative discounts that. He clearly wants to associate Jesus with "*the house and family of David*". He accomplishes this by having Mary accompany Joseph to Bethlehem so that Jesus is seen to be born there.

It is more likely that Jesus was born in Nazareth, but that would not have suited Luke's (or Matthew's) gospel portrait of Jesus as the fulfilment of messianic hopes. There is good reason to see that the internal proof text here is Micah 5: 2-5a:

> "*But you, O Bethlehem of Ephrathah, who are one of the little clans of Judah, from you shall come forth for me one who is to rule in Israel, whose origin is from of old, from ancient days. Therefore he shall give them up until the time when she who is in labour has brought forth; then the rest of his kindred shall return to the people of Israel.*"

There we can see the longing of the writer of the birth story that all Jews inside or outside of Palestine will accept Jesus as Messiah. There is no direct indication in the narrative of Mary's own lineage, especially because it was male ancestral lines that were regarded as significant.

However, a look back to 1:5 tells us that Mary's ancestry includes Aaron, the first High Priest. The link is Elizabeth, who is Mary's "*relative*" (1:36) and is described as "*a descendant of Aaron*". By adding this detail the writer wants his readers to note that Jesus fills the profile of both Messiahs in Jewish tradition. These are clearly represented in the Dead Sea Scrolls as the 'kingly' (Davidic) and the 'priestly' (Aaronic) Messiahs. This tradition is stated plainly in the *Damascus Document* (Scroll CD 12.23-13.1): ... *during the time of ungodliness until the appearance of the Messiahs of Aaron and Israel.* The two messiahs are also expressed as one man (Scroll CD 14.18-19):

This is the exact statement of the ordinances in which they walk until the Messiah of Aaron and Israel appears and expiates their iniquity. The *Damascus Document* is likely to have been written around 150 BCE.

Another scroll (*Manual of Discipline*) adds the figure of a prophet: *They shall not depart from any counsel of the law ... until the coming of the prophet and the anointed ones of Aaron and Israel (Manual of Discipline 9.9b-11).* In Mark, Matthew and Luke, the 'prophet' is represented by John the Baptist/Elijah. The kind of messianic longing expressed in the infancy narratives of Luke is not dissimilar to that found in the Dead Sea Scrolls.

The narrative then involves some shepherds;

2:8-14: *In that region there were shepherds living in the fields, keeping watch over their flock by night. Then an angel of the Lord stood before them, and the glory of the Lord shone around them, and they were terrified. But the angel said to them, "Do not be afraid; for see – I am bringing you good news of great joy for all the people: to you is born this day in the city of David a Saviour, who is the Messiah, the Lord. This will be a sign for you: you will find a child wrapped in bands of cloth and lying in a manger." And suddenly there was with the angel a multitude of the heavenly host, praising God and saying, "Glory to God in the highest heaven, and on earth peace among those whom he favours!"*

In the story of Jesus' birth, the writer is setting out a complex scenario appropriate for the birth of the Messiah. He holds nothing back. The birth of the Messiah is announced in loudest and clearest terms: *"to you is born this day in the city of David a Saviour, who is the Messiah, the Lord."* The reader already knows that this Messiah is born of *"the Holy Spirit"* (1:35), and is the *"Son of God"* (1:35). He is also to bring peace to the earth. It is important to remember that the gospels are not only portraits of the Messiah in a theological sense; they are profoundly political. As in the first verse of the Gospel of Mark, the writer of Luke's infancy narrative can reasonably be seen here as trying to 'top' the designation given to the Roman Emperor at the time (Caesar Octavian/Augustus) who was known as the founder of the 'Pax Romana'. The *"good news"* announced regarding Augustus included his being sent as *"saviour, both for us and for our descendants, that he might end war and arrange all things".*[108] In Luke, God (through the angels) is announcing that it is Jesus who will bring peace to the earth. As Raymond Brown expresses it:

> *It can scarcely be accidental that Luke's description of the birth of Jesus presents an implicit challenge to this imperial propaganda, not by denying the imperial ideals, but by claiming that the real peace of the world would be brought about by Jesus.*[109]

Of significance for non-Lucan authorship of the infancy stories is the fact that after chapter 2 there is no further mention of the 'virgin birth' (as is also the case in Matthew's gospel). Herod (the Great) is mentioned in a purely neutral sense as the ruler of Judea. He is not portrayed as the murderer of Jewish children as per Matthew chapter 2. If the writer of the Gospel of Luke had read the full text of Matthew's gospel (and not just from chapter 3 forward) he made no attempt to refer to the Herodian massacre of children, or to 'correct it'. Nor does his story include an 'escape to Egypt'. The explanation may be that even if Luke had a copy of Matthew to hand in the early second century, as seems very likely, it may not at that stage have included the infancy narratives.

The presentation in the Temple

> 2:29-32: *Master, now you are dismissing your servant in peace, according to your word; for my eyes have seen your salvation, which you have prepared in the presence of all peoples, a light for revelation to the Gentiles and for glory to your people Israel.*

As if the foregoing infancy narrative were not enough to persuade the reader of Jesus' messianic qualifications, the writer adds two vignettes where Mary and Joseph take Jesus to the Temple for his circumcision and presentation to God. First we meet Simeon, a *"righteous and devout"* man waiting for the Messiah. Simeon recites another canticle (the *Nunc Dimittis*), this one reliant on Isaiah (42:6; 49:6; 52:10). Here we see a not-so-subtle hint that this narrative is addressed to Gentiles, as well as to Jews. Simeon's canticle is plainly addressed to both groups. Mary and Joseph are amazed at this, as well they might be, having just had Jesus circumcised as a son of Abraham.

Luke's Simeon character has been identified by Jewish and Christian scholars as a Pharisee, Rabbi Shimon ben Hillel, in other words, the son of the famous Rabbi Hillel, head of the House of Hillel. Other scholars counter that there is no reference in the oral law (before 70CE) of any sayings from Rabbi Shimon ben Hillel. However, the German scholar Wilhelm Bacher has an answer for that. He argues that before the destruction of the Temple in 70, individual rabbis were not quoted in the oral law (which was written down as the *Mishnah*[110] in the 2nd century CE) by name, only by the 'Houses' to which they belonged. Simeon would have belonged to the House of Hillel, so any of his sayings would have been subsumed under that heading.[111] In any case, identification of Simeon as the son of Hillel would mean that this is a very high-ranking Pharisee who regards Jesus as the Messiah. That is obviously a highly significant claim from the writer of the infancy narrative.

After Simeon a prophet appears. Unusually, the prophet is a woman, called Anna. Yet Anna's gender is not as important as the implication of blessings given to Jesus by these three: Zechariah the priest (the Temple), Simeon the Rabbi (the Law) and Anna the prophetess (the Prophets). In the infancy narrative all of them affirm belief in Jesus as the Messiah.

Jesus at twelve years of age

The story about Jesus in the Temple at twelve years of age (Bar Mitzvah age) is the writer's statement that Jesus knew from an early age he was destined to become a prophet and teacher of the

Law of Moses – and the Messiah! There is no necessity to regard
the story as fact, but there is good reason to believe that Jesus
must have spent a good deal of time studying the Law and
Prophets. His most likely teachers would have been Pharisees,
and his liberal interpretation of the Law of Moses carries echoes
of the teachings of the liberal teacher Hillel, who was living at the
time of Jesus. The Pharisees operated not only in the Jerusalem
Temple; they also taught in synagogues in Judea and Galilee.

Regardless of who wrote it, the Temple story adds weight
to Luke's apparent intention to present Jesus as learned in
scripture and (as per the narrative in Chapter 4 about the
synagogue at Nazareth) as literate. That may indicate that Luke
wanted to present a literate Messiah to educated Jews, but given
the depth of Jesus' scriptural knowledge, I think it is more likely
than not that he was able to read the scripture.

The Proclamation of John the Baptist

3: 1-6: *In the fifteenth year of the reign of Emperor
Tiberius, when Pontius Pilate was governor of Judea,
and Herod was ruler of Galilee, and his brother Philip
ruler of the region of Ituraea and Trachonitis, and
Lysanias ruler of Abilene, during the high priesthood of
Annas and Caiaphas, the word of God came to John son
of Zechariah in the wilderness. He went into all the region
around the Jordan, proclaiming a baptism of repentance
for the forgiveness of sins, as it is written in the book of
the words of the prophet Isaiah, "The voice of one crying
out in the wilderness: 'Prepare the way of the Lord, make
his paths straight. Every valley shall be filled, and every
mountain and hill shall be made low, and the crooked
shall be made straight, and the rough ways made
smooth; and all flesh shall see the salvation of God.*

From this point on we are more likely to be reading the
work of the gospel writer who calls himself Luke. Like Mark's
and Matthew's, Luke's gospel from chapter 3 forward contains
no reference to the birth narratives, supporting the likelihood
that they did not form part of the original gospel. As we will see,

chapter 3 contains the Lucan genealogy. It was surely more likely to have been placed in chapter 1 if that had been the original first chapter of Luke's gospel. (Matthew's genealogy forms the first part of the birth narrative itself).

Luke introduces John the Baptist as *"John son of Zechariah"*, giving the impression that the birth narratives were part of the original gospel. It may equally indicate that the text of Luke was altered to include "son of Zechariah" to create continuity with the added chapters 1 and 2. The fact is we simply do not know what the original Gospel of Luke contained. A very important point is that contrary to Mark and Matthew, Luke does nothing here to link John the Baptist with the folk tradition of the returning Elijah. There is no description of John's clothes and desert diet. In fact, as we will see, Luke strongly repudiates the linking of allusions to the Elijah tradition with either John the Baptist or with his portrait of Jesus. Given Luke's more universal, Gentile-oriented potential audience, he appears not to want to associate Jesus as Messiah with a tradition understood to be solely about the restoration of Israel.

If we are correct in locating Luke in the Jewish/Gentile Diaspora outside Palestine, then the preoccupations and needs of his audience would differ markedly from those of the oppressed and sometimes violently suppressed people of the Galilee region. From the time of the Greek conquest in 312 BCE, one of the preferred methods of dealing with devastation caused by conquerors of Palestine was simple avoidance. The more affluent Jews moved to neighbouring territories, among them Syria and Egypt. The result was that Jewish migrants to the Diaspora eventually incorporated an entirely different set of cosmopolitan political, ideological, cultural and social dynamics into their formulation of theology. Jewish children were educated in the Greek system, which eventually necessitated the Greek translation of the Hebrew scriptures (called the Septuagint) in Egypt during the fourth century BCE. It is to such hellenized Jewish people that Luke's gospel looks likely to have been addressed, along with Gentiles in those areas. We ought also to note that contrary to common Jewish attitudes, Luke wants to claim Jesus' openness toward the Samaritans.[112]

For Luke, the problem with the Elijah tradition among the ordinary people in the Galilee region included the fact that, according to the Jewish historian Josephus, Elijah was regarded as a 'zealot'. Originally that simply meant that Elijah was known as having 'zeal' for the Torah. A problem for association with the Elijah tradition arose when Zealots for the Torah were often identified with and associated with the Sicarii, meaning those who wielded daggers and promoted a violent revolt against Rome. Elijah therefore was associated with people whose zeal for their endangered Jewish traditions, plus the fact of their Roman-imposed hardship, meant the prophet was regarded as the folk hero of popular rebellions. Elijah was inspiration for messiah/kings such as Menachem of Galilee, who (prior to the Jewish War against the Romans) set fire to records of debt which were stored in the Temple and Royal Palace. He was hoping to bring about the Jubilee, in which all debts are cancelled and the original kingdom of the twelve tribes is restored under the authority of God.

Given that background, when Jesus appeared and set about 'cleansing' the Temple of corrupt money managers, he was readily identified by many people with the tradition of the returned Elijah. For that reason all synoptic gospels include 'question and answer' scenarios regarding Jesus' identity. Luke's is no exception:

> 9:18-20: *"... Who do the crowds say that I am?" They answered, "John the Baptist; but others, Elijah; and still others, that one of the ancient prophets has arisen." He said to them, "But who do you say that I am?" Peter answered, "The Messiah of God."*

Like Mark and Matthew, Luke wants to lead his readers away from the Jesus-Elijah typology. His aim is to develop his own portrait of Jesus the Messiah as the new (and better) Moses.

We have noted that Matthew also had that intention, but his purpose was to convince Pharisees that Jesus was adhering to the Mosaic Law. For his part, Luke knew that Jews in the Diaspora had a new understanding of Moses through the writings of the hellenized Jewish writer/philosopher Philo of Alexandria. Philo re-interpreted Torah according to hellenistic philosophical principles. He presented Moses as an enlightened philosopher whose Torah/Law could be seen as the basis for philosophical virtues lauded in the Greek-speaking world. Through Philo's writings Moses came to be known as the *Logos*. Moses became the intermediary through whom the divine pre-existent Torah of the transcendent, immutable God of Greek thought was made known to humanity. Moses was regarded by hellenized Jews as personification of Torah, or the 'Word' made flesh. No prizes for guessing who copied that![113] I will say more about the *Logos* in the chapter on the Gospel of John.

The Genealogy of Luke

3:23-38: *Jesus was about thirty years old when he began his work. He was the son (as was thought) of Joseph son of Heli, son of Matthat, son of Levi, son of Melchi, son of Jannai, son of Joseph, son of Mattathias, son of Amos, son of Nahum, son of Esli, son of Naggai, son of Maath, son of Mattathias, son of Semein, son of Josech, son of Joda, son of Joanan, son of Rhesa, son of Zerubbabel, son of Shealtiel, son of Neri, son of Melchi, son of Addi, son of Cosam, son of Elmadam, son of Er, son of Joshua, son of Eliezer, son of Jorim, son of Matthat, son of Levi, son of Simeon, son of Judah, son of Joseph, son of Jonam, son of Eliakim, son of Melea, son of Menna, son of Mattatha, son of Nathan, son of David, son of Jesse, son of Obed, son of Boaz, son of Sala, son of Nahshon, son of Amminadab, son of Admin, son of Arni, son of Hezron, son of Perez, son of Judah, son of Jacob, son of Isaac, son of Abraham, son of Terah, son of Nahor, son of Serug, son of Reu, son of Peleg, son of Eber, son of Shelah, son of Cainan, son of Arphaxad, son of Shem, son of Noah, son of Lamech, son of Methuselah, son of Enoch, son of Jared, son of Mahalaleel, son of Cainan, son of Enos, son of Seth, son of Adam, son of God.*

I make no apology for including this long list of (male)

names; it has great significance for Luke's purpose in writing his gospel. Through his genealogy of Jesus, he widens the scope for Jesus' messianic activity and influence on the affairs of all humanity. Luke does not start Jesus' genealogy from the founders of the nation of Israel as per the Matthean genealogy. Instead, he includes all of humankind by beginning with Jesus and ascending through the patriarchs of Israel to Adam the first man, and finally, to God. Like Matthew's, Luke's genealogy has Jesus descended directly from King David, the first Messiah. This is not 'proof' that Jesus was in fact descended from David, but Luke's genealogy agrees with Matthew's insistence that Jesus fits the traditional expectation of the Messiah as Davidic.

So why deny Jesus was 'son of David'?
In spite of the gospel genealogies, something curious has been inserted into Mark, Matthew and Luke to try to deny that Jesus was 'Son of David'. That insertion is as follows:

- Luke 20:41-44: *"Then he [Jesus] said to them, "How can they say that the Messiah is David's son? For David himself says in the book of Psalms, 'The Lord said to my Lord, "Sit at my right hand, until I make your enemies your footstool." ' David thus calls him Lord; so how can he be his son?"*

- The quotation included there is from Psalm 110:1. This is the NRSV's version, translated into English from Hebrew:

  The LORD says to my lord, "Sit at my right hand until I make your enemies your footstool."

All three synoptic gospels include this curious exchange regarding the title Son of David and Psalm 110. As I often point out, the gospel writers used the Hebrew Scriptures for authority to name Jesus as Messiah. In many instances they simply wrote the story of Jesus' life, death and resurrection from the existing 'script' they found in the Hebrew Scriptures, albeit from the version translated into Greek. Keeping in mind that the gospel writers used the Greek version of the Hebrew Scriptures is crucial for understanding their use of the text. Translations of any sort inevitably become interpretations. Translation as interpretation according to the translator's world view or theology can be very obvious; sometimes it is more subtle. So it is with the gospel writers' use of Psalm 110.

In Mark's Gospel first, then followed by Matthew and Luke, we find that quotation from Psalm 110, in the Greek version of the Hebrew Scriptures (the Septuagint). In all three synoptic gospels this looks very much like an editorial insertion into a series of exchanges between Jesus and Pharisees. The issue is Jesus' puzzling denial that the Messiah is descended from the first Messiah, David. Given that Mark, Matthew and Luke all claim that Jesus is descended from David, what purpose could be served by including this interchange that denies it? This is possibly the work of the same editor(s) who inserted the infancy narratives into Matthew and Luke. Working at a time (possibly up to the fourth century CE) when it was important to separate later claims about the messiahship of Jesus from traditional messianic expectations in mainstream Judaism, the editorial aim is to present Jesus himself denying being 'Son of David'.

To muddy the waters further, even if the work of an editor is the answer to this puzzling exchange, Psalm 110 itself contains a challenge. It is not the body of the Psalm that causes the problem; it is the superscription. In the Greek version and in English, that is rendered (in the NRSV) as: "*Of David. A Psalm*". Yet it is not as clear as that; there is ambiguity in the Hebrew word translated into English as 'of'. In Hebrew the word is composed simply of the letter L (*Lamed*) pointed underneath with two dots arranged vertically – called a *Shewa*. When this functions as a prefix (i.e. placed directly before another word such as the name David), it then becomes *l'david*, which *can* mean '*of* David'. The important point here is that it can also mean '*for* David' (or even '*to* David'). Given that, the superscription to Psalm 110 may just as legitimately read 'For David. A Psalm'. This is not linguistic nit-picking; there is something crucial embedded in the translation of *l'david*.

Before we identify that crucial element, we need to look at the English rendering of Psalm 110:1 in the Hebrew Scriptures/Old Testament. Here the word 'Lord' occurs twice: *"The LORD said to my lord"*. The first instance of the word is capitalized to indicate that this is the name for God; the second is in lowercase, indicating a human being, albeit a very important one. Even so, the reader in English does not know that the original Hebrew version has two different words that have both been translated into English as 'Lord'.

- The first Hebrew word is the word for God which occurs frequently in the Hebrew Scriptures as the so-called *tetragrammaton*, which is four Hebrew consonants with no vowels. The aim is that this word is unpronounceable, so that no one can say the name of God. Translated into English as LORD, it means 'God'.
- The second word, translated as 'lord', does not mean a divine personage, i.e., the Messiah, as per the early Christian interpretation of this psalm. It is actually a translation of the Hebrew word *Adonai*, which is the usual word for a human being who has some high or honourable standing among other human beings. Correctly, it ought to have been translated in Luke 20 as 'lord' with a lower case 'l', as in the English version of Psalm 110. If it had been translated with the lower case 'l', it would have been clearer that 'lord' in Psalm 110 refers not to a divine personage (such as God or a Messiah understood as divine) but to King David.[114]

A further difficulty arises in the New Testament, in which Psalm 110 is quoted from the Greek version of the Hebrew Scriptures. There the Greek sentence in question contains two instances of the word translated as 'Lord' in English. The first is '*Kurios to*' (The Lord), referring to God, and then '*Kurion mou*' (my Lord). This Greek word *Kurios* can mean either 'God' or a person of property or importance, such as a king, depending on the context in which it is used.

In several instances in the New Testament the gospel

writers use *Kurios* (translated into English as 'Lord') to refer to Jesus. By that they imply that Jesus is the Messiah. It is because of that use of *Kurios* for Jesus that Greek-speaking readers of the gospels were likely to read *Kurion mou* (my Lord) in the quote from the Greek version of Psalm 110 as referring to Jesus the Messiah. The editor who inserted this exchange about Psalm 110 knew that very well; in fact he relied on it.

Importantly for his contrived conversation between Jesus and the Pharisees concerning the psalm, there was in those days an unchallenged belief that all psalms were written by David. This view has long been discredited by biblical scholarship.[115] The problem of the Greek word Kurios quoted in the gospels is perpetuated in English versions, where "*the Lord*" (with capital L) as title for Jesus is more often than not read as carrying an exalted or even divine connotation. With that intended meaning, Luke uses "*the Lord*" nine times, to refer to Jesus.

In the hope that my reader is still with me, here is a summary of all this. By altering the superscription to: "*For David. A Psalm*", the psalm then speaks with a different 'voice'. It is no longer David who speaks, but the person who has written a psalm *for* David (or about David or to David). That person addresses David by saying, "*The LORD* (meaning God) *says to my lord* (meaning David), '*sit at my right hand until I make your enemies your footstool.*' " The psalm then continues with the voice of the writer addressing David: "*The Lord* (God) *sends out from Zion your mighty sceptre*", etc. The psalm maintains the writer's address to David until its end.

When the superscription is given that small but crucial different translation, all possibilities of using the psalm for messianic purposes disappear, including using it to deny that Jesus was the Davidic Messiah. The New Testament usage of Psalm 110 enabled it to be a 'proof text' that Jesus was the Messiah/Son of God ('Lord'), but not the Davidic Messiah. After all, the denial that he was Son of David came from Jesus' own mouth – didn't it? The editors knew that most readers would be convinced by that.

Yet surely people who knew about Jesus' family would have disputed anyone calling him Son of David, if in fact his family line was not from David. This would have applied even decades after he died, at the time(s) the gospels were written. It adds more weight to the argument that the editor who added the Psalm 110 interchange was working perhaps centuries after Jesus died. Regarding the virgin birth, the problem with describing Jesus as son of Joseph (who is said to have been descended from David) is dealt with in the genealogy, 3:23: *"Jesus ... was the son (as was thought) of Joseph son of Heli"*. That clearly casts doubt on the idea that Jesus was Son of David.

The words in parenthesis in the genealogy may therefore represent the work of the same editor who added the infancy narratives to the beginning of Luke and who wanted to create consistency in Luke's genealogy with the claim of Jesus' 'virgin birth'. Where there is inconsistency in the gospels, it is reasonable to look for the hallmarks of a later editor. Scholars regard this kind of editorial interference with the New Testament text as far from unusual, particularly when it looks likely to have come from a later (perhaps even third century) period, when the codifying of Christian theology was beginning to take place.[116]

Finally, I want to reiterate how crucial is the fact that the gospel writers used the Greek version of the Hebrew scriptures. The Greek version holds much more potential for a messianic interpretation than the original Hebrew.

- Verse 3 of Psalm 110 as translated into English from the Greek translation of the Hebrew text is an excellent case in point:
  With thee is dominion in the day of thy power, in the splendours of thy saints; I have begotten thee from the womb before the morning.
- Whereas from the Hebrew, it translates as:
  Your people will offer themselves willingly on the day you lead your forces on the holy mountains. From the womb of the morning, like dew, your youth will come to you.

The Baptism and Temptations of Jesus

3:21-22: *Now when all the people were baptized, and when Jesus also had been baptized and was praying, the heaven was opened, and the Holy Spirit descended upon him in bodily form like a dove. And a voice came from heaven, "You are my Son, the Beloved; with you I am well pleased."*

The curious aspect of the baptism of Jesus in Luke is that the text does not actually say it was John the Baptist who baptized him. It is only after Luke tells us that John has been imprisoned by Herod that an almost matter-of-fact reference to Jesus' baptism occurs: *"Now when all the people were baptized and when Jesus also had been baptized ..."* Again, Luke looks uneasy about linking his understanding of Jesus as the Messiah for all nations to the Elijah/restoration-of-Israel prophetic identity of John the Baptist. Accordingly, here John the Baptist does not actually identify Jesus as Messiah. The identification and anointing of Jesus as Messiah comes through the voice of God following his baptism: *"You are my Son, the Beloved; with you I am well pleased."*

4:1-13: *Jesus, full of the Holy Spirit, returned from the Jordan and was led by the Spirit in the wilderness, where for forty days he was tempted by the devil. He ate nothing at all during those days, and when they were over, he was famished. The devil said to him, "If you are the Son of God, command this stone to become a loaf of bread." Jesus answered him, "It is written, 'One does not live by bread alone.'" Then the devil led him up and showed him in an instant all the kingdoms of the world. And the devil said to him, "To you I will give their glory and all this authority; for it has been given over to me, and I give it to anyone I please. If you, then, will worship me, it will all be yours." Jesus answered him, "It is written, 'Worship the Lord your God, and serve only him.'" Then the devil took him to Jerusalem, and placed him on the pinnacle of the temple, saying to him, "If you are the Son of God, throw yourself down from here, for it is written, 'He will command his angels concerning you, to protect you,' and 'On their hands they will bear you up, so that you will not dash your foot against a stone.' " Jesus answered him, "It is said, 'Do not put the Lord your God to the test.' " When the devil had finished every test, he departed from him until an opportune time.*

The idea of Jesus returning from the Jordan to the wilderness echoes the instruction of the "*word of the LORD*", or "*Spirit*" of the LORD, to Elijah, when he was directed to turn east away from the Jordan and toward the Wadi Cherith (1 Kings 17:2f). Elijah's experience here is more compatible with Mark's rendering with than Luke's. Mark's short reference to this Elijah-like activity of Jesus in the wilderness is likely to reflect an oral tradition about Jesus going into seclusion before he began his public proclamation of the kingdom of God on earth. That is congruent with other gospel instances where Jesus went into the wilderness to commune with God. We know nothing of Jesus before his public ministry, but he was probably already inclined to spend long periods in meditation and prayer, during his growing up and earlier adulthood. Given the knowledge of human nature that lies behind his teaching, particularly in the Sermon on the Mount, he must first of all have taken the time to develop deep awareness of his own nature.

Luke's temptations story shows every sign of having been lifted from the Gospel of Matthew, albeit with important modifications. Matthew (copied by Luke) expanded on the tiny Elijah-influenced Gospel of Mark reference to Jesus being tempted in the wilderness. The extended story presents an identification of the Messiah by means of a dialogue between the supernatural 'tester' (Satan) and the messianic Son of God. It is based on texts from Deuteronomy about Moses. It features Jesus overcoming in superior fashion the temptations that were placed before Moses in those texts.

In contrast with Mark's Elijah-based portrait of Jesus in the wilderness, in Matthew and Luke Jesus is clearly associated with Moses. Mark's story has Jesus being fed by angels, as was

Elijah. In Matthew and Luke Jesus fasted, as did Moses on Mount Sinai (Deut. 9:9). This is possibly intended to overcome the problem that 'forty days and forty nights in the wilderness' applies equally to Elijah. Matthew and Luke intend to present Jesus not as Elijah, but as the Messiah who is the 'new Moses'. This subverting of the Elijah tradition that the common people associated with Jesus is dealt with in similar fashion throughout Luke's gospel. We will come across it frequently.

It is no coincidence that the first temptation is for Jesus to turn stones into bread. In 1 Kings 19:6 Elijah is miraculously provided with bread baked on hot stones. Its divine origin is attested by the fact that it is served to Elijah by an angel. But Jesus turns away from Elijah's bread and steadfastly continues to fast, as did Moses.

The second temptation is based on Moses' experience viewing the Promised Land from Mt Pisgah (Deut. 34: 1-3). He is tempted to go into the land and conquer it, but obeys the command of God. Yet the idea of a mountain-top experience involving Jesus' personal spiritual struggle is much more similar to Elijah's 'dark night of the soul' experience on Mount Horeb, than to Moses' experience on Pisgah. Moses' story comes to an end on Pisgah, but after their forty-day fast and testing on the 'mountain-top', Elijah and Jesus both come down from the mountain with a firm understanding of how they are to carry out God's mission in the world. Luke's attempts to subvert the Elijah traditions about Jesus are only partially successful here.

The subject of the third temptation is the enticement to rely on the working of miracles. The biblical Elijah is depicted as inclined to perform miracles to persuade the people that his word was from God. Luke takes care to dissociate the magical practices and easy popularity of figures such as the Samaritan magician Simon Magus (Acts 8:9-24) from the mission and healing miracles of the 'true Messiah'. He also repudiates the spectacular miracles in the Elijah tradition such as 'fire from heaven' (that burned the bullocks), by means of Jesus' reply to Satan's third temptation. His reply puts the story back in touch with the Moses tradition related to Massah: *"It is said, 'Do not put the Lord your God to the test'."* (Deut. 6:16).

The Synagogue at Nazareth

4: 16-30: When he came to Nazareth, where he had been brought up, he went to the synagogue on the Sabbath day, as was his custom. He stood up to read, and the scroll of the prophet Isaiah was given to him. He unrolled the scroll and found the place where it was written: "The Spirit of the Lord is upon me, because he has anointed me to bring good news to the poor. He has sent me to proclaim release to the captives and recovery of sight to the blind, to let the oppressed go free, to proclaim the year of the Lord's favour." And he rolled up the scroll, gave it back to the attendant, and sat down. The eyes of all in the synagogue were fixed on him. Then he began to say to them, "Today this scripture has been fulfilled in your hearing." All spoke well of him and were amazed at the gracious words that came from his mouth. They said, "Is not this Joseph's son?" He said to them, "Doubtless you will quote to me this proverb, 'Doctor, cure yourself!' And you will say, 'Do here also in your hometown the things that we have heard you did at Capernaum.' " And he said, "Truly I tell you, no prophet is accepted in the prophet's hometown. But the truth is, there were many widows in Israel in the time of Elijah, when the heaven was shut up three years and six months, and there was a severe famine over all the land; yet Elijah was sent to none of them except to a widow at Zarephath in Sidon. There were also many lepers in Israel in the time of the prophet Elisha, and none of them was cleansed except Naaman the Syrian." When they heard this, all in the synagogue were filled with rage. They got up, drove him out of the town, and led him to the brow of the hill on which their town was built, so that they might hurl him off the cliff. But he passed through the midst of them and went on his way.

Here Luke actually uses Elijah motifs, but for two distinct purposes. The first is his intention to make his gospel inclusive of Gentiles. For that reason Luke writes a story in the setting of the Nazareth synagogue. Given Nazareth's smallness and poverty, the 'synagogue' was most likely an open-air space in the middle of the village, rather than a dedicated building. Nazareth is situated in the northern area of Palestine (Galilee), the region from which folk traditions about the return of Elijah for the restoration of Israel originated. Luke's Jesus is plainly inclusive of Gentiles, which probably places this gospel in the context of an intra-Christ-movement debate about a mission to Gentiles. Although the Gospel of Luke is directed primarily toward Gentiles and Hellenistic Jews, it appears here to be attempting to persuade 'Hebrews' (Palestinian Jews including Galileans) who see Jesus as Messiah about the rightness of a mission to the Gentiles.

I remind my reader here that like the other canonical gospel writers, Luke is not writing a historical record of events involving Jesus, or a biography of Jesus; he is making his case for Jesus as Messiah. Luke possibly wrote his gospel as late as the early second century, at a time when Gentile involvement in the Christ movement was well developed outside the land of Palestine. He has turned his attention and his gospel to the task of trying to convince Palestinian Jews that Gentiles are to be a part of the proclamation of the Messiah. To that end, in the Nazareth synagogue story he uses Elijah's encounters with Gentiles to devastating effect. He is addressing people at the end of the first century who still link an End-time arrival of the kingdom of God with the return of Elijah. Through his story he claims that Gentiles are more able to recognize Jesus as the expected (Moses-like) prophet/Messiah than were people from his own home village.

In order that Jesus himself can make a claim to be Messiah, Luke gives him the role of reader from scripture in the synagogue.[117] As we have already noted, the 'anointing' in Isaiah 61:1-2 is that of the prophet Isaiah, not of a Messiah. Nonetheless Luke uses it to claim a divine anointing of Jesus, following the description of Jesus' Moses-based messianic credentials in the 'temptations'. Conspicuous by its absence in the Isaiah quotation in Luke is the reference to the "*day of vengeance of our God*" (Isaiah 61:2). By that omission Luke dissociates Jesus from any violent, revolutionary approach to the coming of the kingdom of God. As we have noted, the insurrectionist rebels regarded Elijah as their hero.

Luke's second purpose in creating the story of the Nazareth synagogue is to turn traditions about Elijah on their head. He intends to illustrate for his readers how even Elijah, the prophet to Israel, was inclusive of Gentiles. This was an attitude very much against the grain for mainstream Palestinian Jews. At first the Nazarethites were pleased with the home town boy as he read and interpreted Isaiah 61, even when he said *"Today this scripture has been fulfilled in your hearing"*. This was the kind of prophetic scriptural promise toward which they looked longingly in their downtrodden existence under Roman/Herodian rule. For them the *"release for the captives"* would probably have included the release of their own people in prison for the non-payment of Roman/Herodian taxes. Jesus was on their wave-length and they *"spoke well of him"*.

Then their initial amazement and incredulity that Jesus could speak in this way (*"Is not this Joseph's son?"*) changed. Their subsequent hostility may well have a historical background. It may illustrate a known fact passed on orally that Jesus' own family and other Nazarethites found it hard to accept what was being said about him in his own time – that he was the prophet of the End-time. The End-time or *'Day of the LORD'* was the expected event when God would liberate the people from the Romans and restore divine-human relationship through a renewed covenant. On that day the kingdom of God would be established on earth. My reader will note that nowhere in the quote from Isaiah does this traditional prophetic expectation include the coming of a Messiah. That was a post-crucifixion understanding that developed following news of a 'resurrection' of Jesus. In accordance with that later understanding, Luke's Jesus claims to be 'anointed' as Messiah as he reads the Isaian text.

Luke's written sources for the Nazarethites' hesitation to see Jesus as Messiah are most likely to have been Mark 6:1-6 (where the people merely took offence) and Matthew 13:53-58, (where they were *"astounded"* at Jesus). Even this is in clear contrast with Luke's version, where they were *"filled with (murderous) rage"*. The reason is *not* that after finishing the passage from Isaiah, Jesus says, *"Today this scripture has been fulfilled in your hearing."* They actually *"spoke well of him"* at that point. The hostility arises when Jesus in effect tells them they are not capable of recognizing a prophet when they are looking at him. He supposes they will expect him to perform miracles to prove he is a prophet, and then says, *"No prophet is accepted in the prophet's hometown"*. Luke is indicating here that Jesus' own people did not even recognize him as a prophet, let alone as the Messiah.

Jesus then fulfils Luke's second purpose in telling the story of the Nazareth synagogue. He points out to the citizens of Nazareth how their prophet hero Elijah had performed miracles – with Gentiles! He had not gone to help Israelites during a severe famine, but had gone only to a Gentile widow and to Gentile lepers. Significantly, in contrast with the Israelites, the Gentiles had recognized Elijah as a prophet. The implication and accusation is that while Gentiles did recognize Jesus as divinely anointed prophet/Messiah, the Nazarethites did not. The story is obviously addressed to readers of Luke's gospel at a time when Gentiles had joined the Christ movement. Luke is telling his Gentile readers that like Elijah's miracles, Jesus' teaching is addressed to them also. He is also addressing Galileans who refuse to believe Jesus is the Messiah.

The only kind of miracle Luke has Jesus performing at Nazareth (in accordance with his rejection of the miracle-working temptation in the wilderness) is that when he was in danger of being thrown from a high place by the Nazarethites, he merely *"passed through the midst of them"*. My reader will also note that Jesus' healings and exorcisms as performed in Luke's Gospel are described as deeds of authority, or deeds of power, not as miracles. The problem for Luke is that miracles were traditionally associated with prophets such as Elijah, not with the Messiah.

This story depicts Jesus claiming to be fulfilment of the End-time (or Day of the LORD) announcement in Isaiah 61. There is no Elijah content in the scripture featured in this story, but Luke uses both the prophet Isaiah and the Galilean Elijah tradition to include Gentiles in his proclamation of Jesus as Messiah and to address non-believing Palestinian Jews.

John the Baptist's Question

> 7:18-28: *The disciples of John reported all these things to him. So John summoned two of his disciples and sent them to the Lord to ask, "Are you the one who is to come, or are we to wait for another?" When the men had come to him, they said, "John the Baptist has sent us to you to ask, 'Are you the one who is to come, or are we to wait for another?' " Jesus had just then cured many people of diseases, plagues, and evil spirits, and had given sight to many who were blind. And he answered them, "Go and tell John what you have seen and heard: the blind receive their sight, the lame walk, the lepers are cleansed, the deaf hear, the dead are raised, the poor have good news brought to them. And blessed is anyone who takes no offense at me."*

As I have noted, in contrast with the writer(s) of the infancy narrative, Luke the gospel writer wants to dissociate Jesus from John the Baptist's ministry, which is an Elijah-type call for the redemption of Israel alone. Because of that we find the otherwise odd question conveyed to Jesus by John's disciples: *"Are you the one who is to come, or are we to wait for another?"* When Luke depicts Jesus raising a widow's son from the dead at a town called Nain (7:11-17) as did Elijah at Zarephath (1Kings 17:17-24), the readers of his gospel naturally see Jesus as a prophet like Elijah. Luke corrects this Elijian understanding of Jesus by using a question from John the Baptist to state the terms in which he (Luke) sees Jesus as Messiah.

Significantly, in Luke John the Baptist is locked up in prison from before the time of Jesus' baptism. This tells us that contrary to the birth narrative, Luke himself does not see Jesus and John engaged in any herald/Messiah (or cousin/cousin) relationship. In support of that, John's question of Jesus merely indicates that he has heard about Jesus; not that he has already formed the opinion that Jesus is the Messiah. Even if John had understood himself as the Elijian herald of the End-time, that does not mean he knew the identity of a Messiah ahead of time, let alone from before his and Jesus' own births: (*"For as soon as I heard the sound of your greeting, the child in my womb leaped for joy."* 1:44). The story of Mary's visit to Elizabeth is part of the infancy narrative's christological myth, possibly interpolated from as late as the 4th century CE.

It helps an understanding of all this to remember that messianic identity was probably attributed to Jesus only following his death and 'appearances' to his followers. Jesus' original followers in Galilee most probably saw him as the Elijah-like prophetic figure who would lead Israel to its restoration as people of God in the kingdom of God/heaven on earth. The expectations of Jesus' original followers would probably have been similar to the description of the eschatological prophet (in contradistinction with a Messiah figure) as set out by David Aune:

> *Eschatological prophets ... were expected to play a more thoroughly religious role through such activities as the preaching of repentance in preparation for the Day of Yahweh, the definitive interpretation of Torah, intercession with Yahweh on behalf of Israel, and the performance of miracles as a display of supernatural power and authority.*[118]

That could have been Jesus' understanding of himself, but it should be remembered that none of these expectations necessarily represent Jesus' self-identity. There is little doubt that he was a preacher of repentance as preparation for the coming of the kingdom of God and as such an interpreter of Torah. He was definitely a teacher. To me it is clear that Jesus' teachings were designed to be followed always! They were not meant to be followed only until God intervened in history to establish the kingdom of God. Because of their subversive anti-Empire nature, it is my opinion that Jesus' teachings were meant to be the *means* whereby the kingdom of God would be fulfilled among humanity. It was for them that he risked death and was eventually executed, by the Empire.

Neither is there any necessity to see Jesus historically as a worker of the miracles attributed to him by the gospel writers. Miracle-working was assumed by them as essential in their representation of Jesus as the Messiah, hence their borrowings from depictions of miracles in the Hebrew Scriptures, albeit from writings about prophets. In 7:22, Luke's Jesus responds to the question from John the Baptist with what Luke wants his readers to see as messianic allusions: "*Go and tell John what you have seen and heard: the blind receive their sight; the lame walk, the lepers are cleansed, the deaf hear, the dead are raised, the poor have good news brought to them. And blessed is anyone who takes no offense at me.*"

> 7:24-27: *When John's messengers had gone, Jesus began to speak to the crowds about John. "What did you go out into the wilderness to look at? A reed shaken by the wind? What then did you go out to see? Someone dressed in soft robes? Look, those who put on fine clothing and live in luxury are in royal palaces. What then did you go out to see? A prophet? Yes, I tell you, and more than a prophet. This is the one about whom it is written, 'See I am sending my messenger ahead of you, who will prepare your way before you.' "*

In 7:27 Luke has written his own version of Malachi 3:1 (where God says to Israel through Malachi): "*See, I am sending my messenger to prepare the way before me, and the LORD whom you seek will suddenly come to his Temple.*" The traditional interpretation of this is that the messenger is Elijah, who will prepare the way for the coming of God on the Day of the LORD. Luke has given this quote his own messianic tweak, implying that the "*messenger*" is John the Baptist and the "*LORD*" (expressed in Luke as 'Lord') is Jesus the divinely anointed Messiah/Son of God. Malachi has no mention of a Messiah, only of the coming of Elijah to prepare the people of Israel for the Day of the LORD.

It is crucial for understanding Luke to remember that he is reading the scriptures through the lens of his belief in Jesus as the crucified Messiah. That is obviously more important to him than accurate quoting from the Greek version of his own scripture (Old Testament). Note that Luke acknowledges the prophetic Elijah figure in Malachi, but steps around that by saying that Jesus is a prophet, but *"more than a prophet"* (7:26).

The omission of the Markan passage (9:11-13) where Jesus' disciples comment on scribal (Pharisaic) expectations of Elijah coming first *"to restore all things"*, delivers Luke from difficulties concerning the Elijian role of restoring Israel before the last day, when (Luke expects) the Messiah would appear. As Luke knows, Israel's restoration was clearly not accomplished by John the Baptist/Elijah before his imprisonment and beheading. Luke is therefore attempting to deal with that by dissociating John from the 'returned Elijah' tradition. An additional difficulty for Luke is that as many scholars have pointed out, there is no instance in pre-Christian literature where Elijah (or even a 'messenger' figure) is depicted as the forerunner or precursor of the Messiah. The most likely scenario is that Luke represents a school of thought that saw Jesus combining the characteristics of the Messiah and the 'prophet like Moses'.

That idea is also set out in the Book of Acts, the other source attributed by most scholars to Luke. In Acts beliefs similar to Luke's are placed into the mouth of Peter the apostle:

> Acts 3:19-22: *"Repent therefore, and turn to God so that your sins may be wiped out, so that times of refreshing may come from the presence of the Lord, and that he may send the Messiah appointed for you, that is, Jesus, who must remain in heaven until the time of universal restoration that God announced long ago through his holy prophets. Moses said, "The Lord your God will raise up for you from your own people a prophet like me. You must listen to whatever he tells you."*

Here Jesus is understood to have been carrying out the prophetic role of the prophet like Moses, before assuming his ultimate role of Messiah. That understanding is in the background of Luke's portrayal of a Jesus who carries out both prophetic and messianic roles.

The Feeding of the Five Thousand

9:12-17: *The day was drawing to a close, and the twelve came to him and said, "Send the crowd away, so that they may go into the surrounding villages and countryside, to lodge and get provisions; for we are here in a deserted place." But he said to them, "You give them something to eat." They said, "We have no more than five loaves and two fish – unless we are to go and buy food for all these people." For there were about five thousand men. And he said to his disciples, "Make them sit down in groups of about fifty each." They did so and made them all sit down. And taking the five loaves and the two fish, he looked up to heaven, and blessed and broke them, and gave them to the disciples to set before the crowd. And all ate and were filled. What was left over was gathered up, twelve baskets of broken pieces.*

Although there is no specific "Who is this?" in Luke's account of Jesus' miraculous feeding of five thousand people, the question and the answer are implicit in the incident as described. After all, Luke includes the story following a description (9:7-9) of various answers given to the question of Jesus' identity. Luke is depicting Jesus as the 'prophet like Moses'. The crowds therefore follow a Moses-like Jesus into the desert and rely on him for the provision of their food (as Exodus 16).

Another apparent and typically Lucan aim of this story is to forge a connection with traditions surrounding Elijah, in order to discredit them. This is accomplished by the inclusion of the "*two fish*" in the story originally lifted from Mark and Matthew. It may be that the inclusion of fish in Luke's version of the feeding story alludes to the presidency of Jesus the Messiah at the forthcoming messianic banquet where God will provide fish ('the flesh of Leviathan') for the people who have been living under the invading occupier in the ruins of Jerusalem ("*You crushed the heads of Leviathan;*[119] *you gave him as food for the creatures of the wilderness."* Psalm 74:14). This looks like a nod to Luke's readers; Luke's gospel was written after Jerusalem was reduced to ruins by the Roman occupying force.

Fish were also craved by the Israelites in the wilderness of the desert:

> Numbers 11:4-6: *"The rabble among them had a strong craving; and the Israelites also wept again, and said, "If only we had meat to eat! We remember the fish we used to eat in Egypt for nothing, the cucumbers, the melons, the leeks, the onions, and the garlic; but now our strength is dried up, and there is nothing at all but this manna to look at."*

They complained that they had only manna (bread-like substance from trees) to eat. In Luke's feeding story Jesus the 'prophet like Moses' gives the people not only bread, but also fish, again outdoing Moses and alluding to the forthcoming messianic age of plenty.

Luke may also have told this story as a means of 'topping' the depiction in the Elijah-Elisha tradition of Elisha instructing his disciple/servant to feed only one hundred people (not five thousand) with twenty loaves of barley and some ears of grain in a sack: *"But his servant said, "How can I set this before a hundred people?" So he repeated, "Give it to the people and let them eat, for thus says the Lord, 'They shall eat and have some left.'" He set it before them, they ate, and had some left, according to the word of the Lord."* (2 Kings 4:42-44). Luke's Jesus outdoes that, many times over.

The Transfiguration

> 9:28-36: *Now about eight days after these sayings Jesus took with him Peter and John and James, and went up on the mountain to pray. And while he was praying, the appearance of his face changed, and his clothes became dazzling white. Suddenly they saw two men, Moses and Elijah, talking to him. They appeared in glory and were*

speaking of his departure, which he was about to accomplish at Jerusalem. Now Peter and his companions were weighed down with sleep; but since they had stayed awake, they saw his glory and the two men who stood with him. Just as they were leaving him, Peter said to Jesus, "Master, it is good for us to be here: let us make three dwellings, one for you, one for Moses, and one for Elijah" – not knowing what he said. While he was saying this, a cloud came and over shadowed them; and they were terrified as they entered the cloud. Then from the cloud came a voice that said, "This is my Son, my Chosen; listen to him!" When the voice had spoken, Jesus was found alone. And they kept silent and in those days told no one any of the things they had seen.

In the same sequence as Mark's version, Luke includes the account of Jesus' mysterious transfiguration on the mountain. It comes immediately following the enigmatic words of 9:27 (Mark 9:1), regarding those who *"will not taste death"* before the coming of the kingdom of God. The identity of those who are the object of this saying is ambiguous in Mark, but for Luke they are clearly some of Jesus' disciples. There is a link between the saying about the coming of the kingdom of God and the transfiguration account. It operates as the sign that Jesus is endorsed by both Moses and Elijah as the divinely sent Messiah who will appear when the (apocalyptic) kingdom of God arrives.

Luke may have included this link between the coming of the kingdom of God and the transfiguration as answer to scandalised criticism that erupted from Jewish religious leadership regarding the early Christ movement's messianic claims. There was strong opposition to these claims within Judaism. That was not because the proclamation of a messiah figure was regarded as blasphemous; others had claimed that status before. The scandal was that this particular messianic sect had unusually large obstacles to overcome in its proclamation of Messiah. Those obstacles are clear in the verses of Deuteronomy 18 that follow the often-quoted words of Moses:

18.15: *"The Lord your God will raise up for you a prophet like me from among your own people; you shall heed such a prophet."*

18:18: *"I will raise up for them a prophet like you from among their own people; I will put my words in the mouth of the prophet, who shall speak to them everything that I command."*

The enormous difficulties for proclaiming Jesus as Messiah are obvious as God then goes on to say:

Deut. 18:19-22: *"Anyone who does not heed the words that the prophet shall speak in my name, I myself will hold accountable. But any prophet who speaks in the name of other gods, or who presumes to speak in my name a word that I have not commanded the prophet to speak – that prophet shall die." You may say to yourself, "How can we recognize a word that the Lord has not spoken?" If a prophet speaks in the name of the Lord but the thing does not take place or prove true, it is a word that the Lord has not spoken. The prophet has spoken it presumptuously; do not be frightened by it."*

Members of the early Christ movement, waiting for the reappearance of the Messiah to vindicate their claims, are very awkwardly placed. Their opponents have scripture on their side. They can refer to the words of Moses and of God in Deuteronomy to refute the claim that Jesus is a true prophet, let alone the long-awaited Messiah. We can imagine the arguments used against people proclaiming Jesus as Messiah: "He has not appeared as you say he said he would. Therefore he did not tell the truth. Therefore he is not the Messiah." In view of the well-known criteria for recognition of false prophets, Luke's arguments faced great difficulty, to say the least. Jewish perceptions about the coming of the kingdom of God as a momentous, easily recognizable event, plus the reality of the ignominious death of Jesus as an insurrectionist (the person crucified was stripped naked), ruled out for most Jews any legitimacy in Luke's declaration of him as Messiah.

These potentially fatal flaws in the post-Easter proclamation demanded a creative solution. Luke acknowledged the problem by adopting a literary counter-argument, already partly included in Mark as the 'transfiguration' narrative. In Mark it appears to have been based on the Moses-Sinai, Elijah-Horeb theophanies.[120] Luke uses this argument to bolster his continuing opposition to perceptions of Jesus as the returned Elijah, and his affirmation of him as the 'prophet like Moses'/Messiah. The order in which the two figures appear is the reverse of Mark and Matthew's "Elijah with Moses". Luke has: *"Suddenly they saw two men, Moses and Elijah, talking to him."* (9:30).

That may simply be Luke's use of the chronological order in which Moses and Elijah appear in the Hebrew Scriptures. On the other hand, including Elijah with Moses in a conversation with Jesus affords Luke a priceless opportunity to distance Jesus from popular ideas about him as Elijah returned. Jesus in conversation with Elijah would obviously be impossible if in fact Jesus were to be equated with Elijah returned from the heavenly sphere. Even if Jesus were understood merely to be carrying out his mission in the 'spirit and power of Elijah', as a 'new Elisha', for example, the transfiguration scene is decisive. It pictures Jesus not merely on an equal footing with Elijah, but receiving confirmation from Elijah of his superior status as God's Messiah. (Echoes here of a Lucan 'boom boom'!) Then follows:

> 9:31: *"They appeared in glory, and were speaking of his departure, which he was about to accomplish at Jerusalem."*

In contrast with the other synoptic gospels where they were simply *"speaking"* together, the topic of conversation between Moses, Elijah and Jesus is here included. According to Luke they were speaking of Jesus' *"departure"*, an event he was to accomplish in Jerusalem.

A good deal has been written about this as a 'new-exodus'

motif, given that the key-word in Greek is *exodos,* an obvious reference to Moses. *Exodos* literally means the same as 'exodus', but is mostly translated as 'departure' or 'going out'. The most likely explanation is that Luke is using the expression to refer to Jesus' death and significantly, to his ascension.

Why is the reference to ascension so important? Ascension is a characteristic attributed to the deaths of Elijah and Moses, as well as to Jesus. Elijah was said to have "*ascended in a whirlwind into heaven*" (2 Kings 2:11b). Deuteronomy 34: 5-6 has Moses die in the land of Moab, his body buried "*opposite Beth-peor*". Mysteriously though, "*no one knows his burial place to this day*" (34:6).

Josephus the first century CE Jewish historian has Moses translated to heaven in very mysterious circumstances:

> " ... *while he said farewell to Eleazar and Joshua, and was still communing with them, a cloud suddenly descended upon him and he disappeared in a ravine.*"[121]

Significantly for his anti-insurrectionist and anti-Elijah tradition standpoint, Josephus downgrades the disappearance of Elijah:

> "*Now about that time Elijah disappeared from among men and to this day no one knows his end.*"[122]

Where did the fiery chariot go? This illustrates the Mosaic bias prevalent among Greek-educated Jews (such as Josephus) in the first century CE.

According to the hellenized Jew *par excellence* Philo of Alexandria, Moses did not die, but:

> " ... *was translated by the Word of that Cause by which the whole universe was created.*"[123]

For the hellenized Jew called Luke, parallels between the transfiguration narrative and Jesus' ascension must be made clear. In the final analysis, Luke's belief in the more exalted

status of Jesus is indicated by the fact that of the three great
ones, it is only Jesus whom he depicts as clothed in *"dazzling
white"* garments (9:29). In view of the fact that Luke's
missionary focus included a mission to Jews in the Diaspora, as
well as to Gentiles, for him the exclusively Israel-focussed Elijah
traditions had to be challenged at every possible juncture.

Most importantly, at the time of Luke's writing the
crucified Jesus had still not reappeared. The transfiguration
story carries the message that like Moses and Elijah, Jesus
(having been brought back to life after his death) was
transported alive into heaven, from where he will return to earth,
as have Moses and Elijah in their meeting with Jesus on the
mountain. Jesus, however, will return as Messiah.

The Mission Instructions

9:59–62: *To another he said, "Follow me." But he said,
"Lord, first let me go and bury my father." But Jesus said
to him, "Let the dead bury their own dead; but as for
you, go and proclaim the kingdom of God." Another said,
"I will follow you, Lord; but let me first say farewell to
those at my home." Jesus said to him, "No one who puts
a hand to the plough and looks back is fit for the
kingdom of God."*

This passage contains two references to the sense of
urgency with which Luke invests proclamation of the coming
kingdom of God. The first is Jesus' reply to the man who wished
to bury his father before becoming a follower. The second
instance is to the man who wanted first to say goodbye to his
family. Given the importance of the task of burying the dead,
particularly for a son attending to the burial of his father, the
first response conveys extreme urgency in the task of
proclaiming the kingdom of God before it arrives. The second
request is identical in meaning with Elisha's response to Elijah:
*"Let me kiss my father and my mother, and then I will follow
you."* (1 Kings 19:19-21). Elijah was suitably concerned about
Elisha's family ties and allowed him to bid a proper farewell to
his parents. The fact that Elisha was ploughing when Elijah

called him is another link with the biblical Elijah tradition in Luke's story, where Jesus refers to "*one who puts a hand to the plough and looks back.*"

The way Luke's Jesus responds to both requests indicates that they made the would-be follower "*unfit for the kingdom of God*". There is a strong sense here of Luke's firm belief that Jesus the Messiah would soon (re)appear and establish the kingdom of God on earth. Again, the story dissociates Jesus from an Israel-focussed Elijah role, which Luke fears would rule out his identity as Messiah for the whole world.

It is not by accident that these sayings of Jesus about discipleship follow another incident where Luke denies Elijah-like traits in Jesus. After his rejection by a Samaritan village, 9:51-56 has Jesus refusing to accede to the request of his disciples to "*... command fire to come down from heaven and consume them*". Rather than agree to the Elijian methodology in 1 Kings 18 and 2 Kings 1 (where God sends fire from heaven at Elijah's request), Luke's Jesus rebukes his disciples for this suggestion and, by association, their attempt to align his mission with that of Elijah returned. This story also attributes to Jesus Luke's desire to include the Samaritans in the kingdom of God.

The Entry into Jerusalem

19: 28-44: *When he had come near Bethphage and Bethany, at the place called the Mount of Olives, he sent two of the disciples, saying, "Go into the village ahead of you, and as you enter it you will find tied there a colt that has never been ridden. Untie it and bring it here. If anyone asks you, 'Why are you untying it?' just say this, 'The Lord needs it.'" So those who were sent departed and found it as he had told them. As they were untying the colt, its owners asked them, "Why are you untying the colt?" They said, "The Lord needs it." Then they brought it to Jesus; and after throwing their cloaks on the colt, they set Jesus on it. As he rode along, people kept spreading their cloaks on the road.*

As he was now approaching the path down from the Mount of Olives, the whole multitude of the disciples began to praise God joyfully with a loud voice for all the deeds of power that they had seen, saying, "Blessed is the king who comes in the name of the Lord! Peace in heaven, and glory in the highest heaven!" Some of the Pharisees in the crowd said to him, "Teacher, order your disciples to stop." He answered, "I tell you, if these were silent, the stones would shout out."

As he came near and saw the city he wept over it, saying, "If you, even you, had only recognized on this day the things that make for peace! But now they are hidden from your eyes. Indeed, the days will come upon you, when your enemies will set up ramparts around you and surround you, and hem you in on every side. They will crush you to the ground, you and your children within you, and they will not leave within you one stone upon another; because you did not recognize the time of your visitation from God."

My reader may have noticed that Luke is not the church's choice for a Palm Sunday story. In his version of Jesus entering Jerusalem, Luke makes no mention of *"leafy branches"* or *"palm branches"* being spread on the road. He retains the "cloaks" spread on the road in front of Jesus, but otherwise strips this scene of specific Jewish references to the festival of Sukkot, which are obvious in Mark and Matthew. There are timing issues here for Luke in associating the crucifixion with the Passover, and again his Gentile readership emerges.

Dissociation of Jesus from specifically Jewish messianic traditions comes through Luke's version of the words shouted by the crowd: *"Blessed is the king who comes in the name of the Lord! Peace in heaven, and glory in the highest heaven!"* Luke's source is Psalm 118:26, leaving out the references to the *"festal procession with branches"*. The words in Luke contain no hint of the Davidic messianic understanding that occurs in both Mark ("Blessed is the coming kingdom of our ancestor David!") and Matthew ("Hosanna to the son of David"). Even John's Gospel includes here the palm branches and the crowd's affirmation of *"the king of Israel."*

In Luke the 'king' is clearly the Messiah, but here he is not limited by traditional Jewish expectations. A more obscure and less confrontational reference to Jewish traditions is Luke's inclusion of Mark and Matthew's description of Jesus' mode of transport into Jerusalem. The proof text here is clearly Zechariah 9:9, in which the peaceful king of Israel arrives in Jerusalem riding on a donkey. Significantly for Luke, he will be the king of all the nations, *"and he shall command peace to all the nations."* (Zech. 9:10).

Luke's 'entry into Jerusalem' narrative concludes with a comment from Pharisees who are irritated that Jesus is being proclaimed as king/Messiah. They want Jesus' followers silenced. The answer Luke has Jesus give relates to an ancient tradition regarding 'standing stones'. These are mentioned in various books of the Hebrew Scriptures as witnesses to significant interactions between God and Israel. In Genesis 28:22, after his dream about a ladder stretching from heaven to earth, Jacob says, " *... and this stone, which I have set up for a pillar, shall be God's house ...* " Jacob repeats the setting up of a standing stone in Genesis 35:13-15, where he pours oil on the stone and calls the place Bethel (house of God). In Exodus 24: 2-4, Moses erects standing stones at the foot of Mount Sinai after his encounter with God on the mountain. When Joshua leads the Israelites to the Jordan (Joshua 4), God tells him to arrange stones in the Jordan. They will mark the presence of God as the waters of the Jordan roll back and the Israelites pass over.

In all cases the stones are witnesses to God's presence with the people of Israel. The stones to which Luke has Jesus refer are most likely those that 'stand' in the Temple itself (the house of God). They represent the presence of God, and Luke says they would themselves have witnessed to the coming of the Messiah Jesus, had not Jesus' followers shouted it out themselves.

Luke follows this with a reflection from a weeping Jesus, in which his own retrospective on the events of the Jewish War forms part of Jesus' lament. There is a clear reference to the destruction of Jerusalem, which Luke sees as Israel's punishment *"because you did not recognize the time of your visitation from God."* (19:44). This of course addresses the

Jewish leadership following the Jewish War. "The destruction happened because you did not recognize Jesus as Messiah," says Luke. The belief that God used invading forces to punish a disobedient Israel is expressed over and over again in the Hebrew Scriptures. That belief appears again in this story about the entry into Jerusalem.

The 'cleansing' of the Temple

19:45-48: *Then he entered the temple and began to drive out those who were selling things there; and he said, "It is written, 'my house shall be a house of prayer'; but you have made it a den of robbers."*

Jesus goes into the Temple, where Luke says there were people selling "*things*", not specifically "*doves*" as in Mark and Matthew. There is no mention of money changers, but through his use of the proof texts Isaiah 56:7 and Jeremiah 7:11, Luke makes the same point against the rulers of the Temple. The Temple is meant to have been a "*house of prayer*", but the priests had made it a "*den of robbers*". Luke says Jesus began to drive out the sellers in the Temple. Given the large crowd that would have been in the Temple, this is most likely a prophetic symbolic action, the kind of action that probably was performed by Jesus.

The story relates to the role of the prophet Elijah on the "*Day of the LORD*" (Malachi 3:1-4) in which Elijah is to purify "*the descendants of Levi*" so they can "*present offerings to the LORD in righteousness.*" The story is also based on motifs gleaned from the books of the Prophet Jeremiah and Lamentations. In this scenario both Jesus and Jeremiah are 'weeping prophets' - weeping over the destruction of Jerusalem, including its Temple (Jeremiah 9:1/Luke 19:41). As we know, Luke wrote about this with the benefit of hindsight, from decades after the destruction.

Luke did leave out "*doves*", the direct link in Mark's and Matthew's story with the sacrificial system, but he would probably have preferred to leave out altogether this Elijah-like activity of Jesus in the Temple. His problem is that this episode about Jesus in the Temple is crucial. It creates a link between Jewish charges laid against Jesus concerning opposition to the Temple, and his subsequent crucifixion. Like the other gospel writers, by means of that link Luke wants to place total responsibility for Jesus' execution at the feet of the Temple leadership, not with Rome. No doubt that reflected the perilous social context of the Messiah Jesus movement in the Jewish Diaspora of the Roman Empire.

The Last Supper, Trial and Crucifixion

22:7-13: Then came the day of Unleavened Bread, on which the Passover lamb had to be sacrificed. So Jesus sent Peter and John, saying, "Go and prepare the Passover meal for us that we may eat it." They asked him, "Where do you want us to make preparations for it?" "Listen," he said to them, "when you have entered the city, a man carrying a jar of water will meet you; follow him into the house he enters and say to the owner of the house, 'The teacher asks you, "Where is the guest room, where I may eat the Passover with my disciples?" ' He will show you a large room upstairs, already furnished. Make preparations for us there." So they went and found everything as he had told them; and they prepared the Passover meal.

The Day of Unleavened Bread is said here to be the day on which the Passover lambs were sacrificed. In fact it would have been one of seven days of Unleavened Bread. It relates to the first 'passover' of the Hebrews in Egypt (Exodus 12). At that time God told the Hebrews to make bread for their journey out, but not to wait until it had risen. So they were to add no yeast. They were to eat unleavened bread for seven days before the 'passover' feast. Luke's timing combines the preparation of unleavened bread with the sacrifice of the lambs in the Temple. The lamb is to be eaten as the Passover feast on the same day it is killed, as is set out in Exodus 12:8: *They shall eat the lamb that same night; they shall eat it roasted over the fire with unleavened bread and bitter herbs.*

"When the hour came", the Passover meal for Luke's Jesus and his disciples took place. Here again we see a gospel writer prepared to place Jesus' crucifixion on the Friday, the Day of Preparation for the first Sabbath of the Festival of Unleavened Bread – a high holy day of the Jewish calendar. As we will see, that creates problems of historicity regarding the activities of the Sanhedrin or Council. The Passover itself lasts for only 24 hours during the seven-day Festival of Unleavened Bread. In Luke's scenario it would have lasted from what we would call Wednesday at sunset until Thursday at sunset. The assumption is that Jesus and his disciples ate their Passover meal some time on the Thursday, before sunset. Luke simply says it was *"When the hour came"*. After sunset on the Thursday (on the Day of Preparation for the Sabbath, what we call Friday) they went out to the Garden of Gethsemane. This timing allows for Jesus to rise from the dead on the third day – what we would call the Sunday morning.

> 22:14-23: *When the hour came, he took his place at the table, and the apostles with him. He said to them, "I have eagerly desired to eat this Passover with you before I suffer; for I tell you, I will not eat it until it is fulfilled in the kingdom of God." Then he took a cup, and after giving thanks he said, "Take this and divide it among yourselves; for I tell you that from now on I will not drink of the fruit of the vine until the kingdom of God comes." Then he took a loaf of bread, and when he had given thanks, he broke it and gave it to them, saying, "This is my body, which is given for you. Do this in remembrance of me." And he did the same with the cup after supper, saying, "This cup that is poured out for you is the new covenant in my blood. But see, the one who betrays me is with me, and his hand is on the table. For the Son of Man is going as it has been determined, but woe to that one by whom he is betrayed!" Then they began to ask one another which one of them it could be who would do this.*

Here Luke follows Mark and Matthew in explaining Jesus' coming death as *"the new covenant in my blood"*, an allusion to the Mosaic covenant where (animal) blood was spilled. As the Festival of Unleavened Bread drew near, Jerusalem would have been full of people coming to make their sacrifices and share the festive Passover meal. Some from the Diaspora would have been doing that for perhaps the first and only time in their lives. Some would have come every year from around the land of Palestine. To counter trouble from Jewish insurrectionists mingling with the crowds, Roman governors always ensured that plenty of Roman military were on duty in Jerusalem. Pilate was no exception to that and there would have been an atmosphere of ferment abroad. In one particular year that included the appearance in Jerusalem of the teacher/prophet Jesus from Galilee. Dangerously for him, some of the rebels probably would have wanted to proclaim him king/Messiah and gather around him to stir up the crowds and overthrow the Romans.

All gospels give us a possible associate of those zealot rebels – Judas Iscariot. As I have explained in the section on Mark's Gospel, Judas' name (Iscariot) means 'dagger'. Perhaps Judas meant to force Jesus into declaring himself as King/Messiah. What the gospel writers say is that he offered to lead the Temple police to Jesus. Perhaps the Temple authorities averted Judas' insurrectionist ambitions by insisting that this be done under the cover of darkness, when they could arrest Jesus without fear of a revolt by the people. Jesus was obviously a popular teacher/prophet and his arrest in daylight may well have sparked precisely the kind of revolt Judas wanted, but the Temple and Roman leaders wished to avoid. In any case we can assume that Judas' purpose in betraying Jesus failed.

22:47-53: *While he was still speaking, suddenly a crowd came, and the one called Judas, one of the twelve, was leading them. He approached Jesus to kiss him; but Jesus said to him, "Judas, is it with a kiss that you are betraying the Son of Man?" When those who were around him saw what was coming, they asked, "Lord;*

should we strike with the sword?" Then one of them struck the slave of the high priest and cut off his right ear. But Jesus said, "No more of this!" And he touched his ear and healed him. Then Jesus said to the chief priests, the officers of the temple police, and the elders who had come for him, "Have you come out with swords and clubs as if I were a bandit? When I was with you day after day in the temple, you did not lay hands on me. But this is your hour, and the power of darkness!"

So the scene is set for Jesus' arrest in a quiet place at night. One of the men with Jesus lends weight to the theory that some who followed him around were militaristic zealots; this man deciding to defend Jesus with his sword. In accordance with his own teaching Jesus rebukes the violence and Luke and the other gospel writers say that as prophet/Messiah, he is able to offer healing to the man wounded by the wielder of the sword.

Here Luke is on the horns of a dilemma. He knows Jesus taught non-violence, but he is using the arrest scene from Mark and Matthew, where someone with Jesus uses a sword. For that reason Luke includes his own explanation. In the previous verses (35-38) he attributes to Jesus teaching about equipment the disciples must take with them as they continue his work after his death. In particular, *"And the one who has no sword must sell his cloak and buy one. For I tell you, this scripture must be fulfilled in me, 'And he was counted among the lawless'; and indeed what is written about me is being fulfilled."* They said, *"Lord, look, here are two swords."* He replied, *"It is enough."* (22:36-38). The reference to being *"counted among the lawless"* is from Isaiah 53:12, from the suffering servant narrative the gospel writers use as proof text for Jesus' 'predicted' death.

> 22: 54-62: *Then they seized him and led him away, bringing him into the high priest's house. But Peter was following at a distance. When they had kindled a fire in the middle of the courtyard and sat down together, Peter sat among them. Then a servant-girl, seeing him in the firelight, stared at him and said, "This man also was*

with him." But he denied it, saying, "Woman, I do not know him." A little later someone else, on seeing him, said, "You also are one of them." But Peter said, "Man, I am not!" Then about an hour later still another kept insisting, "Surely this man also was with him; for he is a Galilean." But Peter said, "Man, I do not know what you are talking about!" At that moment, while he was still speaking, the cock crowed. The Lord turned and looked at Peter. Then Peter remembered the word of the Lord, how he had said to him, "Before the cock crows today, you will deny me three times." And he went out and wept bitterly.

Luke includes the curious incident involving the disciple Peter. This scene first appears in Mark, and is found in all gospels. Because of that it may have a historical background. This is not to say that there was an actual conversation in the courtyard of the high priest's house involving Peter, or that denials of association with Jesus were followed by the crowing of a rooster. Mark's story, plus its inclusion in the other gospels, is possibly an attempt to explain Peter's behaviour immediately after the death of Jesus. It is more than likely that at that point neither Peter nor the other close disciples (with the possible exception of Judas Iscariot) saw Jesus as King/Messiah. This is most probably because Jesus did not see himself as the Messiah. It is therefore entirely plausible that Peter actually did 'deny' Jesus (in the sense that Jesus was the Messiah), at the time of the crucifixion. Significantly, at some point in the first decades following the crucifixion it was not Peter, but James the brother of Jesus who assumed leadership of the original, probably non-messianic group of disciples.

That may have been because Peter had by then converted to belief in Jesus as Messiah. This would have necessitated him leaving the original group and joining hellenized Jewish believers in Messiah Jesus who were evangelising in Jerusalem and further abroad. In support of that scenario, in Acts Paul's eventual belief in Jesus as Messiah is related to his association with hellenized Jewish evangelists in Jerusalem and Damascus.

Peter's evangelizing activity is also portrayed in Acts. Following Jesus' prediction that Peter will deny him three times, Luke has Jesus pray for Peter that: *"when once you have turned back, strengthen your brothers."* (22:31-32). Turned back to what? Luke's Jesus surely means 'turned back to belief in me as Messiah'. In accordance with that, Peter's last days were spent in Rome, where he was crucified for his membership of the messianic Jewish community.

> 22:66-71: *When day came, the assembly of the elders of the people, both chief priests and scribes, gathered together, and they brought him to their council. They said, "If you are the Messiah, tell us." He replied, "If I tell you, you will not believe; and if I question you, you will not answer. But from now on the Son of Man will be seated at the right hand of the power of God." All of them asked, "Are you, then, the Son of God?" He said to them, "You say that I am." Then they said, "What further testimony do we need? We have heard it ourselves from his own lips!"*

In Luke's first trial scene the whole assembly of Jewish leadership is present. Chief priests and scribes (i.e. Sadducees and Pharisees) ask Jesus if he is the Messiah. He does not answer 'yes', but claims that if he tells them they will not believe it. Following Mark and Matthew, Luke then has Jesus make the claim (derived from the Book of Daniel, chapter 7) that *"from now on the Son of Man will be seated at the right hand of the power of God."* Because this quote implies Jesus the Son of Man's divinity, they ask if he is the Son of God. At that point he turns the question back on them: *"You say that I am."* The leaders then declare that Jesus has, in effect, condemned himself *"from his own lips!"* If Luke's Jesus had merely declared himself to be the Messiah, that was hardly an offence, let alone a capital offence.

> 23:1-5: *Then the assembly rose as a body and brought Jesus before Pilate. They began to accuse him, saying,*

"We found this man perverting our nation, forbidding us to pay taxes to the emperor, and saying that he himself is the Messiah, a king. Then Pilate asked him, "Are you the king of the Jews?" He answered, "You say so." Then Pilate said to the chief priests and the crowds, "I find no basis for an accusation against this man." But they were insistent and said, "He stirs up the people by teaching throughout all Judea, from Galilee where he began even to this place."

The idea that the whole assembly (Sanhedrin) would be questioning Jesus and then taking him to Pilate (and to Herod) is historically and religiously untenable. It was the Friday morning – the Day of Preparation for the first Sabbath of Passover, the Passover meal having been eaten the night before. Priests would not have been able to enter Gentile territory such as Pilate's headquarters on that day immediately preceding a double high holy day – the first Sabbath of the Festival of Unleavened Bread. They would have been polluted by that contact and unable to celebrate the Sabbath. Given that, we can only follow Luke's story and see why he writes it as he does. As I noted in the chapter on Mark, the gospel writers may have wanted their readers to see Jesus as so significant that the Sanhedrin was prepared to break its own laws to deal with him.

Luke then has the whole assembly take Jesus to Pilate because they want him executed, but do not have the authority to execute him. They lack even the authority to stone him to death for blasphemy, because according to Luke's story he has not committed blasphemy. When Pilate says: *"I find no basis for an accusation against this man"*, the Temple leadership take the fact that many people were following Jesus around and make it look as if he is 'stirring' them to rebellion against Rome. Historically, the fact that Jesus was from Galilee would at least have alerted Pilate to trouble, given that most of the messianic 'kings' who had been inciting rebellion were Galileans. Like the other gospel writers, Luke wants to place the blame for the death of the Messiah on the Jewish leadership. This attitude is likely to be one consequence of his failure to convince most of his fellow

Jews that Jesus was the Messiah.

> 23:6-12: *When Pilate heard this, he asked whether the man was a Galilean. And when he learned that he was under Herod's jurisdiction, he sent him off to Herod, who was himself in Jerusalem at that time. When Herod saw Jesus, he was very glad, for he had been wanting to see him for a long time, because he had heard about him and was hoping to see him perform some sign. He questioned him at some length, but Jesus gave him no answer.*

Even then Pilate is not convinced and Luke has him relieved to be able to send Jesus off to Herod Antipas, the ruler of Galilee, who was also in Jerusalem at that time. Luke is the only gospel writer who includes a trial before Herod, although an insurrectionist probably would have been brought before Herod. Luke's inclusion of the trial before Herod is probably because Luke's community lived outside Herodian jurisdiction, where they need not fear his reaction to Luke's writing. It is also likely that the Herodian dynasty no longer existed at the time of Luke's writing.

In any case it is unsurprising that Herod gets nothing from Jesus with which he could accuse him of insurrection. Again this is most likely because in fact Jesus did not see himself as king/Messiah and was not involved in militaristic rebellion. Luke adds the curious note (23:12) that Pilate and Herod became friends at that point. That can only have been added to focus further the culpability for the death of Jesus on the Jewish Temple leadership.

> 23:13-19: *Pilate then called together the chief priests, the leaders, and the people, and said to them, "You brought me this man as one who was perverting the people; and here I have examined him in your presence and have not found this man guilty of any of your charges against him. Neither has Herod, for he sent him back to us. Indeed, he has done nothing to deserve death. I will therefore have him flogged and release him." Then they*

all shouted out together, "Away with this fellow! Release Barabbas for us!" (This was a man who had been put in prison for an insurrection that had taken place in the city, and for murder.)

The trial continues back at Pilate's headquarters. Luke engages in a comprehensive whitewashing of Pilate, over against the insistent demands of the Jewish crowd that Barabbas the Jewish rebel leader be released and Jesus crucified. Here we have Luke's opposition to violent insurrection against Rome, no doubt because with hindsight he knows it resulted in the destruction of Jerusalem, including the Temple. Pilate insists twice that Jesus is innocent, and proposes that he be flogged and released. Yet the crowd eventually prevails and Jesus is led away to be crucified. The inclusion of the release of Barabbas would serve as information to Roman readers of Luke's gospel that the subsequent Jewish War was instigated by followers of figures like Barabbas, not by followers of Messiah Jesus.

23:26-31: *As they led him away, they seized a man, Simon of Cyrene, who was coming from the country, and they laid the cross on him, and made him carry it behind Jesus. A great number of the people followed him, and among them were women who were beating their breasts and wailing for him. But Jesus turned to them and said, "Daughters of Jerusalem, do not weep for me, but weep for yourselves and for your children. For the days are surely coming when they will say, 'Blessed are the barren, and the wombs that never bore, and the breasts that never nursed.' Then they will begin to say to the mountains, 'Fall on us'; and to the hills, 'Cover us.' For if they do this when the wood is green, what will happen when it is dry?"*

Luke follows Mark's and Matthew's account of the journey to the execution. The Romans are seen here as reasonable people, who even supply a man (Simon of Cyrene) to carry Jesus' cross for him. Further, the Roman centurion in charge of the execution party remains convinced of Jesus' innocence. Along the way to the execution site Luke's Jesus tells people wailing for him in the streets that they should be more worried about the troubles coming for them. Luke has him quote from the prophet Hosea (10:8): *"The high places of Aven, the sin of Israel, shall be destroyed. Thorn and thistle shall grow up on their altars. They shall say to the mountains, Cover us, and to the hills, Fall on us"*.

At the time of his writing, Luke knows that following the disastrous Jewish War against the Romans, when the Temple was destroyed, the authorities expelled the Jewish people from Jerusalem into the countryside. There they faced exposure to the elements, violent persecution and starvation. Luke's quotation from Hosea carries the message that all of this will happen to the people of Jerusalem because they rejected the Messiah. His readers see that all of this has come true, and that Jesus 'predicted' it.

> 23:32-43: *Two others also, who were criminals, were led away to be put to death with him. When they came to the place that is called The Skull, they crucified Jesus there with the criminals, one on his right and one on his left. Then Jesus said, "Father, forgive them; for they do not know what they are doing." And they cast lots to divide his clothing. And the people stood by, watching; but the leaders scoffed at him, saying, "He saved others; let him save himself if he is the Messiah of God, his chosen one!" The soldiers also mocked him, coming up and offering him sour wine, and saying, "If you are the King of the Jews, save yourself!" There was also an inscription over him, "This is the King of the Jews." One of the criminals who were hanged there kept deriding him and saying, "Are you not the Messiah? Save yourself and us!" But the other rebuked him, saying, "Do you not fear God, since you are under the same sentence of condemnation? And we indeed have been condemned justly, for we are getting what we deserve for our deeds, but this man has done nothing wrong." Then he said, "Jesus, remember*

*me when you come into your kingdom." He replied,
"Truly I tell you, today you will be with me in Paradise."*

Luke continues his disapproval of messianic rebellions against Rome at the scene of the crucifixion. Two others are to be crucified with Jesus, both of whom Luke calls 'criminals'. In fact these two are also being executed by crucifixion precisely because they have been involved in insurrection against Rome. They are not 'thieves' as Mark and Matthew have it. Crucifixion is not the punishment for robbery, but for treason against Caesar. Luke wants to make his point that even one of the two being executed with Jesus recognizes him as the true (peacemaking) Messiah, not as the kind of Messiah looked for by the violent rebels. Luke dissociates himself further from the insurrections by having this 'criminal' testify that *"we are getting what we deserve for our deeds"*. There can be little doubt that Luke is intent on presenting a story of Jesus' crucifixion that will not bring Roman persecution on him or on people associated with his gospel.

The mocking of Jesus on the cross by the Jewish people, *"If you are the King of the Jews, save yourself!"* represents all three synoptic gospel writers' dissociation of their communities from rebel elements still abroad in the late first and early second centuries. Characteristically, Luke leaves out Mark's and Matthew's sub-plot about the crowd associating Jesus with Elijah, mistaking his quoting of Psalm 2 with a call to Elijah for help. The idea of Elijah appearing to help people in trouble is expressed in the Talmud and other Rabbinic writings of the second century. The fact that such an idea already had currency in the first century is attested in the writings of Mark and Matthew. Elijah appeared only to help people who were regarded as particularly righteous or pious.[124] But Luke wants to avoid any reference to the first line of Psalm 22, which Mark says the people mistake for Jesus calling for Elijah's help. Instead he substitutes Psalm 22 with Psalm 31:5: *"Into your hand I commend my spirit."*

23:44-49: *It was now about noon, and darkness came*

over the whole land until three in the afternoon, while the sun's light failed; and the curtain of the temple was torn in two. Then Jesus, crying with a loud voice, said, "Father, into your hands I commend my spirit." Having said this, he breathed his last. When the centurion saw what had taken place, he praised God and said, "Certainly this man was innocent." And when all the crowds who had gathered there for this spectacle saw what had taken place, they returned home, beating their breasts. But all his acquaintances, including the women who had followed him from Galilee, stood at a distance, watching these things.

Although Luke distances Jesus on the cross from the Elijah tradition, he is happy to include his version of Mark's testimony from the Roman Centurion. Luke's centurion says: *"Certainly this man was innocent."* Mark's centurion is more specific: *"Truly this man was God's Son!"* Matthew wants no Gentile affirmation of Jesus at all. As in Mark and Matthew, immediately following Jesus' last breath Luke includes the tearing of the veil of the Temple. The way is now open for Jesus the High Priestly Messiah to enter the Holy of Holies and make atonement with his own blood for the sins of the world. For Luke the scope of the atonement is universal; not just for Israel.

23:50-56: *Now there was a good and righteous man named Joseph, who, though a member of the council, had not agreed to their plan and action. He came from the Jewish town of Arimathea, and he was waiting expectantly for the kingdom of God. This man went to Pilate and asked for the body of Jesus. Then he took it down, wrapped it in a linen cloth, and laid it in a rock-hewn tomb where no one had ever been laid. It was the day of Preparation, and the Sabbath was beginning. The women who had come with him from Galilee followed, and they saw the tomb and how his body was laid. Then they returned, and prepared spices and ointments. On the Sabbath they rested according to the commandment.*

Matthew, Luke and John all deal with the problem of the disposal of Jesus' body by including Mark's Joseph of Arimathea, a rich man who is a Pharisee and (fortunately) is also a disciple of Jesus. Historical accuracy would have had Jesus' body removed from the cross after his death and left in a ditch for the wild dogs and vultures, as was the case with all victims of crucifixion. The best case scenario would have been burial in an unmarked mass grave, but neither Roman nor Jewish law allowed traditional burial rites for criminals. By the first decade of the second century (when Luke was probably written) about 80 years had passed since the crucifixion. The truth probably was that when all gospels were written no one living knew what happened to Jesus' body after he died. In accordance with that, aspects of the resurrection story were designed partly to give Jesus a dignified burial as befitting the Messiah and also to solve the problem of the circumstances in which Jesus' body 'disappeared'. Obviously it needed to 'disappear' to lend support to developing ideas about Jesus' bodily resurrection. As we have seen, Matthew's solution is his narrative about soldiers spreading a story that the disciples had stolen Jesus' body (Matt. 28:11-15).

Like Mark and Matthew, Luke had the task of writing a narrative of the last supper, trial and execution of Jesus that would take into account ideas from the Passover meal for their 'last supper' scenario, plus their claim that the Messiah was to die and rise from the dead 'on the third day'. In constructing their stories, the synoptic gospel writers had of necessity to include the unlikely trial of Jesus by the whole Sanhedrin on the Day of Preparation for the first Sabbath of the Festival of Unleavened Bread. Consequently, their promotion of belief in the crucified and resurrected Messiah/Son of God took precedence over historical accuracy.

The Resurrection

24:1-12: *But on the first day of the week, at early dawn, they came to the tomb, taking the spices that they had prepared. They found the stone rolled away from the tomb, but when they went in, they did not find the body.*

While they were perplexed about this, suddenly two men in dazzling clothes stood beside them. The women were terrified and bowed their faces to the ground, but the men said to them, "Why do you look for the living among the dead? He is not here, but has risen. Remember how he told you, while he was still in Galilee, that the Son of Man must be handed over to sinners, and be crucified, and on the third day rise again." Then they remembered his words, and returning from the tomb, they told all this to the eleven and to all the rest. Now it was Mary Magdalene, Joanna, Mary the mother of James, and the other women with them who told this to the apostles. But these words seemed to them an idle tale, and they did not believe them. But Peter got up and ran to the tomb; stooping and looking in, he saw the linen cloths by themselves; then he went home, amazed at what had happened."

Belief in the bodily resurrection of Jesus the Messiah/Christ takes its foundation from gospel depictions of visits to the tomb where Joseph of Arimathea places Jesus' body. On the morning after Sabbath, on the Sunday (first day of the week), the women (in Luke's case, Mary Magdalene, Joanna, Mary the mother of James, and *"the other women with them"*) are witnesses to the empty tomb. The other three gospels also follow Mark (whose original ending has three female witnesses) in saying it was women who first went to the tomb. As in all gospels, the women express amazement or terror at the empty tomb, followed by incredulity on the part of other disciples. This is in complete contradiction with the gospels' reports that Jesus had already told them he was the Messiah, and that he would rise from the dead. If that were in fact the case they would naturally have reacted with joy that it had come true, not with terror or disbelief.

The women are met at the tomb by *"two men in dazzling clothes"*. These two are usually taken to be angels. In Luke it makes better sense to see them as Moses and Elijah, overseeing the 'exodos' (Greek word meaning 'way out') of Jesus from the world as foreseen by Luke's Jesus in the transfiguration narrative (9:31). The two men remind the women that Jesus said he *"must be handed over to sinners, and be crucified, and on the third day rise again."* In Luke's case, Jesus was *"still in Galilee"* when he said this. In Mark and Matthew the two men tell the women that Jesus has gone before them into Galilee, as he said he would. Again I make the point that the territory of Galilee appears to be the locale of Mark's and Matthew's communities. It makes sense for those gospels to tell their readers that Jesus returned to the Galilee, where they are located.

Contrary to that, Luke's gospel says Jesus was in Galilee when he said he would be killed and rise from the dead. Yet the location for the resurrection appearances and eventual ascension of Luke's Jesus is Jerusalem. This is congruent with the Book of Acts, which depicts the spread of the gospel from Jerusalem, not from Galilee. In all cases the resurrection narratives are literary devices designed to allow Jesus to speak following his death. They follow common hellenistic literary practice, where writers have no hesitation in placing their own words into the mouths of religious or other luminaries.

> 24:13-21: *Now on that same day two of them were going to a village called Emmaus, about seven miles from Jerusalem, and talking with each other about all these things that had happened. While they were talking and discussing, Jesus himself came near and went with them, but their eyes were kept from recognizing him. And he said to them, "What are you discussing with each other while you walk along?" They stood still, looking sad. Then one of them, whose name was Cleopas, answered him, "Are you the only stranger in Jerusalem who does not know the things that have taken place there in these days?" He asked them, "What things?" They replied, "The things about Jesus of Nazareth, who was a prophet mighty in deed and word before God and all the people, and how our chief priests and leaders handed him over to be condemned to death and crucified him. But we had hoped that he was the one to redeem Israel. Yes, and*

besides all this, it is now the third day since these things took place."

After the empty tomb is discovered and the women have informed *"the eleven and ... all the rest"* (24:9) Luke changes the scene to the outskirts of the city. Two disciples are depicted walking toward a village outside Jerusalem. The village is called Emmaus, but it is not known as such today. The only clues archaeologists and historians have to the location of Luke's Emmaus is that for the story to work, the village would have to be located within a day's walk from Jerusalem. That points to four or five villages which may have been Emmaus. Emmaus may also have been a literary creation of Luke's to make one of his points about Jesus through resurrection 'appearances'.

Significantly, the Emmaus story looks like another way Luke uses the Elijah tradition, but as always it is designed to highlight Jesus' superiority over Elijah. As in the case of the temptations narrative, here Luke builds on a story which probably came from the original core group of Jesus' followers, post-crucifixion. It appears first in a shorter form in Mark (16:12-13). Even in its revised and expanded Lucan form, this story exhibits strikingly clear characteristics of a Palestinian literary/oral Elijah tradition. During the Rabbinic period (beginning from the late first century CE), many stories about Elijah's return to earth were being told. They formed part of the oral Torah, dating from well before the time of Jesus. Stories about the returned Elijah were recorded in second century CE Jewish writings such as the Talmud and other Rabbinic writings. Given the many references to Elijah in the gospels, it is safe to say that legends about Elijah were self-evidently 'in the air' in the late first century, at the time the gospels were being written. According to Rabbinic literature, Elijah's removal from earth marked:

> *" ... the beginning of his real activity as a helper in time of need, as a teacher and as a guide to Torah."*[125]

Luke's story concerns an encounter experienced by two

disciples with a person they mysteriously fail to recognize as the risen Jesus. It is their curious inability to identify him, plus the nature of their encounter with him, that provides substantial clues to the original inspiration for Luke's expanded story. It has many characteristics in common with Jewish legends regarding the returned Elijah's role as a divinely-sent guide who leads others to enlightenment and redemption through his explanations of scripture. In Luke's story, the returned/resurrected Jesus leads Cleopas and his companion (probably his wife) to enlightenment through a similar process, in this case designed to convince them of his messiahship.

One of the many questions surrounding this story is the problem of why the two disciples of Jesus failed to recognize him. Yet there was a tradition about Elijah in which this kind of thing often happened. The idea of Elijah appearing on earth in 'another form' after he has ascended to the heavenly sphere is a familiar theme of the Jewish legends to which I referred. They contain depictions of Elijah's appearance to human beings in many and varied guises, primarily to improve their understanding of the sacred writings. In most cases Elijah's identity remains unknown to them until after he encourages them in their study of scripture. In Mark's original 'Emmaus' story, Jesus appears *"in another form"* to the disciples on the road (Mark 16:12). In Luke's story Jesus' identity is hidden until after he has explained the scriptures. In this case the explanation is designed to convince the two disciples (plus the readers of Luke's gospel) that their scripture has always pointed to Jesus as the Messiah. Through the same actions Luke's Jesus has usurped Elijah's role as guide to Torah and also proved himself to be the Messiah heralded by Elijah.

By means of this story Luke separates Jesus the Messiah from Elijah the herald of the Messiah. For readers of his gospel this is a conclusive argument that Palestinian Elijah traditions identifying Jesus as Elijah are now invalid: Jesus cannot be both the Messiah and the herald of the Messiah. Luke's further point about Jesus' identity occurs where Jesus asks Cleopas and his companion what they were discussing. They reply, *"The things about Jesus of Nazareth, who was a prophet mighty in deed and word before God and all the people"*. Whether or not the writer of Luke also wrote Acts, this is very similar to a description of Moses included in Acts. In Stephen's address to the Sanhedrin, Moses is described as *"powerful in his words and deeds".* (7:22). We already know that Moses is the prophet with whom Luke wishes to link Jesus.

> 24:28-31: *As they came near the village to which they were going, he walked ahead as if he were going on. But they urged him strongly, saying, "Stay with us, because it is almost evening and the day is now nearly over." So he went in to stay with them. When he was at the table with them, he took bread, blessed and broke it, and gave it to them. Then their eyes were opened, and they recognized him; and he vanished from their sight.*

The scene in Emmaus after Jesus has been persuaded to stay for the night with the two disciples (why not husband and wife?), appears to be the traditional Jewish meal blessing of the bread. The disciples recognize Jesus involved in that familiar practice, before he vanishes. Luke invests the meal with eucharistic significance when the disciples recall Jesus' promise given at the last meal with the twelve that he would *"not drink of the fruit of the vine* (or presumably, eat bread) *until the kingdom of God comes."* In accordance with first century Pharisaic resurrection traditions the dead would rise at the End-time, followed by the appearance of the Messiah. For Luke's community Jesus' resurrection represented revelation of him as Messiah and the inauguration of the kingdom of God.

After Jesus vanishes, the two disciples immediately walk back to Jerusalem to tell the other disciples that Jesus had appeared to them. Although Luke is often described as the gospel writer who is the most 'woman friendly', he chooses to omit Matthew's resurrection scenes where Jesus appears first to the women and later to the men. Luke has only the women finding the empty tomb, but adds a reference to Jesus appearing to Simon (Peter). Jesus then appears among the gathered disciples and says, *"Peace be with you."* Again they register terror, thinking they are seeing a ghost. That is natural enough, but their reaction is incongruent with their supposed knowledge that Jesus said he would rise from the dead. Their reaction should express joyful vindication of their expectation, not fear.

Curiously, all four gospel writers fail to recognize this incongruity. Luke builds on Matthew's resurrection narrative by having Jesus eat a piece of fish, thus adding weight to a growing first century belief in his bodily resurrection. Mark's 'longer ending' resurrection scene would not have been taken into account by Luke, given that it was most likely to have been added to Mark much later than the time of Luke's writing.

The Ascension

24:44-51: *Then he said to them, "These are my words that I spoke to you while I was still with you – that everything written about me in the law of Moses, the prophets, and the psalms must be fulfilled." Then he opened their minds to understand the scriptures, and he said to them, "Thus it is written, that the Messiah is to suffer and to rise from the dead on the third day, and that repentance and forgiveness of sins is to be proclaimed in his name to all nations, beginning from Jerusalem. You are witnesses of these things. And see, I am sending upon you what my Father promised; so stay here in the city until you have been clothed with power from on high." Then he led them out as far as Bethany, and, lifting up his hands, he blessed them. While he was blessing them, he withdrew from them and was carried up into heaven. And they worshipped him, and returned to Jerusalem with great joy; and they were continually in the temple praising God.*

The departure (*exodos*) or 'ascension' of Jesus follows Luke's version of Jesus' commissioning or 'sending out' of his disciples to proclaim "*... repentance and forgiveness of sins ... in his name to all nations.*" The commissioning and farewell occur on the same day as Jesus' resurrection and appearance to the two on the road to Emmaus. The ideas in this narrative reveal their origin in the biblical tradition about Elijah's commissioning of Elisha, and his subsequent ascension into heaven.

In Luke's writings (including the Book of Acts) there is an apparent forty-day delay between the third day farewell in Luke 24 and the final ascension of Jesus:

> Acts 1:3-11: *After his suffering he presented himself alive to them by many convincing proofs, appearing to them during forty days and speaking about the kingdom of God. While staying with them, he ordered them not to leave Jerusalem, but to wait there for the promise of the Father. "This," he said, "is what you have heard from me; for John baptized with water, but you will be baptized with the Holy Spirit not many days from now." So when they had come together, they asked him, "Lord, is this the time when you will restore the kingdom to Israel?" He replied, "It is not for you to know the times or periods that the Father has set by his own authority. But you will receive power when the Holy Spirit has come upon you; and you will be my witnesses in Jerusalem, in all Judea and Samaria, and to the ends of the earth." When he had said this, as they were watching, he was lifted up, and a cloud took him out of their sight. While he was going and they were gazing up toward heaven, suddenly two men in white robes stood by them. They said, "Men of Galilee, why do you stand looking up toward heaven? This Jesus, who has been taken up from you into heaven, will come in the same way as you saw him go into heaven."*

In the gospel the farewell is not the final ascension, but points more to a heavenly base for Jesus, from which he comes and goes over a period of forty days. It is possible that Luke wanted to connect the coming of the Holy Spirit on the disciples with the Jewish festival of *Shavuot*, or Pentecost, which necessitated an interval of 40 days in Luke's timing.[126] The words *"and was carried up to heaven"* (24:51b) do not occur in the oldest complete manuscripts of Luke (e.g. Siniatic Syriac). It is possible that they were added by an editor who wanted to make Luke's Gospel more independent from Acts, or conversely, to 'harmonize' Luke and Acts.

As Jesus did on the road to Emmaus, in the farewell scene he first interprets the law, prophets and psalms for his disciples, so they will believe in his legitimacy as fulfilment of scripture. Although the words *"Thus it is written,"* usually announce a quotation from the Hebrew Scriptures, there is no specific reference in them either to a suffering Messiah or to one who will die and rise, or even that this will occur on the third day. All of these things are claimed by Luke's Messiah as Luke develops his universalist Christology. This is developed further in Acts, (where Paul says):

> Acts 26: 22-23: *"To this day I have had help from God, and so I stand here, testifying to both small and great, saying nothing but what the prophets and Moses said would take place: that the Messiah must suffer, and that, by being the first to rise from the dead, he would proclaim light both to our people and to the Gentiles."*

These ideas represent an intermingling of Pharisaic ideas about the Messiah appearing at the general resurrection of the righteous and the universalist outlook of hellenized Diaspora Judaism. Those hellenized Jews included among their ranks the gospel writer known as Luke.

In Luke the 'promise of God' (24:49) appears to look backwards to John the Baptist's prediction that the Messiah would *"baptize"* with *"the Holy Spirit"* (3:16), and then forward to the ascension scene of Acts chapter 1. The promise in both Luke and Acts is that those who witness Jesus' departure from earth will receive the power of the Holy Spirit. The idea of being *"clothed"* with power from above reflects the symbolism of the prophetic mantle, which was probably nothing more than a sheepskin cloak, worn over the shoulders. It became significant only when the prophet received a blessing on it for his commission from God/the Holy Spirit. When wearing the mantle the prophet was then able to speak the words of the deity.

Significantly, Zechariah 13:4 describes the prophetic mantle as *"hairy"*, like the clothing of Elijah/John the Baptist. No doubt John's hairy clothing (as described in Mark and Matthew) increased the first century perception of him as Elijah returned. When the time came for Elijah to ascend into heaven, he and Elisha his disciple went alone across the Jordan, where Elisha asked Elijah if he could " ... *inherit a double share of (his) spirit"*. Elijah replied that his request would be granted " ... *if you see me as I am being taken from you"*. Elisha did see Elijah ascending in the whirlwind, and his receipt of the divinely-sent spirit of Elijah was symbolised by the prophetic mantle which fell to earth. The watching company of prophets confirmed that now the *"spirit of Elijah rests on Elisha"* (2 Kgs. 2:15) and Elisha continued the work begun by Elijah. The comparison may easily be made with Luke's narrative of the ascension of Jesus, where the close disciples of Jesus witness his being *"... carried up into heaven"*. (24:51b). It is those who see Jesus being taken from them who are to receive *"power from on high"* to continue the mission of Jesus.

Although there is a clear parallel with the Elijah story, the obvious distinction of Luke's narrative concerns the nature of the mission to be carried out by Jesus' disciples. While the mission of Elisha was to continue to speak the prophetic word of God to Israel alone, in Luke Jesus' disciples are to speak to *"all nations"* and in the name of the Messiah. Luke's Gospel is a systematic rewriting of Mark and Matthew plus Luke's own additions, with the primary aim of proclaiming the new Moses/Messiah Jesus to the whole world, including Palestinian Jews, Jews in the hellenized Diaspora, Samaritans and Gentiles.

Whether the original gospel of Luke contained the words *"carried up into heaven"* or not, the same idea applies. When the disciples see Jesus departing from them, if they then go and wait in Jerusalem, they will be *"clothed with power from on high"*. For Luke, that waiting time will be forty days, until Pentecost (as in Acts Chapter 2).

Jesus the Messiah in the Gospel of John

The Gospel of John is rightly in a separate category from the three synoptic gospels; it constitutes a genre of its own. Yet many may have wondered why there is no 'Year of John' in the Common Lectionary. Why not? A look through the other three years will supply the answer. John is actually the backbone of the Lectionary. Through years A, B and C, readings from John illustrate the 'high holy days' of the church's year. John is used to guide the church toward a traditional understanding of church festivals, based on belief in Jesus the Christ. Because of that, John undergirds and emphasises Christian tradition in all three Lectionary years. In particular, John is the preferred gospel for the Easter narratives. The reason for this will become clearer as we look carefully at John's Gospel and recognize that it is the foundational gospel for much of Christian dogma. Because of the mystical literary and theological imagery in John, it is sometimes given the designation 'gnostic gospel'. That was largely discredited in the mid-twentieth century by the discovery of genuine gnostic writings at Nag Hammadi in Egypt in 1945. John is also called the 'signs gospel'.

There are significant questions about John the gospel writer and his specific agenda in writing. Most importantly for the purpose of this book, what does his gospel have to say about the Messiah? How does John portray and imagine Jesus as Messiah? These questions will have answers different from those we encountered looking through Mark, Matthew and Luke. First of all it is essential to be aware that most contemporary scholars are in agreement on a crucial issue regarding the Gospel of John. There is strong scholarly consensus that John's Gospel does not contain the authentic words and actions of Jesus. Rather than a historical record, it is a theological interpretation of the death and resurrection of Jesus as Messiah/Son of God. It is written from the perspective of a hellenized Jew, probably in the early second century, CE.

Needless to say, the author's world view is pre-scientific, with a view from a flat earth to a three-tiered universe, where earth is the sole recipient of God's attention. The people of that era had no knowledge of the universe, even of the nature of the solar system, of which earth is one small planet. That extremely limited view of the universe and therefore of the kind of God who might overlook it, is fundamental to the theology created by an early second century Jewish writer. That context comes into play as John sets out to express the significance of Jesus for himself and his community. We must also acknowledge that Jesus himself was a man of the early first century CE, with first century views of the cosmos.

As in the other canonical gospels, John's God is inclined to intervene in earthly affairs. The God of John's Gospel goes even further than the God of the synoptic gospels, to the point of 'embedding' 'himself' in the body of his 'Son', whom John identifies as a Jewish man from the Galilee region of Palestine. John's Gospel gave a huge amount of stimulus to the development of the 'Christ' of fourth century doctrine.

The first question for our consideration has a large bearing on the content of the gospel. It concerns the identity of the gospel's author. Some commentators would still argue that John the gospel writer was the original apostle John, the brother of James and son of Zebedee. If true, this would mean that the gospel was written from an eye-witness perspective. Most scholars do not take this view of the gospel writer John. The main reason is that the only documentary 'evidence' for it is a quotation from the late first century/early second century CE writer Papias. This quotation does not come from an original manuscript by Papias. It comes second-hand – as included in the writings of the 'church father' Eusebius of Caesarea. As quoted by Eusebius, Papias refers to 'Disciples' and 'Elders' with whom he has spoken:

" ... and again, if anyone came who had been a follower of the Elders, I used to enquire about the sayings of the Elders – what Andrew, or Peter, or Philip, or Thomas, or James, or John, or Matthew, or any other of the Lord's Disciples said and what Aristion and Elder John, the Disciples of the Lord, say."[127]

The above certainly is evidence that in the early writings, including the writing of Papias as quoted, there was common interchange of the words 'Disciples', 'Apostles' and 'Elders'. It is impossible to know whether, when Papias wrote of an "Elder John", that this was the original disciple John or another John, called 'Elder'. It is highly likely that the person who wrote John's Gospel is using a pseudonym. That is, the writer has used the name of one of the disciples to lend credence to his own writings. What looks to us a scandalous practice was by no means unusual in those times. Because of that it is probably best to say that the author of John's Gospel is unknown. I will have more to say about the authorship in my discussion of John chapter 21.

Questions of authorship naturally lead to consideration of the dating of John's Gospel. If it were written by one of the original twelve, specifically by John, that raises questions about attempts to date the gospel toward the end of the first century. Someone who was already adult around the year 30 CE would obviously be very old indeed (i.e. 90 plus) at the end of the first century – incredibly old for that era of history. For that reason commentators in favour of authorship by John the original disciple necessarily date the gospel in the 60s or 70s CE. Even that dating necessitates John writing up to the age of 70, at a time when 40–50 years was the usual life expectancy. One of the crucial limiting factors for aged writers was the absence of aids to vision such as spectacles. Some commentators get around that by imagining John the disciple of Jesus dictating the gospel to scribes, as in the case of Paul's Letter to the Romans.[128] By this extraordinarily slim argument they endeavour to build a case for John's Gospel as a historical eye-witness record of Jesus' words and actions.

There is, however, important historical evidence that

does help to date the gospel after the lifetime of possible 'eye-witnesses'. Around 85 CE one of the Eighteen Benedictions (*Shemoneh Esreh*) recited in all synagogues, including those in the Diaspora, was reformulated to include a curse on 'deviators' (*minim*). The *minim* would have included those hellenized Jews who saw Jesus not only as the Messiah, but as divine Son of God. The curse of the *minim* would have applied to the community of John the gospel writer. John refers to that kind of rejection in the story of the man born blind:

> 9:22: *"His parents said this because they were afraid of the Jews; for the Jews had already agreed that anyone who confessed Jesus to be the Messiah would be put out of the synagogue."*

Other instances are 12:42 and 16:2, which indicate that some followers of Jesus the Messiah were killed by Jewish authorities. This all relates to the time when John was writing his gospel. The 'Jews' here refers to the Pharisees, who were leaders of the Jewish people after the destruction of the Temple in 70CE.

In traditional Judaism the title Son of God did not imply divinity. It merely identified a man divinely anointed to represent God on earth, such as King David. In Psalm 2:7 David speaks: *I will tell of the decree of the LORD: He said to me, "You are my son; today I have begotten you."* On the other hand, in the Gentile Greek world Son of God terminology had its origin in Greek mythology, including tales about sons of the gods who came to earth as messengers of those gods to humanity. A famous example is Hermes, the son of Zeus, the king of the gods. He had wings on his sandals and was authorized to come down to earth from heaven and also to travel to the underworld beneath the earth. All of these ideas needed belief in a three-tier universe with heaven 'up there'.

In John the distinctive non-Jewish understanding of Jesus as divine Son of God is apparent in Jesus' response to *"the Jews"* after he healed a paralysed man on the Sabbath. When they began persecuting him over this, he replied:

> 5:16-18: *"My Father is still working, and I also am working." For this reason the Jews were seeking to kill him, because he was not only breaking the Sabbath, but was also calling God his own Father, thereby making himself equal to God.*

In traditional Judaism, to call God 'Father' did not imply an equal relationship with God. There is plenty of precedent in the Hebrew Scriptures for a parental God in relationship with humanity (e.g. God speaks in Hosea 11:1: *"When Israel was a child, I loved him, and out of Egypt I called my son."*). In the New Testament, Jesus' prayer in Luke beginning *"Our Father"* does not make all who pray it equal with God.

The charge against Jesus in 5:16-18 looks like an attempt to cite reasons in the gospel why the Temple leadership (*"the Jews"* in John means the Temple leadership) were responsible for the death of Jesus. It reflects the hostile attitude of the Jewish leadership (now the Pharisees in John's time after the destruction of the Temple) toward Jews who believed not only that Jesus was the Messiah, but that he was the divine Son of God.

As I have explained in previous chapters, the attitude of the Jewish leadership was in part because of security concerns – the need to distance Jews from messianic groups at the end of a century of disaster for Jews who had followed Messiah/kings. In John's time the hostility of the Pharisee leadership toward his community would have at least partly reflected John's claim for Jesus' divinity. Hostility toward messianic Jews can be seen in their expulsion from synagogues about 85CE, when the curse on the 'deviators' was included in the liturgy. John's Gospel could have been written any time following that development until the early second century.

The church leader Clement of Alexandria noted that John wrote his gospel to 'supplement' the accounts in the other gospels. 'Correct' is probably a better word, given that John's theology includes a more exalted Christology than that of the synoptic gospel writers. John's Gospel shows signs of being focussed on 'correcting' the writings of Luke (Gospel and Acts).

As I have noted, there are scholars who want to date the writing of John from before the Jewish War and the destruction of Jerusalem in 70 CE. They base their case on John 5:2: *"Now in Jerusalem there is a pool, called in Hebrew Bethzatha, which has five porticoes."* The pre-war case hinges on the present tense: *"there is a pool."* Therefore (they argue) the gospel was written before the pool was destroyed in 70 CE. It can also be contended that the writer wanted to present a story conveying immediacy. Naturally then, he depicted Jesus in the year 30 CE, at a time when the pool called Bethzatha still existed. John would not have wanted to remind his readers that he was writing from hindsight as well as from an exalted christological perspective.

For understanding of the length of time between Jesus' death and the writing of John's Gospel, it is helpful to relate that time frame to the 20th and 21st centuries. The time gap is the same as it would be if John's Gospel were being written today (2015), about events that occurred in 1930. A great deal has happened in politics, society, culture and religion since 1930, including wars, mass movement of populations, changing power structures, technological advancement and different political and economic ideologies. Those elements largely determine the way people think in 2015. Similar kinds of change (even though slower to take effect than changes in 20th and 21st centuries) apply to differences between Jesus' Galilean/Judean Jewish society in a Roman province in 30 CE and a hellenized Jewish Diaspora society (possibly in Ephesus) in the early second century. There has also been plenty of time to theologise concerning the identity and meaning of Jesus.

John's Gospel as Gnostic

It is sometimes claimed that the Gospel of John is gnostic. One definition of Gnosticism says it is the doctrine of salvation by knowledge. It has been argued that Gnosticism originated as a variation of Christianity, but many scholars in this area have claimed that it had its origins in Eastern religions, including the religion of Babylonia. The so-called Gnostic Gospels were written from the second to the fourth century CE and are not included in Christian canons of scripture. John's Gospel does contain what is thought of as gnostic language. For example, the concepts of *Logos* and Light, as they are related to Jesus. However, the case for the legitimacy of gnosticism as an established religious tradition has taken a battering recently through the scholarship of Karen L. King. She holds the Hollis Chair of Divinity at Harvard Divinity School and works in the areas of early Christianity and gnosticism. King's position works against the belief that John's Gospel is 'gnostic'. She writes:

> *I have argued that the variety of phenomena classified as 'Gnostic' simply will not support a single, monolithic definition, and in fact none of the primary materials fits the standard of typological definition.*[129]

King also defines what has been called Gnosticism:

> *Gnosticism is a term invented in the early modern period to aid in defining the boundaries of normative Christianity.*[130]

In summary, the term gnostic has been used to refer to any theological idea deemed to be outside of orthodox Christianity as formulated in the fourth century CE. On that basis it is perfectly legitimate to argue that concepts such as Light and *Logos* in the Prologue to John's Gospel are simply the products of Jewish tradition, not ideas alien to Jewish philosophy and theology.

John's intended readers

None of the gospels were written in theological vacuums; they were each a response to other systems of belief, and even a response to other gospels. Mark's audience was Palestinian Jews, including hellenized Jews; Matthew's audience was primarily Palestinian Jews, in particular the Pharisees; Luke wrote for everyone – for Palestinian Jews, for Gentiles, for Samaritans and for hellenized Jews in the Diaspora. There is a good case for arguing that John's intended readers were

hellenized Jews, probably living in Asia Minor and educated in
Greek philosophy. That education would almost certainly have
included the writings of the Jewish philosopher, Philo of
Alexandria. John's Gospel contains sophisticated philosophical
and theological concepts that imply an intended readership well
educated in both Jewish and Greek ideas.

The gospel is the product of a network of Greek-speaking
Christ groups in Asia Minor (known as the Johannine
community) that also produced the three 'pastoral' letters, 1
John, 2 John and 3 John. 'John' is most probably a pseudonym,
used for the purpose of trying to identify the writings of the
'Johannine community' with the original disciple of Jesus called
John, son of Zebedee.

Whoever he or they may be, the writer(s) of John's Gospel
intends to set out a convincing case for Jesus as the Son of God
who 'knows' the Father. John's Jesus is the divine revealer of
secret knowledge concerning the transcendent God. This is
developed throughout John's writing, which itself underpins an
exalted Christology absent from the synoptic gospels. Although
John is clearly Jewish, his gospel was written in an increasingly
hostile Jewish environment. That is in no small part due to his
claims about Jesus as divine Son of God. It is no accident that
John's Gospel is the foundation for trinitarian ideas about Jesus
that developed in the third and fourth centuries CE. The synoptic
gospels do not qualify as foundation for trinitarianism, or for the
Doctrine of the Incarnation. As Canadian theologian Jacob Jocz
wrote:

> The Christology of the Church is essentially Johannine.
> Without the Fourth Gospel, even the Pauline Epistles
> would not have sufficed as a basis for the Trinitarian
> doctrine we have today.[131]

This chapter's description of the way John the Gospel
writer painted his portrait of Jesus as Messiah will argue that
John had knowledge at least of the Gospel of Mark, but probably
of all three synoptic gospels. I will point out where John has
adopted messianic concepts from those gospels, but has also

'corrected' them where he regards their Christology as insufficiently exalted. He uses several names for Jesus as Messiah, including 'Christ', 'Messiah', 'Son of God', 'Son of Man', 'the Prophet', 'the One coming into the world', and 'I Am' (7 times). We will look at all of them as we move along. The most important difference between John's portrait of Messiah Jesus or Jesus Christ and the synoptic gospel depictions, is that John portrays Jesus as divine in himself, as we will see. In accordance with Jewish tradition, Mark, Matthew and Luke see him as divinely anointed Messiah. Matthew and Luke come closest to John's position in their birth narratives, but as I have said, the virgin birth narratives in Matthew and Luke are likely to be later (perhaps third or fourth century) additions from other authors.

The Prologue

1:1-18: *In the beginning was the Word, and the Word was with God, and the Word was God. He was in the beginning with God. All things came into being through him, and without him not one thing came into being. What has come into being in him was life, and the life was the light of all people. The light shines in the darkness, and the darkness did not overcome it. There was a man sent from God, whose name was John. He came as a witness to testify to the light, so that all might believe through him. He himself was not the light, but he came to testify to the light. The true light, which enlightens everyone, was coming into the world. He was in the world, and the world came into being through him; yet the world did not know him. He came to what was his own, and his own people did not accept him. But to all who received him, who believed in his name, he gave power to become children of God, who were born, not of blood or of the will of the flesh or of the will of man, but of God. And the Word became flesh and lived among us, and we have seen his glory, the glory as of a father's only son, full of grace and truth. (John testified to him and cried out, "This was he of whom I said, 'He who comes after me ranks ahead of me because he was*

before me.' "). From his fullness we have all received,
grace upon grace. The law indeed was given through
Moses; grace and truth came through Jesus Christ. No
one has ever seen God. It is God the only Son, who is
close to the Father's heart, who has made him known.

Again we are faced with a gospel opening that in its
essence bears little resemblance to the remainder of the gospel.
As it did with Matthew and Luke, this leads us to ask whether
John's Gospel might have begun with verse 19 of chapter 1,
which introduces John the Baptist. If so, the beginning of John's
Gospel would be consistent in that respect with Mark's,
Matthew's and Luke's. An enormous amount of scholarly
research surrounds the Prologue to John's gospel and I intend to
give my reader only a brief account of what I hope will be helpful
findings.

Many have noted that the language of the Prologue to
John is poetic. Given that, it is likely also to have been a hymn.
Either before or after the gospel was written, it was possibly used
in worship by hellenized messianic Jews. It could have been
composed by another writer and then edited to form the opening
of the gospel. In any case, there are clear additions to the
Prologue itself that interrupt the flow of both concepts and
language.

The first addition concerns the role of John the Baptist:

1:6-8: *There was a man sent from God, whose name was*
John. He came as a witness to testify to the light, so that
all might believe through him. He himself was not the
light, but he came to testify to the light.

The second also concerns John the Baptist:

1:15: *(John testified to him and cried out, "This was he of*
whom I said, 'He who comes after me ranks ahead of me
because he was before me.' ").

The two additions relate to themes in the gospel, so were likely inserted to create thematic connections between gospel and Prologue. Many scholars argue that these verses did not belong in the original poem/hymn. I encourage my reader to read again the Prologue (above) to see the point being made.

The issue of whether the Prologue comprised the original beginning of John remains, but the most important question relates to its content. What does its writer mean when he speaks of the Messiah? Anyone reading the Prologue is left in no doubt that its writer means to increase the status of Jesus the Messiah. Although this writer probably did know Mark, Matthew and Luke, his own Christology was of a different order from theirs.

The first words of the Prologue surely reflect the first words of the Book of Genesis: *"In the beginning"*. In Genesis, *"In the beginning God created"*. In John:

> 1:1-3: *"In the beginning was the Word, and the Word was with God, and the Word was God. He was in the beginning with God. All things came into being through him, and without him not one thing came into being."*

'He' is obviously Jesus Christ, the Messiah/divine Son of God. In the first sentence Jesus is *"the Word"*, *Word* being the English translation of the Greek word *Logos*. The Book of Revelation (19:13) is the only other instance in the New Testament where Jesus is described as *"The Word (Logos) of God"*. The following are three classic meanings commonly suggested for the word *Logos*.

- *Logos* as Torah. For Greek-speaking Jews in the first century CE the *'logos* of God' meant the Hebrew Scriptures, in particular the first five books, or Torah. God's Word *(logos)* was the Law/Torah. The *logos* of God was also made known through the prophets.
- *Logos* as Reason. Behind the Hellenistic Jewish use of the word *logos* was a Greek philosophical understanding. In Greek thought the *logos* was the underlying order of nature. Greek philosophical thought made it more

appealing to understand God or God's *logos* as perfect or orderly reason, than to accept Jewish (biblical) humanized views of God.

- *Logos* as Wisdom. Jewish Wisdom traditions include the idea of the pre-existent Torah. The traditions include the Book of Proverbs, where (in 8:29-30) wisdom (or Torah) speaks: *".... when he assigned the sea its limit, so that the waters might not transgress his command, when he marked out the foundations of the earth, then I was beside him, like a master worker ..."* In an Aramaic paraphrase of Proverbs 8:30 wisdom says, *"I was the skilled tool of the Holy One, blessed be He."*

The rabbinic writer of the biblical interpretation (*midrash*) Genesis Rabbah, wrote:

"Thus, the Holy One, blessed be He, looked in the Torah and created the world, for the Torah says, *"In the beginning, God created"* and there is no 'beginning' except the Torah, as it is written, "The Lord created me at the beginning of his work, the first of his acts of long ago. Ages ago I was set up, at the first, before the beginning of the earth."

It is no accident that Matthew's Gospel includes a reference to Jewish wisdom traditions in the book of Ben Sirach/Ecclesiasticus (6:23-31), where wisdom encourages the putting on of her yoke. Matthew wants to say that Jesus' teaching (for him the 'new Torah') has made the 'yoke of the Torah/Wisdom' light to carry: " *... for my yoke is easy, and my burden is light."* (Matt. 11:30).

Rather than John being inspired by Greek philosophy (as is often assumed) it looks as if the *"Word"* or *Logos* of the Prologue of his gospel reflects a Jewish tradition about the pre-existence of the Torah. For the writer of the Prologue, Jesus the Messiah with his new interpretation of Torah is the personified pre-existent Word/*Logos* of God. He is *"the true light, which enlightens everyone"* (John 1:9). Accordingly the Prologue sets out its Christology in a way that the synoptic gospels do not. It looks gnostic, meaning that it represents salvation as the attainment of sacred knowledge – wisdom that emanates from God through the mediator called the *Logos*. But the Prologue does not actually present Jesus the *Logos* as divine. It interprets Jewish wisdom tradition to recognize Jesus' *teaching as divinely inspired – as the new Torah/Wisdom, pre-existent with God from the beginning of creation. The teaching is represented* by the symbolism of 'Light'.

Most importantly, the Prologue represents Jesus differently from the divine Son of God Christology in the remainder of the gospel. For that reason it is possible to see the Prologue as an addition to the original gospel, which is likely to have begun at 1:19. Raymond Brown's theory concerning this includes the idea that the Prologue may have been a hymn adapted to be added to John's Gospel:

> *(The Prologue) is an early Christian hymn, probably stemming from Johannine circles, which has been adapted to serve as an overture to the Gospel narrative of the career of the incarnate Word.*[132]

British scholar R. P. Casey recognized the difficulties posed by cross-referencing between two different traditions that occurs in the Prologue:

> *... the principal difficulty lies neither in its style nor in its terminology but in the fact that its author has his feet planted firmly in two worlds: that of the Old Testament and that of Hellenistic philosophy and he allows his gaze to wander easily from one to the other. At every important point he has not only two thoughts instead of one, but two sets of allusions in mind.*[133]

Describing Jesus as *"The Word"* is the Prologue's way of saying that the wisdom Jesus taught is what informed God's creative activity from the beginning. This designation of Jesus as teacher of divine wisdom that has existed from before the beginning of creation, functions as an alternative 'birth' narrative. The Prologue proclaims Jesus as representative of God to humanity through his teaching. It is his wisdom that is pre-existent – originating from before the beginning of creation. The Prologue therefore does not say that Jesus (as human or divine, or both) existed from before creation. The remainder of the gospel sees Jesus from a very different perspective, as we will see.

A further reason to see the *Word* in John's Prologue as representing a prior Jewish tradition is its inclusion in the Aramaic Palestinian Targum (Neofiti) translation of Genesis 1:1. Neofiti (originally called Palestinian Targum) is dated early, although scholars argue variously for its origin from the first to the fourth centuries CE. Its language is Palestinian Aramaic, not the Babylonian Aramaic in which the later Targums were written.

As I did with my discussion of Targums in the chapter on Mark's gospel, I will quote first from the English of NRSV and then from the English translation of the Aramaic in Targum Neofiti:

- NRSV Genesis 1:1-2: *In the beginning, when God created the heavens and the earth, the earth was a formless void and darkness covered the face of the deep, while a wind from God swept over the face of the waters.*
- Targum Neofiti Genesis 1:1: *From the beginning with wisdom, the Memra of the Lord created and perfected the heavens and the earth.*[134]

This is an example of a strong first century Jewish movement to remove human-like characteristics from scriptural references to God. Here it is the Aramaic *Memra* (or Word) who does the actual creating, not God (as per John 1:1-3): Psalm 104 expresses the idea of wisdom (in Hebrew *hochmah*) as the creating power of God:

Psalm 104:24: *O LORD, how manifold are your works! In wisdom you have made them all ...*

To help make this clearer, in scripture there are four words for this same creative power that comes from God:
- *Hochmah,* the Hebrew word for wisdom that is used across the Hebrew Bible,
- *Memra,* the Palestinian Aramaic name used in Targums;
- *Logos,* the first century Greek name used in John's Gospel;
- *Word,* the English translation of *Logos.*

I have already noted that the Prologue of John contains what are often recognized as insertions relating to the role of John the Baptist. John's role as herald of the Messiah is woven into a hymn depicting Jesus' wisdom as the pre-existent Word or (in Greek) *Logos.* Verse 8 contains an explicit statement about John that appears to function as a response to those who saw John the Baptist (not Jesus) as the Word/*Logos* of God: "*He himself was not the light, but he came to testify to the light.*" The modified Prologue then looks like a means of asserting a claim to Jesus' messiahship over against those who apparently saw John in this role. Accordingly, in verse 15 there is reiteration of John the Baptist's subordinate role to Jesus the Word/*Logos*: "*He who comes after me ranks ahead of me because he was before me.*"

Verse 18 raises questions of its own. It looks like the writer's summary of his position regarding Jesus' identity: "*No one has ever seen God. It is God the only Son, who is close to the Father's heart, who has made him known*". That language ought to raise reservations about verse 18's place in an original version of the Prologue. It makes a claim for Jesus' divinity even more explicitly than verse 14, where Jesus' "*glory*" is described as glory like that of "*a father's only son*".

In fact, verse 18 makes the most astounding claim about Jesus in the whole of the New Testament. It first acknowledges that "*no one has ever seen God*", then sets out what is recognized as the biblical basis for the Doctrine of the Trinity: "*It is God the only Son, who is close to the Father's heart, who has made him known.*" Here Jesus is not Son of God, he is God the Son. There is therefore good reason to argue that this verse is a later addition to the Prologue, possibly by the writer of the rest of John's Gospel. The addition of this verse would have lent considerable biblical credibility to the formulation of trinitarian doctrine in the fourth century. I reiterate that we simply do not know the original form and extent of the gospels, including John's Gospel.

The gospel writer follows the ideas in 1:18 in chapter 3:18: *"For God so loved the world that he gave his only Son ..."*. Most Christians are familiar with the English translation from Greek in the King James Version of John, where the term is *"only begotten Son"*. Even without 'begotten', this phrase singles out Jesus as the only one who qualifies to be called the actual Son of God. The implication is clear: Jesus is uniquely the Son of God, with attributes of the divine. Even then, it is probably a mistake to equate this understanding of Jesus' divinity with that of the Doctrine of the Trinity, as Raymond Brown points out:

> *The Prologue's hymnic confession "The Word was God" does not have the same ideological content found in Nicea's confession that the Son was "true God of true God." A different problematic and a long philosophical development separate the two.*[135]

The writer of John is clearly Jewish, but he is most probably a hellenized Jew with a broad education in Greek philosophy and literature. It is likely that he is based in Asia Minor, possibly in Ephesus, where Greek was spoken and Jews received an education in Greek philosophy as well as Jewish thought. Another stronghold of hellenized Jews in John's time was Alexandria in Egypt, where Judaism had been increasingly hellenized from at least three centuries BCE. Alexandria was also the base of a strong cohort of Egyptian/Greek philosophers and their schools. Among Jews living in that environment there was a desire to present Judaism as a religion whose philosophy could match that of the classical Greek philosophers. Philo of Alexandria's writings are an example of the paraphrasing of Judaism in philosophical terms. It is not for nothing that it was Alexandria where the Hebrew Bible was translated into Greek in the third century BCE.

Philo worked through the Platonic philosophy he learned in Alexandria, but claimed that Judaism was compatible/equal with the centre of Platonic thought. Platonists also used the concept of *Logos*, which they saw as the spiritual force linking God and the lower world (earth). In that understanding God is remote and inaccessible, except through spiritual mediators. For the Platonists the first act of the *Logos* was creation. As also known in Stoic ideas, the *Logos* became the binding power that made everything in the universe cohere and function. Philo sometimes combined the force of the *Logos* with the spirit of the Torah. It is understandable then, that Philo identified Moses the mediator of a pre-existent Torah as the *Logos*, the 'Word made flesh' (1:14). Philo saw the Platonic *Logos* as '"the Son" and "the first-begotten of God".[136] In hellenized Jewish 'Christ' communities at the end of the 1st century, these ideas began to be expressed about Jesus through the concept of the pre-existent Son, who is the 'Word made flesh'. Philo also saw the *Logos* as an intercessor with God:

To His Word (Logos) His chief messenger, highest in age and honour, the Father of all has given the special prerogative, to stand on the border (between the two worlds) and separate the creature from the Creator. This same Word both pleads with the immortal as suppliant for afflicted mortality and acts as ambassador of the ruler to the subject.[137]

Philo lived until approximately 41 CE, but it is not surprising that he makes no mention of Jesus of Nazareth as the *Logos* made flesh. Philo's writings predate John's thinking about Jesus by at least half a century. Although he makes no mention of Jesus of Nazareth at all, it is clear that Philo's ideas were adopted by Christian writers who believed that the *Logos* had become flesh in Jesus.

It is easy to see how short is the distance between Greek philosophical ideas about a *Logos*, Philo's ideas about a platonized Judaism, the hellenized Paul's vision of Jesus as the Messiah/Christ, John's Gospel's Jesus the divine Son of God, and the doctrines of the Trinity and Incarnation.

In the books of the Apocrypha (following the books of the Hebrew Bible) there is the book of 1 Baruch. In chapter 3, in a section called "In Praise of Wisdom", the role of wisdom in creating is acknowledged. It ends:

> 1 Baruch 3: 35-7: *This is our God; no other can be compared to him. He found the whole way to knowledge, and gave her [Wisdom] to his servant Jacob and to Israel, whom he loved. Afterward she appeared on earth and lived with humankind.*

The idea of Wisdom or *Logos* appearing on earth and living with human beings is a probable precursor to writings about Jesus as the *Logos*. 1 Baruch was probably written in the second century BCE, but there is no certainty about that. An important fact here is that 1 Baruch was written in Greek and included in the Greek version of the Hebrew Scriptures, which was the 'bible' of the gospel writers.

I believe the reader of this book can see in these ideas from Philo and 1 Baruch an outline of the origins of Christology – the use of existing ideas to present Jesus as Son of God. It is possible to identify the blending of traditional Jewish ideas about the Messiah into Greek ideas about a spiritual mediator between humanity and a transcendent God. Those ideas fitted the time and place in which they were formulated – a time and place long gone. Most importantly, they illustrate an ancient Greek view of a transcendent God that has been comprehensively rejected in the development of contemporary spirituality.

From the foregoing it can be seen that the concept of the Son of God/Messiah ('Christ') is a product of human thinking, emerging from the theological/philosophical ideas of a particular era in human history. Increasingly, followers of Jesus are recognizing that christological thinking about him has a 'use by' date that has long passed.

For more details, see Section 4 of this book.

Statements concerning John the Baptist (the beginning of the Gospel of John)

> 1:19-28: *This is the testimony given by John when the Jews sent priests and Levites from Jerusalem to ask him, "Who are you?" He confessed and did not deny it, but confessed, "I am not the Messiah." And they asked him, "What then? Are you the prophet?" He answered, "No." Then they said to him, "Who are you? Let us have an answer for those who sent us. What do you say about yourself?" He said, "I am the voice of one crying out in the wilderness 'Make straight the way of the Lord' " as the prophet Isaiah said. Now they had been sent from the Pharisees. They asked him, "Why then are you baptizing if you are neither the Messiah, nor Elijah, nor the prophet?" John answered them, "I baptize with water. Among you stands one whom you do not know, the one who is coming after me; I am not worthy to untie the thong of his sandal." This took place in Bethany across the Jordan where John was baptizing.*

From chapter 1 verse 19, John the gospel writer begins to lead the reader away from traditional Jewish understandings about the coming of the Messiah. As I have pointed out in chapters on the synoptic gospels, in biblical tradition the Messiah was to have been announced by the returned Elijah, or another of the ancient prophets, usually referring to Moses. In Mark, Matthew and Luke, it is John the Baptist who fits that Elijah expectation. In John's gospel, when the Temple leadership sends emissaries to ask him for his identity, John the Baptist denies being the Messiah. If there had been no belief at that time among Jews that John the Baptist might have been the Messiah, there would have been no need for the gospel writer to include this 'confession' by John.

Then something very different happens. Contrary to the synoptics, John also denies that he is Elijah, or 'the prophet', a reference to the *"prophet like me"* mentioned by Moses (Deuteronomy 18:15). Naturally then, the *"priests and Levites"* demand to know who John the Baptist actually thinks he is, so they will have an answer to take back to Jerusalem. John answers them by quoting Isaiah 40:3 (NRSV English): *"I am the voice of one crying in the wilderness, 'Make straight the way of the LORD'."*

Here the word LORD is capitalized in English so it clearly means God.[138] The Greek version of Isaiah reads in English: *"… make straight the paths of our God."* (40:3). Muddying the waters is the fact that the Greek Old Testament has two words for 'God': *Kurios* and *Theos*. John knows that in the gospels of Mark, Matthew and Luke the word *"Lord"* (in Greek, *Kurios*) is not ambiguous. It means Jesus the Messiah.[139] Accordingly, the meaning of the word 'Lord' in John's Gospel is not specifically 'God', but God's Messiah/Christ, Jesus the Son of God. It effectively changes the meaning of the word *Kuriou* in the Greek Isaiah quote in John 1:23 from *"of our God"* to mean the Messiah: *"of the Lord"*.

All of this is crucial to the purpose of John the gospel writer. It means that for him John the Baptist is not Elijah preparing the way for the (Jewish) Messiah, a human being anointed by God. Instead John the Baptist is the one Isaiah (now) says will prepare the way for God; specifically, for God in the person of Jesus the Son of God "the Lord". Accordingly, John's Gospel from 1:19 onward is not only messianic in its proclamation, it is explicitly christological, with claims to Jesus' divinity. In traditional Jewish usage, Son of God does not imply divinity;[140] in John's Gospel it does. John uses this title again and again to make his claim that Jesus the Messiah/Christ is divine.

The further question from the Jerusalem representatives about John the Baptist's identity (1:22) is met with an enigmatic response. John implies that someone of enormous significance and standing is already *"among you"*, even if you don't recognize him. This surely was picked up and placed by an editor into the Prologue at 1:10: *"He came to what was his own, and his own people did not accept him"*, *"his own people"* being the Jews.

Consistent with that statement, John's Gospel contains anti-Jewish rhetoric encapsulated in the writer's frequent use of the term *"the Jews"* when referring to 'enemies' of Jesus – those who did not recognize him as Messiah/Son of God. Many scholars have translated the obviously negative use of the term *"the Jews"* in this context as 'the Judeans'. The explanation is that the Jewish gospel writer John came from outside of Judea, and looked on the Judeans as those responsible for Jesus' crucifixion and the persecution of followers of Jesus (now the Christ) in the late first century. While I agree that the writer of John's Gospel came from outside of Judea (probably from Ephesus in Asia Minor) I want to narrow down the designation *"the Jews"* further still. In each instance where it is used, a strong case can be made that by *"the Jews"*, John means the Jews who constituted the leadership of the Jerusalem Temple (Sadducees and Pharisees). For that reason, from here on I will use the term 'the Temple leadership' wherever the term *"the Jews"* is found in the gospel.

From his point of view, it is understandable that John the hellenized Jewish gospel writer and believer in Jesus the Messiah/Son of God should criticize non-messianic Jews in this fashion. John's negativity is all the more enhanced by persecution inflicted on messianic Jews by the Jewish leadership, at the time his gospel was written. Because his writing is necessarily retrospective, written at least 70 years after Jesus' death and probably 30-40 years after the destruction of the Temple, John uses the term *"the Jews"* whenever he refers to Jewish leaders *at the time of Jesus*. At that point they were the Temple leadership. What looks like anti-Jewish rhetoric in John's Gospel reflects John's hostility toward the Temple leadership who rejected Jesus as Messiah around 30CE. Yet there was more to it than that. John was apparently experiencing similar rejection and persecution from the Jewish leaders of his own time at the end of the first century – the Pharisees who succeeded the Temple leadership after the Temple's destruction in 70CE. All of that naturally influenced the way his portrait of Jesus as Messiah was written.

Jesus' baptism in John

1:29-34: *The next day he saw Jesus coming toward him and declared, "Here is the Lamb of God who takes away the sin of the world! This is he of whom I said, 'After me*

*comes a man who ranks ahead of me because he was
before me.' I myself did not know him; but I came
baptizing with water for this reason, that he might be
revealed to Israel." And John testified, "I saw the Spirit
descending from heaven like a dove, and it remained on
him. I myself did not know him, but the one who sent me
to baptize with water said to me, 'He on whom you see
the Spirit descend and remain is the one who baptizes
with the Holy Spirit.' And I myself have seen and have
testified that this is the Son of God."*

The synoptic gospels reflect an increasing uneasiness in
depicting John the Baptist baptizing Jesus with a baptism of
repentance. Matthew has John arguing that it is Jesus who
should baptize him! This difficulty reaches its synoptic peak in
Luke 3:21-22, where it is quickly glossed over as *"when Jesus
also had been baptized"*. John takes this difficulty with Jesus'
baptism a huge step further. Congruent with his depiction of
Jesus as divine, he dismisses the baptism altogether and has
John the Baptist say that Jesus is the one who *"baptizes with the
Holy Spirit"* (1:33). In accordance with the Christology of John's
gospel, John the Baptist then calls Jesus the Son of God. In
reality the baptizer would have had no problem calling the
Messiah the Son of God, but meaning the anointed
representative of God on earth (the *mashiach*), not the divinized
sense in which this gospel writer meant it. The placing of the
words in 1:30: *"After me comes a man who ranks ahead of me
because he was before me."*, as *"he who comes after me ranks
ahead of me"* in the Prologue (1:15), is quite likely to serve an
editorial purpose in linking the ensuing text of the gospel itself
with the Prologue.

Jesus' divine messianic powers in John's Gospel
From here on we will look for John's 'signs' that Jesus is not only
the Jewish Messiah or Anointed One, but the divine Son of God.
Seven signs are usually identified by scholars, but there appear
to me to be ten.

- The first sign: Jesus 'knows' Nathanael:
  1:47-48: *"When Jesus saw Nathaniel coming toward him, he said to him, "Here is truly an Israelite in whom there is no deceit!" Nathanael asked him, "Where did you get to know me?" Jesus answered, "I saw you under the fig tree before Philip called you."*

This sign endows Jesus with divine omniscience, which is God's capacity to know everything. The story of Jesus calling Nathaniel is the first instance where John attributes divine powers to Jesus. As God knows everyone inside and out, even from before they were born (as in Psalm 139), Jesus has the capacity to 'know' Nathaniel before they were introduced. In John's Gospel, Nathaniel's natural response to this is to call Jesus *"King of Israel"* (or Messiah), and *"Son of God"* (1:49).

- The second sign: Jesus changes water into wine:
  2:1-11: *And Jesus said to her, "Woman, what concern is that to you and to me? My hour has not yet come." His mother said to the servants, "Do whatever he tells you." Now standing there were six stone water jars for the Jewish rites of purification, each holding twenty or thirty gallons. Jesus said to them, "Fill the jars with water." And they filled them up to the brim. He said to them, "Now draw some out, and take it to the chief steward." So they took it. When the steward tasted the water that had become wine, and did not know where it came from (although the servants who had drawn the water knew), the steward called the bridegroom and said to him, "Everyone serves the good wine first, and then the inferior wine after the guests have become drunk. But you have kept the good wine until now." Jesus did this, the first of his signs, in Cana of Galilee, and revealed his glory; and his disciples believed in him.*

This sign occurs at the celebrated *"wedding in Cana of Galilee"*, where Jesus is accompanied by his mother (never named as 'Mary' in John's Gospel) and his disciples. Why is *"the mother of Jesus*" not called 'Mary'? In accordance with John's high Christology, he may have wanted to create distance between "the mother of Jesus" and the Mary of the synoptics, around whom there was more than a hint of scandal. Verse 12 implies that "*his brothers*" were present also, as after the wedding they go to Capernaum together. There is no mention of Joseph. Where John's portrait of the divine Jesus Christ is concerned, Joseph would have been a distraction.

The wedding scene sees Jesus reluctant to reveal his divine powers until pushed by his mother when the wine ran out. This scenario looks like a foretaste of the messianic banquet described in Isaiah,[141] over which John wants his readers to believe that Jesus the Messiah will preside. Then he will give his followers the very best of the heavenly feast, including bread and the best of wine. John says this "*reveals his glory*" (meaning Jesus' divinity) and on this basis his disciples "*believed in him*".

- The third sign: the 'cleansing' of the Temple:
  2:13-25: *The Passover of the Jews was near, and Jesus went up to Jerusalem. In the temple he found people selling cattle, sheep, and doves, and the money changers seated at their tables. Making a whip of cords, he drove all of them out of the temple, both the sheep and the cattle. He also poured out the coins of the money changers and overturned their tables. He told those who were selling the doves, "Take these things out of here! Stop making my Father's house a marketplace!" His disciples remembered that it was written, "Zeal for your house will consume me." The Jews then said to him, "What sign can you show us for doing this?" Jesus answered them, "Destroy this temple, and in three days I will raise it up." The Jews then said, "This temple has been under construction for forty-six years, and will you raise it up in three days?" But he was speaking of his body. After he was raised from the dead, his disciples remembered that he had said this; and they believed the scripture and the word that Jesus had spoken. When he was in Jerusalem during the Passover festival, many*

believed in his name because they saw the signs that he was doing. But Jesus on his part would not entrust himself to them, because he knew all people and needed no one to testify about anyone; for he himself knew what was in everyone.

In an attempt to give his gospel a more accurate chronological sequence, John locates the so-called 'cleansing of the Temple' at the beginning of Jesus' ministry, not toward the end as in the synoptic gospels. The Passover of the Jews is announced as the reason for Jesus' visit to Jerusalem. According to John and unlike the synoptics, this is the first of three Passovers in which Jesus is present in Jerusalem. Also unlike the versions of Mark and Luke in which he 'begins' to drive out the animal sellers and money changers, in John (and Matthew) Jesus drives them all out. The big difference (and third sign) occurs in what Jesus says as he wields his whip: *"Take these things out of here! Stop making my Father's house a marketplace!"*

In accordance with his divine Son of God portrait of Jesus, John's is the only gospel in which Jesus calls the Temple *"my Father's house"*. It is also the only gospel in which the disciples 'remember' the passage from Psalm 69:9 (a Psalm of David): *"It is zeal for your house that has consumed me."* That verse continues its intimate association of Jesus with God: *"the insults of those who insult you have fallen on me."* In the background are the critical Temple leadership, called chief priests and scribes in the synoptic gospels. I have noted in chapters on the synoptic gospels that the writers use internal proof texts. We can see from this scenario in the Temple that the writer of John uses them also.

The leaders of the Temple then demand Jesus' credentials for his action there. They ask for a 'sign' (that he is the Messiah). He declares that if the Temple is destroyed (as John knows it already has been), he could raise it again in three days. For John, Jesus' response probably refers to his crucifixion and then to his resurrection as the restored 'Temple of his body'. After his death his disciples 'remember' what he said about that, and based on that 'sign', they believe in him. Many others in Jerusalem also *"believe in his name"* because of (unnamed) 'signs' he was doing. Then follows John's nod back to the first 'sign' - the calling of Nathanael. The implication here (1:24-25) is that Jesus did not trust anyone, since because of his divine omniscience, he knew what they were thinking.

- The fourth sign: Jesus 'knows' about the woman at the well.
  4:16-19: *Jesus said to her, "Go, call your husband, and come back." The woman answered him, "I have no husband." Jesus said to her, "You are right in saying, 'I have no husband'; for you have had five husbands, and the one you have now is not your husband. What you have said is true!" The woman said to him, "Sir, I see that you are a prophet."*

Another link with the first sign occurs as Jesus converses with a Samaritan woman. When he asks her to bring her husband to talk with them, she says she has no husband. Jesus exercises his divine omniscience in telling her: *"You are right in saying, 'I have no husband'; for you have had five husbands, and the one you have now is not your husband."* On the basis of this the woman does not identify him as Son of God or Messiah, but does see him as a prophet with divinely-inspired insight. The aftermath of the conversation bears fruit; other Samaritans believe Jesus to be *"the Saviour of the world"* after hearing the woman's account of her conversation with him. Here is John saying that as Son of God, Jesus is not just Saviour of the Jews, but of the whole world (see also 3:16: *"For God so loved the world ... "*). As a hellenized Jew himself, associating with Gentiles, John had a wider view of the significance of Jesus than Matthew, for whom Jesus was the Jewish Messiah sent to restore Israel's covenantal relationship with God, full stop!

- The fifth sign: Jesus cures a dying boy.
  4:46-53: *Now there was a royal official whose son lay ill in Capernaum. When he heard that Jesus had come from*

Judea to Galilee, he went and begged him to come down and heal his son, for he was at the point of death. Then Jesus said to him, "Unless you see signs and wonders you will not believe." The official said to him, "Sir, come down before my little boy dies." Jesus said to him, "Go; your son will live." The man believed the word that Jesus spoke to him and started on his way. As he was going down, his slaves met him and told him that his child was alive. So he asked them the hour when he began to recover, and they said to him, "Yesterday at one in the afternoon the fever left him." The father realized that this was the hour when Jesus had said to him, "Your son will live." So he himself believed, along with his whole household.

This sign sees Jesus having the power of life over death for the son of a 'royal official'. It is not strictly a raising from death, but a healing to avert death. Unlike the synoptic reports of healings or raisings from death, this instance does not even require Jesus' presence with the child. Significantly, the royal official represents a different class of people from those with whom Jesus usually associated. This is John's way of giving more status to Jesus for those who will read his gospel. They will see that as a result of the 'signs', even people in the court of King Herod came to believe in Jesus as Messiah/Son of God: *"So he himself believed, along with his whole household."* (4:53).

- The sixth sign: Jesus heals the 'sick' man.
  5:2-18: *Now in Jerusalem by the Sheep Gate there is a pool, called in Hebrew Bethzatha, which has five porticoes. In these lay many invalids – blind, lame, and paralyzed. One man was there who had been ill for thirty-eight years. When Jesus saw him lying there and knew he had been there a long time, he said to him, "Do you want to be made well?" The sick man answered him, "Sir, I have no one to put me into the pool when the water is stirred up; and while I am making my way, someone else steps down ahead of me." Jesus said to him,*

"Stand up, take your mat and walk." At once the man
was made well, and he took up his mat and began to
walk.

One of the reasons for the exclusion of a person from the
life of the Temple was a physical imperfection such as lameness,
blindness or a skin disease (usually leprosy). Although his illness
is not specified, the man lying beside the pool at the Sheep Gate
was one such excluded person. It was thought that the first
person to step into the pool when its water was stirred up –
ostensibly by an angel - would be healed of their physical
affliction. No one had ever helped this man into the water when
it was stirred up. When Jesus met him he had been ill and
coming to the pool for thirty-eight years. Jesus rejected the need
for an angel to stir up the water and simply told the man to
"Stand up, take your mat and walk." (5:8).

As I have said in chapters about the synoptic gospels,
healing was the traditional role of prophets, not of the Messiah.
In John's Gospel we are also viewing Jesus as Messiah/Son of
God, with apparent divine powers of healing.

That was not the end of the matter. The healing occurred
on the Sabbath, when it was not lawful to pick up one's sleeping
mat and carry it. The Temple leadership took issue with Jesus
over that but he told them that God (*"My Father"*) was still
working on the Sabbath and therefore he also was working on
the Sabbath. According to John the Temple leadership plotted to
kill Jesus because they saw him as committing blasphemy when
he called God *"My Father"*, which implied his own divinity.

Here is testimony in John's writing that he sees Jesus as
divine Son. If Jesus had actually said *"My Father"*, the Temple
leadership could have regarded him as committing blasphemy.
First century Jews (including leaders of the Temple) would not
have had a problem with Jesus calling God 'Father' (calling God
"Our Father" in the Lord's Prayer was obviously acceptable). In
fact there are instances in the Hebrew Scriptures where God is
depicted as a father, such as Malachi 2:10: *"Have we not all one*
father? Has not one God created us?" This is a communal
understanding of God as 'father' or progenitor of Israel.

On the other hand, the individualist and intimate implication of calling God *"My Father"* would have been seen by the Jewish leadership of John's time as extremely presumptuous, even blasphemous. Doubtless this was one of the reasons John's community found itself in fierce conflict with mainstream Judaism. John, however, needed to depict Jesus calling God *"My Father"* in order to build on his portrayal of Jesus as exalted Son of God.

- The seventh sign: Jesus feeds five thousand.
  (6:4-14) *Now the Passover, the festival of the Jews, was near. When he looked up and saw a large crowd coming toward him, Jesus said to Philip, "Where are we to buy bread for these people to eat?" He said this to test him, for he himself knew what he was going to do. Philip answered him, "Six months' wages would not buy enough bread for each of them to get a little." One of his disciples, Andrew, Simon Peter's brother, said to him, "There is a boy here who has five barley loaves and two fish. But what are they among so many people?" Jesus said, "Make the people sit down." Now there was a great deal of grass in the place; so they sat down, about five thousand in all. Then Jesus took the loaves, and when he had given thanks, he distributed them to those who were seated; so also the fish, as much as they wanted. When they were satisfied, he told his disciples, "Gather up the fragments left over, so that nothing may be lost." So they gathered them up, and from the fragments of the five barley loaves, left by those who had eaten, they filled twelve baskets. When the people saw the sign that he had done, they began to say, "This is indeed the prophet who is to come into the world."*

The feeding of the five thousand is one of the few stories from the synoptic gospels that turns up in John. This alone indicates that John was conversant with at least some of Mark, Matthew and Luke. Given its miraculous nature, his decision to include this story is not hard to understand – it is a fitting activity for the Son of God. John gives us the detail that Jesus and his disciples did not merely go to a quiet place; they went to the opposite side of the Sea of Galilee. They were there to escape the crowds who followed Jesus because of his healing 'signs'.

Then John tells us (alone among the gospel writers) that *"The Passover, the festival of the Jews, was near."* (6:4). The significance of this is not clear, but may well be related to the large crowd of people who approached Jesus, even in such an isolated place. Perhaps John saw these people as travellers from the Jewish Diaspora going to Jerusalem for the Passover meal (hence the mention of it). This was a common annual movement of people, which means the Diaspora crowd theory is not beyond credence. If this were John's meaning, the crowd in John's gospel represents Jews from beyond Israel who also came to believe in Jesus as Messiah/Son of God. For them, the proof of that was in the miracle of the loaves and fishes.

The imagery in the synoptic gospels is that Jesus fed them as Moses fed the people in the wilderness. Contrary to that, John goes to considerable lengths to explain the feeding of the crowd as a feeding not by a prophet like Moses, but as *"bread from heaven"*, through Jesus the Son of God. The story and the bread are both highly symbolic, as we will see.

- The eighth sign: Jesus walks on the sea.
  6:16-24: *When evening came, his disciples went down to the sea, got into a boat, and started across the sea to Capernaum. It was now dark, and Jesus had not yet come to them. The sea became rough because a strong wind was blowing. When they had rowed about three or four miles, they saw Jesus walking on the sea and coming near the boat, and they were terrified. But he said to them, "It is I; do not be afraid." Then they wanted to take him into the boat, and immediately the boat reached the land toward which they were going.*

The 'walking on water' sign is probably the best known of the messianic miracles in Mark, Matthew and John. In John this sign again indicates one of Jesus' divine attributes. He can walk among the waves of the sea as God does. Imagery of this sort is contained in the Psalms. Problematically for John, those psalms also continue the synoptics' Moses connection from the feeding of the five thousand into the story of Jesus walking on water. Psalm 77 makes the link, in speaking of God:

> Psalm 77:19: *"Your way was through the sea, your path, through the mighty waters; yet your footprints were unseen. You led your people like a flock by the hand of Moses and Aaron."*

The Moses connection notwithstanding, John apparently regards the walking on water 'sign' as too important to leave out of his gospel.

After the feeding and the 'walking on water', the crowds catch up with Jesus back on the shore of the Sea of Galilee near Capernaum. He tells them they are only looking for more food, whereas whoever believes in him as the symbolic *"bread of life"* will never be hungry or thirsty. Jesus says he has *"come down from heaven, not to do my own will, but the will of him who sent me."* He also says that everyone who believes in *"the Son"* will have eternal life. He will raise them up on the *"last day"*. He then makes another claim about himself as bread of heaven:

> 6:51: *"Whoever eats of this bread will live forever; and the bread that I will give for the life of the world is my flesh."*

Here we have John claiming that the Eucharist originated from Jesus himself. I remind readers of this book that John's Gospel does not contain the authentic words of Jesus; rather they are John's theological reflection on Jesus as Son of God, and the implications for that view of Jesus' life and death.

For the Temple leadership in John's time, the idea of consuming Jesus' flesh and blood, even symbolically as *"bread of heaven"*, would have been anathema. John says many of the people following Jesus also were turned off by this idea. Historically speaking, this eucharistic rhetoric from John's

Jesus, and the subsequent dropping out of some followers, probably reflects reality. Some messianic Jews were unable to adopt eucharistic symbolism as it had developed by the end of the first century. We will see more of that eucharistic symbolism in John's version of the crucifixion of Jesus.

- The ninth sign: Jesus gives sight to a blind man.
  9:1-7: *As he walked along, he saw a man blind from birth. His disciples asked him, "Rabbi, who sinned, this man or his parents, that he was born blind?" Jesus answered, "Neither this man nor his parents sinned; he was born blind so that God's works might be revealed in him. We must work the works of him who sent me while it is day; night is coming when no one can work. As long as I am in the world, I am the light of the world." When he had said this, he spat on the ground and made mud with the saliva and spread the mud on the man's eyes, saying to him, "Go, wash in the pool of Siloam" (which means Sent). Then he went and washed and came back able to see.*

John includes this sign concerning the man "*born blind*" to demonstrate further Jesus' divine attributes. In 9:3 when people ask whether the blind man or his parents have sinned so that he is born blind, Jesus says, "*Neither!*" The man was born blind so that "*God's works might be revealed in him.*" Those works of God will of course be done by Jesus, God's own Son.

After the healing miracle is carried out, the rest of the chapter is devoted to a conversation between the formerly blind man and the Pharisees. Their problem is partly that the healing occurred on the Sabbath, and partly that some people had begun to believe in Jesus as Son of God. John wants to make a point that even though the Jewish people saw miracles from Jesus, most still did not believe in him ("*his own did not receive him*"). Even though they 'saw', they were in fact blind.

John then says that the man's parents were too afraid to speak to the Jewish leadership about the healing because "*the Jews had already agreed that anyone who confessed Jesus to be the Messiah would be put out of the synagogue."* (9:22). This kind of expulsion was not happening in Jesus' time, but it certainly was the case at the end of the first century when John was writing. Declaring someone to be the Messiah before the Jewish War in 66-70CE was not regarded as a problem, certainly not one incurring expulsion from religious life.

- The tenth sign: Jesus raises Lazarus from death.
  11: 1-45: *And Jesus looked upward and said, "Father, I thank you for having heard me. I knew that you always hear me, but I have said this for the sake of the crowd standing here, so that they may believe that you sent me." When he had said this, he cried with a loud voice, "Lazarus, come out!" The dead man came out, his hands and feet bound with strips of cloth, and his face wrapped in a cloth. Jesus said to them, "Unbind him, and let him go."* (41-44).

The 'raising of Lazarus' is the first instance where John has Jesus bring someone back from the dead. The royal official's son was merely dying when he recovered. This sign is usually regarded as John's ultimate indication of Jesus' divine credentials. The story is not in any of the synoptic gospels, which is sufficient reason to see its huge symbolic significance for John. It is important to see the story as a message from John to his fellow Jews at the end of the first century CE. It speaks to Jews who have not embraced the claim that Jesus is Messiah, let alone divine Son of God. They are represented in the story by Lazarus, the brother of Jesus' good friends Mary and Martha. Whereas Mary and Martha have believed in Jesus as Son of God, able to raise the dead, the story implies that Lazarus has not.

For John, Lazarus may represent Jews who did not believe in Jesus as Messiah and as a result have been destroyed (in the Jewish War). In John's time their leaders (the Pharisees) still reject Jesus as Messiah, which means that the true Judaism meant to have been led by Jesus the Messiah is dead. John sees it as dead long enough to have become decayed and stinking; in other words, corrupted.

In his story, Mary and Martha ask Jesus to prevent Lazarus/Judaism from dying, but now (at the end of the first century when John's Gospel is being read) they believe it is too late. John's Jesus does not believe it is too late to raise the 'dead'. He tells Martha that:

> 11:25: *"I am the resurrection and the life. Those who believe in me, even though they die, will live ... "*

He then goes to the tomb and says what is for John a very significant prayer. It ends:

> 11:42: *"I have said this for the sake of the crowd standing here, so that they may believe that you sent me."* (11:42).

He then 'calls' Lazarus to *"come out"* from the dead. This is a sign for the Jewish people who have not yet followed Jesus as Messiah (including the readers of John's gospel). When Lazarus actually listens to Jesus calling him, he is able to rise from 'death' – the symbolic death of the Jewish people's relationship with God. When Lazarus sees what has happened to him – that he has come back to 'life' – he believes in Jesus. We see no more of him until Jesus is again at the home of Martha and Mary and Lazarus is with them.

The aftermath (and point) of the story is revealed when John says crowds of Jews so far uncommitted to Jesus, flock to see Lazarus, who has found new life in believing in Jesus. The problem this gives the Temple leadership is that because people are given new life and hope through following Jesus the Messiah/Son of God, *"many of the Jews were deserting and were believing in Jesus."* (12:11). This appears to represent John's situation in the late first century, where Jewish authorities (Pharisees) were unhappy that some Jews were converting to follow Jesus the Messiah.

Reading back into Jesus' time, John has the chief priests (Temple leadership) planning to put Lazarus to death so that he could not influence anyone else to believe in Jesus. In John's own time the Jewish leaders who were persecuting followers of Jesus the Messiah/Son of God were the Pharisees. The point is the same: followers of Messiah Jesus were in danger of being expelled from Jewish life (including their violent ejection from synagogues) by the leaders of mainstream Judaism. All of this is in the background of John's symbolic stories.

The historical background

The Gospel of John must always be read with careful attention to the historical situation in which followers of Jesus as Messiah and the Jewish authorities found themselves, after the Jewish War in 66-70CE. They all had strong memories of the Jews being led to catastrophic defeat by messianic figures. The followers of Jesus the Messiah/Son of God considered that had mainstream Judaism believed in him and followed the 'real Messiah', the defeat would not have happened.

Various implications of messianic belief were crucial, given Roman persecution of messianic Jewish groups and the additional Jewish discouragement of those groups. This discouragement was based partly on a departure from messianic tradition in claims made about Jesus as Messiah. To be fair, it was also an attempt on the part of the leadership to keep the Jewish people safe from Roman persecution of Jews who continued to follow messiahs, including followers of Messiah Jesus. As I noted before, John the Baptist's refutation of claims about himself as Messiah in John's Gospel, indicates that toward the end of the first century CE some Jews apparently were still following the late John the Baptist as a messianic figure. Probably they were waiting for him to 'return' as Messiah, in the same way that followers of Messiah Jesus expected his return.

The entry into Jerusalem

12: 12-19: *The next day the great crowd that had come to the festival heard that Jesus was coming to Jerusalem. So they took branches of palm trees and went out to meet him, shouting, "Hosanna! Blessed is the one who comes in the name of the Lord – the King of Israel!" Jesus found a young donkey and sat on it; as it is written: "Do not be afraid, daughter of Zion. Look, your king is coming, sitting on a donkey's colt!" His disciples did not understand these things at first; but when Jesus was glorified, then they remembered that these things had been written of him and had been done to him. So the crowd that had been with him when he called Lazarus out of the tomb and raised him from the dead continued to testify. It was also because they heard that he had performed this sign that the crowd went to meet him. The Pharisees then said to one another, "You see, you can do nothing. Look, the world has gone after him!"*

John's version is consistent with synoptic gospel versions in its context at the Festival of Passover, with crowds waving branches of palm trees, and in the biblical quotes they shouted. (Curiously, this is much more associated with the Festival of Sukkot, where the people bring palm branches to the altar in the Temple.)[142] Also as per the synoptics, John says the disciples did not understand what this greeting from the crowds meant. Later, when Jesus was 'glorified', meaning he was resurrected from the dead and therefore revealed as Son of God, they 'remembered' that certain biblical passages had been written about him. This is John, giving credence to his own use of scripture as proof texts.

John's version differs most clearly from the synoptics where he explains why there was a large crowd in the street greeting Jesus as King of Israel (in other words, as Messiah). The people were there because they had been present when Lazarus was called out of the tomb and raised from the dead. They were continuing to testify, as were others who had not been present at Lazarus' raising, but had "*heard*" about it. This is all symbolic, representing those who converted to belief in Jesus the Son of God in John's time. John knows he is not writing historical fact here, but is in effect 'preaching' to the readers of his gospel.

John's version ends the entry into Jerusalem with the scene where some Greeks, who had come to worship at the festival, are asking to talk with Jesus. They are obviously hellenized (Greek-speaking) Jews. Why else would they have worshipped at the Jewish Festival of Passover? John includes them as representative of hellenized Diaspora (possibly Egyptian) Jews who were drawn to believe that Jesus was the Messiah.

John uses a quotation from Isaiah chapter 6 to tell his readers why it was that so many Jews did not believe in Jesus as Messiah, even after all the 'signs' he performed:

> 12:39-40: *"And so they could not believe, because Isaiah also said, 'He has blinded their eyes and hardened their heart, so that they might not look with their eyes, and understand with their heart and turn – and I would heal them'."*

When Isaiah asks God how long this blindness and hardness of heart must continue, the reply is: *"Until cities lie waste without inhabitant"* (Isaiah 6:1-11). There can be little doubt that this is John's way of telling his Jewish readers that now is the time (following the 'laying waste' of Jerusalem) to believe in Jesus the Son of God.

The Discourses
As I have noted, the Gospel of John is in a genre of its own. John makes very little attempt to align it with the synoptic gospels aside from particular events such as the 'cleansing' of the Temple and the entry into Jerusalem. There is of course a narrative concerning the crucifixion and resurrection, but it too is plainly the work of John in its language and ideas. From start to finish, John is painting his own portrait of Jesus the Messiah as Son of God. Accordingly, Jesus is portrayed as in no doubt regarding his own identity and purpose:

> 12:32: *" ... I have not spoken on my own, but the Father who sent me has himself given me a commandment about what to say and what to speak."* (12:49). In John the same certainty applies to Jesus' death: *" 'And I, when I am lifted up from the earth, will draw all people to myself'. He said this to indicate the kind of death he was to die."*

In consequence of that, John's Gospel is replete with christologically-influenced discourses or sayings from Jesus.

These are not the words of the historical Jesus. They are written by John to create opportunities for putting his own thoughts (and the thoughts of like-minded Jews,) into the mouth of Jesus. The authority this methodology gives those words has proved to be resoundingly successful. Even today the majority of Christians believe that Jesus actually said every word John places in his mouth. Several of the Jesus sayings in John have been held up as examples of Jesus' true thoughts about God and about the way Christians ought to think about Jesus. Having been so long established, that belief is very hard to discredit. These 'sayings of Jesus' also undergird triumphalist understandings of Christianity which have persisted for two millennia.

I will discuss three examples only. Readers of this book and of John's Gospel will be able to identify more examples of fundamental Christian beliefs in words that were placed in Jesus' mouth by John the gospel writer.

- John 3:16: *"For God so loved the world that he gave his only Son, so that everyone who believes in him may not perish but may have eternal life."*

Here is the endlessly quoted 'saying' which is foundation for John's expression of the purpose of Jesus' crucifixion. God loves the world so much that he 'gives' Jesus to die so that those who believe he is divine Son of God will have eternal life. He will be the atoning sacrifice (the Lamb of God) who is the offering to pay for human sin. Jesus knows this is true; he says so.[143]

All of this relies on the gospel reader's belief that the words spoken by Jesus in the Gospel of John are authentically his. It also relies on the reader's belief that a human sacrifice, entailing being tortured to death, equates with God's love. I and many other followers of Jesus in this age regard that as blatant blasphemy. Those who want to believe it have sometimes resorted to believing that as Jesus is divine Son of God, "he wouldn't feel pain as we do."

- John 14:6: *"Jesus said to him (Thomas), "I am the way, and the truth, and the life. No one comes to the Father except through me."*

This 'saying' has been used to claim Christian superiority throughout the history of Christianity. It includes two statements. The first, "I am the way, and the truth, and the life", was written from John's Greek-philosophical/Jewish perspective. He would have invested its meaning with gnostic-like ideas about Jesus as revealer of divine wisdom for salvation. The concepts of 'way', 'truth' and 'life' are capable of all the countless positive or negative interpretations to which this passage has been subjected through the history of the church. It is the second statement in this saying which has caused immeasurable problems, because of the belief that it should be read literally.

"No one comes to the Father except through me." The first thing to remember is that John did not write those words for us in the twenty-first century! He certainly wrote them for his fellow Jews (primarily for men) in the Middle East at the end of the first century. These would have included Jews living in the land of Palestine and Jews living in the Diaspora (Asia Minor, Egypt, etc.). Given that John also wrote a story about Jesus encountering Samaritans who 'believed in him', we can add Samaritans to John's intended audience. Given too, that John wrote a story about the healing of a son of a 'royal official', we can assume that he had in mind Jewish people previously associated with the (by then extinct) Herodian dynasty.[144]

At the time John's Gospel was written, Paul's mission to the Gentiles had been running for approximately thirty years. Yet John's Gospel does not explicitly claim that Gentiles 'believed' in Jesus as Messiah. If John meant to include Gentiles in his intended audience, he does not make that clear.

Because of that, the saying attributed to Jesus: *"No one comes to the Father except through me"*, is directed at least primarily, and probably exclusively, to Jews. John naturally knew nothing of Christianity or Islam, neither of which existed in his time. Christianity (meaning the religion of followers of Jesus the Christ) was still a sect of Judaism in the late first century. The names 'Christian' or 'Christianity' were not coined and used until at least another two decades after John wrote his gospel. John may have heard of Buddhism and Hinduism, but it is unlikely, given his probable location in Ephesus.

Therefore, the saying, *"No one comes to the Father except through me"*, most likely indicates only that John wanted Jesus the Christ to be the means by which all *Jews* were in relationship with God. For that reason this saying belongs specifically in the context of first century Judaism. Unfortunately, over millennia it has been taken as a warrant for Christian proselytizing among people of other religions. Whereas it has doubtless resulted sometimes in a life-affirming new faith in God, in countless instances it has had the effect of dividing people from one another on the basis of religion.

In the fifteenth and sixteenth centuries the Spanish Inquisition tried to force Jews to 'come to the Father' through Christ, by forced baptisms. The alternative being death, many Jews submitted to baptism. The Inquisition subsequently burnt alive hundreds of baptised Jews who were thought to have reverted back to Judaism. The net effect of such barbaric behaviour by the church, which was driven by attitudes completely opposed to the teachings of Jesus, caused immeasurable further harm. Christian feelings of superiority generated by this 'saying' in John's Gospel, and the aggressive proselytizing that resulted, caused hundreds of years of Christian hatred of people of other religions, especially of Jews.

The *Apostolic Constitutions (Book VII)* a record of writings of the 'church fathers' from the second to the fourth centuries, expressed hatred toward Jews because they were believed to have been solely responsible for the death of Christ. This appears in Section 38, which is headed, 'A Prayer for the Assistance of the Righteous': *"For you have delivered us from ... the heresy of the murderers of Christ"*.[145]

Where were the Roman executioners in Jerusalem, with their charge of treason, in this version of the crucifixion? In the end, christological beliefs and their outcomes laid a firm foundation for the Holocaust in Christian Europe. We can easily imagine how Jesus would have viewed all that!

- 17: 22-23: *"The glory that you have given me I have given them, so that they may be one, as we are one. I in them and you in me, that they may become completely one, so that the world may know that you have sent me and have loved them even as you have loved me."*

Any cursory reading of John chapter 17 cannot miss the fact that 'Jesus' prayer' here is first of all for his eleven disciples (Judas will be out of it). Then it is for *"those who will believe in me through their word."* (17:20). The prayer is that *"they may be one"*, which seems to presuppose that in John's time the followers of Jesus were by no means 'one'. They were interpreting the Christian message in their own ways, in different places. Disunity among the followers was happening at the time of Paul, some thirty years before John's Gospel was written. It was still happening at the end of the first century. John is concerned about that and wishes all who believe in Jesus the Messiah/Son of God to see this belief in accordance with the way he sees it; hence this prayer. Doubtless the scope of the prayer for unity includes all of the Jews who have rejected Jesus as Messiah.

Although it is patently not about Christian ecumenism, an uncritical acceptance of this prayer as from Jesus has been the foundation for many efforts at church unity, both in the past and (still) in the twenty-first century. Ecumenism based on this prayer in John has led to preoccupation with the unity of all Christians everywhere, often resulting in frustration and a tremendous waste of energy and the church's resources.

Yet there never has been a unified Christian Church. From the beginning there have been many variations on Christian belief. 'Unity in Christ' has proven to be next to impossible in a religion with such immensely diverse theological, doctrinal, hierarchical, liturgical, social, political, cultural and institutional characteristics. From John the gospel writer's group onward, each church has been convinced its way is the right way, which means that very little in the way of compromise has been or can be made, for the sake of unity. On the other hand, belief in the God of love taught by Jesus and a unity of purpose based on the universal ethical teachings of Jesus, is indeed possible.[146]

The 'I am' sayings
In John 8:58, Jesus says, *"Very truly I tell you, before Abraham was, I am."* This is John's clearest statement of the meaning of the *"I am"* sayings in his gospel. Seven others are recognized, but 8:58 is definitive of them all.
The seven are symbolic, where Jesus says: "I am":
- *"bread of life"* (6:35);
- *"light of the world"* (8:12);
- *"gate"* (10:9);
- *"good shepherd"* (10:11);
- *"resurrection and the life"* (11:25);
- *"the way, and the truth, and the life"* (14:6);
- *"the true vine"* (15:1).

Scholars have reached a solid consensus that John's view of Jesus as divine Son of God is represented in the *"I am"* sayings. *"I am"* has a clear biblical precedent in the book of Exodus 3:14, where Moses asks for the name of God. The reply is spectacularly enigmatic: *"I am who I am"* (or even more indefinite is the possible alternative rendering: "I will be who I will be"). Either way, ancient writers knew that this was all Moses was going to get from God regarding the divine identity. John probably had in mind this designation from Exodus as his Jesus explains his divine role to reconcile humanity with God.

The 'Son of Man' sayings
The Hebrew for 'Son of Man' (*ben adam*) simply means 'human being', or 'mortal' as opposed to 'immortal', meaning divine. It appears ninety four times in the sixth century BCE book of the prophet Ezekiel, where Ezekiel is addressed by God as *"son of man"*. By the second century BCE, when the book of Daniel was written, 'son of man' appeared in relation to ideas about an apocalyptic End-time (Daniel 7:13-14). Those ideas reflected the

JESUS THE MESSIAH IN THE GOSPEL OF JOHN

situation of the Jews under Greek, Syrian and Egyptian rulers. The people naturally wanted to believe that God would rescue them from foreign domination at the End-time. This End-time did not mean the end of the world, but the end of exploitation and tyranny, replaced by a new world of freedom for the Jews to live as independent people of God.

The *"one like a son of man"* (Daniel 7:13) is most likely to represent the righteous Jews who suffered and died under foreign domination, and are now vindicated by God and raised to the heavenly throne to be given dominion over the foreign powers. This section of Daniel is written in Aramaic in its oldest manuscripts, where 'son of man' is rendered *bar enash*, simply meaning 'humanity', or 'a human being'. The second century BCE book of 1 Enoch does include a more messianic figure called 'Son of Man' (46:1-4; 48:2-10). In the Hebrew scriptures themselves, 'son of man' does not appear to have messianic meaning.

That brings us to ask why the gospel writer John put this title twelve times into the mouth of Jesus. Wherever it appears in John, Jesus is using it to refer to himself. As I have noted, John is likely to have had access to the synoptic gospels. The title Son of Man appears sixty-nine times in the synoptics, often indicating a messianic and apocalyptic (or End-time) role for Jesus. At other times, in accordance with traditional usage it seems to operate merely as an Aramaic term for 'someone', or even as a self-designation.[147] Jesus says: *"Foxes have holes, and birds of the air have nests, but the Son of Man has nowhere to lay his head."* (Luke 9:58). There is no scholarly consensus about the Son of Man title given to Jesus in the synoptic gospels.

In John's Gospel the designation has a different meaning. It relates specifically to messianic and apocalyptic ideas: *"No one has ascended into heaven except the one who descended from heaven, the Son of Man."* (3:13). This gathers up the idea of Jesus as the pre-existent Son of God, plus the idea in Daniel of the Son of Man's return or 'ascending' to heaven. The same applies to: *"Then what if you were to see the Son of Man ascending to where he was before?"* (6:62). For John, the title is far less ambiguous than it is for the synoptic writers. For him,

Son of Man borrows apocalyptic imagery and refers to the Word made flesh, that is, to the Son of God who has taken on human flesh to bring the Word of God to humanity. In his flesh, Jesus is *seen* as Son of Man who is also Son of God.

The Last Supper, Arrest, Trial and Crucifixion of Jesus

John's story of the arrest, trial and crucifixion of Jesus follows the basic outlines in the synoptics, but with several important variations. It is not the purpose of this book to dwell on every detail, but simply to point out what John's Easter narrative tells us about his system of belief in Jesus as Messiah/divine Son of God.

The Last Supper

13:1-11: *Now before the festival of the Passover, Jesus knew that his hour had come to depart from this world and go to the Father. Having loved his own who were in the world, he loved them to the end. The devil had already put it into the heart of Judas son of Simon Iscariot to betray him. And during supper Jesus, knowing that the Father had given all things into his hands, and that he had come from God and was going to God, got up from the table, took off his outer robe, and tied a towel around himself. Then he poured water into a basin and began to wash the disciples' feet and to wipe them with the towel that was tied around him. He came to Simon Peter, who said to him, "Lord, are you going to wash my feet?" Jesus answered, "You do not know now what I am doing, but later you will understand." Peter said to him, "You will never wash my feet." Jesus answered, "Unless I wash you, you have no share with me." Simon Peter said to him, "Lord, not my feet only but also my hands and my head!" Jesus said to him, "One who has bathed does not need to wash, except for the feet, but is entirely clean. And you are clean, though not all of you." For he knew who was to betray him; for this reason he said, "Not all of you are clean."*

John's narrative of the last supper Jesus ate with his disciples begins with a reminder that (for the third time) Jesus is in Jerusalem at the time of the festival of the Passover. That will have significance later in the story. Nothing is said here about the preparation for the Passover meal, including buying a sacrificial lamb. That is because John's version locates the 'last supper' on the night before the Day of Preparation for Passover, a full twenty-four hours before the supper occurs in the synoptic gospels. It is therefore not the Passover meal that John depicts Jesus eating with his disciples. John reiterates this point in several instances where he depicts the Jewish leaders who tried Jesus as reluctant to enter Gentile territory before Passover. For example:

> 18:28: *Then they took Jesus from Caiaphas to Pilate's headquarters. It was early in the morning. They themselves did not enter the headquarters, so as to avoid ritual defilement and to be able to eat the Passover.*

Here it is the Passover they are concerned about. In the synoptics it is the Day of Preparation for the first Sabbath Day after the Passover meal. The sacrificial lamb associated with Passover will, however, become symbolically present at the 'foot washing', in John's interpretation of the Suffering Servant of Isaiah. The earlier time slot for the supper relieves John of difficulty in depicting the religious leaders meeting on the Day of the Passover or even on the Eve of the Sabbath, which they were forbidden to do.[148] In John the crucifixion itself therefore happens on the Day of Preparation for the Passover, not on *Yom Pesach*, the Day of the Passover. The Mishnah, the compilation of Jewish Law, gives very clear instructions concerning the hearing of charges by the Sanhedrin (the Council):

> K. (8) *In property cases they come to a final decision on the same day [as the trial itself], whether it is for acquittal or conviction. In capital cases they come to a final decision for acquittal on the same day, but on the following day for conviction.*

*L. (Therefore they do not judge [capital cases] either on
the eve of the Sabbath or on the eve of a festival.)*[149]

Given that it is on the Day of Preparation for the Passover
that the Passover lamb is sacrificed, John is able to integrate this
symbolism into his story of the death of Jesus on that day, rather
than on the Passover itself.

John claims that Jesus' divine omniscience means he
knows what is going to happen to him. The disciples say:

> 16:30: *"Now we know that you know all things, and do
> not need to have anyone question you; by this we believe
> that you are from God."*

This is in response to Jesus saying:

> 16:28: *"I came from the Father and have come into the
> world; again, I am leaving the world and am going to
> the Father."* (16:28).

Uniquely in the gospels, John's story has Jesus get up in
the middle of the (non-Passover) supper and wash the feet of his
disciples. Here is John's representation of the 'ordination' of
eleven disciples to the mission of Jesus the Messiah/Son of God.
Jesus is to be sacrificed on the Day of Preparation (as the lambs
were) as the ultimate 'Passover lamb' for the sins of Israel.
Before that happens he appoints the eleven as apostles. To do
that, he washes their feet. The significance of this is not that it is
the action of a humble servant who puts his own ego needs aside
to do the most menial task imaginable, for others. John has
something else in mind. He is relying for his imagery here on
Isaiah chapters 52 and 53. Along with others who believed Jesus
to be the Messiah/Son of God, John has turned to the
description of *"the messenger"* who brings good news of peace:

> Isaiah 52:7: *"How beautiful upon the mountains are the
> feet of the messenger who announces peace, who brings
> good news, who announces salvation, who says to Zion,
> 'Your God reigns'."*

This is an English translation of the Hebrew text. Again it is important to remember that John was a hellenized Jew, whose scripture was a Greek translation of the Hebrew Bible. There is a crucial difference between the Greek version of Isaiah 52:7 and the original Hebrew. There is also a difference in the meaning of the English translation from the Hebrew (as above). The Greek version is:

> Isaiah 52:7: *"I am present as a season of beauty upon the mountains, as the feet of one preaching glad tidings of peace, as one preaching good news: for I will publish thy salvation, saying, O Sion, thy God shall reign."*

The important phrase is *"a season of beauty upon the mountains"*. The Greek word *hora*, translated into English as 'season' carries a wealth of meaning. *Hora* can mean 'the blooming season', 'the right, fitting time or hour', 'due season'. Of fruits or of people it can mean 'in the spring, or prime of life', 'blooming', 'mature'. In other words, it means that these things are at their most beautiful.

We can see now that the feet of people who carry the good news, or the message of peace, are 'mature', 'ready' to go out at 'the right time'. In that sense they are like ripened fruit – complete and beautiful. This is how John saw it in his reading from the Greek version of Isaiah. When Jesus washes his disciples' feet, John is saying that Jesus is preparing them to carry the good news of salvation to Zion. By preparing or beautifying their feet, John's Jesus is in effect ordaining the eleven to carry on after he dies; to carry the message that God has come among them in Jesus, the Word made flesh.

When Peter objects to the foot washing it is because he does not understand its significance for Jesus. So Jesus tells Peter that unless he allows him to wash his feet, he (Peter) cannot share in carrying the good news to others. Peter and the other disciples must go on to wash the feet of other people so that they too can be 'messengers of peace'.

In effect, this is the passing on of 'apostolic succession' from Jesus to his disciples and from them to others. Much has been made of this by the Roman church, which probably included an extra chapter in John's gospel (Ch. 21) to reinforce the primacy of Peter. We will discuss that further in the resurrection section. Again I remind the reader of this book that a substantial majority of modern scholars believe John's Gospel contains none of the authentic words and actions of Jesus. After the foot washing Jesus 'proves' his divine omniscience once more by predicting who among the twelve will betray him to the authorities. In that scenario John does follow the synoptics.

Now John is 'on a roll' with the Isaiah Suffering Servant imagery, as we will see in his story of the death of Jesus. Isaiah's words look to him like a prophecy of the kind of death Jesus dies. John's response is to write his trial and crucifixion story in accord with ideas and imagery in Isaiah 53. Before that, he writes several more discourses in which Jesus speaks about his coming death and return to God (13:31-17:26). These are written to depict Jesus as certain that his death will embody God's will and action. It will happen to 'glorify' God's divine Son and by that means, to bring about the conversion of all Jews to belief in him as Messiah/Son of God.

John picks up the Greek word *doxazo* ('glorify') from his Greek version of Isaiah 52:13. Whereas the original Hebrew word *kabod* means literally to be 'lifted up' or 'exalted' (usually associated with kings), the Greek word includes the meaning of brightness, splendour, majesty and radiance, particularly associated with God. John clearly intends his messianic portrait of Jesus to exude divine authority.

Jesus also predicts that his followers will be put out of synagogues, as John knows has already happened. Through this 'prediction' of Jesus, John means to encourage the readers of the gospel to remain loyal to the Messiah Jesus movement by placing words of encouragement in Jesus' own mouth. As John has Jesus put it: "*In the world you face persecution. But take courage; I have conquered the world!*" (16:33).

John also includes a conversation where Jesus predicts that Peter and the other disciples will not follow him 'where he is going'. As he does in all of the synoptic gospels, Peter insists that he will not betray Jesus:

13:36-38: *Simon Peter said to him, "Lord, where are you going?" Jesus answered, "Where I am going, you cannot follow me now; but you will follow afterward." Peter said to him, "Lord, why can I not follow you now? I will lay down my life for you." Jesus answered, "Will you lay down your life for me? Very truly, I tell you, before the cock crows, you will have denied me three times."*

Another prediction appears: *"Before the cock crows, you will have denied me three times."* This is first included in Mark, probably to deal with the historical truth that Jesus' disciples did not try to rescue him from the authorities. In such circumstances they would understandably have distanced themselves from the environs of the Temple and Roman court. John's version includes Jesus' promise that he will not leave the disciples *"orphaned"* after his death; he will return to them. This has special significance for the primacy of Peter in the later Roman church (see discussion of chapter 21).

The Arrest and Trial

Based on Isaiah 52 and 53, John expresses Jesus' understanding of the coming crucifixion throughout the discourses in chapters 13 – 17. John continues to take his inspiration from Isaiah (chapters 18-19) through his story of the arrest and trial. Following a long 'prayer' in which Jesus reiterates his intimate relationship with God and his desire that his disciples take part in that relationship with God, he and they go to a garden across the Kidron valley. Mark and Matthew call it Gethsemane; Luke simply says he goes to the Mount of Olives. All are pointing to an area outside the city walls, where Jesus was possibly in the habit of sitting with his disciples.

18:1-11: *After Jesus had spoken these words, he went out with his disciples across the Kidron valley to a place where there was a garden, which he and his disciples entered. Now Judas, who betrayed him, also knew the place, because Jesus often met there with his disciples. So Judas brought a detachment of soldiers together with police from the chief priests and the Pharisees, and they came there with lanterns and torches and weapons. Then Jesus, knowing all that was to happen to him, came forward and asked them, "Whom are you looking for?" They answered, "Jesus of Nazareth." Jesus replied, "I am he." Judas, who betrayed him, was standing with them. When Jesus said to them, "I am he," they stepped back and fell to the ground. Again he asked them, "Whom are you looking for?" And they said, "Jesus of Nazareth." Jesus answered, "I told you that I am he. So if you are looking for me, let these men go." This was to fulfill the word that he had spoken, "I did not lose a single one of those whom you gave me." Then Simon Peter, who had a sword, drew it, struck the high priest's slave, and cut off his right ear. The slave's name was Malchus. Jesus said to Peter, "Put your sword back into its sheath. Am I not to drink the cup that the Father has given me?*

Immediately a detachment from the Roman and Jewish authorities arrives, led there by Judas. Already there is a big difference between John's arrest scene and the synoptic versions. There is no narrative where Jesus agonizes alone over whether or not he will allow himself to be arrested. John's Jesus would never be so humanly terrified or unsure about whether God wanted him to go through a trial and possible crucifixion. As we have learned, this Jesus 'knows' that all of these things will happen, and accepts what is happening as foreordained. So the story goes immediately to the arrest, where Jesus tells the arresting party to take him only and leave his followers alone. The person identified in the synoptics as 'one who was standing by', a man who cuts off the ear of one of the arresting party, is clearly named by John as Peter, who draws his sword and cuts off the ear of the high priest's slave. Jesus tells Peter to put away his sword, because what is happening is meant to take place. This is *"the cup that the Father has given me."* (18:11). As in Matthew and Mark, it is police and soldiers from the Temple and Pilate's court who arrest Jesus, not the 'elders', 'scribes' and 'chief priests' whom Luke depicts in this unlikely police duty.

18:12-14, 19-24: *So the soldiers, their officer, and the Jewish police arrested Jesus and bound him. First they took him to Annas, who was the father-in-law of Caiaphas, the high priest that year. Caiaphas was the one who had advised the Jews that it was better to have one person die for the people.*

John says the arresting party takes Jesus first to Annas, father-in-law of Caiaphas. Annas and Caiaphas are mentioned in Luke 3:2 as high priests at the time of Jesus' birth. Apparently the two held this office at the same time. As Annas was patriarch of a high-priestly family, it looks appropriate for a Jewish prisoner to be taken to him first, then to the high priest actually in service, Caiaphas. In any case it looks as if this scenario is designed to make Jesus' case clearly exceptional. Annas questions Jesus about his disciples and his teaching, and then sends him to Caiaphas.

18:28-38a: *Then they took Jesus from Caiaphas to Pilate's headquarters. It was early in the morning. They themselves did not enter the headquarters, so as to avoid ritual defilement and to be able to eat the Passover. So Pilate went out to them and said, "What accusation do you bring against this man?" They answered, "If this man were not a criminal, we would not have handed him over to you." Pilate said to them, "Take him yourselves and judge him according to your law." The Jews replied, "We are not permitted to put anyone to death." (This was to fulfil what Jesus had said when he indicated the kind of death he was to die.). Then Pilate entered the headquarters again, summoned Jesus, and asked him, "are you the King of the Jews?" Jesus answered, "Do you ask this on your own, or did others tell you about me?" Pilate replied, "I am not a Jew, am I? Your own nation and the chief priests have handed you over to me. What have you done?" Jesus answered, "My kingdom is not from this world. If my kingdom were from this world, my followers would be fighting to keep*

me from being handed over to the Jews. But as it is, my
kingdom is not from here." Pilate asked him, "So you are
a king?" Jesus answered, "You say that I am a king. For
this I was born, and for this I came into the world, to
testify to the truth. Everyone who belongs to the truth
listens to my voice." Pilate asked him, "What is truth?"

John gives us nothing about what took place with
Caiaphas. He simply states that early in the morning Jesus was
taken from the house of Caiaphas to Pilate's headquarters. He
then adds the detail that the Jews who took Jesus to Pilate
remained outside Roman territory to avoid being 'polluted' by a
Gentile environment and as such be unable to take part in the
Passover, due to begin at sunset on that night. John also avoids
the awkwardness of having the Sanhedrin convene on the
Passover (as the synoptic gospels have it) when no such activity
would have been allowed by Jewish law. The only Jewish 'trial' of
Jesus then takes place on the Day of Preparation for Passover.

These details do lend more historical credibility to John's
story of the trial and execution of Jesus. That possible historical
correctness regarding Jewish practice has led countless
Christians to regard the rest of John's Gospel as more likely to be
historically correct. However, as our quotation from the
Mishnah (in the comments on the Last Supper) points out, even
these differences from the synoptic gospels do not explain how
the Sanhedrin could meet on the Day of Preparation for the
Passover. In case it might be thought that the whole story of
Jesus' trial and crucifixion is a complete fiction, the only
practical possibility is that the 'last meal' (not a Passover) took
place on what we would call 'Wednesday night'. That would
mean the trial could happen the day before the Day of
Preparation for Passover (the Thursday). The Day of Preparation
was on the Eve of Passover and therefore off-limits for the trial
of a 'capital' case.

John then explains that the Jews who take Jesus to Pilate
insist on Pilate taking responsibility for trying Jesus as a criminal.
The reason for this is so Jesus can be crucified by the Romans, as
they (the Temple leadership) are *"not permitted to put anyone to*

death." 'They' could in fact stone to death Jewish prisoners accused of blasphemy, but this would not fit with predictions John has Jesus make. Crucifixion will fulfil John's version of Jesus' prediction about the way he will die ('lifted up' i.e., crucified, John 12:32). Crucifixion is also the way Jesus died, a historical fact that could not be altered by John. It was of course already testified to in the synoptic gospels, which would be hard to refute. Yet somehow the death of the Messiah by Roman crucifixion had to be explained, while including culpability by the Temple leadership. That was the challenge for all gospel writers.

Like the synoptic gospel writers, John makes no attempt to explain to his reader that crucifixion was a Roman execution method reserved for those regarded as insurrectionists, or rebels against Rome. In John, Jesus is crucified because the 'people' demand it. The inference (in 18:33-38) is that this is because Jesus has claimed to be the king of Israel, another title for the Messiah. Jesus replies in terms that would have been understood by gnostic or philosophical readers of John's Gospel – that he brings salvation by knowledge of the 'truth':

> 18:37: *"For this I was born, and for this I came into the world, to testify to the truth."*

Pilate is portrayed as a reasonable man, a philosophical thinker: *"What is truth?"* he asks, reluctant to have Jesus put to death. This view of Pilate is most probably included because John wishes to protect his own group and his readers from persecution by Rome. There is no mention of Herod in the trial scene, probably because by the time John's Gospel was written the Herodian dynasty was extinct (from 92 CE). John can therefore see no point in adding Herod to those who 'try' Jesus.

> 18:38b-40: *After he had said this, he went out to the Jews again and told them, "I find no case against him. But you have a custom that I release someone for you at the Passover. Do you want me to release for you the King of the Jews?" They shouted in reply, "Not this man, but Barabbas!" Now Barabbas was a bandit.*

Pilate the gentleman-philosopher then offers to have Jesus released in accordance with a custom of releasing a prisoner at the Passover Festival. Instead the crowd chooses to have Barabbas released, a man the Greek text of John describes as a *lestes*. There are two possible meanings for this word: 1. Robber. 2. Insurrectionist. The King James version of John translates lestes as 'robber', a choice which has added to Christian readers' outrage and incredulity that the 'Jews' chose a robber over Jesus the Messiah. Mark counts Barabbas among insurrectionists against Rome who had committed murder. Luke also adds murder to charges against the insurrectionist Barabbas and Matthew calls him a *"notorious prisoner"* 27:16)

The point made in all gospels is that the 'Jews' calling for crucifixion do not understand Jesus and his purpose as Messiah and it is that which seals his fate. I have argued that 'the Jews' means the Temple leadership and John makes that clear when he says *"the chief priests and the police"* were those who shouted *"Crucify him!"*. The truth was that Jesus had many friends and supporters among his own ordinary (Jewish) people.

The Crucifixion and Burial

19:1-11: *Then Pilate took Jesus and had him flogged. And the soldiers wove a crown of thorns and put it on his head, and they dressed him in a purple robe. They kept coming up to him, saying, "Hail, King of the Jews!" and striking him on the face. Pilate went out again and said to them, "Look, I am bringing him out to you to let you know that I find no case against him." So Jesus came out, wearing the crown of thorns and the purple robe. Pilate said to them, "Here is the man!" When the chief priests and the police saw him, they shouted, "Crucify him! Crucify him!" Pilate said to them, "Take him yourselves and crucify him; I find no case against him." The Jews answered him, "We have a law, and according to that law he ought to die because he has claimed to be the Son of God." Now when Pilate heard this, he was more afraid than ever. He entered his headquarters again and asked Jesus, "Where are you from?" But Jesus gave him no answer. Pilate therefore said to him, "Do you refuse to speak to me? Do you not know that I have power to release you, and power to crucify you?" Jesus answered him, "You would have no power over me unless it had been given you from above; therefore the one who handed me over to you is guilty of a greater sin."*

Here we return to 'suffering servant' passages to understand the way John has written the crucifixion and burial scenes. The most obvious and well-known sections of Isaiah 53 have the servant:

53:3: *"despised and rejected by others".*
53:5: *"wounded for our transgressions, crushed for our iniquities; upon him was the punishment that made us whole."*
53:8a: *"By a perversion of justice he was taken away".*
53:8b: *"... for he was cut off from the land of the living, stricken for the transgression of my people"*

Most significantly, the servant is *"oppressed"* and *"afflicted"*, *"yet he did not open his mouth; like a lamb that is led to the slaughter."* As we can see, John's 'lamb of God' Christology is borrowed from Isaiah's suffering servant passages. John's Jesus is the ultimate Passover sacrifice for the sins of the people. The Jesus of this gospel knows that, which is why he does not resist his arrest and execution. He knows this is all part of God's plan of salvation (*"Yet it was the will of the Lord to crush him with pain."* 53:10). In verses 10-11 John makes his claim that Pilate has power over Jesus only because of the *"greater sin"* of the Temple leadership. If they had believed Jesus was the Messiah, he would not have been delivered into Pilate's hands and to crucifixion.

An attentive reader will find here a huge incongruity regarding the 'sin' of the Temple leaders and John's conviction that Jesus' death was pre-ordained by God. Does that not indicate that in accordance with John's belief, the 'sinful' Jewish leaders are 'agents' of God's plan for human salvation? Again

John's anti-Temple rhetoric fuels the flames of anti-Jewishness (and ultimately antisemitism) in later Christian understanding of his gospel. Then, in accordance with his sacrifice motif, John reminds the reader again that it is not the Day of the Passover when Jesus is crucified, but the Day of Preparation, when the Passover lambs were sacrificed (19:14).

To facilitate this, the Sanhedrin would have had to meet at a prohibited time during the night of the Day of Preparation (it beginning at sunset on the Thursday). Again that raises difficulties for historical credibility. The most important point for John is that his reader sees Jesus' death as the perfect sacrifice of the Son of God for the sin of the people. In the end, for John historical accuracy is secondary to his theological proclamation, as it is for the synoptic gospel writers.

> 19:25b-37: *Meanwhile, standing near the cross of Jesus were his mother, and his mother's sister, Mary the wife of Clopas, and Mary Magdalene. When Jesus saw his mother and the disciple whom he loved standing beside her, he said to his mother, "Woman, here is your son."* *Then he said to the disciple, "Here is your mother." And from that hour the disciple took her into his own home. After this, when Jesus knew that all was now finished, he said (in order to fulfil the scripture), "I am thirsty." A jar full of sour wine was standing there. So they put a sponge full of the wine on a branch of hyssop and held it to his mouth. When Jesus had received the wine, he said, "It is finished." Then he bowed his head and gave up his spirit.*

In accord with synoptic gospel accounts, John adds the sequence borrowed from Psalm 22:18 about the soldiers casting lots for Jesus' clothing (19:23-24): " ... *they divide my clothes among themselves, and for my clothing they cast lots.*" Immediately following this is a scene about women standing near the cross. They are Mary the mother of Jesus, Mary the wife of Clopas and Mary Magdalene. No other people are mentioned. It looks as if this scene has been inserted by the writer for the purpose of identifying himself as 'the disciple whom Jesus loved'. It differs markedly from Mark's, Matthew's and Luke's accounts, where the women stand "*at a distance*". In reality they would have been too far away for Jesus to have had a conversation with them, even if he had been capable of conversing with anyone.

In the synoptics, Jesus' mother is not named as such among those standing there, nor is "*Mary, the wife of Clopas*". However, "*Mary the mother of James and Joseph*" (also in Matthew 27:56) is named. Mark's version calls her: "*Mary the mother of James the younger and of Joses, and Salome.*" (15:40) Some have said that James and Joseph (or Joses) were Jesus' brothers, and so this Mary is also Jesus' mother. If so, why would the synoptics not have named her as such? Instead, they mention that there were several other women watching from a distance – women from the Galilee who had supported Jesus all along.

The most important omission from John's narrative is that although he names three women "*standing near the cross*", he does not name any male disciple as being present. Yet the words of Jesus from the cross are addressed to "*the disciple whom he loved*". It would therefore make sense if (in the original version of this scene) the disciple whom Jesus "*loved*" were Mary Magdalene. It would be understandable if Jesus *had* wanted another (younger) woman whom he loved and trusted, to look after his mother following his death.

It would make sense too, if the 'beloved disciple' was Jesus' brother James, who headed the Jerusalem group after Jesus died. It would be logical if it were James who took Jesus' mother Mary (also James' own mother) into his home following Jesus' death. In reality James probably did take on the role of the eldest son, with traditional responsibility for his parents, after his brother Jesus died. As it stands, this looks very much as if an editor of this section, in his "*disciple whom Jesus loved*" persona, has installed Jesus' mother into his own home. That lends credibility to his gospel claim to know the details of the crucifixion and all other events related to Jesus.[150]

Unsurprisingly, John's Jesus does not utter the words

quoted in Mark and Matthew from Psalm 22:1: *"My God, my God, why have you forsaken me?"* The Jesus of this gospel is supremely in control of himself and of the events occurring, and would never admit to loss of faith in God his *"Father"*. Accordingly Jesus says he is thirsty, but only to *"fulfil the scripture"* (*" ... my mouth is dried up like a potsherd, and my tongue sticks to my jaws"* Ps. 22:15). Jesus then declares that his purpose has been fulfilled: *"It is finished"*. He bows his head and dies.

> 19:31-37: *Since it was the day of Preparation, the Jews did not want the bodies left on the cross during the Sabbath, especially because that Sabbath was a day of great solemnity. So they asked Pilate to have the legs of the crucified men broken and the bodies removed. Then the soldiers came and broke the legs of the first and of the other who had been crucified with him. But when they came to Jesus and saw that he was already dead, they did not break his legs. Instead, one of the soldiers pierced his side with a spear, and at once blood and water came out. (He who saw this has testified so that you also may believe. His testimony is true, and he knows that he tells the truth.) These things occurred so that the scripture might be fulfilled, "None of his bones shall be broken." And again another passage of scripture says, "They will look on the one whom they have pierced."*

John's former allusions to Jesus as sacrificial lamb (1:29; 1:36) are spelt out more fully as he describes the scene where the Temple leadership ask Pilate to have the legs of the crucified men broken so they can be taken down before the Passover begins. When the soldiers get to Jesus, they find he has already died. Therefore his legs did not need to be broken, and he is fit to be the unblemished ultimate Passover sacrifice for the sins of Israel. The soldiers make sure Jesus is dead by pushing a spear into his side. Blood and water come out, often explained as symbols of baptism (the water) and Eucharist (the blood). Then follows a break in the narrative. In parenthesis a message is inserted, ostensibly from the author of the gospel, claiming to have been an eye-witness to these events. (19:35). The message is more likely to be from the editor who claims to be "*the disciple whom Jesus loved*".

The continuing narrative relies here on two more allusions to scripture. The first concerns Jesus' unbroken leg bones (Psalm 34:20: "*He keeps all their bones; not one of them will be broken*"). The second concerns the 'piercing' of Jesus' side: " *... when they look on the one whom they have pierced, they shall mourn for him.*" (Zechariah 12:10). That is followed by a likely scriptural connection to the water coming from Jesus' side: "*On that day a fountain shall be opened for the house of David and the inhabitants of Jerusalem, to cleanse them from sin and impurity.*" (Zech 13:1). According to John the sacrificial 'lamb' has brought about forgiveness from sin by the blood of his sacrifice and by the baptism of water to wash away the sin.

> 19:38-43: *After these things, Joseph of Arimathea, who was a disciple of Jesus, though a secret one because of his fear of the Jews, asked Pilate to let him take away the body of Jesus. Pilate gave him permission; so he came and removed his body. Nicodemus, who had at first come to Jesus by night, also came, bringing a mixture of myrrh and aloes, weighing about a hundred pounds [45kgs]. They took the body of Jesus and wrapped it with the spices in linen cloths, according to the burial custom of the Jews. Now there was a garden in the place where he was crucified, and in the garden there was a new tomb in which no one had ever been laid. And so, because it was the Jewish day of Preparation and the tomb was nearby, they laid Jesus there.*

A further borrowing from Isaiah 53 occurs in John's burial narrative, as it does in the synoptics. It describes the appearance of Joseph of Arimathea, described by Matthew as a "*rich man*", and by Mark and Luke as a member of the Sanhedrin or "*Council*". He is a secret disciple of Jesus and (Luke says) did not agree with the decision of the Sanhedrin regarding charges against Jesus. In all gospels he goes to Pilate to ask for Jesus' body, for burial. The quotation each gospel writer uses is Isaiah 53:9: *"They made ... his tomb with the rich."*

This gospel burial tradition is at odds with the customary fate of bodies of those crucified. They were usually taken down after death occurred and buried in mass graves with other 'criminals' or simply tossed into the ditch surrounding the city for wild dogs to eat. They were not to be given dignified burial rites. The problem for the gospel writers is that a burial scenario in a tomb is essential background to the resurrection narratives.

In John it is two Pharisees, Joseph of Arimathea and Nicodemus, who prepare Jesus' body for burial with *"a hundred pounds"* of spices. The synoptic gospels do not include this; in their narratives the preparation of the body could not be done on the Sabbath, especially on the Sabbath which is also the first Sabbath of the Festival of Unleavened Bread. For the synoptic stories, the preparation had to wait until the day after the Sabbath. In John the crucifixion and burial, including preparation of Jesus' body, take place on the day before the Sabbath (the Day of Preparation for the first Sabbath of the Festival of Unleavened Bread), which allows for this work to be done. John's timing of the crucifixion to coincide with the sacrifice of the Passover lambs on the Day of Preparation of the Passover means he has had to make several changes to the synoptic narratives. In so doing, he has probably placed the narrative in a more realistic historical sequence. This would aid his purpose in writing for educated hellenized Jews aware of Jewish traditions surrounding trials and their proximity to Jewish festivals.

The Resurrection (Chapters 20-21)

> 20:1-10: *Early on the first day of the week, while it was still dark, Mary Magdalene came to the tomb and saw that the stone had been removed from the tomb. So she ran and went to Simon Peter and the other disciple, the one whom Jesus loved, and said to them, "They have taken the Lord out of the tomb, and we do not know where they have laid him." Then Peter and the other*

disciple set out and went toward the tomb. The two were running together, but the other disciple outran Peter and reached the tomb first. He bent down to look in and saw the linen wrappings lying there, but he did not go in. Then Simon Peter came, following him, and went into the tomb. He saw the linen wrappings lying there, and the cloth that had been on Jesus' head, not lying with the linen wrappings but rolled up in a place by itself. Then the other disciple, who reached the tomb first, also went in, and he saw and believed; for as yet they did not understand the scripture, that he must rise from the dead. Then the disciples returned to their homes.

John's Gospel continues to place the disciple "*whom Jesus loved*" at the forefront of witness and participation in the events of Easter. On the first day of the week, while Mary Magdalene is allowed to be first to see that the stone has been removed from the entrance to the tomb, she is not allowed to be the first to see that Jesus' body is no longer there. She apparently deduces that the tomb is empty, although the gospel does not say that. She runs to tell Peter and the disciple "*whom Jesus loved*" that Jesus' body has gone. She does not understand that it means he has risen from the dead. Instead, it is Peter and the 'beloved disciple' who are witnesses to the empty tomb. Peter goes first into the tomb and sees the linen wrappings, followed by the "*other disciple*". Like Mary Magdalene, they too do not understand the significance of this. All they know is that Jesus' body has gone.

20:11-18: *But Mary stood weeping outside the tomb. As she wept, she bent over to look into the tomb; and she saw two angels in white, sitting where the body of Jesus had been lying, one at the head and the other at the feet. They said to her, "Woman, why are you weeping?" She said to them, "They have taken away my Lord, and I do not know where they have laid him." When she had said this, she turned around and saw Jesus standing there, but she did not know that it was Jesus. Jesus said to her,*

"Woman, why are you weeping? Whom are you looking for?" Supposing him to be the gardener, she said to him, "Sir, if you have carried him away, tell me where you have laid him, and I will take him away." Jesus said to her, "Mary!" She turned and said to him in Hebrew, "Rabbouni!" (which means Teacher). Jesus said to her, "Do not hold on to me, because I have not yet ascended to the Father. But go to my brothers and say to them, 'I am ascending to my Father and your Father, to my God and your God.'" Mary Magdalene went and announced to the disciples, "I have seen the Lord"; and she told them that he had said these things to her.

So it is that in John's gospel Mary Magdalene becomes the real witness to the resurrection. When she goes into the tomb she sees two angels who apparently were not seen by Peter and the other disciple. Then she sees Jesus. Her refusal to believe Jesus' words before his crucifixion – that he would return – leads her to mistake him for a gardener until he speaks to her. She thereby becomes the sole first witness to the resurrection and the first to take the news to the other disciples:

20:18: *Mary Magdalene went and announced to the disciples, "I have seen the Lord".*

Here John follows Mark and Matthew in depicting Mary Magdalene encountering the resurrected Jesus before he appears to the male disciples. It is she who announces the resurrection to the men. This may well be because of a well-established tradition in the first century CE that Mary Magdalene was the first to experience the presence of Jesus after his death. For that reason, in early Christian art works she was often depicted teaching male disciples. An example is an illustration from the Albani Psalter, Hildesheim, 12th century. In this painting Mary Magdalene is standing with right index finger raised (in teacher fashion) instructing the 11 remaining male disciples, who are listening intently to her. In following centuries patriarchal church officials changed her identity from highly respected teacher to 'fallen woman' (prostitute). That view is mostly discredited among biblical scholars today.

> 20:19-23: *When it was evening on that day, the first day of the week, and the doors of the house where the disciples had met were locked for fear of the Jews, Jesus came and stood among them and said, "Peace be with you." After he said this, he showed them his hands and his side. Then the disciples rejoiced when they saw the Lord. Jesus said to them again, "Peace be with you. As the Father has sent me, so I send you." When he had said this, he breathed on them and said to them, "Receive the Holy Spirit. If you forgive the sins of any, they are forgiven them; if you retain the sins of any, they are retained." But Thomas, (who was called the Twin), one of the twelve, was not with them when Jesus came. So the other disciples told him, "We have seen the Lord." But he said to them, "Unless I see the mark of the nails in his hands, and put my finger in the mark of the nails and my hand in his side, I will not believe." A week later his disciples were again in the house, and Thomas was with them. Although the doors were shut, Jesus came and stood among them and said, "Peace be with you." Then he said to Thomas, "Put your finger here and see my hands. Reach out your hand and put it in my side. Do not doubt but believe." Thomas answered him, "My Lord and my God!" Jesus said to him, "Have you believed because you have seen me? Blessed are those who have not seen and yet have come to believe."*

John's resurrection narrative expands here to speak more directly to the readers of his gospel. Almost the first thing said is that the disciples are behind locked doors for *"fear of the Jews"*. Again this is anti-Pharisaic rhetoric (directed toward the successors to the Temple leadership at the time of John's writing), but as expressed in the gospel this phrase has contributed to centuries of murderous Christian hostility toward all Jews.

After Jesus appears to the rest of the disciples, John introduces Thomas, who had been absent when Jesus appeared in a locked room. Thomas demands proof that Jesus has been raised from death, proof which is provided when Jesus appears and shows Thomas the crucifixion wounds on his hands and feet. Thomas then believes. The word for Thomas, but more particularly for the sceptical reader of the gospel, is that although Thomas was blessed by believing after he had proof of the resurrection, those who believe without that proof are even more blessed by God. In that way John appeals to his readers to believe in Jesus as the Messiah, divine Son of God, some sixty to seventy years following the crucifixion.

First Postscript

20:30-31: *Now Jesus did many other signs in the presence of his disciples, which are not written in this book. But these are written so that you may come to believe that Jesus is the Messiah, the Son of God, and that through believing you may have life in his name.*

Chapter 20 ends with what many scholars believe is the original ending of John's Gospel. It gives every indication that such was the case. The writer is telling the reader that Jesus did a lot more "*signs*" (i.e. messianic miracles) in the presence of his disciples. John has written down some of them so that the reader will "*believe that Jesus is the Messiah, the Son of God, and that through believing you may have life in his name.*" That sounds remarkably like the ending of the gospel. In fact there is a small amount of documentary evidence that John's Gospel may have ended at 20:31. One such is in the writings of the 'church father' Tertullian, (c.160 – c.225 CE) on the conclusion to the Gospel of John: "And wherefore does this conclusion of the gospel affirm that these things were written unless it is that you might believe, it says, that Jesus Christ is the son of God?"[151] There can be little doubt that this refers to the end of chapter 20, not to the end of chapter 21.

Another piece of evidence is the discovery in 2006 of the Bodleian (Oxford) Library's manuscript '*Bodleian MS*

Copt.e.150(P)'. It is one leaf only of a fourth century CE codex which has a large space at the bottom of the page after John 20: 30-31. That is intriguing, but by no means conclusive evidence about where John's Gospel ends. The question is, what difference does it make, one way or the other? To answer that, it is useful to consider the significance of chapter 21 for the developing church in the first four centuries CE.

Chapter 21

Whether or not chapter 21 was added at a later point to lend weight to the claim for primacy of the Bishop of Rome, it contains John's story of the commissioning of Peter as leader of the Christ movement.[152] Regardless of its dating, that is its clear purpose. Yet there is a gap of approximately 100 years between Peter's death in Rome and Anicetus (155-166), the first bishop documented as being in charge of all of the messianic Jesus groups in Rome. Peter was in Rome in the mid-first century CE, but is highly unlikely to have been the first bishop of Rome (or Pope). At that point there had been nowhere near enough development of the church in Rome to necessitate an over-arching headship of the leaders (a bishop). In any case, the earliest lists of Popes from Roman writers in the *Liber Pontificalis* and the fourth century *Apostolic Constitutions*, have Peter and Paul listed together as co-founders of the Roman church. The *Liber Pontificalis* has lately undergone intensive scholarly scrutiny which has pronounced it as: "an unofficial instrument of pontifical propaganda."[153] As Australian biblical scholar Robert Crotty points out:

> *It is clear that there has been serious confusion among the writers about the succession. We have already noted that neither Peter nor Paul could have had anything to do with the foundation of the Church in Rome. That was the work of others. In fact, there is no evidence for an overall bishop-leader in Rome until the mid-second century, long after their deaths. These lists are fictive; they belong to the Church Story not to history.*[154]

If chapter 21 were a part of the original gospel, it is curious that it follows what looks like a postscript to the gospel at the end of chapter 20. Some scholars say it must have been written by the author of John because its Greek has 'Johannine' characteristics. Yet it would not be difficult to copy John's style in order to produce an 'authentic' chapter 21. That would include using words and grammatical expressions often used by John.

> 21:1-8: *After these things Jesus showed himself again to the disciples by the Sea of Tiberias; and he showed himself in this way. Gathered there together were Simon Peter, Thomas called the Twin, Nathanael of Cana in Galilee, the sons of Zebedee, and two others of his disciples. Simon Peter said to them, "I am going fishing." They said to him, "We will go with you." They went out and got into the boat, but that night they caught nothing. Just after daybreak, Jesus stood on the beach; but the disciples did not know that it was Jesus. Jesus said to them, "Children, you have no fish, have you?" They answered him, "No." He said to them, "Cast the net to the right side of the boat, and you will find some." So they cast it, and now they were not able to haul it in because there were so many fish. That disciple whom Jesus loved said to Peter, "It is the Lord!" When Simon Peter heard that it was the Lord, he put on some clothes, for he was naked, and jumped into the sea. But the other disciples came in the boat, dragging the net full of fish, for they were not far from the land, only about a hundred yards off* (91.44m).

Chapter 21 does serve a geographic (and evangelical) purpose related to the time of its writing. It takes the resurrection narrative from Jerusalem, where it had been located exclusively until the end of chapter 20. The action now shifts to Galilee *"by the Sea of Tiberias"*. Perhaps the writer of chapter 21 wanted to include Galileans in the readership of the gospel. In any case, it describes a group of Jesus' disciples who had gone back to Galilee after the crucifixion and resurrection appearances in Jerusalem. Significantly, they were not 'out there' proclaiming the good news of the resurrection. They were together on a beach, going about their lives as fishermen, as they had been before Jesus called them to follow him.

This may well be a historically realistic glance at the situation of Jesus' original followers following the crucifixion. Given the fate of Jesus, they would most probably have returned home and found comfort in each other's company and in familiar territory and activities. Yet contrary to chapter 20, where Jesus is reported as appearing in a locked room in Jerusalem (20:19-29), when he appears on the beach in the narrative of chapter 21, the disciples don't recognize him. They do not even recognize him when he gives them fishing instructions. Only after they follow the instructions and haul in a huge catch in their nets, does someone realise it is Jesus on the beach. Guess who recognizes Jesus? It is none other than "*the disciple whom Jesus loved*" (the one the author of John 21 will claim to be). It is he who tells Peter "*It is the Lord*", and only then does Peter leap into action to go to Jesus.

> 21:9-14: *When they had gone ashore, they saw a charcoal fire there, with fish on it, and bread. Jesus said to them, "Bring some of the fish that you have just caught." So Simon Peter went aboard and hauled the net ashore, full of large fish, a hundred fifty-three of them; and though there were so many, the net was not torn. Jesus said to them, "Come and have breakfast." Now none of the disciples dared to ask him, "Who are you?" because they knew it was the Lord. Jesus came and took the bread and gave it to them, and did the same with the fish. This was now the third time that Jesus appeared to the disciples after he was raised from the dead.*

There is a fire burning on the beach with fish cooking (apparently the actions of Jesus) and Jesus offers the disciples fish and bread for breakfast. They are asked to bring to him the fish they had just caught and Peter does that. The bread and fish are probably meant to be reflective of the messianic feeding story in 6:1-14. The one hundred and fifty three fish would have represented something significant for the writer of chapter 21, but there is no conclusive argument for any of the many reasons proposed by biblical scholars. One proposal is that perhaps the number 153 represented the known number of species of fish at the time. The symbolism is that when the disciples take instruction from Jesus, he will make them "fishers of men" – from all groups of humanity. For that reason this looks like another 'commissioning' of the disciples to proclaim Jesus the Messiah/divine Son of God in the region of Galilee and beyond.

One likely reason for the inclusion of chapter 21 is that it includes a commissioning from Galilee rather than from Jerusalem, where Luke's Gospel ends. In fact this story appears to be based on Luke 24:42-43, where Jesus meets his disciples on a beach and eats some cooked fish. In John 21 Jesus prepares a meal of fish and bread for the disciples but does not eat it himself. The implication is that as divine Son of God he is going back to "*the Father*" and has no need for the food of mortals.

> 21:15-19: *When they had finished breakfast, Jesus said to Simon Peter, "Simon son of John, do you love me more than these?" He said to him, "Yes, Lord; you know that I love you." Jesus said to him, "Feed my lambs." A second time he said to him, "Simon son of John, do you love me?" He said to him, "Yes, Lord; you know that I love you." Jesus said to him, "Tend my sheep." He said to him the third time, "Simon son of John, do you love me?" Peter felt hurt because he said to him the third time, "Do you love me?" And he said to him, "Lord, you know everything; you know that I love you." Jesus said to him, "Feed my sheep. Very truly, I tell you, when you were younger, you used to fasten your own belt and to go wherever you wished. But when you grow old, you will stretch out your hands, and someone else will fasten a belt around you and take you where you do not wish to go." (He said this to indicate the kind of death by which he would glorify God.) After this he said to him, "Follow me."*

By far the most important reason for the addition of chapter 21 appears to be the scandalously ambiguous position in which the end of chapter 20 leaves Peter. In accordance with all three synoptic gospels, Peter three times denies knowing Jesus (18:15-27). That fulfils Jesus' prediction that this will happen (13:36-38). Peter's situation remains unclear after the crucifixion. Even though (after the 'beloved disciple' beat him to the empty tomb) Peter saw the discarded grave clothes in the tomb, he "*did not understand the scripture, that he (Jesus) must rise from the dead.*" Chapter 20 then concludes at verse 31 with no further mention of Peter. He is left in a most inconclusive situation, particularly for one who was by John's time upheld as leader of the Christ movement. That 'Peter problem' alone may have been sufficient motivation for the writer of chapter 21.

The problem is dealt with specifically in 21:15-17, where Peter is 'commissioned' by Jesus three times in clear response to his three denials. There is also a reference to what was obviously already known at the time of writing – the manner in which Peter was to die by execution (21:18-19). Although chapter 21 has been claimed as biblical 'proof' for primacy of the Bishop of Rome (because Peter went to Rome and was executed there), it does not actually name the place of Peter's execution.

> 21:20-25: *Peter turned and saw the disciple whom Jesus loved following them; he was the one who had reclined next to Jesus at the supper and had said, "Lord, who is it that is going to betray you?" When Peter saw him, he said to Jesus, "Lord, what about him?" Jesus said to him, "If it is my will that he remain until I come, what is that to you? Follow me!" So the rumour spread in the community that this disciple would not die. Yet Jesus did not say to him that he would not die, but, "If it is my will that he remain until I come, what is that to you?" This is the disciple who is testifying to these things and has written them, and we know that his testimony is true. But there are also many other things that Jesus did; if every one of them were written down, I suppose that the world itself could not contain the books that would be written.*

Given that John's Gospel itself was probably written at the end of the first century or early in the second century, chapter 21's comments by the writer about himself create difficulty. It stretches credibility that a contemporary of Jesus in 30 CE could have written a gospel 70 – 80 years later. Because of that the writer's claims (in chapter 21) to be *"the disciple whom Jesus loved"* are without plausible foundation and would surely have provoked incredulity in the gospel's first readers. A possible explanation is that chapter 21 was added to John by someone intent on claiming that the original gospel was written much closer to the time of Jesus. That would have entailed the 'other hand' writing not only chapter 21, but adding the sections where the *"disciple whom Jesus loved"* appears at other points in the gospel (e.g. 13:23, 19:26 and 20:2). Given the lack of documentary evidence for the earliest full versions of all gospels, additions to a later version such as those mentioned here, need not be ruled out.

Corroborating this argument, the references to *"the disciple whom Jesus loved"* can be recognized as interruptions to the flow of the narrative. In 13:21, as in all three synoptic gospels, Jesus says, *"Very truly, I tell you, one of you will betray me."* It is only in John (13:22-25) that Peter unnecessarily prompts the 'beloved disciple' reclining next to Jesus, to ask Jesus who will betray him. Why would Peter not put the question directly to Jesus? In the synoptics it is *"the disciples"* who wonder among themselves about who the betrayer might be. In John, at 13:26 Jesus continues with: *"It is the one to whom I give this piece of bread when I dipped it in the dish."* This is a clear continuation of 13:21. There is no christological purpose to the 'beloved disciple' insertion, but it can be seen to corroborate the eyewitness claim of the writer of chapter 21.

Following 19:25, another such insertion occurs when the *"disciple whom he loved"* is asked by Jesus to take his mother into his home. This interrupts the narrative concerning the scriptural basis for the crucifixion, which then continues at 19:28.

A third example is 20:2, where the disciple *"whom Jesus loved"* is inserted into the narrative when Mary Magdalene is informing Peter that Jesus' body is missing from the tomb. This makes the claim that the 'beloved disciple' saw the empty tomb before Peter, even though Peter went into it first. In Luke it is Peter who reaches the tomb first, possibly meaning that the writer of John 21 has used and altered Luke's narrative in order to establish his own 'eyewitness' credentials.

In chapter 21 the 'beloved disciple' continues to appear at crucial moments. It is he who first recognizes Jesus on the beach (21:7). Most importantly, it is he who is the sole subject of the last fifteen verses of chapter 21. After Jesus has again commissioned Peter to be shepherd of the sheep (the followers of the Messiah) and has predicted the way Peter would die (known to the writer because it occurred under Emperor Nero who died in 68CE) attention is fixed on *the disciple whom Jesus loved*. Peter asks Jesus what will happen to this disciple. It is here that an apocalyptic End-time element enters chapter 21. Jesus' answer to Peter indicates that he (Jesus) *will come*, meaning Jesus will return, presumably as triumphant Messiah. Jesus says the 'beloved disciple', also identified as the writer of this chapter, will *remain until I come*. The writer then further claims that it is he 'the beloved disciple' who is writing all of this from his own knowledge. In verse 24 he claims that *we* know he tells the truth about all of this.

Could it be that this conversation about the 'beloved disciple' remaining *until I come* is the author of chapter 21's way of saying that the writer of the gospel lived to an extraordinarily old age? Perhaps this is a response to people in the second century objecting to a claim that the author was one of Jesus' first disciples. If Jesus said this beloved disciple would remain *until I come*, might that be meant to say he lived to a very old age indeed, and therefore was able to write a gospel from his own eyewitness testimony?

Through this statement from Jesus (21:22) the author of chapter 21 sets out to 'prove' that he is John the beloved disciple, who happens to be the author of the entire gospel. Everything written in the gospel is therefore 'true', having been remembered by him and now written down. In verse 24 he claims that *we* know he tells the truth about all of this. The *we* is an attempt to claim that others would verify his account as true. There is no attempt to identify who "*we*" might be, which does tend to weaken his claim.[155]

His final word for the reader is that he knows Jesus did many more miraculous things. This further 'eyewitness' claim is intended to strengthen the purpose of the entire Gospel of John – to proclaim that Jesus is the Messiah/Christ, the divine Son of God.

Conclusions about the
Gospels as 'made on earth'

My purpose in the preceding four chapters has been for the reader of this book to see the how, when, where and why of the gospel writers' aims in writing their quite different gospels. My hope is that the differences will now be much clearer, and that they can be seen to be related to the particular contexts in which the four writers were living and working. I have intended to help the reader see more clearly how theological, historical, literary, philosophical and cultural norms and developments determined the faith of the early church. Each gospel writer had a similar belief in Jesus as the Messiah/Christ, but needed to convince his readership of the reasons for his own belief. Naturally that entailed extensive use of scripture to verify messianic claims, although we have seen that this can be explained easily as gospels written in accordance with scripture.

Given the traditional Christian belief that the New Testament is at least inspired by God, if not actually 'dictated' by God to the writers, it is often very difficult for Christians to see these writings as originating from the (sincere) beliefs of human beings. In particular, it is difficult for many people to understand that the gospel writers had no problem with placing their own words into the mouth of Jesus. To people of a later era and different (Western) context, that seems close to fraud. But for people in the late first century and early second century CE, particularly among writers of Greek literature, that practice was not scandalous at all. It was widely understood that various writers used this practice to add weight to their claims. It was commonly the practice among writers of religious literature in that era, such as the 'Testaments' of Abraham, Isaac and Jacob. First written in Greek in the late first and early second century CE (as were the gospels), these books are also based on scripture, such as the 'blessing of Jacob' (Genesis 49:1-27).

Certainly the gospel writers were sincere in their belief that the significance of Jesus among his own people qualified him to be regarded as the Messiah. They were among many who saw Jesus that way, following the events of Easter. They no doubt knew of the conviction of the Apostle Paul regarding Jesus the Anointed One. They would have known about the Pharisaic tradition regarding the general resurrection of the righteous and the appearance of the Messiah at the End-time Day of the LORD. Given the time frame in which the gospels were written, it seems very likely that their inspiration for writing as they did was the destruction of Jerusalem and the Temple, after which they expected the return of Jesus as the Messiah. That they were quite simply wrong in this expectation has never really been acknowledged by the church.

However, what we have from the gospel writers and other New Testament writers is a genuine attempt to put into words what they believed, that in his words and deeds Jesus somehow represented God, and that he would return to vindicate this belief. There must also be room for acknowledgment that the earliest complete gospel texts are edited versions, altered to create harmony in basic belief regarding Jesus as Messiah/Christ.[156] That editing process of New Testament texts probably continued through the second and third centuries CE, after which (in the fourth century) extensive attempts were made to formulate the tenets of Christian belief, including the creeds of the church and the beginnings of trinitarian doctrine. At that time (382CE) St Jerome translated older Latin versions of the gospels (and the whole Bible) into what is known as the Vulgate, which eventually (at the Council of Trent in 1545-63) became the official bible of the Catholic Church. Jerome had a huge number of manuscripts to contend with, the Latin texts having been translations from earlier Greek, Coptic, Syriac, Arabic and Gothic versions of the gospels.

The earliest complete gospel manuscripts are the Codex

Sinaiticus and Codex Vaticanus, from the early 4th century CE. So far scholars have discovered 25,000 hand-written copies of the New Testament, both fragmentary and complete. There are also numerous quotes from the New Testament in the writings of the early (second to fourth century CE) 'church fathers'. They were often used as basis for new copies and translations.

I realise that some of my readers may be regarding all of this as esoteric information, but I include it to illustrate the huge amount of translation and copying of the gospels that took place in the early centuries of the Common Era. Although it is agreed that most translations and copies have accurately preserved an early view of Jesus as Messiah, the second last verse of Matthew's Gospel (28:19: the 'Great Commission') contains the trinitarian formula of Father, Son and Holy Spirit. That can only have been added during the third or fourth centuries CE. Evidence for that includes the fact that the version of Matthew 28:19 written 17 times by Bishop Eusebia of Caesarea (263-339 CE) has: "*Go disciple ye all the nations in my name.*" No trinity in that.

Although a good deal of the gospels consists of messianic 'proof texts' from the Hebrew Scriptures, they also include authentic teachings from Jesus of Nazareth. In particular, we can only be grateful that Matthew the probable Pharisee saw Jesus as the deliverer of a 'fulfilled Torah', what Christians call the Sermon on the Mount. Along with corresponding parables, that corpus of Jesus' teachings has changed the world for the good in uncountable and immeasurable ways.

Unfortunately, in the church of the second and later centuries CE, those priceless teachings *of* Jesus were counted as secondary to the development of teachings *about* Jesus. Although unwittingly, the gospel writers contributed fundamentally to the development of christological doctrine through their narratives about the resurrection (and ascension) of Jesus Christ. In particular, John's Gospel has been the biblical foundation for doctrine concerning the divine Christ.

South Australian scholar Paul Trudinger, formerly Senior Professor of New Testament Studies at the University of Winnipeg, regards the idea of Jesus' divinity as quite unhelpful:

I can find a very central place for Jesus in my thinking, and I can account for what he was and did, without resorting to deifying him, turning him into God. If I make him God, I find his place in my thinking much less significant, in fact; of much less help to me, and to humanity.[157]

The gospel section of this book has been written to help the reader make a clearer distinction between the Gospel (good news) from Jesus himself and the Gospel of Christ that came to be based on the four canonical gospels. My aim is to provide good reason to see that although the canonical gospels were produced by people convinced they were inspired by God to write, the gospels were unmistakably 'made on earth'. Although they contain the treasures of Jesus' teachings, they are the literature of their own era, expressing messianic beliefs that belong in that time and that context.

For my readers who are questioning the absolute authority of doctrine concerning Jesus the Christ, my hope is that this exploration of the gospels may provide some clarity regarding the human origins of such doctrine. It may also help to clear away christological obstacles to a more intentional focus on Jesus' teachings about the best possible world.

Section 4

What's in a name?
The church without
Christ

What would it mean for Christianity if it disclaimed the Christ and reclaimed the Teacher?

What difference would it make to the church if 'Christ' were recognized as a theological construction born of first to fourth century human imagination and creativity? What if later theologians, basing their beliefs on Mark, Matthew, Luke and John, were found not to be describing an actual divine/human entity sent from heaven to redeem humanity to a judgmental God? Would it mean that the church must cease and desist from that teaching forthwith? Would it mean that the church itself must cease to exist? Apart from obvious problems with the name, what would be left of the foundations of Christianity if christological propositions and beliefs were lifted from Jesus? Even taking into account the many interpretations of Christology that have tried to restate the tradition for the current age, Christology's historically-bound doctrinal baggage remains. It continues to stand in the way of fully understanding and embracing the teachings of Jesus.

In all cases the gospel writers would have believed themselves divinely inspired to develop their portraits of Jesus as Messiah/Christ the Son of God. By and large that belief has been accepted by the church for two millennia. Yet quests of the historical Jesus have opened up cracks in the acceptance of a literal reading of the Bible, including the gospels; this has led to the widespread growth of critical biblical studies. Increasingly, scholars have unfolded the first century world of meaning that influenced the gospel writers.

As I pointed out in the Introduction to this book, the male-controlled production of scripture and doctrine led not only to the exclusion of the female point of view; it enshrined and even made sacrosanct male structures of society that encourage hierarchies and relegate all people to rungs on a hierarchical ladder. The church's embrace of that ancient system disempowered the poor, but more particularly, it declared women to be inferior to men. It need hardly be said that this took the church in the opposite direction from the way Jesus' inclusive teachings were pointing. These days many men working for reform alongside female scholars and female church leaders are trying to overcome that enormous obstacle to Jesus' teaching in the church's own life. One such obstacle is called 'tradition'. Tradition in the church became traditionalism, an ideology that is often ranked ahead of the need for re-thinking a faith for today.

In Section 1 I explained my difficulty with what I recognized as contradiction in the message proclaimed by the church of my childhood and early adulthood. I have no doubt that this was the proclamation commonly received across the length and breadth of the church in the mid-twentieth century. One of the contradictory messages preachers through the ages have delivered concerns the term 'gospel'. This is the English translation of the Greek word *euangelion*, meaning 'good news'. The word *euangelion* is itself derived from the Greek word *aggelos* ('*angelos*') meaning 'angel'. The implication is clear: through their titles the gospels are claimed to be divinely-sent messages of good news from God.

In classical Greek an *euangelion* was a message of victory from the gods. It could also be a message of victory sent by the leader of a victorious army to the king or the people. It does not stretch the meaning too far to see the idea of divine victory behind the application of *euangelion* to the title of books written by all four gospel writers. Mark, Matthew, Luke and John are all intent on proclaiming the divine victory in Jesus the Messiah/Christ – not only over other claimants to divine truth, but over the ultimate human foe – death. Cue the strains of the old Easter hymn: "Thine be the glory, risen conquering Son, endless is the victory thou o'er death hast won".

Nonetheless, contradiction has been perpetuated in the church concerning the term 'gospel'. Preachers in all ages have used and still use the term liberally and triumphantly, as if it had only one meaning. Yet gospel as 'good news' has always carried highly ambiguous meaning. In incarnational Christology the 'good news' concerns the arrival on earth of a divine/human male Christ, sent from heaven by a male Father God through the employment of a compliant human virgin's womb. Whether intended to be seen in metaphysical or symbolically Jewish terms, the gospels promote an other-worldly, miracle-working nature for Christ. The alternative gospel option for Christ's arrival on earth is that he appeared through ordinary human agency, as Mark seems to have been content to leave it. My investigation of the birth narratives in Matthew and Luke points to a distinct possibility that their gospels began in a similar way to Mark's, that they did not in fact write the 'infancy narratives'.

In any case the gospel tradition says the man who appears is Jesus of Nazareth. Regardless of the christological nature of the birth narratives, it is not until long after belief in Jesus' victory over death (resurrection) that the gospels say he is recognized by his followers to have been divine (or at least divinely appointed) as well as human. He is henceforth known as the Messiah/Christ, or, as John's gospel in particular expresses it, divine Son of God. John Bodycomb notes in his book *No Fixed Address* that this developing belief in Jesus' divinity would have been foreign, if not blasphemous, to Jesus himself:

> *We are told in the gospels that Jesus announced the arrival of God's kingdom. He is alleged to have said "The kingdom is already among you." If he did make this statement (which many scholars believe to be the case), this could have been enough for some of his followers to have thought Jesus saw himself as embodying this kingdom. Hence they may have given him the title 'Christ', meaning one anointed as God's agent. All this is somewhat speculative, but it is not implausible. However, it is quite impossible that during his lifetime anyone would have seen Jesus as more than this. They*

would not have seen him as 'God'. That idea would have been preposterous to them – indeed a blasphemy, as it would have been to him.[158]

Since the gospel writers formulated their ideas about the resurrection of Jesus, the salvific package has contained an extra bonus for repentant believers – eternal life in heaven. From the fourth century onward the 'good news' officially included the message that the fully divine/fully human Jesus the Christ was crucified to appease the wrath of his heavenly Father toward humanity and thereby to save and reconcile inherently sinful humans with God. The two ideas of resurrection to eternal life for believers in Christ, plus Christ's sacrificial appeasement of divine wrath, have together constituted the essence of 'good news' passed on by the traditional church since the fourth century CE. It is those beliefs that are correctly meant when people speak of the 'gospel of Christ'. This same term is often wrongly applied to the teachings of Jesus; it is one of the sources of contradiction in the church's proclamation. Which 'gospel' do you mean? It is essential for the church's future that this 'good news' (the gospel of Christ) be examined not only for its content, but for its effect on human society over almost two millennia. Here are three major reasons for doing that.

- **A religion of fear**

The first reason is that the 'gospel of Christ' is in essence a religion of fear. Countless Christians have lived in fear and trembling that in their death they will be found not to have lived up to the church's criteria for entering heaven. The whole edifice of Christology is founded on the doctrine of Original Sin, which requires a Saviour figure to rescue humanity from its inherent sinfulness. That has invested an inordinate amount of power in Catholic clergy in particular, whom the Catholic Church claims to have power to control the process of confession and forgiveness of sin and therefore escape from hell. It should be added that clergy of other denominations are not entirely blameless in this regard, particularly through the process of preaching 'hellfire and brimstone' sermons.

In the Protestant and Catholic churches, the view of Jesus as Christ the Saviour has had the effect of distracting people from their attempts to follow Jesus. Attention to attendance at church, to adhering to 'correct' doctrine, to believing that people of all other faiths are condemned by God and must be converted to Christianity or they will go to hell, has built barriers between people instead of creating a harmonious human community over the earth. These are all consequences of the religion of fear built around belief in Christ the Saviour.

•   The Effect on the Jewish people

Secondly, through the power of Christian empires, beginning with the Roman Empire, the influence of traditional christological beliefs has permeated the wider society, as well as the lives of believers in Christ. Belief in Christ has had a profoundly toxic effect on the well-being and physical safety of the Jewish people, as well as on adherents of Islam, the third major faith that emerged in the Middle East. It is difficult to over-estimate the profundity of the effect christological beliefs have had on the people most intimately related to the new faith of Christianity. Jews who did not consider Jesus as Messiah (let alone as the universal Christ) were the majority of the mainstream Jewish population in the first centuries of the Common Era.

As I have noted, it is reasonable to argue that many Jews of his time regarded Jesus of Nazareth as a prophet. No historical information has appeared which indicates that Jesus' own Galilean contemporaries saw him as the Messiah. The gospels can be regarded as statements of belief in Christ, or even as 'sermons' written to make a case for validity of belief in Jesus as the Messiah/Christ. They cannot be regarded as any kind of 'proof' that Jesus saw himself as the Messiah. Nor do they constitute proof that Jesus' original Galilean followers saw him that way.

It was probably inevitable that a growing belief in Jesus the Messiah/Christ among hellenized Jews and Gentiles would be responsible for the gospel writers' development of an anti-Jewish point of view, particularly in the Gospel of John. By the last two decades of the first century CE, the mainstream of Jewry, along with its leadership, was viewed by the Christ followers as the opposition, even as the enemy. There is nowhere near sufficient scope in this book for an adequately detailed description of the effect of christological beliefs on the Jewish people through Christian history until the 20th century. Suffice it to say that when belief in Jesus as the Christ developed into certainty that he was not only fully human but fully divine, that is, God incarnate, then the stage was set for the systematic and often savage persecution and murder of the Jewish people for the crime of 'Deicide': 'murder of God'.

In uncountable ways, the church has visited its wrathful revenge on the people it most wanted to acknowledge and believe in its Christ. When the Jewish people refused to believe that the theology of Nicea was divine revelation of Israel's fulfilled salvation history, the church's disappointment and anger reached its peak.

An early example of Christian hostility against the Jews is preserved in the writings of John Chrysostom, Presbyter in Antioch and subsequently Archbishop of Constantinople. In the late fourth century Chrysostom delivered eight homilies '*Against the Jews*'. They were most probably directed against the practice whereby some Antiochian Christians 'fraternized' with Jews and attended Jewish festivals. Unfortunately for countless Jews (and their descendants) who had fled Roman Palestine for Europe in the second century, Chrysostom's homilies were phrased in violent and hate-filled antisemitic rhetoric. One example will suffice.

> *The synagogue is a criminal assembly of Jews, a place of meeting for the assassins of Christ, a house worse than a drinking shop, a den of thieves, a house of ill fame, a dwelling of iniquity, the refuge of devils, a gulf and abyss of perdition. Whatever name even more horrible could be found, will never be worse than the synagogue deserves. I would say the same things about their souls. It is unfit for Christians to associate with a people who had fallen into a condition lower than the vilest animals. Debauchery and*

drunkenness had brought them to the level of the lusty
goat and the pig. They know only one thing, to satisfy
their stomachs, to get drunk, to kill and beat each other up.
God hates them, and indeed has always hated them. But
since their murder of Jesus He allows them no time for
repentance. When it is clear that God hates them, it is the
duty of Christians to hate them too.[159]

That view of all Jews as vile and hated by God is the first written example of Christian antisemitism. It was passed on as authoritative in following centuries as Chrysostom's homilies against the Jews were taught to succeeding generations of Christian priests. This was one of the many ways the idea that the Jews had been rejected by God for their 'terrible crime' was perpetuated in Christian societies throughout Europe.

Those antisemitic ideas from a 'church father' laid a firm foundation upon which Christian rulers and church leaders in Europe formulated and carried out persecution of the Jews, who were regarded as of no account and rejected by God. Martin Luther's already drastic measures to punish the Jews for their refusal to convert to Christianity were far outweighed by the 'final solution' to the 'Jewish problem' developed by Hitler and his Nazi followers. Hitler used Luther's writings to justify his attitude to the Jews. In an audience with two Catholic churchmen in 1933, he explained that by removing Jewish influences from the life of the German nation, he merely intended to accomplish what the church had for so long attempted.

In his 2010 book Roots of *Theological Antisemitism: German Biblical Interpretation and the Jews*, German theologian Anders Gerdman makes the point that unchallenged theological traditions in German university departments of theology have operated as "transmitters of anti-Semitism":

The church wittingly or unwittingly in passing on its
tradition was also implicitly or explicitly promoting
anti-Semitism ... In the earliest period, emergent
Christianity struggled as a tiny minority to develop its

own image and identity over against the ongoing faith of Judaism ... But when Christianity emerged triumphant within the Roman Empire, its earlier tradition of fighting for its own freedoms over against Jewish patterns of life was not discontinued, but was transmuted to regarding the Jews as heretics in an empire where Christianity now had power. Jews as minorities in many European countries were henceforth generally regarded as having no real right to exist since Christianity with its political success was perceived to be obviously its superior successor.[160]

It is beyond denial that this happened because Jesus was declared by the early church to be 'God' – the second 'person' of the Holy Trinity. From this outcome alone, the development of Christology and its consequences can with good reason be described as the central tragedy of Western civilization. For the reader who wishes to pursue a full description of the rise and effect of Christian antisemitism, I would suggest *Constantine's Sword: the Church and the Jews. A History*, by former Catholic priest James Carroll. In his comments about the need to rethink traditional doctrine that undergirds antisemitism, he asks:

How can we stand by and continue to develop theologies of the church and the tradition as if the Holocaust did not happen?[161]

- **The Church embraces the Empire**

Thirdly, the church's embrace of the Roman Empire to assist its own growth, created a further ugly blot on human history. From the time of Constantine onward, the church's attention focussed primarily on the identity of Jesus as the divine Christ. The Book of Revelation contains imagery whereby the conquering Christ defeats the 'beast', the Roman Empire. Revelation has often been regarded as prediction of the way the church would conquer Rome through its triumphant Christ. The reverse is true. The rhetoric of Revelation was influential in the development of a triumphalist church, looking remarkably like an empire in itself, with the emperor Pope and his princely bishops. In consequence, it was Rome that conquered the church!

It was out of an imperialist theology that the Popes conquered and subdued their subjects and authorized forced baptisms of the Jews, through the power of the 'Holy Roman Empire'. Popes crowned the emperors of Europe from Charlemagne in 800 to Charles V in 1530. The Holy Roman Empire itself lasted until 1806, when it was dissolved by Emperor Francis II, after he was defeated by Napoleon.

From Constantine on, soldiers of various Christian empires have seen themselves as 'soldiers of the Cross'. The triumphalist flavour of Christology easily lent itself to the conquering and subjugation of people in colonies established by Christian empires. The most infamous and shameful example of imperialist Christian theology was the endorsement of slavery. During the apartheid system of government in South Africa, churches used scripture to excuse their shameful treatment of black South Africans. That could only have happened in a church where the teachings of Jesus were secondary to an alliance between church and state.

The former slave and abolitionist Frederick Douglass wrote about the unholy coupling of the slave trade with what passed for Christianity in America:

> I love the pure, peaceable, and impartial Christianity of Jesus. I see no reason, but the most deceitful one, for calling the religion of this land Christianity. The man who wields the blood-clotted cowskin during the week fills the pulpit on Sunday, and claims to be a minister of the meek and lowly Jesus. The slave auctioneer's bell and the church-going bell chime in with each other, and the bitter cries of the heart-broken slave are drowned by the religious shouts of his pious master. The slave prison and the church stand near each other. The clanking of fetters and the rattling of chains in the prison, and the pious psalm and solemn prayer in the church, may be heard at the same time. The dealer gives his blood-stained gold to support the pulpit, and the pulpit, in return, covers his infernal business with the garb of Christianity.[162]

Ironically, alongside the destruction of the Jerusalem Temple and the associated end of its system of priesthood and sacrifices, the development of Christology supported ideas about a renewed priesthood in the new faith, albeit without a Temple. An altar was installed in every church and the 'last supper' became the re-enactment of the sacrifice of Christ for the sins of humanity. The priesthood, in offering the elements of bread and wine as 'body and blood of Christ', became *'in persona Christi'*.

In his Apostolic Exhortation of 1980, Pope John Paul II wrote concerning this:

> *The priest offers the holy sacrifice in persona Christi. Awareness of this reality throws a certain light on the character and significance of the priest celebrating who, by confecting the holy Sacrifice and acting 'in persona Christi' is sacramentally (and ineffably) brought into that most profound sacredness, and made part of it, spiritually linking with it in turn all those participating in the eucharistic assembly.*[163]

In the twenty-first century the belief that priests of the Catholic Church are *'in persona Christi'* has hardly diminished. History has shown that this clerical understanding has given unchallenged power to priests in the belief that they can do no wrong, as they are representatives of Christ. In his book about sexual abuse of children by Catholic priests, retired Catholic Bishop Geoffrey Robinson names what he calls the 'messiah complex' among recently ordained priests in Australia:

> *One of the saddest sights in the Church today is that of some young, newly-ordained priests insisting that there is an 'ontological difference' between them and laypersons, and enthusiastically embracing the mystique of a superior priesthood. Whenever I see young priests doing this I feel a sense of despair, and I wonder whether we have learned anything at all from the revelations of abuse.*[164]

Former Catholic priest Kieran Tapsell notes that the 'messiah complex' is still being taught in seminaries in Sydney:

> *This is a systemic problem arising from the doctrine and theological culture of the Church. It may not be a cause of child sexual abuse, but it is one of the matters that make it easier to occur because Catholic children are also taught to have this kind of respect for priests.*[165]

The priesthood of first century Judaism died along with the destruction of the Temple. The hierarchical priesthood of the Christian church remains, the clerical caste from the Pope down representing a last vestige of the medieval court. Most Christians are now eager to agree that the church has moved on beyond Christendom that incorporated an unholy alliance between church and state. Curiously, the leadership of mainstream denominations continues to hold fast to the theology of Christendom. However, an inevitable crisis is approaching for christological beliefs. As membership of major denominations steadily diminishes, the Christology that has been their mainstay will disappear along with the institution upon which it is based. Each is dependent on the other. The theology of the institution will not survive the disappearance of the institution itself.

Ironically, a temporary reprieve from the traditional church's last gasp in Australia will come via the importation of clergy (and the immigration of Anglican, Catholic, Methodist and Presbyterian laity) from the old colonial mission fields of Christendom. The tables have turned and post-colonial missionaries are being sent to congregations of the contemporary church in Australia, to perpetuate for a season the faith of Christendom. Most of those congregations are composed of migrant groups from Korea, China, the Philippines, Africa, Tonga, Fiji, Sri Lanka and Indonesia. The Caucasian congregations are shrinking fast, with a clear end point on the horizon.

On the other hand, progressive or evolving Christians are moving irreversibly toward developing a post-Christendom faith. This movement may well be described as following the teachings of Jesus and finding spiritual inspiration from his God, without 'Christianity'. The main reason for hope in a post-Christendom community of faith is deeply ironic. Almost incidentally, along with traditional christological 'good news', good news of a totally different kind has also been passed on through the church. Banished to second ranking in importance after the christological teaching, this 'secondary' good news of the church is the core teaching of the Jewish teacher of the Law, Jesus of Nazareth. When the church has turned its focus to the teachings of Jesus over and above the 'gospel of Christ', it has been an enormous power for good in the world, as Jesus would have intended.

As we have noted, Matthew's primary intention was to present Jesus as the new Moses who reveals the fulfilled Torah. Unwittingly, that writer has ensured a future for the countless Christians now leaving the diminishing church of Nicea. By including the Sermon on the Mount and associated parables of Jesus, Matthew's Gospel has preserved the priceless heritage from Jesus for his followers (Matthew 5-7).[166] A truncated version appears in Luke 6:17-49, known as the Sermon on the Plain, along with the parables of the Good Samaritan and the Prodigal Son.

As I pointed out in the Preface, the church historically has tried to take the two meanings of gospel 'good news' and mix them together in one religion. The result has been an inevitable contradiction of understandings in a religion about God and Jesus and its effect on human relationships. The 'two gospels' church is what science calls an emulsion,[167] where irreconcilable elements mixed together inevitably separate back to their original forms. The two gospels of the church have been revealed to be like oil and water – simply incompatible. A common contribution to the confusion is to call the teachings of Jesus 'the teachings of Christ'. For that reason many are reluctant to set aside christological doctrine for fear that they are also discarding Jesus. More clarity about this confusion is greatly needed in all of the churches.

This Section's heading asks, 'What's in a Name?' For increasing numbers of church members or former church members who are discarding christological tradition *about* Jesus in favour of the teachings *of* Jesus, the name Christian represents a dilemma. A 'Christian' is, after all, a believer in Christ. At present there are attempts to find alternative names for gatherings of Jesus' followers who want to find a non-christological way of being church. A popular suggestion is 'The Church of The Way', referring to the most ancient title for Jesus' post-Easter disciples. According to the Book of Acts they were known as followers of the Way.[168] For the Jewish people, the word 'Torah' means the way of life they follow. Given that Jesus was a teacher of Torah, who encouraged following the spirit of Torah to its ultimate potential for life, 'Followers of The Way' seems an appropriate name for his 21st century followers. Another possibility gaining popularity is 'Friends of Jesus'.

Yet even given the importance of a name, that issue is not the most critical one to be addressed in coming decades as the institutional church recedes in numbers and influence. What must be faced head-on are the ideas about God that form the basis of christological beliefs. There is inherent contradiction between the teachings of Jesus about humility in relationships and care for the other, and teaching about the conversion of unbelievers to belief in Christ the sacrificial 'lamb of God', who will conduct the believer to eternal life. For understanding of God and for the development of a Jesus-inspired spirituality for the 21st century, the difference is crucial and could not be greater.

The time has come
It is high time to remove from the church all beliefs and doctrines that stand in contradiction to the teachings of Jesus. Whether Jesus' 21st century post-Christianity followers gather in homes, halls, old churches or cafes, they have the 'good news' of the gospel of Jesus. In his teaching they have a peerless basis for spiritual depth in their relationship with the sacred (God). They have unmatched guidance for personal and community life, ethical judgment grounded on the rule of love, and hope for a harmonious future with all the peoples of the world.

Given the boundless human misery caused by the old triumphalist religion of certainty based on Christ, it is well past the time to allow it to be consigned to history, including the name 'Christ'. It is time for it to be numbered among other religions that emerged in ancient times and ran their courses, until societies changed their understandings of the sacred.

Most importantly, let my reader not confuse putting aside the 'Christ' as throwing out Jesus and God! Jesus will forever remain the foundation for his followers' understanding of God. His teachings belong in this century as in any other. They in no way preclude continuing scientific investigation of the universe. They complement the discoveries of science in developing a human understanding of existence. As John Bodycomb is inclined to say: *"Jesus is to the art of living as Einstein is to cosmology."*

My ultimate aim in writing a book about how gospel writers created 'Christ', is to help my readers let go of 'Christ' and embrace the future gladly as followers of the Way of Jesus. Jesus' teaching requires no institution, no doctrine, no priesthood to enforce it. It can be discussed and learned and put into practice by worshipping/learning groups dedicated to creating the best possible world. Worshipping and learning resources for such groups are emerging from followers of Jesus around the world. History has always shown that once clearly known, Jesus' teaching is freely received and followed gladly. No wonder! It is sacred wisdom for life.

GLOSSARY OF TERMS

- APOCALYPTIC
  In biblical terms, this word describes or prophesies the destruction of the present world, when hidden or heavenly things will be revealed. In the New Testament, the apocalyptic scenario is when the Kingdom of God is revealed on earth, at the re-appearance of Jesus as Messiah/Christ.
- BODILY RESURRECTION
  The belief that although the physical body dies, after death it will be replaced by a 'resurrection body', that will not die.
- DAY OF THE LORD
  The biblical Day of the Lord is God's victory over evil. In the Hebrew Scriptures the prophets (e.g. Is. 2:12) warned that on the Day of the Lord, Israel would be destroyed because of its sin. The concept continues into Christian scripture, where the tumultuous event is closely tied with the coming of the Messiah to judge the world. The imagery of the sun turned to darkness and the moon to blood is copied from Joel 2:28-32 into Acts 2:19-21.
- DIASPORA
  The place of the dispersion of Jews beyond Israel. OR of any people from their original homeland.
- DIVINITY OF CHRIST
  The belief that Jesus Christ was made both Son of God in the spirit and Son of man in the flesh – that is, both God and man. (Lactantius, Divine Institutes 4:13:5).
- DOCTRINE OF THE INCARNATION
  The belief that God reconciled human beings to 'himself' by coming among them in the person of his Son. God 'incarnate' was then vulnerable to all aspects of human life, including human death.
- ESCHATOLOGY
  The branch of theology concerned with the final events in the history of the world or of humankind.
- GOSPEL OF CHRIST
  The central content of traditional Christian revelation – the proclamation of redemption through the death and resurrection of Christ.

- GOSPEL OF JESUS
  The good news taught by Jesus about creating the best possible world – what he called the kingdom of heaven on earth.
- HEBREW BIBLE
  The Jewish scriptures, originally written in Hebrew and called the Old Testament by Christians.
- KINGDOM OF HEAVEN/GOD
  The state of affairs on earth when Jesus' teachings have been fully accepted and put in place. As if God were the ruler of the earth.
- LAW OF MOSES
  The Torah = the first five books of the Hebrew Scriptures, plus the oral Law, first written in the Mishnah and encapsulated in the Talmud (2nd century CE). It defines God's way of life.
- MESSIANIC SECRET
  The 'messianic secret' is a theme of biblical criticism developed in 1901 by the German Lutheran theologian Wilhelm Wrede. It is Wrede's explanation for Jesus wanting to hide his messianic identity, particularly as set out in the Gospel of Mark.
- POST-EASTER
  The time following the events of Easter – the crucifixion and resurrection.
- PRE-EASTER
  The period during the lifetime of Jesus, up until his crucifixion.
- RESTORATION PROPHET
  A prophet (such as Jeremiah) whose aim is to call the people of Israel to repentance for sin, and so to reconciliation with God.
- SAVIOUR CHRIST
  Traditionally, the redeemer of human beings from their sin and the saviour of their souls from destruction at the day of judgment.
- SON OF MAN
  Title for the humanity of Jesus, alongside Son of God, being the description of the divinity of Jesus.
- SUPERSESSIONISM
  Belief that Christians have superseded the Jewish people as the true people of God. It entails reading the Hebrew Scriptures as prediction of the coming of Jesus Christ.
- THE WAY
  The name given to the way of life taught by Jesus, especially in the Sermon on the Mount. The title 'followers of the Way' occurs in the Book of Acts.

PRIMARY SOURCES

Scripture:
> *The Holy Bible: containing The Old and New Testaments with The Apocryphal/Deuterocanonical Books,* New Revised Standard Version, London, Harper Collins Publishers, 1989.

> *The Septuagint with Apocrypha: Greek and English,* Sir Lancelot C.L. Brenton (Trans.), United States of America, Hendrickson Publishers, 1995.

> *Biblia Hebraica Stuttgartensia,* Stuttgart, Germany, Deutsche Bibelgesellschaft, 1984.

> *Greek Text with Critical Apparatus,* London, The British and Foreign Bible Society, 1952.

Targums:
> *The Aramaic Bible,* Translation with Notes by Michael Maher M.S.C., A Michael Glazier Book, The Liturgical Press, Collegeville, Minnesota, 1994.

Dead Sea Scrolls:
> The Complete Dead Sea Scrolls in English, Seventh Edition (Penguin Classics), Geza Vermes (Translator), Penguin Books, 2012

Rabbinic Writings:
> *Pesikta Derab Kahanna,* W. G. Braude (Trans.), Jewish Publication Society of America, 2nd Edition, 2002.
> *The Mishnah: A New Translation, Jacob Neusner,* Yale University Press, New Haven and London, 1988.
> *The Talmud of Babylonia. An American Translation,* Jacob Neusner, Tzvee Zahavy (Translators), Atlanta, The Scholars Press, Brown Judaic Studies, 1995.

Historical:
> *Josephus,* Loeb Classical Library, H. St. J. Thackeray (Translator), Cambridge Mass., Harvard University Press, 1997.
> *Philo of Alexandria,* Loeb Classical Library, F. H. Colson and G. H. Whitaker (Translators), 10 Vols., Bury St Edmunds, Suffolk, UK, St Edmundsbury Press, Hunter & Foulis Ltd., 2001 edition.
> *Historia Ecclesiasticus,* (History of the Church) Kirsopp Lake, J.E.L. Oulton, H.J. Lawler, William Heinemann (Eds.), Cambridge, Mass., Harvard University Press, 1932.

> *Ante-Nicene Fathers,* Alexander Roberts, James Donaldson, A. Cleveland Coxe (Eds.), Buffalo NY, Christian Literature Publishing Co., 1886.

> *The Fathers of the Church,* Paul W. Harkins (Translator), Washington DC, The Catholic University of America Press, 1979.

GENERAL BIBLIOGRAPHY

Anderson, Robert A., *Quite Some Time: A Memoir*, Melbourne, 2011.

Asmussen, Ryan, "The Persistence of Memory: An Interview with Paula Fredriksen", *Focus*, Spring 2003, The Boston University School of Theology.

Aune, David E., *Prophecy in Early Christianity and the Ancient Mediterranean World*, William B. Eerdmans Publishing Company, Grand Rapids, Michigan, 1991.

Bacher, B. Z. (Wilhelm), *Aggadot HaTanna'im*, (A. S. Rabbinowitz Tr.), Jerusalem, 1922.

Baylis, H. J., *Minucius Felix and His Place Among the Early Fathers of the Latin Church*, London, 1928.

Bieler, Andrea and Schottroff, Luise, *The Eucharist: Bodies, Bread and Resurrection*, Minneapolis, Fortress Press, 2007.

Bodycomb, John, *No Fixed Address: Faith as Journey*, Melbourne, Spectrum Publications, 2010.

Brown, Raymond E., *The Birth of the Messiah: A Commentary on the infancy narratives in Matthew and Luke*, London, Geoffrey Chapman, 1977.
– *Jesus God and Man: Modern Biblical Reflections*, London, Geoffrey Chapman, 1968.
– *The Gospel According to John*, Anchor Bible Series, Vol. 29, Garden City, NY, Doubleday, 1966.

Campbell, William S, "Reflections on the transmission of traditions in interaction with Anders Gerdmar"; *Roots of Theological Anti-Semitism: German Biblical Interpretation and the Jews, from Herder and Semler to Kittel and Bultmann*, Leiden and Boston, Brill, 2010, xviii – 675, in 'Book Reviews', *Journal of Beliefs & Values: Studies in Religion and Education*, Vol. 36, Number 2, August 2015, Routledge, Taylor and Francis Group, pp.220-223.

Carroll, James, *Constantine's Sword: the church and the Jews, a History*, Boston, Houghton Mifflin Company, 2001.

Casey, R. P., "The Earliest Christologies", in *The Journal of Theological Studies*, New Series, Vol. 9, No. 2, October 1958.

Charlesworth, James, *The Pseudepigrapha and Modern Research*, Scholars Press for The Society of Biblical Literature, Stanford University Press, Stanford, California, 1976.
– *The Historical Jesus: An Essential Guide*, Nashville, Abingdon Press, 2008.

Crossan, John Dominic and Reed, Jonathan L., *Excavating Jesus: Beneath the Stones, Behind the Texts*, San Francisco, HarperSanFrancisco, 2001.

Crossley, James, "Mark, Paul, and the Question of Influences", in *Paul and the Gospels: Christologies, Conflicts and Convergences*, Michael F. Bird and Joel Willitts (Eds.), Library of New Testament Studies 411, London: T & T Clark, 2011.

Crotty, Robert, *Peter the Rock: What the Roman Papacy was, and what it might become*, Melbourne, Spectrum Publications, 2015.

Douglass, Frederick, *My Bondage and My Freedom*, New York and Auburn, Miller, Orton and Mulligan (1885), John Stauffer (Ed.) Random House, 2003.

Eliot, T. S., 'Little Gidding', in *Four Quarters*, London, Faber & Faber, 2001.

Fosdick, H. E., *Adventurous religion and Other Essays*, London, Student Christian Movement, 1926.

Fiorenza, Elizabeth Schüssler, "Between Movement and Academy", in Elizabeth Schüssler Fiorenza (Ed.), *Feminist Biblical Studies in the Twentieth Century: Scholarship and Movement*, Society of Biblical Literature, Atlanta, Georgia, USA, 2014.

Fitzmyer, Joseph, *The Gospel According to Luke X-VVIV, 2 Vols.*, The Anchor Bible, Garden City, New York, Doubleday and Company Inc., 1958.

Fortin, A. H., and Barnett, K. G., "Medical School Curricula in Spirituality and Medicine", in *Journal of the American Medical Association*, 2004, 291(23).

Funk, Robert W. and the Jesus Seminar, *The Acts of Jesus: What did Jesus really do?* New York, Polebridge Press, HarperSanFrancisco, 1998.

Gerdmar, Anders, *Roots of Theological Anti-Semitism: German Biblical Interpretation and the Jews, from Herder and Semler to Kittel and Bultmann*, Leiden and Boston, Brill, 2010.

Ginzberg, Louis, *The Legends of the Jews*, Philadelphia, Jewish Publication Society of America, Twelfth Impression, 1987.

Hooker, M. D., *The Gospel According to Saint Mark*, BNTC; London, A. & C. Black, 1991.

Horsley, Richard, *The Prophet Jesus and the Renewal of Israel: Moving beyond a diversionary debate*, William B. Eerdmans Publishing Company, Grand Rapids, Michigan, 2012.

Jensen, Morten H, "Climate, Droughts, Wars, and Famines in Galilee as a Background for Understanding the Historical Jesus", in *Journal of Biblical Literature Vol. 131*, No. 2, 2012.

Jocz, J, "The Invisibility of God and the Incarnation", *Judaica 17*, 1961.

Knohl, Israel, "The Gabriel Revelation and the Birth of Christianity", presented at the conference Dead Sea Scrolls and Contemporary Culture: Celebrating 60 years of Discovery, Jerusalem, 6 – 8 July, 2008.

Krause, Neil, "Reported Contact with the Dead, Religious Involvement, and Death Anxiety in Later Life", in *Review of Religious Research*, Vol. 52, No. 4 (June 2011).

Levine, Amy-Jill, *The Misunderstood Jew: the Church and the Scandal of the Jewish Jesus*, New York, HarperOne, 2007.

Lightfoot, J. B. (Translator and Editor), *The Didache or Teaching of the Apostles, in Apostolic Fathers Part 1* (two vols), London, MacMillan & Co., 1885.

Mack, Burton L., *Who Wrote the New Testament? The Making of the Christian Myth*, San Francisco, Harper, 1996.

Maher, Michael, (Translator with Notes), *The Aramaic Bible*, Vol. 2, Targum Pseudo-Jonathan: Deuteronomy, A Michael Glazier Book, The Liturgical Press, Collegeville, Minnesota, 1994.

Metzger, Bruce, *A Textual Commentary on the Greek New Testament*, United Bible Societies U.S.A, Stuttgart, 1971.

Meyers, Robin, *The Underground Church: Reclaiming the subversive way of Jesus*, London, SPCK, 2012.

Morwood, Michael, *It's Time: Challenges to the Doctrine of the Faith*, Toronto, Kelmore Publishing, 2013.

Neusner, Jacob, *The Rabbinic Traditions About the Pharisees before 70: The Houses*, Book III, Conclusions, Netherlands, E. J. Brill, 1971.

Parkinson, Lorraine, *The World According to Jesus : his blueprint for the best possible world*, Melbourne, Spectrum Publications, 2011.
   - *Jesus as Moses or Elijah: Two Divergent Typologies*, Unpublished dissertation, Melbourne College of Divinity, 1996.

Plaskow, Judith, *Sex, Sin and Grace: Women's Experience and the Theologies of Niebuhr and Tillich*, Washington DC: University Press of America, 1980.

Pope John Paul II, *Dominicae Cenae*, Apostolic Exhortation, 1980.

Robinson, Geoffrey, *For Christ's Sake: End Sexual Abuse in the Catholic Church for Good*, Melbourne, John Garratt Publishing, 2013.

Robinson, John A. T., *Jesus and His Coming: The Emergence of a Doctrine*, London: SCM, 1957.

- *Honest to God*, London, SCM Press Ltd., 1963.

- *Redating the New Testament*, London, SCM Press, 1976.

Schneiders, Sandra M., *Written That You May Believe*, New York, Crossroads, 1999.

Schniewind, Julius, *Das Evangelium nach Markus*, Das Neue Testament Deutsch, Vol. 1, Göttingen, Vandenhoeck & Ruprecht, 1933.

Schroer, Silvia, "The Spirit, Wisdom and the Dove, Feminist-Critical Exegesis of a Second Testament Symbol Against the Background of its History in Ancient Near Eastern and Hellenistic-early Jewish Traditions", in *Wisdom has Built Her House: Studies on the Figure of Sophia in the Bible*, Silvia Schroer (Ed.), Linda M. Maloney and William McDonough (translators), Collegeville, MI, Liturgical Press, 2000.

Schürer, Emil, *The Literature of the Jewish People in the Age of Jesus Christ* (175 B.C.-A.D. 135), a new English version revised and edited by Geza Vermes and Fergus Millar, Edinburgh, T & T Clark Ltd., 1973.

Schweitzer, Albert, *Von Reimarus zu Wrede*, Tübingen, J.C.B. Mohr, 1906.

- (English Edition) *The Quest of the Historical Jesus: A Critical Study of its Progress from Reimarus to Wrede*, W. Montgomery (Trans.), New York, Macmillan, 1948.

Scott, Bernard Brandon, *Re-Imagine the World: An Introduction to the Parables of Jesus*, Santa Rosa, Polebridge Press, 2001.

- *The Real Paul: Recovering his Radical Challenge*, Salem, Oregon, Polebridge Press, 2015.

Smith, Dennis E., and Tyson, Joseph B., (Eds.), *Acts and Christian Beginnings: The Acts Seminar Report*, Salem, OR, Polebridge Press.

Smith, John W. H. and Hunt, Rex A. E. (Compilers and Editors), *New Life: Rediscovering Faith. Stories from Progressive Christians*, Preston, Melbourne, Mosaic Press, 2013.

Tapsell, Kieran, *Potiphar's Wife: The Vatican's Secret and Child Sexual Abuse*, Adelaide, ATF Press, 2014.

Trudinger, Paul, *A good word for Jesus: A heretic's testimony*, London, Open Gate Press, 2007.

- *Honest to Jesus*, Winnipeg, Canada, Frye Publishing, 1983.

Walck, Leslie W., *The Son of Man in the Parables of Enoch and in Matthew*, Review by Donald Senior in 'Jewish Christian Texts in Contexts and Related Studies 9', New York, T & T Clark, 2011.

Wellhausen, Julius, *Das Evangelium Marki, übersetzt und erklärt*, Berlin, 1903.

Wrede, William, *Das Messiasgeheimnis in den Evangelien: Zugleich ein Beitrag zum Verständnis des Markusevangeliums, Göttingen*, Vandenhoeck & Ruprecht, 1901.

- *Messianic Secret*, English Edition, J.C.G. Grieg (Trans.), Cambridge, James Clarke & Co., 1971.

Wright, N. T., "The Historical Jesus and Christian Theology", Sewanee Theological Review 39, 1996.

Yardeni, Ada, "Gabriel's Vision", Biblical Archaeology Review Magazine, 34:01 Jan/Feb 2008.

Endnotes

1 Lorraine Parkinson, *The World According to Jesus: his blueprint for the best possible world,* Melbourne, Spectrum Publications, 2011.

2 The English name Christ is derived from the Greek name *Christos. Christos* is the Greek translation of the Hebrew word *Mashiach,* meaning Messiah, or anointed representative of God. In its original Hebrew meaning 'Messiah' did not include the idea that the one divinely anointed was himself divine.

3 Christological dogma is regarded as an essential and (in Catholic belief) infallible set of central principles laid down by the church to define its belief in Jesus as the Messiah/Christ. The church's christological dogma is thought to be incontrovertibly true.

4 Nicea (called Iznik in modern Turkey) was the place where 4th century bishops gathered to formulate the dogma of the church, in particular, the Doctrine of the Trinity and the divinity of Christ.

5 John A. T. Robinson, *Jesus and His Coming: The Emergence of a Doctrine,* London: SCM, 1957, p.10-11.

6 Ken Fletcher, "My journey has made me question a lot of things ...", in *New Life: Rediscovering Faith. Stories from Progressive Christians,* John W. H. Smith and Rex A. E. Hunt (Compilers and Editors), Preston, Melbourne, Mosaic Press, 2013, pp.203-4.

7 Judith Plaskow, *Sex, Sin and Grace: Women's Experience and the Theologies of Niebuhr and Tillich,* Washington DC: University Press of America, 1980.

8 Elizabeth Schüssler Fiorenza, "Between Movement and Academy", in Elizabeth Schüssler Fiorenza (Ed.), *Feminist Biblical Studies in the Twentieth Century: Scholarship and Movement,* Society of Biblical Literature, Atlanta, Georgia, USA, 2014, p.15.

9 Robin Meyers, *The Underground Church: Reclaiming the subversive way of Jesus,* London, SPCK, 2012, pp.9-10.

10 T. S. Eliot, 'Little Gidding', in *Four Quarters,* London, Faber & Faber, 2001.

11 Michael Morwood, *It's Time: Challenges to the Doctrine of the Faith,* Toronto, Kelmore Publications, 2013, p.43*

12 H. E. Fosdick, *Adventurous Religion and Other Essays,* London, Student Christian Movement, 1926, p.309

13 John A. T. Robinson, *Honest to God,* London, SCM Press Ltd., 1963, p.64.

14 John A. T. Robinson, *Honest to God,* p.9.

15 Amy-Jill Levine, *The Misunderstood Jew: the Church and the Scandal of the Jewish Jesus,* New York, HarperOne, 2007, p.56.

16 For the readers' information, CE means Common Era; i.e. the era common to both Judaism and Christianity. BCE, then, means the era before that. These neutral terms can therefore be used by Jewish scholars as well as Christians. This designation replaces the exclusively Christian BC (Before Christ) and AD (Anno Domini – 'the year of our Lord').

17 The word 'Messiah' is translated into English from the Hebrew word *Mashiach,* which means 'anointed by God'. It was translated from Hebrew into Greek as *Christos,* or 'Christ'.

18 Some scholars link the Dead Sea Scrolls to the development of Christianity, but most see the non-biblical scrolls from Qumran as having been written up to 200 years before the time of Jesus.

19 In the NRSV English version of the Hebrew Bible, the Hebrew names for God are translated as LORD, in capitals to distinguish the name from other references to 'lords' or important figures. Because of that, the name 'Lord', although not expressed in capitals in New Testament quotes from the Hebrew Bible, is often read as referring to a divine Jesus Christ. I will illustrate those occurrences later in this book.

20 Supersessionism is the term that describes Christian belief that Israel has been 'succeeded' by Christianity, and that therefore the 'old covenant' has been replaced by a 'new covenant'. This is part of the so-called 'teachings of contempt' which laid the foundation for hostile Christian attitudes toward Jews that led to the Holocaust.

21 Apocalypse mean the unveilling of hidden things. An apocalyptic End-time is understood as the time when hidden (usually heavenly) things will be revealed. It does not mean the end of the world, only its renewal by God.

22 In rabbinic writings Elijah, in the disguise of an old man, teaches Eleazar the whole of the extraordinarily difficult Sifra – rabbinic teachings on the Book of Leviticus (*Pesikta d'Rav Kahanna* 11:22).

23 Although some were apparently claiming that he was the Messiah/King at the time of his arrest, given the 'King of the Jews' inscription the gospel writers say was placed above his head as he was being crucified. That is in accordance with the reason for crucifixion – the penalty for political rebellion.

24 'Day of the LORD' references can be found in the prophetic books of Isaiah, Zephaniah, Zechariah, Jeremiah, Ezekiel, Joel, Obadiah, Amos and Malachi. They also occur in Paul's writings in 1 Cor., 2 Cor., and 1 Thess., and in 2 Peter.

25 The Book of Enoch contains parts from different eras, including the third century BCE and the first century CE (the Parables). It is known as a pseudepigraphal work because its name is a pseudonym. Its name (falsely) claims that the book was written by Enoch, the great grandfather of Noah.

26 Leslie W. Walck, *The Son of Man in the Parables of Enoch and in Matthew*, Review by Donald Senior in 'Jewish and Christian Texts in Contexts and Related Studies 9', New York, T & T Clark, 2011.

27 4 Ezra is also known as 2 Esdras. It is included in the apocryphal books contained in the Catholic Old Testament.

28 Zealots were a militaristic Jewish political party dedicated to inciting the Jewish people to rebel against the Romans, particularly during the 'Jewish War' (66-70 CE). Their name comes from the idea of having 'zeal' for the Law of Moses.

29 Ryan Asmussen, "The Persistance of Memory: An Interview with Paula Fredriksen", *Focus*, Spring 2003 (Boston School of Theology, p.10, quoted in Paul Trudinger, *A good word for Jesus: A heretic's testimony,* London, Open Gate Press, 2007, p.25.

30 Flavius Josephus, *The Life of Josephus,* 374-384.

31 See Morten H. Jensen, "Climate, Droughts, Wars, and Famines in Galilee as a Background for Understanding the Historical Jesus", in *Journal of Biblical Literature* Vol. 131, No. 2, 2012, pp.307-324.

32 Flavius Josephus, *Jewish War* (2.169-74).

33 Flavius Josephus, *Jewish Antiquities* (18.55-59)

34 Josephus and Philo of Alexandria both include those words to emphasise that these were popular and well-organized protests, not merely spontaneous and opportunistic: Flavius Josephus, *Jewish War,* (2.185-203), and Philo of Alexandria, *Embassy to Gaius,* (203-348).

35 John Dominic Crossan and Jonathan L. Reed, *Excavating Jesus: Beneath the Stones, Behind the Texts,* HarperSanFrancisco, 2001.

36 Outlined in Lorraine Parkinson, *Jesus as Moses or Elijah: Two Divergent Typologies,* Unpublished dissertation, Melbourne College of Divinity, 1996.

37 Richard Horsley, *The Prophet Jesus and the Renewal of Israel: Moving beyond a diversionary debate,* William B. Eerdmans Publishing Company, Grand Rapids, Michigan, 2012, p.128.

38 Dennis E. Smith and Joseph B. Tyson (Eds.), *Acts and Christian Beginnings: The Acts Seminar Report,* Salem, OR, Polebridge Press, 2013, p.3.

39 Flavius Josephus, *Jewish War,* 2.8.14

40 Flavius Josephus, *Jewish Antiquities,* 18.1.3

41 Professor Israel Knohl, "The Gabriel Revelation and the Birth of Christianity", presented at the conference Dead Sea Scrolls and Contemporary Culture: Celebrating 60 years of Discovery, Jerusalem, 6 – 8 July, 2008. The full translation on the stone can be accessed through Ada Yardeni, "Gabriel's Vision', *Biblical Archaeology Review Magazine,* 34:01 Jan/Feb 2008.

42 The word *diaspora* refers to neighbouring countries to which the Jews of Palestine were dispersed by the Romans in the second century CE. Jews also went voluntarily to other territories (the diaspora) during the time of the Greek occupation of Palestine in the second and first centuries BCE.

43 The University of Michigan's Neil Krause reports that a nationwide survey of older Americans says 21 per cent say they have seen a dead loved one. Those people tend to cope better with the death of the loved one. Neil Krause, "Reported Contact with the Dead, Religious Involvement, and Death Anxiety in Later Life", in *Review of Religious Research,* Vol. 52, No. 4 (June 2011), pp.347-364.

44 'Christian apologetic' means the defence of Christian ideas in speech or in writing.

45 Bernard Brandon Scott, *The Real Paul: Recovering his Radical Challenge,* Salem, Oregon, Polebridge Press, 2015, p.9.

46 Tim LaHaye and Jerry B. Jenkins, *Left Behind: a novel of the earth's last days,* Illinois, Tyndale House Publishers, 1995.

47 Synoptic means they hold to a basically common view of the Jesus story.

48 Robert Crotty, *Peter the Rock: What the Roman Papacy was, and what it might become,* Melbourne, Spectrum Publications, 2015, pp.22-30.

49 The Jewish Diaspora in the first century of the Common Era consisted of substantial Jewish communities in Egypt, Asia Minor and around the Mediterranean.

50 Many scholars see oral sources used by Matthew and Luke as having been gathered together into a written document called Q, which stands for the German word quelle, meaning 'source'. I do not see the necessity for such a document, given that Matthew used Mark plus his own ideas and Luke almost certainly used much of Mark and Matthew and added his ideas. Mark did not need to use a so-called 'Q' sayings source.

51 Fragments of 1 Enoch were discovered among the Dead Sea Scrolls, but an entire manuscript in Ethiopic was discovered in the Abyssinian church and translated into English in the 19th century. It is quoted in the New Testament in Jude 1:14-15.

52 James Charlesworth, *The Pseudepigrapha and Modern Research,* Scholars Press for The Society of Biblical Literature, Stanford University Press, Stanford, California, 1976, p.98.

53 Flavius Josephus, *Antiquities of the Jews,* 18.5.3 136.

54 "In accordance with the traditional Jewish understanding of apocalyptic, actualization of the 'day of the LORD' promise would have entailed a radical transformation of the world order. This was nothing less than a complete reversal of the world as it was, including its social order and power structures, as well as the relationships between human beings and the rest of creation. There is no place in this scenario for the destruction of the world itself, but rather for its profound renewal." Lorraine Parkinson, *Jesus as Moses or Elijah: Two Divergent Typologies,* unpublished doctoral dissertation, Melbourne College of Divinity, 1996.

55 Targum Pseudo-Jonathan was originally called Targum Jerusalem, and originates in Palestine. Its dating is fiercely contested, with scholars dating it from as early as 2nd to 4th centuries CE, while others date it from the 8th century – post-Islamic era. In any case, it is a written version of earlier oral versions.

56 *The Aramaic Bible*, Vol. 2, Targum Pseudo-Jonathan: Deuteronomy, Translation with Notes by Michael Maher M.S.C., A Michael Glazier Book, The Liturgical Press, Collegeville, Minnesota, 1994.

57 Luke also has John the Baptist announcing the coming of the Messiah, but he identifies John not with Elijah, but with the prophetic voice in Isaiah 40.

58 The New Revised Standard Version of the Bible uses upper case letters to designate the word LORD as referring to God in the Hebrew Scriptures. In the New Testament quotes from the Hebrew Scriptures the letters in the word Lord are in lower case with a capital L. This indicates Jesus, not God.

59 Josephus (*Jewish War* vii.3 6) reports that exorcisms were carried out by administering drugs made from poisonous root extracts or by making sacrifices.

60 Then follows the story of the woman with the constant flow of menstrual blood. She is restored to her community and her religion through her healing by Jesus the Messiah. Her 'polluting' association with blood has gone.

61 'Manna' in the Bible possibly refers to a hardened edible sugary substance exuded by trees of the African and Asian deserts such as flowering ash trees.

62 William Wrede, *Das Messiasgeheimnis in den Evangelien: Zugleich ein Beitrag zum Verständnis des Markusevangeliums,* Göttingen, Vandenhoeck & Ruprecht, 1901; William Wrede, *Messianic Secret,* English Edition, J.C.G. Grieg (Trans.), Cambridge, James Clarke & Co., 1971.

63 Julius Wellhausen, *Das Evangelium Marki, übersetzt und erklärt, Berlin, 1903.*

64 William Wrede, *Das Messiasgeheimnis,* p.236.

65 Albert Schweitzer, *Von Reimarus zu Wrede,* Tubingen, J.C.B. Mohr, 1906; English Edition, Albert Schweitzer, *The Quest of the Historical Jesus: A Critical Study of its Progress from Reimarus to Wrede,* W. Montgomery (Trans.), New York, Macmillan, 1948, p.337.

66 Julius Schniewind, *Das Evangelium nach Markus,* Das Neue Testament Deutsch, Vol 1, Göttingen, Vandenhoeck & Ruprecht, 1933, p.175.

67 N. T. Wright, *"The Historical Jesus and Christian Theology"*, originally published in Sewanee Theological Review 39, 1996.

68 Morna D. Hooker, *The Gospel According to Saint Mark, Black's New Testament Commentaries,* London, A. & C. Black, 1991, p.69.

69 Sukkot comes (in the autumn) immediately following the Day of Atonement. It is the most joyful of Jewish festivals. It celebrates the time when the ancient Israelites gathered in their fruit harvest and offered thanks to God. During Sukkot in the 21st century, many Jews eat their meals and spend part of their time in a sukkah (a booth or hut outdoors with an open roof of branches and leaves). The booths represent the temporary shelters in which the ancient Israelites lived as they followed Moses on their journey from Egypt to the Promised land. In synagogues on Sukkot people wave palm branches in all directions to show that God is everywhere. Sukkot occurs in the northern hemisphere autumn, not in springtime, when Passover is celebrated.

70 Refer back to chapter headed 'Messianic Belief in 1st century CE Judaism for a fuller description of the Davidic Messiah.

71 See chapter headed, 'Jesus the Messiah in the Gospel of Luke', in the section on Luke's genealogy, for a full discussion of an alternative interpretation of this verse (Psalm 110:1).

72 Among the Dead Sea Scrolls there are six texts which witness to a literally clear messianic expectation on the part of their authors. Among them are *The Community Rule* (1QS): " ... until there shall come the Prophet and the Messiahs of Aaron and Israel." 1QS IX 8-11.

73 James Crossley, "Mark, Paul, and the Question of Influences", in *Paul and the Gospels: Christologies, Conflicts and Convergences,* Michael F. Bird and Joel Willitts (Eds.), Library of New Testament Studies 411, London: T&T Clark, 2011, pp.10-29.

74 Orthodox Jews were simply ordinary Jews who adhered to the Torah and the oral law of Judaism in that era.

75 As the first gospel, Mark established the tradition that Jesus' last meal with his followers was a Passover meal. The other synoptic writers followed Mark's example, which led to problems with the timing of the trial and crucifixion in a Jewish context. John's gospel also follows the Passover meal setting, but changes its timing to suit the historical context.

76 This accusation is featured in a conversation called *The Octavius of Minucius Felix* (c.160CE), Codex Parisinus Latinus 1661 (9th century CE), in H. J. Baylis, *Minucius Felix and His Place Among the Early Fathers of the Latin Church,* London, 1928, 274-359. The Octavius of Minucius Felix was probably first referred to in the writings of Tertullian.

77 *The Didache or Teaching of the Apostles,* in Apostolic Fathers Part 1 (two vols), J. B. Lightfoot (translator and editor), London, MacMillan & Co., 1885.

78 Burton L. Mack, *Who Wrote the New Testament? The Making of the Christian Myth,* San Francisco, Harper, 1996, 240-241.

79 John A. T. Robinson, *Redating the New Testament,* London, SCM Press, 1976, argued that the Didache was dated between 40 and 60 CE.

80 Exodus 24 combines the two concepts of covenant and sacrifice. To express the people's acceptance of the covenant with God, Moses offers an animal sacrifice, sprinkles blood on the people and says, "See the blood of the covenant that the LORD has made with you ..." These biblical motifs come together in Mark's account of the Last Supper. Jesus' death is being interpreted as a covenant sacrifice.

81 In Hebrews 9 Jesus offers himself in the heavenly sanctuary as a perfect sacrifice for sin.

82 Richard Horsley, *The Prophet Jesus and the Renewal of Israel*, pp.156-7.

83 Feminist theologians Andrea Bieler and Luise Schottroff have proposed a contemporary political interpretation of the Eucharist as a resisting response to the politics of the state. They link the martyrdom of Jesus with the martyrs of Maccabees 4, and with the 'diseappeared' of Pinochet's Chile, plus Guantanamo Bay and Abu Ghraib. See Andrea Bieler and Luise Schottroff, *The Eucharist: Bodies, Bread and Resurrection,* Minneapolis, Fortress Press, 207, pp.144-146.

84 There may be another explanation for the charge of blasphemy. For that see my comments on Matthew 26:65-68, in the chapter on Jesus the Messiah in the Gospel of Matthew.

85 Eloi is neither Hebrew nor Aramaic. It indicates that Mark is working from a Greek transliteration of this Hebrew phrase from Psalm 22. His source is neither a Hebrew nor an Aramaic text; it is the Greek translation of the Hebrew Scriptures, the Septuagint. If he had obtained this quote from an Aramaic source it would have read 'elahi', and he would have transliterated it into Greek as elahai.

86 Bruce Metzger, *A Textual Commentary on the Greek New Testament,* United Bible Societies U.S.A, Stuttgart, 1971, p.123-5

87 Irenaeus was Bishop of Lyons, in what was then known as Gaul. Most of his writings date from the second half of the second century CE.

88 Raymond E. Brown, *The Birth of the Messiah: A Commentary on the infancy narratives in Matthew and Luke,* London, Geoffrey Chapman, 1977, pp. 48ff.
89 Another discussion of the likelihood that the birth narratives of Matthew and Luke were added to those gospels by later editors may be found in *The Acts of Jesus: What did Jesus really do?,* Robert W. Funk and the Jesus Seminar, New York, Polebridge Press, HarperSanFrancisco, 1998, 497-526.
90 *B'tulah* (virgin) is the word which describes Rebekah, "whom no man had known" (Genesis 24:16).
91 Plutarch, "Numa Pompilius", in *The Parallel Lives,* Loeb Classical Library edition, Vol. 1, 1914, 43-44.
92 Greek does not have the letter 'h', hence the spelling of the English transliteration.
93 The dove is a very common symbol in the ancient near east, with meanings ranging from the biblical dove in the Noah story, to its symbolism of various goddesses, among them Caananite Asherah, Phoenician goddess Tanit and Roman goddesses Venus and Fortunata.
94 See Silvia Schroer, "The Spirit, Wisdom and the Dove, Feminist-Critical Exegesis of a Second Testament Symbol Against the Background of its History in Ancient Near Eastern and Hellenistic-Early Jewish Traditions", in *Wisdom Has Built Her House: Studies on the Figure of Sophia in the Bible,* Silvia Schroer (Ed.), Linda M. Maloney and William McDonough (translators), Collegeville, MI, Liturgical Press, 2000.
95 Robert A. Anderson, *Quite Some Time: A Memoir,* Melbourne, 2011, pp.111-112.
96 A. H. Fortin and K. G. Barnett, "Medical School Curricula in Spirituality and Medicine", in Journal of the American Medical Association, 2004, 291(23) 2883.
97 For an extended explanation of the ways the Beatitudes explain the essence of the 'kingdom of heaven', see Lorraine Parkinson, *The World According to Jesus: his blueprint for the best possible world',* Spectrum Publications, Melbourne, 2011.
98 It is likely that Luke selected 'Sermon on the Mount' sayings from oral/written sources and probably also from Matthew, for inclusion in his own gospel (the Sermon on the Plain), in accordance with his own agenda.
99 Bernard Brandon Scott, *Re-Imagine the World: An Introduction to the Parables of Jesus,* Santa Rosa, Polebridge Press, 2001, pp.35-40.
100 Scott, *Re-Imagine the World,* pp.29-34.
101 Flavius Josephus, *War of the Jews,* 2:8.14.
102 By this means Matthew distances the Sanhedrin from Gentile territory, overcoming at least the historical objection that the priests and Pharisees would have been polluted by entering Pilate's headquarters. This applies also to Mark's narrative. Luke has the Sanhedrin enter the headquarters and talk with Pilate.
103 I will have more to say about the horrendously dark shadow those words have cast across Jewish and Christian history, in the final chapter of this book.
104 Philo of Alexandria, *The Embassy to Gaius 299-305,* as discussed in Emil Schürer, *The Literature of the Jewish People in the Age of Jesus Christ (175 B.C.-A.D. 135),* A new English version revised and edited by Geza Vermes and Fergus Millar, Vol. 1, Edinburgh, T. & T. Clark Ltd, 1973, pp.383-386.
105 James H. Charlesworth, *The Historical Jesus: An Essential Guide,* Nashville, Abingdon Press, 2008.
106 Dennis E. Smith and Joseph B. Tyson (Eds.), *Acts and Christian Beginnings: The Acts Seminar Report,* Salem, Oregon, Polebridge Press, 2013, p.2.
107 A superscription is usually a paragraph or less that comes first, separate from the following book or literary work. It functions to introduce the writing, sometimes by setting it in a particular time and place. In Luke's case, the superscription sets out the purpose of the gospel.

108 The Priene Calendar Inscription (c.9BCE) with those words was displayed throughout the Roman Empire, M. D. Hooker, *The Gospel according to Saint Mark,* BNTC; London, A. & C. Black, 1991, p.34.

109 Raymond Brown, *The Birth of the Messiah,* p.415.

110 The Mishnah is the first major written version of the Oral Law/Torah. It was compiled by Rabbi Yehuda HaNasi (Judah the Prince) in the late 2nd century CE. This was done because it was feared that the oral traditions of the Pharisees up until 70CE would be forgotten.

111 B. Z. (Wilhelm) Bacher, *Aggadot HaTanna'im* (A. S. Rabbinowitz Tr.), Jerusalem, 1922, pp.1-17, in Jacob Neusner, *The Rabbinic traditions about the Pharisees before 70: The Houses, Book iii, Conclusions,* Netherlands, E. J. Brill, 1971, p.355.

112 For example, the parable of the Good Samaritan (10:29-37); the one leper who thanked Jesus was a Samaritan (17:16); Jesus rebuked disciples who wanted God to punish a Samaritan village because the villagers refused to welcome him (9:51-55).

113 Given that Philo of Alexandria's dating is c.20BCE – c.50CE, his writing well predates that of the gospel writer John.

114 *Adonai* is the word commonly used by Jewish people to say out loud the name of God. That way they avoid adding vowels to the unpronounceable tetragrammaton, and so avoid saying God's actual name.

115 Even if the original version of Psalm 110 contained a superscription that read 'Of David. A Psalm', it could still be interpreted as being a psalm 'about' David, not as a psalm from David. The word *l'david' can also mean* 'To David'. Again this can mean that the psalm has been written about David, and is now given 'to David'. It is, after all, about David who was called Messiah, not about any subsequent Messiah.

116 The earliest manuscripts of the Gospel of Luke are five 3rd century papyrus fragments. The earliest complete text is in Codex Sinaiticus and Codex Vaticanus. See the Introduction to Section 3 of this book.

117 Luke is also claiming here that Jesus was literate, although some contemporary scholars see him as illiterate. I support Jesus' literacy, given his apparent comprehensive knowledge of scripture. I would argue that this cannot be attributed entirely to the tradition of remembering scripture and passing it on orally.

118 David E. Aune, *Prophecy in Early Christianity and the Ancient Mediterranean World,* William B. Eerdmans Publishing Company, Grand Rapids, Michigan, 1991, p.126.

119 Leviathan is the name given to a mythic sea monster. Job 41:1-34 contains a detailed description of Leviathan. Only God is able to control it.

120 Theophany is a Greek word meaning the appearance of a deity (or god) to a human being.

121 Josephus, Loeb Classical Library, *Antiquities of the Jews,* 8.48.

122 Josephus, Loeb Classical Library, *Antiquities of the Jews,* 9.2.2,28.

123 Philo of Alexandria, Loeb Classical Library, "De Sacrificiis Abelis et Caini", 8-10.

124 BT *Kiddushin* 40a contains a story about a particularly pious man whom Elijah helped to escape from moral danger. BT *Sanhedrin* 108b and BT *Berakhot* 58b tell of Elijah rescuing innocent Israelites from certain death. The Markan passage about Elijah coming to Jesus' aid is the earliest known evidence of this belief.

125 Louis Ginzberg, *The Legends of the Jews,* Philadelphia, Jewish Publication Society of America, Twelfth Impression, 1987, Vol. IV, pp.203-32.

126 Joseph Fitzmyer, *The Gospel According to Luke X-VVIV, 2 Vols.,* The Anchor Bible, Doubleday and Company Inc, Garden City, New York, 1985, p.1588.

127 Eusebius Caesariensis, *Historia Ecclesiasticus* [The History of the Church]. 3.23.3ff and 4.14.3-8.

128 Romans 16:22 indicates that Paul worked with a scribe called Tertius, who actually wrote down Paul's words.
129 Karen L. King, *What is Gnosticism?* Cambridge MA, Harvard University Press, 2005, p.226
130 Karen L. King, *What is Gnosticism?* Introduction, pp.1-4
131 J. Jocz, "The Invisibility of God and the Incarnation", *Judaica 17*, 1961, p.196. Jacob Jocz was born of a Jewish father and Christian mother. He was Professor of Systematic Theology for 16 years, at Wycliffe College, University of Toronto.
132 Raymond E. Brown, *The Gospel According to John,* Anchor Bible Series No. 29, Garden City, NY, Doubleday, 1966, p.1.
133 R. P. Casey, "The Earliest Christologies", in *The Journal of Theological Studies,* New Series, Vol. 9, No. 2, October 1958, p.270.
134 Alejandro Dièz Macho, *Neophyti I: Targum Palestinense MS de la Biblioteca Vaticana, R. Le Déaut (French Tr.), Martin McNamara and Michael Maher (English Tr.), Consejo Superior de Investigaciones Científicas, Madrid-Barcelona, 1970.*
135 Raymond E. Brown, S.S., *Jesus, God and Man: Modern Biblical Reflections,* London, 1968, p.27.
136 Philo of Alexandria, *De Confusione Linguarum,* 146.
137 Philo of Alexandria, Loeb Edition, p.385-7.
138 The Hebrew word for God consists of consonants only, deliberately unpronounceable. Some Christians have inserted vowels and created the word 'Jehovah'. This is an illegitimate use of the Hebrew word. Some Jews simply say 'ha-Shem' (the name) to avoid saying the name of God. Others use the word 'Adonai', which means 'Lord' – an important person.
139 The Greek word *Kurios* can mean a master, or someone having ownership or authority. It can also mean 'God'.
140 Nor does verse Psalm 2:7 imply a virgin birth for David.
141 The messianic banquet is mentioned in Isaiah 25: 6-9, when God will feed all with rich (fatty) food and "well-aged wines". This is based on Deuteronomy 32: 37-38, where the fatty food and wine are related to liturgical rituals in the Temple. The messianic banquet is therefore most likely to have been seen as occurring in the Temple.
142 It is the Festival of Sukkot where people cut palm branches and take them into the synagogue, as part of a thanksgiving to God for the fruits of the harvest. It is held as summer fades into autumn, not in the spring, when Passover is celebrated.
143 This belief is stated explicitly in the Johannine Epistle 1 John 4:10: *"In this is love: not that we loved God but that he loved us and sent his Son to be the atoning sacrifice for our sins."*
144 The last Herod (Agrippa II) died in 92 CE, after which the Herodian kingdoms were incorporated into the Roman province of Judea.
145 James Donaldson (Tr.), *Apostolic Constitutions,* in *Ante-Nicene Fathers,* Vol. 7, Alexander Roberts, James Donaldson and A. Cleveland Coxe (Eds.), Buffalo, NY: Christian Literature Publishing Co., 1886.
146 See Lorraine Parkinson, *The World According to Jesus,* pp.228-229.
147 In contemporary parlance, someone might complain: "A man has to wait all night for his dinner". The speaker is obviously referring to himself.
148 Some scholars argue that because of the tensions abroad in Jerusalem at the Passover Festival, in order to shut down a growing disturbance around Jesus, the Jewish leadership may have made an exception to the rules regarding working on Passover. John's Gospel has the more likely historical scenario for the crucifixion.
149 *The Mishnah: A New Translation,* Jacob Neusner, Yale University Press, New Haven and London, 1988, Tractate Sanhedrin: the Fourth Division: the Order of Damages, 4.1.K, L, p.590

150 I will examine this further and other references to *"the disciple whom Jesus loved"* in my discussion of John chapter 21.

151 Tertullian, *Against Praxeas,* Ante-Nicene Fathers, Vol. 3, Alexander Roberts, James Donaldson, and A. Cleveland Coxe, (Eds.), Buffalo, NY, Christian Literature Publishing Company, 1885, Ch. 25.

152 Pope Damasus I was the first to claim that Rome's primacy rested solely on Peter. It is significant that he was Pope in the fourth century (366-384).

153 Philippe Levillain and John W. O'Malley (Eds.), *The Papacy: An Encyclopedia,* 3 volume set, NY, Routledge, 2002, p.941.

154 Robert Crotty, *Peter the Rock: What the Roman Papacy was, and what it might become,* Melbourne, Spectrum Publications, 2015, p.73. Robert Crotty was formerly Professor of Religion and Education in the University of South Australia, His new book *Peter the Rock* contains a detailed examination of the Catholic Church's claims about the primacy of Peter as first Pope.

155 Sandra M. Schneiders, (*Written that you may believe,* Crossroads, New York, 1999), has argued that the 'we' of chapter 21 is the writer's way of including the readers of the gospel in encounters with the risen Christ. She suggests that the 'beloved disciple' is a literary device to represent every disciple.

156 In 170 CE the Assyrian Christian writer Tatian created a synthesis or 'harmony' of the four gospels in what is known as the Diatessaron. It was used in the Syrian churches until the 5th century CE.

157 Paul Trudinger, *Honest to Jesus,* Winnipeg, Canada, Frye Publishing, 1983, p.10.

158 John Bodycomb, *No Fixed Address: Faith as Journey,* Melbourne, Spectrum Publications, 2010, p.56

159 John Chrysostom, Sermon VI.1, in *The Fathers of the Church Vol. 68, St John Chrysostom, Discourses against Judaizing Christians,* The Catholic University of America Press, 1979, Paul W. Harkins (translator), p.147ff.

160 Anders Gerdmar, *Roots of Theological Antisemitism: German Biblical Interpretation and the Jews, from Herder and Semler to Kittel and Bultmann,* Leiden and Boston, Brill, 2010, xviii – 675.

161 James Carroll, *Constantine's Sword: the Church and the Jews, a History,* Boston, Houghton Mifflin Company, 2001, p.598.

162 Frederick Douglass, *My Bondage and My Freedom,* New York and Auburn, Miller, Orton and Mulligan (1855), John Stauffer (Ed.) Random House, 2003.

163 Pope John Paul II, *Dominicae Cenae,* Apostolic Exhortation, 1980.

164 Geoffrey Robinson, *For Christ's Sake: End Sexual Abuse in the Catholic Church for Good,* Melbourne, John Garratt Publishing, 2013, pp.83-84.

165 Kieran Tapsell, *Potiphar's Wife: The Vatican's Secret and Child Sexual Abuse,* Adelaide, ATF Press, 2014, p.174.

166 For a full examination of the Sermon on the Mount as foundational teaching for 'making disciples', see my book *The World According to Jesus.*

167 The Oxford Dictionary defines 'emulsion' as 'A fine dispersion of droplets of one liquid into another in which it is not soluble or miscible'.

168 See Acts 9:2; 18:25; 18:26; 19:9; 19:23; 22:4; 24:14; 24:22.

INDEX

www.ingramcontent.com/pod-product-compliance
Lightning Source LLC
Chambersburg PA
CBHW060239100426
42742CB00011B/1578